D1569364

WINNER OF THE PAUL A. BARAN – PAUL M. SWEEZY
MEMORIAL AWARD

Established in 2014, this award honors the contributions of the founders
of the *Monthly Review* tradition: Paul M. Sweezy, Paul A. Baran, and
Harry Magdoff. It supports the publication in English of distinguished
monographs focused on the political economy of imperialism. It also
applies to writings previously unpublished in English, and includes
translations of new work first published in languages other than English.
Please visit monthlyreview.org for complete details of the award.

PAST RECIPIENTS

*Imperialism in the Twenty-first Century:*
*Globalization, Super-Exploitation, and Capitalism's Final Crisis*
John Smith

*The Age of Monopoly Capital:*
*Selected Correspondence of Paul A. Baran and Paul M. Sweezy, 1949–1964*
Edited and annotated by Nicholas Baran and John Bellamy Foster

*Value Chains: The New Economic Imperialism*
Intan Suwandi

THEORY, HISTORY, AND THE PRESENT

# Capital and Imperialism

## Utsa Patnaik
## Prabhat Patnaik

MONTHLY REVIEW PRESS

*New York*

Library of Congress Cataloging-in-Publication Data
available from the publisher

ISBN paper: 978-158367-890-9
ISBN cloth: 978-1-58367-891-6




Typeset in Bulmer Monotype

MONTHLY REVIEW PRESS, NEW YORK
monthlyreview.org

5 4 3 2 1

# Contents

*For Akeel Bilgrami and C. P. Chandrasekhar*

# *Preface*

The pervasive tendency on the part of practitioners of theoretical economics has been to analyze capitalism as a closed self-contained system. This is logically untenable, and it also gives a misleading picture of its actual history. The purpose of this book is to counter this theoretical perspective. Here we put forward the proposition that not only has capitalism always been historically ensconced within a pre-capitalist setting from which it emerged, with which it interacted, and which it modified for its own purposes, but additionally that its very existence and expansion is conditional upon such interaction.

The first five chapters of the book, which mainly deal with and provide critiques of accepted theory, argue that a closed self-contained capitalism in the metropolis is a logical impossibility. In later chapters we discuss the specific ways in which capitalism has shaped, and continues to shape, its pre-capitalist environment to suit its needs. This provides a reading of the history of capitalism that is very different from the usual reading. This history is captured from our particular theoretical perspective, and is not meant to be an attempt to provide a comprehensive account of the system in all its facets.

This book is the product of a long period of thought and work, in the course of which we have accumulated a large intellectual and personal debt to numerous friends and colleagues. It is not possible to mention all of them, but it would be invidious not to mention some.

For any student of political economy belonging to our generation, the intellectual debt to Irfan Habib and Amiya K. Bagchi is incalculable. In addition, we gratefully acknowledge the interaction and encouragement we received from Akeel Bilgrami, Sayera Habib, Sunanda Sen, Carol Rovane, Radhika Desai, Akbar Noman, C. P. Chandrasekhar, Jayati Ghosh, Indu Chandrasekhar, Praveen Jha, Nishad Patnaik, and Rajendra Prasad. None of them, however, bears any responsibility for the views expressed in this book, which, whatever their worth, are our own.

Finally, we owe a deep debt of gratitude to Michael Yates, Colin Vanderburg, and Erin Clermont for their help in bringing the manuscript to its present shape.

—UTSA PATNAIK
—PRABHAT PATNAIK

# PART 1

# CHAPTER 1

# *A Money-Using Economy*

The conceptual representation of capitalism that is analyzed in economic theory in almost all its major strands has not only been significantly different from the reality of the system but is also logically flawed. Such a claim on our part may appear as hyperbole at first sight, but we make it in all seriousness. And in making it, we do not wish to cast any aspersions on the luminaries of the discipline; we only wish to underscore that economics has been perennially afflicted by a blind spot caused by being developed essentially within a metropolitan location. The purpose of this book is to establish the limited, and hence flawed, nature of this perception that afflicts the subject, and to provide an alternative conceptual representation of capitalism that is both theoretically and empirically better grounded than what economic theory has offered till now.

The conceptual representation in economic theory, from its inception, has basically been of an isolated capitalist economy, where, in its simplest version, only capitalists and workers exist, with the state ensuring that law and order prevails and the rules of the game of the system are followed. When international trade has been introduced into this picture, it has been trade among such isolated capitalist economies, and therefore, though enlarging the unit of analysis, adds little of substance to the basic conclusions. Now, a major logical flaw in this representation is that such an isolated capitalist economy simply cannot be a money-using capitalist economy in any meaningful sense. A money-using capitalist economy, in other words, has requirements that no isolated capitalist economy of the sort highlighted in economic theory can possibly fulfill. Let us examine some of the implications of money-use.

### Say's Law and the Wealth Demand for Money

Money has long been a medium of circulation. A money-using economy, above all, is one in which a certain amount of money is always kept in the possession of economic agents for managing transactions, meeting what economists call the "transaction demand for money."

The money held for transaction purposes can be visualized as follows: Economic agents sell commodities, including in the case of workers their labor-power, obtain money in exchange for the sale, and use this money for buying the commodities they need. Since there is a time-lag in the case of each agent between sale and purchase, money is held by each in the interim period. Aggregated across all economic agents at any point of time, this is the total amount of money-stock held for managing transactions in an economy.

Some money, however, may be held by each economic agent in excess of what the agent would normally hold at any point of time for transaction purposes alone. It represents a command over goods and services that is never actually transformed over any given period into goods and services. It is simply a form in which economic agents hold their wealth.

Economic theory, apart from certain heterodox traditions that we will discuss later, posits that though money is certainly held for transaction purposes, it cannot possibly be held as wealth, since it is a barren asset that earns nothing. Any individual holding wealth in the form of money is certainly not acting in his or her best interests, since if this wealth would have been held in some non-money form, it would have fetched the owner a positive rate of return, which money in itself does not.

But non-heterodox economic theory does not hold this view as a plausible reading of the world. The very foundations of non-heterodox economic theory rest upon the assumption that money is not held as a form of wealth, above and beyond what is needed for transaction purposes. Let us see why.

The amount of money held for transaction purposes can be said to have a certain fixed ratio to the money value of the total transactions of goods and services in the economy. The wealth demand for money, however, if there is such a wealth demand, would depend upon all sorts of other factors, a prominent one among which must be the expected rate of return on other assets in terms of which wealth could alternatively be held. In short, the wealth demand for money would depend *inter alia* upon expectations about the future.

Now, there could be occasions when, starting from a state where wealth is held by individuals in the form of both money and capital stock, the expected rate of return on capital stock (or claims upon capital stock in the form of equity and bonds) falls. This would prompt wealth-holders to hold more of their wealth in the form of money than in the form of capital stock (or claims on capital stock). When this happens, then *ceteris paribus* the price of capital stock will decline in terms of money.

This would lower the production of *new* capital goods, because, assuming for simplicity that old and new capital goods are identical in terms of their effectiveness, since their prices must be the same and equal, in a competitive situation, to the marginal cost of producing new capital goods, a fall in the price of existing capital stock would also mean a fall in the price of new capital goods. This would push the latter price below the marginal cost at the old level of production, and that would cause a fall in production.[1] In an oligopolistic situation where the price of new capital goods is a markup over (a constant) unit prime cost, a fall in the prices of old capital stock would shift demand away from new capital goods, causing a fall in the latter's output.

This would entail lower employment and incomes in the capital-goods (or investment goods) producing sector, which in turn will have "multiplier effects." Lower incomes in the investment goods sector would lead to lower demand for consumption goods, lower output of the latter, and hence would further lower demand, and so on, causing higher unemployment alongside higher unutilized capacity in the economy as a whole.

An objection to this argument may be raised on the grounds that it has assumed given money wages. But if money wages fall in a situation of higher unemployment, then not only would the marginal cost of producing new capital goods also move down, but the original expectation of a reduced rate of return on capital goods in the future could also get reversed if the stream of expected prices of the goods produced by the capital goods falls less than the stream of expected costs of producing them (the latter being dependent upon the stream of expected money wages). The fall in money wages therefore could negate any reduction in employment arising because of a greater desire to hold wealth in the form of money rather than in the form of capital goods or claims on capital goods. From this, one can argue that if money wages are *flexible* then involuntary unemployment caused by a deficiency of aggregate demand for produced goods need not arise at all.

There is, however, no reason, taking the above example, why the expectation of a relative decline in the rate of return on capital stock, should *necessarily* reverse itself with a fall in money wages, that is, why expectations should exactly pan out in such a manner. And if they do not pan out, then though the recession will continue, money-wage flexibility will only entail a continuous fall in money wages and prices in a futile bid to eliminate this problem, which will destroy the price system, and with it the economy. An additional factor aiding this destruction will be the havoc it will cause owing to the inability of economic agents to fulfill fixed monetary contracts inherited from preceding periods.[2]

The problem therefore lies not in the absence of money-wage flexibility, as is often thought, but in the very existence of a wealth demand for money, which is what makes possible such "involuntary unemployment" (which we define as unemployment coexisting with unutilized capacity). And since non-heterodox economic theory has generally asserted that markets function in a manner that prevents the system settling at a state of involuntary unemployment, it has tended to assume away altogether any wealth demand for money.

This entire matter can be looked at in a different way. The view that there can never be a deficiency of aggregate demand for the produced goods and services in an economy because "supply creates its own demand" was put forward by J. B. Say and is called Say's Law. Non-heterodox economics generally accepts Say's Law (not always explicitly or consciously) and rejects the view that capitalism is a system that can settle at a state of involuntary unemployment in a world of flexible prices and in the absence of "policy mistakes." Ricardo was a believer in Say's Law, and the Walrasian equilibrium, which postulates that all markets "clear," including the labor market, if prices are flexible, necessarily accepts Say's Law.

Now, an *ex ante* excess supply of produced goods and services can arise only if there is an *ex ante* excess demand for something else outside the circle of produced goods and services (since all *ex ante* excess demands, positive or negative, must always add up to zero). The obvious entity outside the circle of produced goods and services for which there could be such an *ex ante* excess demand is money. But if there is no wealth demand for money at all, but only a transaction demand that bears a fixed ratio to the total value of the produced goods and services being transacted, then there is no question of any *ex ante* excess demand for money arising, which would cause a corresponding *ex ante* excess supply of produced goods and services and invalidate Say's Law.

This was most clearly expressed in the Cambridge quantity equation of the pre-Keynesian days that made the demand for money a function of the money income, with a constant $k$ linking the two, that is, $M_d = kY$. Though several attempts have been made since then to make $k$ a variable and establish that the functioning of the market-system rules out involuntary unemployment, these have been marked invariably by logical infirmities, which we need not go into here.[3] Non-heterodox theory requires for its logical tenability the absence of a wealth demand for money (which has the effect of making $k$ a constant). Putting it differently and more precisely, if there are no restrictions on the form that expectations about the future can take, then Say's Law would hold if, and only if, there is such an absence of the wealth demand for money.

The existence of a wealth demand for money, however, is not only a real-life phenomenon in a money-using economy but is in fact logically entailed by the transaction demand itself. In other words, money cannot be a medium of circulation without also being a form of holding wealth. In the C-M-C circuit mentioned earlier, with individuals converting commodities into money and the latter back into commodities, money is the form in which wealth is held at least for a fleeting moment. But if wealth is held in this form for a fleeting moment, then there is no reason why it cannot be held in this form for more than a fleeting moment. It follows therefore that postulating a transaction demand for money but not a wealth demand for money is logically untenable.

A money-using economy would typically have a stock of money being held by economic agents whose magnitude is not just a fixed ratio of the value of the produced goods and services. In other words, in such an economy money will typically be one of the forms in which wealth is held. This in turn implies that a money-using economy can settle at a state of involuntary unemployment—with the givenness of the money wages in any period being not the cause of such unemployment but rather providing a perch that ensures the price-system does not hurtle down because of the existence of such unemployment.

The wealth demand for money and its corollary that the economy can settle at a state of involuntary unemployment have a number of theoretical implications. Let us turn to these now.

### Accumulation and the Market Question

If an economy has unutilized capacity that every capitalist producer faces, then adding to capacity seems scarcely justified for such a producer. And even if some addition takes place because of the belief that the magnitude of unutilized capacity will shrink, there is no denying that the amount of addition to capacity is likely to be less when there is greater unutilized capacity. It follows therefore that net investment, aggregating across the producers as a whole, is likely to be inversely related to the level of unutilized capacity in the economy.

So much has been written, especially within the Marxist tradition, about competition between capitals spurring the accumulation process, starting from Marx's own comment "Accumulate, accumulate, that is the Moses and the Prophet!" that any suggestion that demand may influence investment may appear strange at first sight. Nikolai Bukharin's criticism of Rosa Luxemburg concerned precisely this point. Her suggestion that capitalism required an "external market" to stimulate expanded reproduction was, according to Bukharin, at variance with the reality of capitalism, where competition between capitals was the stimulus behind accumulation.[4]

But what is missed in this discussion, including Bukharin's, is that capitalists may wish to go on *accumulating* money capital even when they do not *invest*.[5] Accumulation can occur in the form of money as well, and not just in the form of additions to physical capital stock, whence it follows that even when owing to competition capitalists may wish to go on accumulating, how much they add to *capacity* can still depend upon the state of capacity utilization. Dragging in the fact of competition to deny the relevance of an investment function is to deny that accumulation can take different forms, a fact that Marx had emphasized through his rejection of Say's Law and recognition of the wealth demand for money.[6]

The fact that net investment depends upon the level of capacity utilization, increasing when capacity utilization increases and falling when it falls, has two extremely important implications. First, it makes the system unstable. Suppose for some reason capacity utilization happens to fall. Then it lowers investment compared to what it otherwise would have been, which in turn would reduce aggregate demand and hence lower capacity utilization still further. If the economy in the absence of the original fall in capacity utilization would have continued at some particular level of utilization, then it would keep going downhill because of this original fall.

In other words, there may be some level of capacity utilization such that, if the economy happens to be placed at that level, then that level will continue—which is analogous to Roy Harrod's "warranted rate of growth." But if the economy deviates from that level then it will go on deviating. That level is then said to have a "knife-edge" property.[7]

The second implication is that if the economy is in a stationary state, (that is, a state of "simple reproduction" with zero growth) then there is nothing *within the system* to pull it out of that state. In a world where net investment depends solely upon capacity utilization and is not stimulated by something else from outside this endogenous circle, of demand leading to investment which in turn determines demand, there is nothing to pull the economy out of a stationary state. Put differently, there are endogenous stimuli and there are exogenous stimuli. The former refer to the stimulus for growth in a system that arises because of the very fact of growth having occurred. Endogenous stimuli cannot therefore lift a system out of a stationary state. Exogenous stimuli, by contrast, operate independently of whether growth had been occurring. In the absence of exogenous stimuli, an economy that is at simple reproduction will remain stuck there.

But that is not all. Simple reproduction, or a stationary state, is not someplace at which the economy *may* get stuck in the absence of exogenous stimuli. It will *necessarily* get to that state in the absence of exogenous stimuli.[8] Given the instability of the system, if the economy is growing then it must be propelling itself forward. In the process it is bound sooner or later to hit some supply-side constraint, either labor scarcity, or a capacity constraint on the production of investment goods that limits investment.[9] In such a case, it begins a downward journey which will end only when gross investment equals the level of depreciation, that is, at the stationary state. Once aggregate demand has been factored in, there is no state where the economy can remain perched other than the stationary state in the absence of exogenous stimuli. (The other possible perch, corresponding to Harrod's "warranted rate of growth," is, as we have seen, an unstable one, with a "knife-edge" property.)

Because a money-using capitalist economy is characterized by a wealth demand for money and can settle at a state of involuntary unemployment, it also means that in the absence of exogenous stimuli it will move ultimately toward a state of simple reproduction, and remain stuck there.

The three exogenous stimuli that have figured in theoretical discussions are incursions into pre-capitalist markets, state expenditure, and innovations. While the conceptual representation of capitalism in much of economic theory leaves out the first two, since the system is supposed to be isolated and the role of the state is confined to providing law and order and upholding the rules of the game, the last one, innovations, cannot strictly be considered exogenous, even though it has been widely recognized as one.

In a world in which firms cannot simply assume that they face a horizontal demand curve at the going price, which is what "perfect competition," a mythical state of affairs, entails, they would have to lower their price to sell more. This in turn would invite retaliation from other capitalist firms that do not want to lose their market share. The fact that firms might have unutilized capacity despite the price exceeding marginal cost, the more common scenario, suggests that the fear of retaliation prevents them from attempting to steal market shares from their rivals. Even if a new process or a new product becomes available to a firm, this same fear of retaliation would make that firm use the new process or product in the place of the older process or product *to sell only what it would otherwise have sold.* Innovation does not make the firm attempt to sell more at the expense of its rivals. It follows that innovation does not *per se* warrant additional net investment; it contributes to a change in the *form* of investment (new machines in place of the old).[10] An economy stuck in a stationary state cannot hope therefore to get out of such a state even if innovations become available.[11]

The fact that innovations do not constitute a genuine exogenous stimulus, with the exception perhaps of what Baran and Sweezy called "epoch-making" innovations, such as the railways and the automobiles, is attested to by economic historians.[12] The period between the First and Second World Wars had seen the development of several new innovations, but these were not introduced into the production process because of the Depression.[13] They got introduced only in the years of postwar boom, which suggests that innovations get stifled in recessions rather than helping overcome recessions.

If the conceptual representation of capitalism prevalent in much of economic theory was correct, then such an economy, being a money-using economy, and therefore capable of settling at a state of involuntary unemployment, would get pushed down toward a stationary state and remain stuck there. Being stuck in such a state, however, is palpably uncharacteristic of capitalism, which underscores the incompatibility between this conceptual representation and its money-using character.

## The Value of Money and the Question of Inflation

Let us now turn to another implication of the wealth demand for money. Once it is recognized that there is a wealth demand for money and hence no fixity of ratio between the level of money income and the demand for money, then it necessarily follows that the value of money in terms of goods and services cannot be determined by the interaction between the supply of money and the demand for money arising from the world of goods and services, as is presumed by monetarism and expressed clearly by the Cambridge Quantity Equation.

Let us see what the Cambridge equation says. With the demand for money being equal to k.Y, which can be further split up as k.p.Q where p is the price-level and Q the full employment output (full employment is assured because Say's Law must hold in the absence of a wealth demand for money), equality between demand and supply in the money market entails that M= k.p.Q where M denotes money supply. The price level $p$, which is the reciprocal of the value of money, therefore can be said to be determined by the demand and supply of money. And in this case, any rise in money supply results in an equi-proportionate increase in the price level, since $Q$ and $k$ are given. It follows that a rise in the supply of money lowers its value vis-à-vis commodities.

But once we recognize a wealth demand for money, then it follows that a rise in money supply does not necessarily increase, let alone increase equi-proportionately, the price level of commodities in terms of money. In other words, a rise in money supply does not necessarily lower the value of money vis-à-vis commodities. Since the economy is not at full employment, a rise in money supply, if it raises the demand for goods and services at all, can bring forth larger supplies of these goods and services even without any increase in their price, that is, if the marginal cost curve is flat or if price exceeded marginal cost to start with.

Put differently, in the presence of a wealth demand for money, and hence involuntary unemployment, there must be some other rule, other than the demand and supply of money, that must be determining the value of money vis-à-vis goods and services. Both Marx and Keynes, who recognized the wealth demand for money, had correspondingly alternative rules for determining the value of money. In Marx, this rule was provided by the labor theory of value, which held that the value of a commodity in terms of another was determined by the relative quantities of labor directly and indirectly embodied in a unit of each. The value of money in terms of a unit of the non-money commodity accordingly was determined by the relative quantities of labor directly and indirectly embodied in a unit of the money commodity compared to a unit of the non-money commodity. (Marx was talking about a commodity money world.) In Keynes, this rule was the fixity of money wages, that is, the fixity of the value of one com-modity (labor-power), which goes into the production of all other com-modities, in money terms. We will discuss this issue later, but the point here is that in a money-using economy where there is a wealth demand for money and hence involuntary unemployment, there is nonetheless always a determinate value of money in terms of goods and services, even though this is not based on the demand and supply of money.

Likewise, any economy where wealth is held in the form of money and a host of other money-denominated assets also requires that the value of money should be somehow protected. It must not only not fall, for that would have serious consequences for the system, but it must also not be *expected to fall*, for in such a situation wealth-holders would move away from holding money (and even money-denominated assets) into hold-ing commodities which would impair the money-using character of the system. And since any actual fall in the value of money also generates expectations about a further fall, it becomes all the more important to pre-vent such an actual fall.

To be sure, some fall, even a steady fall, in the value of money can be taken by the system in stride, as long as the rate of such fall remains below a certain bound. But above a certain threshold, inflation in the prices of goods and services will accelerate as the expected rate of inflation exceeds the carrying cost of goods that can be substituted most readily for money. The value of money in such a case can fall precipitously. Therefore, a money-using economy must ensure that inflation is kept below this thresh-old, and in general, since nobody quite knows this threshold, as low as possible.

Since a money-using economy typically experiences involuntary unem-ployment (which coexists with unutilized capacity), and, save in excep-tional circumstances such as wars (when there are price-controls and rationing anyway) is scarcely ever supply-constrained, the threat to the value of money arising from an excess demand for the produced goods and services is not very serious, as long as raw materials whose sources are located outside this economy can be obtained at non-increasing prices. (We'll postpone this last point for discussion later.) The existence of involuntary unemployment, a feature of a money-using economy, itself acts therefore as a means of sustaining the value of money. But even in a demand-constrained system, such as what a money-using economy would typically be, there can be a threat to the value of money arising from conflicts over distributive shares.

Inflation, even accelerating inflation, can occur in an economy nowhere close to full employment. This fact is scarcely recognized in economic theory, even to this day. The monetarists see the economy as spontaneously arriving at a "natural rate of unemployment" that is de facto full employment, and they visualize accelerating inflation if the unemployment rate is pushed below this level and decelerating inflation if it is pushed above. At this level, the economy experiences steady inflation that is determined, leaving aside parametric changes in the income velocity of circulation of money, by the difference between the rate of growth of money supply and the "natural rate of growth" of the economy.[14]

According to the monetarists' conception, then, there can never be accelerating inflation when employment is anywhere below this de facto full employment level. And even Keynesians, because of their belief that the capitalist system can be taken close to full employment, do not visualize any serious constraint by way of accelerating inflation before near-full employment has been reached. (Joan Robinson's "inflationary barrier" was an exception to this, which we discuss later.)[15]

There is no reason, however, why the level of employment determined by aggregate demand in any period may not be such that money-wage claims, with labor productivity given, must either entail an accommodating reduction in the non-labor share of output, or, in the absence of such an accommodating reduction, an inflation rate that, once it begins to get anticipated, starts accelerating. If there is a reduction in the non-labor share of output with the rise in money wages, then this rise, since it is unaccompanied by a proportionate rise in prices, must entail a rise in real wages.

Thus, in a money-using economy, where accelerating inflation undermines such an economy, a rise in money wages, if it at all occurs, must be accompanied by a rise in real wages to forestall accelerating inflation. Of course, a rise in money wages compared to the previous period, which occurs at exactly the same rate as the rise in labor productivity, leaves the unit labor cost in money terms unchanged. In such a case, even at the same price of the previous period, there will be both a rise in real wages and a maintenance of the non-labor share of output. What we are talking about is a rise in money wages *for raising the labor's share in output.* In a money-using economy, if such a rise in money wages occurs at all, then it must lead to a rise in wage-share, because, if it did not, inflation would occur, which would threaten the value of money and hence the wealth held in the form of money and money-denominated assets; and a money-using economy can scarcely tolerate such inflation.

Keynesian economics sidestepped this proposition. Since Keynes believed that real wages equal marginal productivity of labor in "equilibrium" and that the curve for the short-run marginal productivity of labor was downward-sloping, an increase in aggregate demand, which he wanted state intervention to bring about, would raise employment only by lowering real wages. It was essential for the Keynesian position that if employment was to increase a lowering of real wages be accepted by the workers. To buttress his position, he put forward his concept of "money illusion," namely that as long as the money-wage rate was not cut, then even if there was a cut in the real wage rate through a rise in prices—as would happen when employment and output increase along an upward-sloping marginal cost curve—workers would take little cognizance of it.

This "money illusion" theme was carried forward and given an empirical backing by the Phillips Curve, which suggested on the basis of historical data that the rate of growth of money wages and the unemployment rate had a stable inverse relationship. In effect, no matter what increases in money wages workers demanded and obtained, if these increases were negated through corresponding price rises, the workers took little cognizance of it—and never incorporated the price rises into their money-wage demands. It was "money illusion" in a new garb: workers were satisfied getting money-wage increases, which could be higher at lower levels of unemployment because of their greater bargaining strength, even if these brought no real wage increases.

But this immediately raised the question: What good were trade unions if they did not succeed in raising real wages? And the equally pertinent question: Why were the employers so opposed to trade unions and why

did they create so much hullaballoo against them if the unions achieved
nothing real?

Michał Kalecki was also deeply affected by this question. He did not
accept the proposition that real wages equaled the marginal productivity
of labor in "equilibrium." On the contrary, he had a theory of distribution
according to which the share of wages—real wages divided by the (given)
labor productivity—was determined by capitalists' pricing behavior, the
markup over the unit prime cost that reflected "the degree of monopoly."
Money wage increases, therefore, could not increase real wages, but could
only increase prices, which again raised the question: What was the point
of trade unions? The answer given by Kalecki to this question, that the
markup itself was constrained by trade union strength, provided no indi-
cation of how exactly this came about.[16]

This question was raised by Ashok Mitra and answered through a
theory of distribution of his own, one different from Kalecki's.[17] But the
question continued to trouble Kalecki, and he came back to it in one of his
last articles, "Class Struggle and the Distribution of Income,"[18] where he
reiterated, again without explaining exactly how, that trade union action
had a role in restraining the size of the markup.

But if money-wage increases do not increase real wages but only raise
prices, then, in a world where trade unions insist on real wage increases,
accelerating inflation would ensue, which is impermissible in a money-
using economy. *Such an economy therefore must be characterized by the fact
that money-wage increases for raising the wage share must give rise to real
wage increases that do raise the wage share.*

Capitalists, of course, prefer a situation where such money-wage
increases do not occur. This is why the system maintains (not necessarily consciously or through deliberate machinations) a substantial level of
unemployment, or in Marx's terminology a "reserve army of labor," that
weakens trade unions adequately. The maintenance of the value of *money*,
in other words, requires the maintenance of a substantial reserve army of
*labor*. But if perchance there is a rise in the money-wage rate for raising the
labor-share in output, then the requirement of a money-using economy is
that it should give rise to an increase in the real wage rate, and hence in the
share of labor in output.

Now, in the conceptual representation of a capitalist economy as consisting only of workers and capitalists, any rise in labor-share can only lead to a fall in the profit share and therefore in the profit rate as well. Hence, if any increase in money wages occurs beyond what the increase in labor productivity allows, then the capitalists have to suffer a fall in profit margin (if accelerating inflation had to be avoided in order to prevent a collapse in the value of money). From their point of view, the best scenario would be if there were no increases in money wages, which means maintaining the size of the reserve army of labor to ensure that there were no such increases. But, for another reason, even this would not be enough. Let us turn to it.

### Increasing Long-Run Supply Price

Large numbers of primary commodities are subject to increasing supply price, not just in the short run when production cannot in any case be easily augmented, but even in the long run. The size of the tropical and semi-tropical land that produces large numbers of crops for consumption purposes or for commercial use in the capitalist sector of the world is limited. Even though land-augmenting investment and technological change can increase the effective supply of land, it typically requires state action, which is ruled out by the conceptual representation of capitalism. (And in any case, there is the real-life opposition to state action by financial interests that insist on "sound finance" and minimal state expenditure of this sort.) Also, minerals like oil are subject to increasing long-run supply price in the absence of new discoveries.

Increasing long-run supply price can be accommodated only through a fall in the profit share or a fall in the wage share within the capitalist sector. David Ricardo believed that since the real wage rate was bounded from below by a certain subsistence level,which alone would ensure an adequate supply of labor, an increasing supply price of primary commodities (what he called "diminishing returns") would squeeze profit share and hence the profit rate until it fell to zero in a stationary state, and accumulation would come to a halt.

Even with given money wages, an increasing supply price would still have to reduce profit margins and profit rates if the value of money is to be kept intact and accelerating inflation avoided. It is not enough, in other words, that money wages are not allowed to increase autonomously. Even if they are not, capitalists are still faced with the prospect of either reductions in profit margin or accelerating inflation. Even a reserve army of labor large enough to prevent autonomous increases in money wages is not adequate to rescue capitalists from reduced profit margins if the value of money is to be protected.

There is, however, a further point of importance here. With increasing supply price of primary commodities, even if there is a reduction in the capitalists' profit margin and profit rate and hence no accelerating inflation in the final product price and no threat to the value of money because of inflation in such final product price, *there would still be a direct threat to the value of money because of the inflation in primary commodity prices.* Primary commodities, or goods whose prices are supposed to move in tandem with their prices, will replace money as a form of wealth-holding as people come to expect a secular increase in their money prices. And even with profit margin and profit rate falling in the primary commodity–using sector, there would still be a threat to the value of money, which would cease to be a form of wealth-holding, and therefore the system would cease to be money-using.

Therefore, as a money-using economy, capitalism must have recourse to some ways of protecting the value of money. However, these ways are incapable of being captured in the standard conceptual representation of capitalism that economic theory has conjured up over the years.

### Summing Up

The specificity of a money-using economy, which capitalism preeminently is, is not captured in the conceptual representation of it as an isolated sector, consisting only of workers and capitalists, that much of economic theory has dealt with. If capitalism was only an isolated sector, then it would be stuck forever in a stationary state or a state of simple reproduction. And in the event of accumulation, it would not even be able to protect the value of money in the face of the increasing long-run supply price to which several of the primary commodities are subject. The fact that capitalism has not had such dire experiences is because its reality has been quite different from the conceptual representation of it in most strands of economic theory. But before examining this reality, we'll take a brief look at some of these strands and see how, specifically, economic theorists have failed to take account of capitalism's money-using character.

# CHAPTER 2

# Money in Some Theoretical Traditions

I n the previous chapter we discussed that the conceptual representation of capitalism as an isolated sector consisting only of capitalists and
workers cannot capture its character as a money-using economy. Yet
much of economic theory has stuck to this representation, which is why
its treatment of money has been flawed in various ways. In this chapter, we
examine some major strands of economic theory to establish this point.

## The Walrasian System

Let us take the Walrasian system first. In the simplest exposition of this
system an auctioneer arrives at market-clearing prices, and all sales occur
only at these "equilibrium" prices, and there is no need for money in
transactions. Money is only a *numeraire*, in terms of which all prices are
expressed, a role that any other good can play as well. There is nothing *sui
generis* about money; indeed, there is no reason why some special thing
called "money" needs to exist in such a world at all.

Ironically, the Walrasian system, with money being used for the circulation of commodities at a constant velocity, with a transaction demand
for it that bears a constant ratio to the total value of the transactions carried out, has been the staple of much monetary theory. It has been the
bedrock of the particular tradition called "monetarism," so much so that
Frank Hahn described monetarism as synonymous with the belief that

the world conforms to a Walrasian equilibrium.[1] But in grafting a transaction demand for money into a Walrasian universe, the question remains: In a world where transactions occur only at market-clearing prices, why should there ever be a transaction demand for money? The only possible answer can be that the bids by market participants, which the auctioneer has to consider, are affected by their possession of money; that is, the money balance held by an individual affects his or her demand function. The question is how can it do so in a manner compatible with the notion of a transaction demand for money?

Robert Clower sought to answer this question through this example:[2] The market meets only once a week, and the sale proceeds of one particular week cannot be used entirely for buying goods in the same week. Only a part of such proceeds, a fixed part at that, can be used, and the remainder must be carried over to the next week, where demand consequently becomes dependent upon the money-stock in the possession of the buyers. The total value of transactions on any market day in such a case will clearly be constrained by the amount of money stock in the possession of the people, as monetarism postulates.[3]

However, this constraining role of money supply on the value of transactions, which restores some role to money even in a world where all markets clear simultaneously through an auctioneer, arises entirely because of the assumption that only a fixed ratio of current proceeds can be spent on purchases in the current week. Unfortunately, to assume such a fixed ratio is completely arbitrary. Monetarism and its assumption of a constant (income) velocity of circulation of money, collapses if this ratio became a variable. Besides, if it does become a variable there is no reason why it cannot reach 100 percent, that is, why the entire proceeds of a given day cannot be spent the same day, in which case the constraining role of money on transactions, and with it *any role of money*, would disappear altogether. In such a case we would be back to the Walrasian world with an auctioneer, a world where money is not needed.

Moreover, a variable time lag between sale and purchase by market participants gives rise to a deeper problem. If money is held for a variable period of time between sale and purchase, then the obverse of this period for which it is held, namely the velocity of circulation of money, also becomes a variable. But this immediately raises the possibility of a deficiency of aggregate demand for produced commodities, and Say's Law, which denies such deficiency of aggregate demand, breaks down.

This is so because Say's Law, by which there can never be a deficiency of aggregate demand as "supply creates its own demand," amounts to saying the following. There can never be an *ex ante* excess supply of produced commodities because, for this to happen, there has to be something outside the circle of produced commodities for which there is a corresponding *ex ante* excess demand; and there is nothing outside this circle of produced commodities for which there can possibly be such an *ex ante* excess demand. Money, the only obvious entity that stands outside of the charmed circle of produced commodities, and one for which an *ex ante* excess demand could cause an ex ante excess supply for produced goods, thus nullifying Say's Law, cannot play this spoiling role if the demand for money is a fixed ratio of the value of produced commodities.

In short, *ex hypothesi*, there can never be an *ex ante* excess demand for money if there is a fixed time lag between sale and purchase. Such an excess demand can arise only when the time lag between sale and purchase by a representative market participant becomes a variable. And if that happens and Say's Law ceases to hold, then the Walrasian equilibrium, which assumes that all markets clear and that there is no involuntary unemployment (which would occur if there was an *ex ante* excess supply of produced goods), loses its relevance.

Summing this up, if there is no time lag between a market participant selling goods and buying goods, as is the case if all transactions occur at the same time at the market-clearing equilibrium prices arrived at by the auctioneer, then there is in effect no money in the economy. Money comes into the picture only when there is a time lag between a person's sale and purchase. If this time lag is fixed, then one can perhaps tell some sort of a coherent story about the Walrasian equilibrium. But there is no earthly reason why this time lag should be constant. And if it is not, then the Walrasian equilibrium loses its relevance since there is no reason for Say's Law to hold. In other words, giving money a role in the Walrasian system, a role that does not destroy the relevance of the system itself, can occur only under stringent and unrealistic assumptions.

The unrealism of this fixed–time lag assumption can be seen in a different way. During the time lag between sale and purchase in the C-M-C circuit, wealth is being held, no doubt fleetingly, in the form of money. But if wealth can be held fleetingly in the form of money, then there is absolutely no reason why it cannot be held in the form of money more than fleetingly. There can indeed be a whole range of circumstances that induce people to wish to defer their purchases, to hold their sale proceeds in the form of money, though this would nullify Say's Law.

Say's law and the Walrasian equilibrium assume that such a denouement, namely an *ex ante* excess supply of produced commodities, *never happens,* not that it may happen at certain times while other things happen at other times. It follows that the most "mainstream" strand of economic theory, which is the Walrasian one, is based on a conception that is not possible in a money-using economy.

## *The Ricardian System*

Ricardo wrote much on money, including on monetary issues being debated in his time. But we shall be concerned here with discussing his monetary theory not with reference to his position in monetary debates of his time, but with reference to his overall economic theory.

Adam Smith had put forward his theory of price. which has often been referred to as an "adding up" theory of price,[4] in which the price of corn determines the prices of all other commodities. When the corn price rises, money wages rise to keep the corn wage intact; hence the cost of production rises everywhere, and this gets passed on in the form of higher "natural prices" of all commodities.

This theory, however, which said that a "general enhancement of the price of all commodities" occurs "in consequence of that of labor,"[5] made the level of money wages and money prices indeterminate, even in a world where the corn wage was a given. Now, such indeterminacy in a paper money or credit money world, where the level of money wages and prices could be anywhere but happened to be at some perch at any given time, could be understandable. But Smith was not talking about a paper or credit money world.

He was talking about a commodity money world, which was relevant for his time, and which was clear from the use he made of Hume's ingenious theorem on gold flows to refute the mercantilist claim that a nation grew richer by amassing precious metals.[6] He argued based on Hume that if a country accumulated more gold, then its price level would rise (based on the Quantity theory of money), which would make its commodities uncompetitive, resulting in a current account deficit, which would be settled only through its gold flowing out. And in a commodity money world, Smith's adding up theory could not hold. The value of money in such a world, where the production of the money commodity got augmented if it became more profitable, had to be linked to the conditions of production.

This was the starting point of Ricardo's theory.[7] In a commodity money world (or where paper money is convertible to the money commodity), money became part of the charmed circle of produced commodities, with the wage rate and the profit rate being identical between the money and non-money sectors (in a situation of free mobility of capital and labor across sectors). The equilibrium value of money, which constitutes the "center of gravity" of the "market price" of money, is given by its price of production, that is, the relative price vis-à-vis non-money commodities at which the profit and wage rates in the money sector are equal to those in the non-money sector (though Ricardo generally used relative labor values as an approximation for this equilibrium value).

It followed from this that when money wages rose, the rate of profit fell. Indeed. instead of all money prices rising as Adam Smith had suggested, if the money commodity was produced with labor alone, and all other commodities required some means of production, then a rise in money wages would mean *a fall in all money prices of all non-money commodities*, which was the exact opposite of what Smith had suggested.

Ricardo's monetary theory, however, had no role for any wealth demand for money, which also explains why Ricardo was an adherent of Say's Law. His carrying over of the entire array of concepts—"market price," "natural price," and "center of gravity"—to his theory of money, which was the consequence of analyzing money as a produced commodity that was used only as a means of circulation, made him a monetarist in the short run though not in the long run.

This is because if perchance there was an increase in the supply of money, then the market price of money would fall, meaning that the market prices of all non-money commodities in terms of money would rise, exactly in accordance with what monetarism postulates. But this would mean a lowering of the rate of profit of the money-producing sector compared to the other sectors, and hence a shift of capital and labor away from producing money into producing other goods, which would lower the supply of money and thereby ensure once more that prices of production prevail and that the supply of money is no greater or no less than what is required for circulating commodities at those prices of production.

Therefore, in the short run, commodity prices depend upon the supply of money. In the long run, the supply of money adjusts to the demand, with commodity prices being equal to the prices of production. In Joan Robinson's telling phrase, the Quantity equation MV= PQ is read by Ricardo from the left to the right in the short run, which is what monetarists do, but from the right to the left in the long run, which is of course contrary to monetarism.[8]

But a constant income velocity of circulation of money was central to Ricardo's theory, both his theory of market prices of commodities in terms of money and his theory of prices of production, as indeed it was for Hume. James Mill, who was Ricardo's interpreter and popularizer, tried to justify this assumption of a constant income velocity of circulation by suggesting that even though the different components of the money stock made different numbers of circuits in the process of circulation, there had to be an average number among them, a justification against which Marx had rightly remarked that an *average* did not mean a *constant*.[9] And once this assumption of constancy of the income velocity of circulation is dropped, we have to reckon with a wealth demand for money, which makes a belief in Say's Law logically untenable.

The Ricardian theory of money, like that of Walras, ignored the basic property of a money-using economy. Ricardo's conceptual representation of capitalism consisted, in the core of his theoretical discussion, of an isolated sector with capitalists and workers, and in analyzing it he abstracted, not surprisingly, from the central features of a money-using economy.

Exactly the same can be said of the Marshallian system, which we looked at in chapter 1 through the Cambridge equation. Though money in this system, as in the Walrasian, is not a produced good, so that there is no "natural price" of money and no need to distinguish between that and its "market price," the assumption of a constant $k$ (or a constant income velocity of circulation of money) rules out any wealth demand for money and hence any possibility of a deficiency of aggregate demand for produced goods. And whether it be in the Walrasian or the Ricardian or the Marshallian theories, ruling out any wealth demand for money and recognizing only a transaction demand for it, is logically untenable. This is because if money is held "fleetingly," then there is no earthly reason why it cannot be held more than "fleetingly."

### The Keynesian System

The Keynesian system, like the Marxian one, rightly recognizes the wealth demand for money, because of which it rejects both monetarism and Say's Law. According to Keynes, the value of money in any period is given not by the demand for and supply of money but by the level of the money-wage rate, that is, by the fact that the exchange ratio between a unit of money and a unit of one particular commodity, "labor-power," to borrow Marx's terminology, which is used directly or indirectly in the production of all produced commodities, is given.

Some assumption of this sort is essential to make for a paper money world, once we recognize the wealth demand for money and abandon the view that the value of money is determined by its demand and supply. Since money in such a world is not a produced commodity and is not even convertible at a fixed exchange rate into a produced commodity like gold or silver, there is no cost of production to provide any anchorage to the value of money. And if demand and supply play no role in determining its value, then the only way for there to be a determinate value of money is if this value is tied to one particular commodity. And a commodity that has to be used for producing all other commodities is an ideal candidate for this purpose. Labor-power is such a commodity. Hence money wages being given in any period makes eminent sense in this context.

A problem, however, arises from the fact that the stability of the value of money, which is essential for it to play the role of a wealth-form, then becomes dependent upon the stability of the money-wage rate or the "wage unit" as Keynes called it. And in the isolated capitalist sector that is the conceptual universe for analysis there is no reason to expect the wage unit to be constant irrespective of the level of employment, whether within a given period or across periods.

This is precisely the assumption that Keynes made in the context of his single period analysis and it is crucial for his theory. The whole point of his theory was that a capitalist economy can settle down at any level of employment, depending upon the level of aggregate demand; and since unemployment was socially unacceptable, the state should nudge the economy toward a higher level of employment. But if a higher level of employment meant a higher money wage, then the stability of the wage unit, and with it the entire role of money as a form of wealth-holding, would get jeopardized.

On the other hand, since Keynes accepted the equality of real wages and the marginal product of labor at the "equilibrium" level of employment where the economy settled (given the level of aggregate demand), higher levels of employment would necessarily mean lower real wages (as the marginal product of labor curve was assumed to be downward-sloping). This meant assuming that the workers would be willing to accept the same money-wage rate no matter what the level of employment, even though the real wage rate would be different at different levels of unemployment.

There was thus a basic contradiction between Keynes's assumption that multiple employment equilibria were possible in the single period he was considering, and that the wage unit nonetheless remained stable in this period. This is the contradiction that was later exploited by his critics to bring about a revival of monetarism.

Keynes glossed over this contradiction, through postulating a "money illusion" that afflicted the workers. He put forward the proposition that any lowering of real wages as employment increased would go unnoticed by the workers as long as the money wages remained unchanged, because workers were focused only upon the money-wage rate—wherein lay their "money illusion." If their real wage rate were to be cut through a cut in the money-wage rate, then they would resist it, but they would not notice a cut in real wage rate through a rise in prices at a *given* money-wage rate.

Keynes thus sought to reconcile, through his theory of money illusion, the requirement that the wage unit should be stable in a money-using economy with his theory that such an economy could settle at any one of a range of levels of employment, and therefore should be pushed toward full employment by state intervention in aggregate demand. The Phillips Curve supported Keynes's idea of a "money illusion" afflicting the workers.

This last point can be seen as follows: If the rate of growth of money wages is a function of the unemployment rate, that is, $[(dw/dt)/w] = f(u)$, and if the rate of growth of prices is the same as the rate of growth of unit labor cost, that is, $[(dp/dt)]/p = [(dw/dt)/w] - \beta$, where $\beta$ is the rate of growth of labor productivity, then it follows that at every level of unemployment the workers' effort to raise the wage share of output is frustrated. Real wage growth can never rise above productivity growth, even though in demanding and obtaining money wage increases, *this is what workers are aiming to achieve.* They believe that prices will not change while obtaining money wage increases, but this is precisely what happens, preventing them from getting any real wage increases in excess of productivity growth.

Taking $\beta$ to be zero, what this means is that the workers never actually get any real wage increase, even though the whole point of their demanding and getting higher money wage increases was to raise their real wage. They are frustrated by price increase, and yet the Phillips Curve postulates that *they never notice the price increase,* for if they did then they would anticipate inflation and incorporate it into their money-wage demand, which would make inflation accelerate. The basic underlying assumption behind the Phillips Curve, as is well known, is static price expectations on the part of the workers, which means that they do not notice inflation and therefore do not expect it. This is a form of "money illusion."

But it is obvious that though "money illusion" among workers may prevail temporarily, it cannot be assumed to be a permanent feature of a capitalist economy, in which case Keynesianism gets into difficulties, a point perceived by Joan Robinson when she postulated an "inflationary barrier."[10] She saw that the rate of unemployment could not fall below a certain level, the level at which unbounded inflation set in. That is, unbounded inflation set a floor for the level of unemployment to which an increase in aggregate demand (including through state intervention) could push the economy.

The "inflationary barrier," however, does not do away with the idea of "money illusion." All it suggests is that at some level of unemployment, when the real wages have fallen sufficiently low, the fall will be noted, the "illusion" will break, and workers will wake up to demand higher money wages, which, if offset by price increases, will go on and on rising, resulting in a veritable explosion. Before the point at which the "illusion" breaks, it must be there.

Put differently, the following three propositions, each of which characterizes the Keynesian system, cannot *logically* hold together without workers being afflicted by "money illusion" at least over a certain range: (1) Real wages = marginal productivity of labor (with a downward-sloping MPL curve); (2) money wages are given in the period in question; and (3) the level of employment can be altered by state intervention through altering aggregate demand. And if "money illusion" is seen to be an unreal phenomenon, then this makes the Keynesian system, at least in its original form as developed by Keynes,[11] *logically* untenable.

One can, of course, go along with the Kaleckian formulation, rather than the Keynesian one, and do away with number 1 above. One can postulate instead that the price is a markup over unit prime cost, which in the case of an isolated capitalist economy producing *ex hypothesi* all its own raw materials internally, is simply the unit labor cost that is constant as long as all production coefficients are given and unchanging. The fixity of the money-wage rate even in this case, however, cannot hold since the workers' real wage demand (for given productivity) will be negatively related to the rate of unemployment, with there being a certain floor real wage rate which it cannot fall below. At the level of unemployment where the real wage demand begins to exceed this floor, money wages will rise, and since they will be "passed on" in the form of higher prices, accelerating inflation will ensue (because there is no "money illusion"). But this level of unemployment will then become the floor below which unemployment cannot fall (analogous to the "inflationary barrier"). And since it is at this

level of unemployment that money wages start increasing through workers' bargaining for higher real wages, this floor unemployment rate can be
quite high, which means that the capacity of the government to push down
unemployment remains correspondingly constricted.

But for the same reason that pushing down unemployment remains
constricted, any buoyancy in aggregate demand that pushes the unemployment level below this threshold also pushes the economy into accelerating inflation. In an isolated capitalist economy with no regulation of
aggregate demand, there is nothing to prevent such accelerating inflation.

We can distinguish here between two cases. One, where at the prevailing level of aggregate demand and hence output, there is both unutilized
capacity and unemployment above this threshold rate the wage unit will
be stable in such a case. Two, where at the prevailing level of aggregate
demand, there is either an *ex ante* excess demand at full capacity or an *ex
ante* tendency for unemployment to fall below the threshold level. In this
case the wage unit will get destabilized through accelerating inflation.

The stability of the wage unit therefore requires both things: the maintenance of unutilized capacity (so that there is no tendency toward a rise
in prices through demand-pull pressures) and the maintenance of sizable
unemployment, above the threshold where money wages start rising. This
dual requirement is impossible to meet in a capitalist economy in which
aggregate demand is not planned by some central authority.

Besides, if both these conditions held then we would never witness
any increase in money wages above the rise in labor productivity, for that
would simply engender accelerating inflation. Since we do see increases
in money wages above the rate of growth of labor productivity, and yet no
accelerating inflation, as Phillips has shown through his empirical analysis,
it follows that unless we believe in "money illusion," the conceptualization of capitalism as an isolated system with only workers and capitalists
is wrong.

Even the Keynesian analysis of a money-using economy, which recognizes its characteristics so much better than the other theoretical systems
we have analyzed, the Walrasian, Marshallian, and Ricardian, is fraught
with logical contradictions. True, these would not arise if we believe with
Keynes that workers suffer from "money illusion," but once we abandon

this concept as unreal (thereby rendering Keynes's original system logi-cally untenable) and introduce an alternative pricing-distribution system in its place that is compatible with "involuntary unemployment," it turns out that the stability of the wage unit, without which a money-using economy cannot survive, becomes difficult to explain. Clearly the problem lies with the conceptual universe in terms of which we are looking at capitalism.

Capitalism cannot be conceived as an isolated system consisting only of workers and capitalists, as economic theory in all its different traditions has done. But before going further into how it should be conceptualized, we will examine the Marxian theoretical system in the next chapter.

# CHAPTER 3

# The Marxian System and Money

The Marxian system, like the Keynesian, recognizes that people hold a part of their wealth in the form of money, and consequently Say's Law does not hold and involuntary unemployment can and does occur in such an economy. It also recognizes that because there is a wealth demand for money, the value of money vis-à-vis the world of commodities cannot be determined by the demand for and the supply of money. Rather, it is fixed independently of its demand and supply.[1] Since Marx, unlike Keynes, was talking not about a paper money or credit money world, but about a commodity money world (with paper money being statutorily convertible into the money commodity at some fixed rate), he saw the relative amounts of labor directly or indirectly embodied in a unit of the money commodity, as compared with a unit of the basket of non-money commodities being produced, as the determinant of the value of money. In short, he saw the value of money vis-à-vis commodities as being determined by the labor theory of value.

## Ricardo and Marx on Money and Value

It is often taken for granted that the labor theory of value of Marx is more or less identical with that of Ricardo. This is untrue. Indeed, it simply cannot be true in view of Marx's total rejection of Say's Law, which Ricardo accepted. Rejection of Say's Law entails accepting that money has a wealth demand, quite apart from its transaction demand; the magnitude of this wealth demand can change even when there is no change in the value of the commodities being circulated through the medium of money. Marx saw people hoarding money, quite apart from the money that was circulating, the size of which could fluctuate for independent reasons having nothing to do with the value of the total magnitude of commodities circulating. If there is such a wealth demand for money, then an increase in the supply of money also need not enter immediately into circulation (at least not the whole of it) and create additional demand for commodities, raising their prices in the short run, as Ricardo believed.

The value of money, or its obverse, the price level of commodities, does not respond to an increase in the supply of money, either fully (as monetarism, including that of Ricardo, would suggest), or even at all, since all the addition to the supply of money may simply be added to the hoard that people hold. Correspondingly, if there is an increase in the transaction demand for money owing to an increase in the value of commodities circulating in the economy, this need not cause an increase in the value of money, since this extra transactions demand may be accommodated through a fall in the relative size of the hoard.

What is more, even if the supply of money remains unchanged, as does the supply of commodities that have to be circulated with the help of money, a desire on the part of people to hoard a larger amount of money, that is, not throw it back into circulation, can lead to an *ex ante* change in the aggregate demand for commodities and hence in their price level (to be followed by quantity adjustment). Since neither an increase in the supply of commodities (and hence in the transaction demand for money required to circulate them) nor an increase in the supply of money need make any difference to the value of money, it follows that in a money-using economy the value of money has to be explained by some factor other than the demand for and supply of money. Then, whatever effect the changes in the demand and supply of money have on the economy has to be examined independently. Supply and demand do not provide any anchorage to the value of money.

This other factor determining the value of money cannot be the obverse of the "prices of production" of commodities, as in Ricardo. This is because monetarism, as we have seen, is a necessary ingredient of Ricardo's theory, indeed of any theory that determines the value of money in terms of these prices of production (or "Sraffa prices," as some may prefer to call them).

It follows that Ricardo's acceptance of monetarism even in the short run cannot characterize the Marxian system. This in turn means that money in the Marxian system cannot be part of the charmed circle of commodities across which the rate of profit and the wage rate are equalized in a free competition economy. The value of money has to be independently determined, and *the determination of all the prices of production of non-money commodities has to be based on this independent specification.* The relative exchange rate between money and non-money commodities in Marx is not determined as the relative exchange rates within the world of non-money commodities, but is determined independently, and underlies the latter. This determination is by the relative quantities of labor embodied directly and indirectly in a unit of the money commodity relative to a unit of the basket of non-money commodities.

It follows from this that when the prices of production deviate from labor values in the case of the non-money commodities, this does not mean any change in the rate of exchange between money and the non-money commodities, which, in the Marxian system, continues to equal the relative labor values. This exchange rate remains unchanged, unaffected by the transformation of values into prices; rather it constitutes the basis on which the transformation of values into prices within the non-money commodities world occurs.

Putting it differently, even if labor values do not actually determine the long run (or "center-of-gravity") equilibrium prices among the non-money commodities, the relative quantities of labor embodied still constitute the determinant of the exchange ratio between money and the world of non-money commodities in the Marxian system. The prices of commodities in terms of money, in other words, are determined on the prior specification of an independent meta-rule that determines the value of money. The labor theory of value provides such a meta-rule.

An example will clarify the point. If 100 units of the money commodity require as much labor directly and indirectly as the total output of non-money commodities, then the money value of the latter is 100; or the value of money in terms of the basket of commodities produced is .01. If the money wage rate is 0.5, then the prices of production can be determined, given this value of money. If the value of money was not given by this meta-rule, then, unlike in the Ricardian system where money enters the charmed circle of commodities across which the wage rate and the rate of profit are equalized, prices of production could not be determined.

Of course, the exchange ratio between money and the basket of other commodities need not empirically correspond to the relative quantities of labor directly and indirectly embodied in a unit of each. This empirical fact may suggest that we need an alternative explanation for this exchange ratio. But any different explanation can always be subsumed under a relative labor–embodied explanation by bringing in, say, the monopoly rent of gold mine owners, which may explain why the gold-versus-commodity ratio is not exactly identical with the relative quantities of labor embodied.

In other words, a fixed ratio between money and the world of non-money commodities, even if it does not empirically correspond to the relative quantities of labor embodied, can still be explained as being based upon it. It is this fixed ratio that is an essential part of Marx's theory, as underlying even the determination of the prices of production of the non-money commodities on the basis of given money wages. Thus there is a fundamental difference between Ricardo and Marx on the question of money and value theory. This in turn arises from their difference over the wealth demand for money, and hence Say's Law, and the possibility of generalized *ex ante* overproduction.

### The Marxian and the Keynesian Systems

On the basic issue of a wealth demand for money and the possibility of generalized *ex ante* overproduction (or what Keynes called "involuntary unemployment"), there is much in common between the Marxian and the Keynesian systems. Indeed, one can say without exaggeration that almost seventy years before Keynes's *General Theory*, the basic conclusions of that opus had been anticipated by Marx, although, having recognized the possibility of generalized overproduction, Marx did not theorize about where the economy would settle in such a situation. That is, he lacked a theory of income determination based on the "multiplier," which is what Richard Kahn and Keynes provided in the 1930s.

But Marxists saw deficient aggregate demand only as a *cyclical* phenomenon that would reverse itself, so that *on average*, the system would function at a certain level of capacity utilization, on the basis of which the input coefficients that go into the determination of labor values could be worked out. This was an error, because once the possibility of a deficiency of aggregate demand is admitted, then an isolated capitalist system acquires a "knife-edge" property and gets pushed toward a stationary state or simple reproduction (a zero trend situation), a possibility seen only by Rosa Luxemburg (1913) and later theorized by Kalecki.[2] For a long time, Marxian economics remained handicapped due to not following up on Marx's insights into the theory of aggregate demand.

This similarity between the Marxian and Keynesian systems may appear surprising to many because they have very different notions of money. Indeed Nicholas Kaldor has argued that though monetarism does not hold in a credit money world, since such a world is characterized by money supply "endogeneity" (where money supply adjusts to the demand for money), it is likely to characterize a commodity money world since money supply there is exogenously given.[3] But the existence of a hoard, which signifies a wealth demand for money even in a commodity money world, can have exactly the same implications, by way of negating monetarism and Say's Law, as occur in a credit money world.

However, one fundamental difference between the Marxian and the Keynesian systems exists, even in this terrain. Whereas in Keynes an increase in money wages gives rise to an increase in prices, leaving real wages unchanged, begging the question why trade unions existed at all, in Marx, as in Ricardo, a rise in money wages increases real wages at the expense of profits. In a famous pamphlet, *Wages, Prices and Profits,* which is the text of his speech at a meeting of the International Working Men's Association, Marx had argued against Citizen Weston, a follower of John Stuart Mill, who had suggested on the basis of Mill's "Wages Fund" theory that workers could not raise their real wages, and that the gains of some could only come through losses of others. But this was not the case, Marx said, contending that all workers could gain through trade union action at the expense of the capitalists. This was probably the first explicit formulation of what later came to be called the "factor-price frontier," that is, the inverse relationship between the real wage rate and the rate of profit. What was striking, however, was that this formulation was made for a world that could, by Marx's own recognition, be characterized by "involuntary unemployment."

In a world with "involuntary unemployment," since output is demand-constrained, a rise in real wages could simply raise output—the rise in real wages leads to an increased demand for output, which, in turn, raises the quantity produced without altering the magnitude of profits and hence the rate of profit. A downward-sloping "factor-price frontier" can be postulated here only in the following sense: if real wages increase *at a given output,* then the rate of profit will fall. Or put differently, a rise in real wages would lower the "given-output rate of profit," and a rise in money wages, since it necessarily raises real wages, would also do so. In interpreting Marx's "factor-price frontier," which shows an inverse relationship between money wages and the rate of profit, we are not asking the question what happens if money wages rise in an economy; we are asking the question what happens if money wages rise in an economy with given output?

Let us now pull together the threads of Marx's argument with regard to money. Marx's view of the characteristics of a money-using capitalist economy can be summed up in three propositions:

- Proposition 1: Money is held in a capitalist economy not just for circulating commodities but also as a form of wealth, so that the money held on average over any period may far exceed what is needed for circulation.
- Proposition 2: For any given level of capacity utilization of the fixed capital stock, there is a unique money value of the aggregate output produced, which is independent of the total money supply.
- Proposition 3: For any given level of capacity utilization, a rise in the money-wage rate lowers the maximum realizable rate of profit.

Although the Keynesian system accepts the first two propositions, the Marxian system accepts all three, and therein lies its uniqueness.

The difference between the two systems, which relates only to the third of these propositions, would be attributed immediately to the fact that Marx is dealing with a commodity money world. In it, the value of the money commodity in terms of non-money commodities is fixed independently, whereas Keynes is dealing with a credit money world where there is no such fixity.

Although this is certainly true, the question to ask of the Marxian system is: If money wages increase, why should prices not increase? *What is the mechanism through which the fixity or the relative fixity of the value of money is maintained when money wages increase?*

To say that money consists, say, of gold, and that the value of gold in terms of other commodities is determined by their relative labor costs (either immediately or in some refracted fashion) is not enough. This amounts to asserting that any increase in money wages *ipso facto* results in a rise in real wages (because the value of money in terms of commodities is fixed). The question here is: Why does the value of money in terms of commodities not change when the money wage rate rises?

Looked at differently, suppose the money-wage rate rises, and suppose the capitalists put up their prices proportionately, so that the profit margin and hence the profit rate do not fall. What is there to prevent such a denouement in the Marxian schema, while such precisely is what is supposed to happen in the Keynesian-Kaleckian schema (though the manner in which it is supposed to happen is not identical for Keynes and Kalecki)?

The immediate answer might be that since Marx was talking about "free competition," raising prices by capitalists in view of the money wage increase should be ruled out because that is not the way "free competition" is supposed to operate. This answer, however, is unconvincing for two reasons. First, it would amount to saying that trade unions can raise real wages under free competition but not under oligopoly (where there is markup pricing), which then raises the same question as before: Why is there so much hullaballoo over trade unions under oligopolistic capitalism? Second, a focus on the nature of *competition* obscures that the answer is supposed to lie in the nature of *money*. Indeed, that would have been Marx's own answer, emphasizing that the money he was talking about was commodity money. Hence, dragging in the distinction between "free competition" and oligopoly/monopoly is inapposite here.

So, if in a commodity money world there is a rise in money wages and the capitalists mark up their prices equiproportionally, then what is there to prevent it? There is no point saying that they cannot, given the fixity of the value of money, since the whole point is to investigate how this fixity in the value of money is sustained.

Oddly, Marx does not say much on how exactly this fixity in the value of money is actually maintained in the economy. An implicit answer in *Wages, Prices and Profits* goes as follows: If the economy is not a gold-producing one but imports its gold against a certain bundle of other commodities, there is no reason whatsoever why the gold exporters should accept any smaller bundle of commodities in exchange for what they supply just because money wages have gone up inside the gold-importing economy. The fixity of the value of money in the face of money-wage changes arises, in other words, because the terms of exchange between its gold imports and commodity exports remain unchanged when money wages change. This argument is plausible, though it does not cover the case where gold is domestically produced.

The Marxist tradition has not been concerned with this question at all.[4] Typically, the tendency has simply been to take this fixity for granted and argue on its basis that a rise in money wages must raise real wages. But this, as we have maintained, does not amount to proving the point.

### Fixity of the Value of Money

Although Marx did not specify how exactly the fixity in the value of money is sustained, we can adduce a possible mechanism for it. Suppose everyone in the economy believes that this fixity will be maintained, because it actually has been maintained in the past. Then if money wages rise by 10 percent, say, and the money prices are also marked up by 10 percent, the value of money falls by 10 percent. Since economic agents believe that the usual value of money will be maintained, they would expect that the value of money would rise by 10 percent from the level to which it has currently fallen; that is, they would expect commodity prices to fall by 10 percent.

There would, therefore, be a reduction in the demand for commodities, as people postpone purchases and reduce commodity stocks in order to increase money holdings. This will have the actual effect of pushing commodity prices back to their old level, and ensuring that the increase in money wages actually results in a corresponding rise in real wages, and hence a fall in the "given-output rate of profit."

It may be felt that with this mechanism it would become difficult for any change to occur in the market prices of commodities, such as would arise as a prelude to involuntary unemployment. After all, before any quantity adjustment occurs, there is likely to be some fall in prices in general owing to *ex ante* overproduction; but if every fall gives rise to an expectation of a price increase and to a larger demand for commodities, then there can scarcely be a deficiency of aggregate demand (or fluctuations in the level of aggregate demand).

We can, however, salvage Marx's theoretical vision from this logical problem by adopting one of two possible routes. One, which can be borrowed from Kalecki, does not visualize any actual divergence of market prices from the "equilibrium" (or markup) prices. Variations in demand directly affect inventories and through them capacity utilization without causing any price changes. At the same time, any rise in money wages, if it is fully passed on as a general price rise, is doomed to failure, since everyone will believe that money prices will come back to their earlier level in the future, no matter what their current level may be. This route entails what some would call a "fix-price" economy. Though a far cry from Marx's own formulation, it can be one way of ensuring that his various propositions on money hold together.

The other route is to assume that economic agents can distinguish between "cost-induced" changes in the price level and "demand-induced" changes in the price level. Where the money commodity is domestically produced and thus affected by a rise in money wages, like all other commodities, they would expect money prices of non-money commodities to remain more or less unchanged even when money wages rise, and this would prevent any actual rise in money prices of non-money commodities. Money-wage increases in this case will lead to real wage increases. But aggregate demand–induced changes in the price level affect only the non-money commodities vis-à-vis the money commodity. The expectation then would be that the change in money prices would continue for some time, instead of reversing itself. And this would cause output adjustment, or involuntary unemployment.

We can thus adduce possible ways of defending Marx's position on money in the context of an isolated capitalist sector. But even these, no matter whether they are persuasive, are not enough. The irreconcilability between a closed capitalist sector and the three propositions advanced by Marx, which are valid propositions in a money-using economy, becomes obvious when we consider paper money, as Marx himself had done.

### A Problem with Paper Money

It would appear at first sight that the Marxian system is immune to one important strand of the general criticism we have been making here of the various theoretical systems in economics. Our general criticism has been that the isolated capitalist economy, consisting only of workers and capitalists, with the state not *directly* intervening in any significant way in economic life, which is the usual conceptual representation of it in the economic literature, is incompatible with a money-using economy. This is so for a number of reasons, one of which is that two properties of a money-using economy cannot both be satisfied in an isolated capitalist sector. First, a rise in money wages must lead to a reduction in the "given-output rate of profit," otherwise we cannot understand the reality of class struggle and the employers' persistent efforts to roll back trade union rights. And second, the economy cannot avoid the possibility of involuntary unemployment.[5]

The Marxian system appears to be immune to this particular strand of our criticism. It seems that there can both be involuntary unemployment, and at any level of such unemployment *if* there is a rise in money wages enforced by the workers, then it would lead not to a rise in the price level but to a reduction in the rate of profit. In other words, with an invariance of money-price to money-wage changes at every level of unemployment, the system can settle at alternative levels of unemployment. (And, typically, lower levels of unemployment are associated with lower "given-output rates of profit." In such a system, it is clear why employers are dead-opposed to trade unions.

But there is still a problem here. To go back to our previous discussion, if money wages rise and prices rise *pari passu,* then, with people expecting that the value of the money commodity will come back to the old level, there will be an actual reduction in the demand for commodities to bring the price level back to the original position and reduce the given-output rate of profit. But if money consists not just of the money commodity but also of paper currency convertible into it, then we are dealing with two sets of expectations, not one, namely the expectation of the value of the money commodity vis-à-vis the non-money commodities, *and* the expectation of the value of paper currency vis-à-vis the money commodity. Even if the paper currency is statutorily convertible, people still may not always be confident that it will remain so when the crunch comes.

Though people may confidently expect that commodity prices will come down vis-à-vis the money commodity if there is a rise in prices because of a rise in money wages, they may also expect that paper currency will not maintain its value. That is, it may not remain convertible at the old rate for long. There would then be a rush to gold from both directions, from those holding commodities and from those holding paper currency. And with every flight from paper currency to gold, the confidence in its remaining convertible at the old rate would diminish, which would trigger further flight. Indeed, maintaining convertibility would actually become impossible in such a situation.

In the Marxian system, despite commodity money and convertible paper currency, we therefore have something of the same problem that afflicted the Keynesian system. A rise in money wages, if it is passed on through higher prices, threatens the value of the part of money that consists of paper currency. On the other hand, there is no reason why capitalists should not wish to pass on the higher wages in the form of higher prices and meekly accept a lower rate of profit. And if higher money wages are passed on as higher prices, with no fall expected in these prices vis-à-vis the paper currency, which is also depreciating, then wealth held in the form of paper currency will be subject to losses. *Thus, if the economy has paper currency, even though convertible to the money commodity at a fixed rate, and some wealth*

*is held in the form of such currency, then a rise in money wages threatens the*
*value of such currency and hence the wealth held in this form.*

Reconciling three obvious and observable phenomena, namely money as a form of wealth-holding, the possibility of involuntary unemployment, and trade unions' ability to raise real wages through higher money-wage bargains, all three of which characterize capitalism and are recognized within the Marxian system, seems impossible within an isolated capitalist sector.

It follows, then, that even the Marxian system faces a problem in reconciling a conceptual representation of capitalism as an isolated sector consisting only of workers and capitalists with the reality of a money-using economy, though it is more keenly aware of this reality than other theoretical systems, including even the Keynesian one.

### A Critique of the Marxian System: Summing Up

Notwithstanding Marx's deep understanding of the relationship between capitalism and the surrounding pre-capitalist segments of the world economy that were forcibly dragged into its orbit, Marx's basic concept of capitalism in *Capital* is of an isolated capitalist sector. This understanding gets expressed in his numerous writings on the colonial question but makes only fleeting appearances in *Capital*, especially Volume I, which he completed in his lifetime. As a result, the tendency has been to see Marx, like the other economic theorists, as conceptualizing a capitalist economy basically as a closed sector (with the pre-capitalist environment being simply an add-on but not in any sense essential to this core sector).

This perception has also influenced subsequent Marxist writings on economics in an unfortunate direction. An obvious example of this is the belief widely held in Marxist circles that the process of primitive accumulation of capital occurred only in the prehistory of capitalism and that once the system was in place, subsequent accumulation occurred only on the basis of the generation of surplus value within it. The reality, however, is that primitive accumulation occurs throughout the history of capitalism, and even in a wholly explicit form, of a tax-based appropriation of surplus by the metropolis, under colonialism.[6]

It is this understanding of the Marxian system, for which one cannot altogether exonerate Marx from blame, that we are critiquing. And our overall critique of the Marxian system, including what was said in earlier chapters, focuses on three points. First, since Marx rightly rejects Say's Law and visualizes the possibility of *ex ante* overproduction, the capitalist sector he is examining would settle down at a state of simple reproduction. Or, to be more precise, in such a universe where aggregate demand can be deficient, if we have an investment function that takes adequate cognizance of demand, then the only stable equilibrium is one with a zero trend.' Sustained growth, or expanded reproduction, in the capitalist sector therefore cannot be explained unless we go beyond its isolated existence. We have, in sum, a theoretical contradiction between the concept of a money-using economy (which causes *ex ante* overproduction) and an isolated capitalist sector if sustained growth is seen, as it must be, as one of its characteristics.

A second contradiction between the concept of a money-using economy and the concept of an isolated capitalist sector arises from the fact that if the sector uses any paper currency, even if deemed statutorily convertible into the money commodity, an increase in money wages, enforced by trade unions for enlarging the wage share, will make the system unworkable. This is because capitalists would naturally resist any decline in their share by jacking up prices, which would trigger an exodus from paper currency to gold, and therefore make the wealth held in the form of paper currency worthless. Since wealth *is actually held* in the form of paper currency, it follows that there must be something that prevents its value from collapsing even when there are money-wage increases. This "something" has to be located outside the isolated capitalist sector, which means that this sector represents an inadequate conceptualization of capitalism.

A third contradiction arises between a money-using economy and an isolated capitalist sector, even within the Marxian schema, once we take cognizance that there are a whole lot of goods used by this sector but produced outside it, all of which are subject to the phenomenon of increasing supply price at given money wages.

Expanded reproduction of the capitalist sector in such a case would run into a cul-de-sac. Ricardo had visualized this dead end as consisting in the arrival of a stationary state, which was the culmination of a process of declining rate of profit. But long before this dead end arrived the value of money would have fallen, since capitalists would try to maintain their rate of profit by jacking up money prices. In this case, there would be no expectation of a return of the value of money to its old level; on the contrary, because everyone would know about the increasing supply price, any initial fall would create expectations of a further fall, so that the value of money will fall precipitously as wealth-holders flee from holding money to holding precisely the commodities that are subject to increasing supply price. Hence to ensure that a money-using economy continues to remain a money-using economy under these circumstances, the phenomenon of increasing supply price must be prevented from making an appearance.

Ways of preventing increasing prices must involve imposing a certain economic regime upon the outside world from which commodities are imported, for which in turn political control, whether direct or indirect, over this outside world becomes necessary. Looking at the capitalist sector in isolation, and assuming that even when in the natural course of things it buys goods from outside, the idea that we can justifiably analyze its expanded reproduction in its isolated state ceases to be valid.

Increasing supply price is a matter we discuss in detail in a later chapter. But the point of this chapter is that even the Marxian system, like other theoretical systems, gets beset with serious contradictions if its extraordinarily insightful analysis of a money-using economy is combined with a conceptualization of capitalism as an isolated sector consisting only of capitalists and workers.

# CHAPTER 4

# Capitalism and Its Setting

We have argued that because capitalism is a preeminently money-using economy any conceptual representation of it as an isolated capitalist sector, consisting only of capitalists and workers, with the state playing no direct role in managing the economy, creates serious logical contradictions. And yet seeing capitalism as an isolated capitalist sector has been the common practice in economic theory. Furthermore, the various ways to overcome these logical contradictions are palpably unsatisfactory. The Walrasian and the Ricardian traditions, for instance, do not even take full cognizance of the fact that capitalism is a money-using economy; they admit only the role of money as a medium of circulation while denying its role as a medium of holding wealth (which itself is a logical contradiction, for money cannot be the one without being the other as well). On this basis these traditions accept Say's Law and the impossibility of "involuntary unemployment."

The Keynesian and Marxian traditions, on the other hand, which do take cognizance of, and see the implications of capitalism being a money-using economy, are hamstrung in other ways by the "isolated-capitalist-sector" perception. Within this perception, they cannot explain how sustained growth occurs within this sector, since such growth requires exogenous stimuli that have to come from outside the sector; and if the perception of capitalism precludes any "outside," then it *ipso facto* precludes sustained growth. They also cannot explain how the system accommodates money-wage increases, enforced by workers to raise their share in national income, without jeopardizing the value of money. And as this sector requires a set of commodities subject to increasing supply price (at any given money-wage rate), it is impossible to explain how the system continues to experience expanded reproduction without the value of money collapsing.

The way out of these logical contradictions is to see capitalism not as an isolated entity, but as one that exists within a setting that it not only interacts with but with the help of which, and at the expense of which, it overcomes all the problems that would otherwise confront it because of its being a money-using economy. Let us see how each of these problems in the context of the Marxian and Keynesian systems (we ignore the Walrasian and Ricardian systems because they do not even come to terms with capitalism being a money-using economy) is overcome once we see capitalism within this broader setting.

## The Problem of Exogenous Stimuli

The need for exogenous stimuli for sustained growth arises, as we argued in an earlier chapter, because the system is subject to "involuntary unemployment." Once the possibility of involuntary unemployment is recognized, then, in the absence of exogenous stimuli, capitalists add to capacity only if they expect demand to increase And whether they expect demand to increase depends upon whether it has been increasing, that is, upon current experience.

If the current period's demand is such that it gives capitalists their "desired" degree of capacity utilization (Steindl had argued that capitalists always desire to hold some unutilized capacity[1]), then they take investment decisions that give them a rate of growth of capital stock in the next period that is the same as in the current period. If current capacity utilization is less than "desired," then they reduce the rate of growth of capital stock in the next period; if it is more, then they increase their rate of addition to capital stock in the next period.

But the current period's capacity utilization depends upon the current period's investment relative to capital stock. It follows that there is some particular rate of growth of capital stock that gives the "desired" level of capacity utilization, and that, if experienced, continues to persist. If the rate of growth of capital stock is less than this, then the economy will keep experiencing a lower and lower rate of growth of capital stock over time, until this rate falls to zero, that is, until gross investment just equals the rate of depreciation of capital stock and the economy reaches a stationary state, or a state of simple reproduction.

Even if the rate of growth of capital stock exceeds this particular rate, and hence increases over time, because capacity utilization exceeds the desired level, it will eventually hit a ceiling when either the labor reserves or unutilized capacity get exhausted. When it does so, it will not stay at this ceiling; it will keep coming down because capacity utilization keeps falling from this ceiling, until it again reaches a state of simple reproduction.

Thus, once the effect of demand upon investment is recognized, the economy can only experience two possible trends: a particular growth rate that gives the "desired" level of capacity utilization (which corresponds to what economist Roy Harrod had called the "warranted rate of growth"[2]), and a zero trend or a state of simple reproduction. The first of these is unstable in the sense that a chance deviation of the rate of accumulation in either direction from this trend takes the economy to simple reproduction; the second, simple reproduction, is stable in the sense that a chance deviation from it brings the economy back to it.[3]

Purely on the basis of endogenous stimuli therefore, that is, on the basis of the impetus for growth that arises from the fact that the economy has been growing in the past and hence is expected to grow in the future, we cannot explain sustained growth in the system.[4] Such growth requires some additional, exogenous, stimuli, which add an amount to investment that is unrelated to the growth occurring in the past.

Now, there has long been a view that even an isolated capitalist sector generates exogenous stimuli from within itself through innovations, which raise the level of gross investment, and thus net investment, beyond what would otherwise be warranted by the expected growth of markets alone. This, however, happens only if those introducing innovations undertake some extra investment, over and above what the expected growth of the market would have otherwise warranted, in the belief that they would be able to sell more because they introduce an innovation their rivals lack.

But in a situation where the rivals are strong enough to resist a snatching away of their market, and, despite not introducing the innovation, can still resort to and survive price cuts if the innovator among them lowers prices on the strength of the innovation, snatching away any market becomes impossible. And the innovator, knowing this, will not make any extra investment over and above what the expected growth in its market would warrant. An innovation will only affect the *form* that investment takes—for example, new innovated machines rather than the old machines—but not its *amount*, in which case it ceases to be an authentic exogenous stimulus.[5] The rivals, in turn, will feel the need to innovate because of the original innovation, but they too will introduce innovated machines for old machines without raising the *amount* of investment. Innovations do not act as an exogenous stimulus increasing investment beyond what the growth of the market would have dictated; on the contrary, the growth of the market determines the pace of introduction of innovations.

Economic historians, as we have discussed earlier, have been saying this for some time. Several innovations that had become available during the interwar period waited to get introduced until after the Second World War boom was underway, which is attributed by W. Arthur Lewis to the dampening effect of the Great Depression on the tendency to introduce innovations.[6] If a period of deficiency in demand dampens the introduction of innovations, then innovations clearly are not playing the role of an exogenous stimulus.

Baran and Sweezy made a distinction between routine innovations and "epoch-making" innovations like railways and automobiles.[7] They had thought that the latter could provide an exogenous stimulus to growth, but not the former. It is significant, however, that the automobile, whose spread after the First World War could have been expected to thwart the onset of the Great Depression, or to have truncated the depth and the duration of the Depression after it had set in, failed to do so. It was only in the post–Second World War boom that automobile sales spread dramatically. One has therefore to take the potential of even these epoch-making innovations to thwart the onset of, or to break out of, a state of stagnation with a degree of skepticism. In short, innovations are poor examples of an exogenous stimulus.

No doubt, booms have been characterized by vigorous adoptions of innovations, which give the impression of innovations causing the boom itself, but this is more likely to be a case of mistaken identity. Booms initiated by other, genuinely exogenous stimuli have called forth a vigorous spread of innovations, but there is little evidence of innovations themselves initiating a boom. The obvious exception to this is when the introduction of innovations has been supported by the state, as the introduction of the railways was over much of the nineteenth century. But here it is the state that should be seen as providing the exogenous stimulus rather than the innovations themselves.

If we leave aside innovations, then the only two genuinely exogenous stimuli are state expenditure and the imperial arrangement, which was the focus of Rosa Luxemburg's analysis. While both entail breaking out of the conceptualization of capitalism as an "isolated capitalist sector," it is the imperial arrangement, emphasized by Luxemburg, that has played the role of an exogenous stimulus over much of capitalism's history.

By "imperial arrangement" we mean something more than just the colonial markets. Incursions into the colonial markets were part of the imperial arrangement, but this arrangement must be seen in its totality. We have to distinguish, to start with, between the colonies of conquest, such as India, Indonesia, Malaya, and the West Indies (and semi-colonies like China), and the colonies of settlement like the United States, Canada, Australia, and New Zealand. Sales of goods produced by metropolitan capitalism to the former at the expense of their local crafts producers, who were driven out of their traditional occupations as a result (a process called "deindustrialization"), was an important part of the imperial arrangement.

But it is not as if all metropolitan capitalist countries made use of such colonial and semi-colonial markets. Britain, as the leading capitalist country and colonial power, accessed these markets, which economic historian S. B. Saul calls "markets on tap,"[8] and allowed other capitalist countries, especially the newly industrializing ones, to access its own markets. All capitalist countries therefore had access to the colonial and semi-colonial markets, whether directly, or indirectly via Britain.

In the colonies of settlement, on the other hand, the indigenous inhabitants were driven off their land, which got occupied by migrants from Europe. Many local inhabitants perished, and those who survived were herded into reservations. An enormous migration of white persons from Europe, around fifty million in the period between the end of the Napoleonic Wars and the First World War,[9] occurred. And along with such migration of persons, there occurred a complementary migration of capital for setting up railways, creating infrastructure, and pushing the frontier further outward.

Now, it may appear at first sight that this spread of metropolitan capitalism from Europe provided the exogenous stimulus so that the tropical and subtropical colonial and semi-colonial markets played no essential role in this respect. However, this is not true. The commodity-composition of demand from these new regions of settlement was different from what could be supplied from the European metropolis, and this mismatch became increasingly acute as these regions got industrialized and started exporting manufactured goods to Europe. The colonial and semi-colonial markets were essential to resolve this problem. For instance, Britain in the nineteenth century increasingly sold goods in the colonial and semi-colonial markets (historian Eric Hobsbawm uses the term "flight to colonial markets" to describe this phenomenon)[10] and got them to export their goods to the temperate regions of white settlement in order to balance its payments through this triangular pattern of trade..

But that is not all. Britain got its colonies like India to export more goods than they absorbed (and such absorption too was at the expense of their own local craftsmen), and this surplus, in the form of raw materials and other primary products, was simply appropriated by Britain to pay for its own capital exports to these regions. This surplus, in other words, was not credited to the account of the colonized countries. It was taxed away from them by the colonizing power, a phenomenon called the "drain" of surplus, to finance its own capital exports.[11]

The colonial and semi-colonial markets, in other words, did not play the role of providing an exogenous stimulus in the simple and obvious manner visualized by Rosa Luxemburg. The markets became part of an overall imperial arrangement that kept the process of accumulation going by providing it with an exogenous stimulus. But, in order to understand this arrangement and how sustained accumulation could occur under metropolitan capitalism, we need to break out of the conceptualization of an isolated capitalist sector.

Let us clarify the respective roles of exogenous and endogenous stimuli. One has to distinguish between the quantitative and the qualitative importance of the exogenous stimuli. Even though these stimuli are qualitatively important, in the sense that in their absence the isolated capitalist sector would experience only simple reproduction, its actual growth rate, in the presence of such stimuli, would be larger than the rate of growth of capital stock directly engendered by such stimuli, just as the size of output in any period of time would be much larger than, say, the sales to the pre-capitalist sector *per se* because of the multiplier effect. This therefore may create an optical illusion that exogenous stimuli are not very important, when in fact the opposite is the case, and the system would be mired in stagnation in their absence.

## *The Cushion Against Inflation*

Let us now look at the case of money-wage increases. We argued earlier that in an isolated capitalist sector, if money wage-increases occurred in an effort to increase the workers' wage share, then such increases, in the face of capitalists' resistance to any cut in their profit share, would destabilize the value of money. Because in this scenario the value of money did not actually get destabilized, this could only be possible if no money wage increases were enforced by workers in excess of productivity increases or if capitalists meekly accepted cuts in their profit share. Neither of these being the case in reality, it followed that there was a logical incompatibility between a money-using economy (where the value of money does not get destabilized), which capitalism preeminently is, and its representation as an isolated capitalist sector.

But if we get out of the conceptualization of an isolated capitalist sector, then the problem of destabilization of the value of money owing to money wage increases does not arise. If there exists a class of claimants on total output who cannot defend their share in it, then the competing claims of workers and capitalists can always be reconciled at their expense. Workers can indeed obtain money-wage increases in excess of labor productivity growth that are not simply "passed on," in the sense that prices do not increase in tandem with the increase in unit labor costs, for if that happened then their share in output could not increase. They can therefore succeed in enlarging their share of output. And this cannot happen through a reduction of the capitalists' share in output, but through a reduction in the share of this other group of claimants.

This is not to suggest that workers consciously squeeze the shares of these other claimants. But the system works in such a way that the higher-money wage demands of the workers are accommodated at the expense of these claimants without jeopardizing the capitalists' share. Put differently, the claims enforced by both the workers and the capitalists can be met without causing accelerating inflation and a destabilization in the value of money if there is another category of claimants that acts as a mere "price-taker." Locating capitalism within a broader setting, where purchases are made of raw materials, current inputs and even foodstuffs from a group of producers who lack any bargaining strength and therefore have a claim on output that is compressible, is an essential condition for the viability of the system.

The reason the claim of this group is compressible is obviously because it is located within an ocean of labor reserves that forces its members to act as price-takers. And this has always been the case with capitalism, which has obtained a set of goods from petty producers outside of the metropolitan center. The deindustrialization that capitalism had imposed upon the outlying economies in its quest for markets created an enormous mass of unemployment. This made it possible for the petty producers to pass on the burden of reduced claims on output to which they were subjected to those lower down, namely the laborers they employed. In addition, even when they did not employ laborers, any resistance to reduced claims on their part became impossible since they could not get organized. Given the large labor reserves, any attempt at organization on their part would mean that the landowners (who are not the same as the petty producers) would replace them with others waiting in the wings.

We referred earlier to Keynes's idea of the "money illusion," which was essential in his schema for the stability of the wage-unit despite that employment could rise through an increase in aggregate demand. It is not some psychological trait of the workers, some limitation on their part that makes them fixated on money wages. Money illusion, which has the effect of making the workers' share compressible, is an ill-founded concept (which is why monetarism could carry out a counterrevolution against the Keynesian Revolution with such ease). The real reason why the share of workers is compressible is because of the existence of a vast labor reserve. This exists mainly in the outlying regions, outside of the capitalist sector proper, and afflicts not all workers employed by capital (for then we would not see any trade unions at all, let alone successful wage increases enforced by them), but only *some* workers (or more accurately petty producers), those located in these outlying regions and supplying the capitalist sector with numerous products it requires. But to recognize their presence, we have to abandon the conceptualization of capitalism as an isolated sector and see it in its overall setting, located amid a set of petty producers that meet its demands for their goods.[12]

The point at issue can be seen as follows. If the product of the capitalist sector has price $p$ and is produced with the help of labor that gets a money wage rate $w$, and raw materials "imported" from outside the capitalist sector which have a price $m$ per unit (in the currency of the metropolis), then we have:

$$p = (am+wl) (+\pi) \ldots (i)$$

where $a$ and $l$ denote respectively the raw material and labor required per unit of output and $\pi$ the markup factor. The above equation can be alternatively written as:

$$1 = (am/p+wl/p)(1+\pi)$$

It is clear that the share of wages in output $wl/p$ can be increased without any fall in the share of profits $(\pi/(1+\pi))$ if the share of the raw material producers $(am/p)$ is driven down; that is, if the raw material producers allow this to happen (because they are price-takers).

The same result, namely successful increases in the money wages of one group of workers being accommodated by the system through the compression of the share of another group of workers, without destabilizing the value of money, could be achieved even if both groups were located within the isolated capitalist sector. But a sustained and even a growing dichotomy between two groups of workers who are in close geographical proximity with free mobility is difficult to preserve. Besides, squeezing workers who are employed directly by capital, even those who are unorganized, has limits, since capital also has to ensure that there is a continuous flow of labor-power, which is endowed with a certain minimal strength and ability. But petty producers, located outside its frontiers amid an ocean of labor reserves, so that one group can be replaced by another without much inconvenience to capital, are quite another matter. They constitute an "ideal" group upon which a squeeze can be imposed (not necessarily directly but mediated through the market) to ensure the stability of the value of money.

It is remarkable that with so much written on the theory of inflation in the last few decades, hardly a word has been said on the possibility of inflation being controlled through a squeeze on the primary-commodity-supplying petty producers. So committed has economics become to the vision of an isolated capitalist sector that, working within this paradigm, it even declared that there was only one level of unemployment (NAIRU) at which the economy could experience non-accelerating inflation. (It could experience non-accelerating inflation at unemployment rates higher than this unique one if there were ratchet effects to prevent decelerating inflation, that is, if capitalists did not allow prices to *fall* in absolute terms; at all such rates there would be no money-wage increases.) The possibility of the economy settling down at any one of a set of possible unemployment rates, with varying money-wage increases associated with each, such as what Phillips found and what corresponds to the reality of capitalism (no matter what one thinks of the theory in support of the Phillips Curve), is simply brushed aside.

But once we go beyond the isolated capitalist sector idea, and see capitalism as ensconced within a setting of pre-capitalist producers that were enlisted for supplying some requirements it cannot produce, then it follows that for every level of the terms of trade (m/p in the above example), there would be a corresponding NAIRU. There is not one unique NAIRU, but a multiplicity of them. What is more, if the claims of these petty producers are compressible, then the economy can settle at any level of unemployment without being plagued by accelerating inflation, exactly as Keynes had visualized, though for the wrong reason (namely, money illusion).

Michal Kalecki's work was significant for its explicit introduction of distant raw material producers into an analysis of capitalism, though he did not carry this to its logical conclusion.[13] In fact, he explained the alleged stability of the share of wages in the national income of metropolitan capitalist economies as the outcome of two factors pulling in opposite directions[14]: a rise in the "degree of monopoly" (the markup margin), which has the effect of lowering the wage share in the national income, and a fall in the ratio of raw material prices to unit wage costs, which has the opposite effect. This theory was a breath of fresh air, especially in contrast to the contrived explanation in terms of the Cobb-Douglas Production Function, which apart from all its logical infirmities arising from capital being a value-sum, is also afflicted by the logical problems we have been discussing (such as assuming Say's Law), for it sticks stubbornly to the idea of an isolated capitalist sector.

Kalecki, however, did not see the fall in raw material prices relative to the unit wage-cost as being *caused* by, say, the increase in the degree of monopoly. In other words, he saw the two factors he highlighted as operating independently of each other; the alleged constancy of the share of wages was a happenstance because the effects of these two forces acting in opposite directions happened exactly to balance each other. But he did not go further to talk of the system stabilizing itself through effecting a reduction in raw material prices relative to unit wage-cost as an offset against the rise in the degree of monopoly.

To say this, of course, does not mean a planned move on the part of the system, to turn the terms of trade deliberately against the raw material producers to ensure that the wage share did not fall as a consequence of the rise in the degree of monopoly. The "spontaneous" working of the system in a world where there are price-takers would automatically bring about such a denouement. This can be seen in the following example.[15]

Suppose workers bargain for, and obtain, a money-wage that gives them at an expected price $p^e$ a certain target share of output, which, at any given level of trade union organization, is a function of the employment rate $e$, but raw material producers lack this strength. They bargain and obtain a share of output but only at, say, last period's price. Then we can alter (i) to

$$p_t = (a\mu p_{t-1} + f(e)p^e_t)(1+\pi) \ldots (i')$$

in which $(a\mu)$ is the targeted output share of the raw material producers. Their actual share however equals $(a\mu\, p_{t-1}/p_t)$, which means that the higher the rate of inflation the lower is their actual share. Now, assuming that

$$p^e_t = P_{t-1}.P_{t-1}/P_{t-2}$$

which is a case of adaptive expectations, at any given level of employment $e$ and any markup margin in the capitalist sector there would be a unique rate of steady inflation and hence a unique actual output-share of the raw material producers. This steady inflation rate will be:

$$r^* = [a.\mu(1+\pi)/\{1-(f(e).(1+\pi))\}] - 1 \ldots (ii)$$

If there is an increase in the degree of monopoly, then the employment rate can remain unchanged and the share of workers remain unchanged. but since the right-hand side in (ii) goes up, there will be an increase in the new rate of steady inflation and therefore a lower share of the raw material producers. Here the share of raw material producers would have fallen *spontaneously* to offset the effect of the rise in the degree of monopoly upon the workers' share.

The period from the last quarter of the nineteenth century to the Second World War was characterized by an adverse shift in the terms of trade between manufacturing and primary commodities against primary commodities.[16] This was also the period in which the wage share is supposed to have remained more or less constant even as the degree of monopoly increased. These two factors, namely the rise in the degree of monopoly and the shift in the terms of trade against primary commodities, instead of being two independent phenomena, were related. The rise in the degree of monopoly increased the mark up margin, but workers in the metropolis could prevent a fall in their share by bargaining for and obtaining higher money wages; this process did not cause accelerating inflation because the terms of trade could be shifted against primary commodity producers, who were price-takers and whose share in output was compressible.

Hence, the fact that a secular rise in the degree of monopoly did not desta-bilize the value of money under capitalism, despite a near constancy in the share of wages, is because capitalism was not identical with an isolated capitalist sector, but was embedded within a group of price-taking petty producers.

### Concluding Observations

Of course, as the share of the primary producers in the total value of output declines, a further compression in this share becomes more dif-ficult. Hence turning the terms of trade against primary commodities as an instrument for stabilizing the value of money in the event of a rise in the degree of monopoly at a given unemployment rate (and hence wage-share), or in the event of a rise in workers' money wages in excess of the rise in labor productivity, with the markup being given, loses its efficacy. When the share of the value of primary products in the total value of the output produced is extremely small, a compression in this share can hardly act as an effective counter to accelerating inflation that any change in these factors can initiate.

But the fact that a certain factor becomes less efficacious in playing the role of a stabilizer does not mean it has been absent. It is only by recog-nizing the role it has played in the past that we can see the problems that late capitalism faces in stabilizing the value of money, problems that mani-fest themselves for instance in its maintaining *on average* higher levels of unemployment than in the immediate post–Second World War period. The point is that whatever changes may be occurring within the capital-ist system, it simply cannot be analyzed as it has been in various strands of economic theory as an isolated sector that is not entrenched within a certain setting.

Finally, the analysis of capitalism as an isolated capitalist sector creates serious problems for another reason. It completely ignores the phenomenon of increasing supply price for many of the primary commodities it uses. This phenomenon is extremely important but can be appreciated only when we see capitalism in its overall international setting. We take up a discussion of this phenomenon in the next chapter.

# CHAPTER 5

# Increasing Supply Price and Imperialism

avid Ricardo was the first major economist to have incorporated what he called "diminishing returns" into a theoretical analysis of capitalism.[1] Since "diminishing returns" is a misleading term that can be mistaken to mean "diminishing returns to scale," which, strictly speaking, is a logical impossibility. Since a production unit can always be replicated instead of building one twice as big for doubling output, we prefer to use the term "increasing supply price" (at given money wages). Increasing supply price is acknowledged to affect primary commodities, among which minerals, especially oil, have received much attention. As an exhaustible resource, greater and greater exploitation not only leaves less for further exploitation, but also entails an increasing supply price because the more easily exploitable sources of supply are presumed to be used up first.

Marx had opposed this last presumption.[2] He saw no reason why, taking Ricardo's example, the more fertile land would get cultivated first by people entering an island. It was much more likely that the land closest to the shore would be first cultivated, and as the settlers moved farther inland they may chance upon land of greater fertility, in which case the supply price would not increase steadily but would move up and down around a trend that has no reason not to be flat.

Marx is perfectly right in what he says about the island example, but this example is misleading. To see this, we must remember that oil and other minerals are the "leading species of a large genus" (to paraphrase Alfred Marshall), which includes products of the tropical and semi-tropical landmass. In the case of these products, we are not talking about virgin territory being settled, but territory upon which millions have lived for millennia, and which, even if not fully used up to start with, does get used up as the demands of the capitalist metropolis are met. That is, the more easily cultivable land gets used up, pushing the margin toward less accessible and less fertile land. Increasing supply price, and even a near-vertical supply curve, in the case of such products is thus a perfectly realistic presumption. In this chapter we consider the issue of increasing supply price, especially in the case of tropical and semi-tropical products that are not producible everywhere, that have a family resemblance with oil in this regard, but have scarcely got the attention they deserve.

## Land Augmentation and the State

Just as there would be no increasing supply price if land of equal fertility was available aplenty, there would be no increasing supply price if technological progress of the "land-augmenting" kind could occur easily. In fact, even if there were no technical progress, in the sense of the arrival of entirely new methods of production and new practices, but investment, such as irrigation, which allows multiple cropping and thus increases the effective supply of land, could occur to the required degree, there would again be no cause for increasing supply price. So, when we talk of increasing supply price as a problem facing the capitalist sector, we are asserting that land-augmenting investment and land-augmenting technical progress do not occur to the required degree. The question is, why not?

Before answering, we should be clear about the social setting of our discussion, which is provided by a number of elements. First, capitalism, which developed in the temperate region of the world, Europe, and got diffused to the temperate regions of white settlement in North America, Australia, and New Zealand, uses a whole range of goods produced in the tropical and semi-tropical regions of the world, which it can neither produce itself or produce in adequate quantities, nor do without.

When we say it cannot produce, we also include the case where it can produce the products in one season but has to import them in the other part of the year from the tropical and semi-tropical regions that can produce them at that time. We also include the case where certain products can be produced, and are produced, in the capitalist metropolis but the requirement of the metropolis for these products far exceeds what it can itself produce, so that *at the margin* the entire additional supply has to come from the tropical and semi-tropical regions. In short, there is a whole range of goods the metropolis cannot do without but whose supplies at the margin must come from the tropical and semi-tropical regions.

Secondly, within the tropical and semi-tropical regions, it is largely a group of peasants who are engaged in the production of these goods. In the densely populated tropics, a replication of what was done to the original inhabitants of the temperate regions when European migration occurred to these regions, is not possible. Besides, the tropics are not the region to which much European migration occurs. We therefore have a situation where the old practices and the old modes of production continue, but metropolitan capital simply uses them for its own purposes. The sheer scale of disruption involved in displacing the existing peasant producers and taking over their lands for capitalist cultivation is so large that capital is not too keen to embark upon it. We thus have capital using peasant production for its own purposes in the tropical and semi-tropical regions to produce a whole range of goods that it requires, but from a landmass that is already largely cultivated.

In this context land augmentation requires above all the intervention of the state. Irrigation, historically the main land-augmenting measure, cannot be done by individual peasant farmers unless water is supplied to entire villages through canals fed from the tropical river systems. The scale of the requisite investment for such canals is too large to be undertaken by individual peasants. Once canals are constructed, feeder channels to individual farms, or even wells whose water tables are nourished by these canals, can be constructed by the peasants. However, for constructing the canals or even reservoirs for storing water, and maintaining them, a supra-village, supra-peasant authority is needed.

The state in earlier times had played this role, prompting Marx's remark in the context of India that there have been in Asia since time immemorial three main departments of government: a department of Finance whose aim was plundering its own inhabitants, a department of War whose aim was plundering other countries, and a department of Public Works, since "artificial irrigation" was "the basis of Oriental agriculture."[3]

Likewise, even land-augmenting technical progress, which involves new practices, new varieties of seeds, and new methods of cultivation, requires research and experimentation beyond the capacity of an individual peasant cultivating a tiny strip of land in the densely populated tropical agricultural tracts. The spread of such new practices and methods to peasants on a large scale also requires extension services that only the state can provide. In short, land augmentation on the tropical landmass can occur only through state intervention and state expenditure. Though it might be thought that genetically modified plants, by raising yields, provide one way out of the difficulty through private expenditure, the results of such adoption of GM crops are highly disputed as they both increase seed dependence of farmers on transnational companies and also tend to increase output volatility.

Under capitalism, however, state effort of this sort is precisely what is eschewed. There are at least three reasons for this: first, the entire ideological trappings within which the capitalist state, or its offshoot, the colonial state, is supposed to function, namely that it must balance its budget, that it can undertake any investment only if such investment earns a minimum rate of return, preclude any state effort toward land augmentation. Second, though the state makes allowances for projects that are of benefit to the capitalists, it follows these rigid rules when it comes to projects that would bring larger incomes to the peasants. The same Indian colonial state that used this rate of return criterion (a minimum rate of 5 percent had to be earned to make it worthwhile for the state to invest in a project) to avoid making any significant investment in irrigation in colonial India (with the sole exception of the "canal colonies" in Punjab), actually subsidized foreign companies to build the Indian railway system (which was essential to open up the economy to extraction by the metropolis of minerals, foodstuffs, and raw materials) by guaranteeing a 5 percent rate of return.

The *formal* rules governing state action, in other words, rest upon the *substantial* reality of class relations, which brings us to the third point.

Faced with two options, either to take a part of the products of the tropical landmass, through imposing taxes or other exactions on the peasants and other classes within this region, or to expand the output of such products through larger state expenditure on "land augmentation," which would entail either state borrowing or reduction in state expenditure benefiting the capitalists, the preference under capitalism would be for the former.

The upshot is that the means by which land augmentation could occur on the tropical landmass are foreclosed under capitalism because of the rules governing state expenditure within this system (which, in turn, have their basis in the material reality of class relations). Increasing supply price (or even a vertical supply curve) for tropical and semi-tropical products therefore is a reality capitalism has to deal with.

## *Increasing Supply Price and the Value of Money*

David Ricardo's argument was that increasing supply price, or what he called "diminishing returns," would have two basic effects. First, it would give rise to a falling rate of profit as accumulation occurred. Since less and less fertile land would be used for cultivation as accumulation increased the demand for corn, say, on which the average productivity of labor would be less and less, and since the real wage rate was given in the sense that it could not fall below the long-run supply price of labor determined by a subsistence wage basket, the rate of profit would keep falling, until it fell to zero (when the wage rate equaled the average product of labor on the marginal land). This meant the onset of a "stationary state."

Second, there would be a shift in the terms of trade in favor of corn and against the manufacturing, or non-corn, sector (that is, the sector not subject to diminishing returns), which would mean that the rate of profit in the latter would keep falling, in tandem with that in the corn sector, until it fell to zero.

But this idea of the rate of profit falling until it finally falls to zero is entirely unrealistic. If there are "diminishing returns" because of which certain products experience a rise in their relative price not only with respect to other, non-diminishing returns products, but also, in the Ricardian system, with respect to money, and if everybody knows that this is going to happen period after period, then the value of money would crash vis-à-vis such products long before any stationary state is reached. A money-using economy would become an impossibility, with everybody wishing to hold the diminishing returns products, in lieu of either the money commodity or any other commodity for that matter, long before the economy got to a stationary state. It is essential for the system, therefore, as we saw in chapter 1, that increasing supply price must not be allowed to manifest itself.

Ricardo, of course, was writing in the context of a commodity money economy and assuming free competition, that is, equal wages and an equal rate of profit across sectors through free mobility of labor and capital. More pertinent for us is to look at a world with paper money and mark up pricing, where the effect of increasing supply price in destroying the value of money emerges even more clearly. We argued in chapter 4 that in such a world, with given production coefficients, the *ex ante* claims of capitalists and workers on output can be reconciled through an appropriate shift in the terms of trade against primary commodity producers. Such a shift is brought about through inflation. Since primary commodity producers are price-takers, the price they get is not indexed to the manufactured goods price; it gets adjusted only sluggishly, so that a higher rate of inflation entails worse terms of trade for primary commodity producers and hence a lower share in total output for them. In short, they have to be content with the "leavings" of the others.

Increasing supply price means an increase in the labor coefficient per unit of output in the primary commodity sector. This will be absorbed by the system without any reduction in the share of workers or capitalists in the manufacturing sector, through a reduction in the real incomes of the primary producers via a higher rate of inflation, *but without any shift in the terms of trade*. Since the trigger for higher inflation is not increased claims by the workers or capitalists but a rise in the labor coefficient in the primary producing sector, this rise will be exactly offset by reduced income per unit if labor, which will raise the rate of inflation but leave the terms of trade unchanged.

While a once-for-all increase in labor coefficient in primary commodity production will entail a higher, but not accelerating, rate of inflation, if the labor coefficient keeps rising, which is what increasing supply price means, then the rate of inflation will accelerate.[4] This destroys the value of money.

People switch from holding money as a form of wealth to holding commodities as a form of wealth. Of course, such a shift may happen even when there is steady inflation, provided it exceeds a certain threshold rate. But with accelerating inflation occurring, and then becoming expected, because of a rising labor coefficient in primary commodity production, a shift from holding money to holding commodities *is bound to happen*.

If we denote the inflation rate by r, then an anticipation of accelerating inflation implies that $r^e_{t+1} > r_t$. Suppose last year's price (for period t  1) is 100; then if the current year's price is 105, that is, the current rate of inflation is 5 percent, then next year's expected inflation rate must be more than 5 percent, meaning that next year's expected price must be more than 110.25. Similarly, if the current year's price is 110, that is, the current inflation rate is 10 percent, then the next year's price must be more than 121. Thus, a 4.8 percent increase in the current price, from 105 to 110, causes a rise in the expected price by at least 9.8 percent, from 110.25 to 121. The elasticity of price expectation thus exceeds unity, and with an elasticity of price expectation greater than unity, there cannot be any stability in the value of money vis-à-vis commodities.

This, incidentally, answers the question that may be raised by many, namely since money has no carrying cost while commodities have a carrying cost, how can money be supplanted by commodities unless inflation exceeds some threshold level? This argument becomes irrelevant when accelerating inflation is expected. No matter what the current level of inflation, even if it is below the carrying cost, if accelerating inflation is anticipated, then there can still be no equilibrium, and the value of money would still plummet to zero.

The reason for this is that all commodities do not have identical carrying costs, and all persons do not have identical price expectations. As long as there is even one person who expects the next period's price of a certain commodity to exceed the current period's price by a margin larger than the carrying cost of the commodity in question, then that person would move to the commodity from money (for simplicity we are ignoring the risk premium here). This would raise the price of the commodity further, which because of elastic price expectations would make more people shift to this commodity, which would raise its price further, and so on. Likewise, what is happening to this commodity would also affect the price expectations for other commodities, with the result that *even if the initial rate of inflation was lower than the carrying cost, the economy still could not possibly reach an equilibrium.* It follows that anticipation of accelerating inflation, which increasing supply price would engender, would simply destroy the value of money. It is incompatible with the continuance of a money-using economy.

It becomes essential for capitalism, therefore, quite independently of the Ricardian falling rate of profit, to ensure that the shadow of increasing supply price does not fall on the economy.[5]

## *Negating the Threat of Increasing Supply Price*

One obvious way that increasing supply price can be warded off is through a depreciation of the exchange rate of the tropical region's currency vis-à-vis the metropolitan currency. A simple example will make the point clear. Let us assume that we are talking about a vertical supply curve, that is, the tropical land-mass is fully used up and the output of its products cannot be increased at all. With accumulation, as the demand for these products rises in the metropolis, domestic absorption of them within the tropical region must be curtailed to make more supplies available for the metropolis. An obvious way for this to happen, which has happened in history, is through what Keynes had called "profit inflation."

With the rise in demand, since supply remains unchanged, there is a rise in price relative to money wages. The profit margin widens, hence the term "profit inflation," forcing reduced consumption by the workers, whose money wages are not indexed to prices, and thus larger releases of the good in question for use in the metropolis. Of course, it is not just the workers, or peasants in this case, who have sold their products at pre-contracted prices but who have to buy the same or substitute products at higher prices, whose consumption is squeezed. All consumers of the product who have fixed money incomes, or money incomes that do not go up *pari passu* when the price of the product increases, have to curtail their consumption with the rise in the price, releasing more of the product for the metropolitan market. Profit inflation therefore acts to release supply for the metropolitan market in response to growing demand, even when the output of the product cannot go up.

But profit inflation in the tropical region will not pose a threat to the value of money in the metropolis if there is a corresponding depreciation of the exchange rate of the region vis-à-vis the metropolis. In a world where capital is free to move across frontiers, this will happen spontaneously. With inflation in the tropical region, there will be an expectation on the part of the wealth-holders of a corresponding decline in its nominal exchange rate. They would then shift from the tropical currency to the metropolitan currency, precipitating a depreciation of the tropical currency that would be of the same order as the inflation (if the original real effective exchange rate of the tropical currency was an equilibrium one and perceived to be so).

With regard to the tropical and semi-tropical products, produced, with the exception of a few plantation crops, by peasant agriculture, which capitalism requires and which are subject to increasing supply price because of the fixed size of the tropical land, it is essential that there be a regime binding the tropical region with the metropolis, which satisfies two characteristics. First, this region must be "opened up" for trade with the metropolis so that there are no restrictions on the flow of goods from it to meet metropolitan demands. And second, it must also be open to capital flows into and out of its borders, so that exchange rate changes occur that insulate the metropolitan currency from the effects of inflation in the periphery.

But even having such a regime would not be enough for two reasons, one of which is quite straightforward, but the other less so. The straightforward reason is that if the tropical product being released from domestic absorption is for use in the metropolis, it suggests that the metropolis requires only those products that were already being produced in this region, even before it was opened up for trade. This, however, is not necessarily the case. The metropolis also requires, apart from the goods the tropical region already produced, a whole range of other goods, which, though producible only on the tropical landmass, were not being produced on it earlier. The peasants in the tropical region have to be made to produce these goods, diverting area from the goods they were already producing toward these new goods.

Of course, once the production of these goods has been introduced, then relative price changes might perhaps be enough to make peasants produce more of such goods in response to a larger demand from the metropolis (though this would not negate the necessity for profit inflation). But to introduce them at all requires some mechanism. In colonial India, this mechanism was a system of advances by traders (themselves linked to exporting agencies). These advances had to be taken by the peasants in order to pay *in time* their land revenue to the colonial administration or land rent to their local landlords—the *zamindars* who, in turn, were required to pay the bulk of rent as revenue to the colonial administration. If these payments were not made in time, then the peasants would forfeit whatever rights they had to the land, which is why they were forced to depend on the traders' advances. The traders then specified what crops they would grow and the price at which these crops should be made available to them. The market signals, in short, were relayed to the peasantry through the traders who gave them advances. The regime imposed on the tropical region thus included not just openness to trade and openness to capital flows but an arrangement for dictating the production pattern.

But even this was not enough for a deeper reason, namely that relying on profit inflation with offsetting exchange rate depreciation was itself not enough to get supplies of tropical goods for the metropolitan market out of a given landmass, We discuss this in the next section.

### The Need for Income Deflation

There are two obvious reasons why the mechanism of profit inflation alone would not be enough for extracting tropical products for metropolitan requirements. The first is that even though the metropolis might be made free of any accelerating inflation caused by increasing supply price because of the exchange rate depreciation accompanying such inflation in the periphery, the periphery itself would now get characterized by accelerating inflation for exactly the same reason. The currency of the periphery would not just depreciate vis-à-vis the metropolis, but it would collapse as people move to commodities or the currency of the metropolis.

Now, just because a collapse happens in the periphery, capitalism cannot be indifferent to it. What capital requires is an arrangement, and not sheer chaos. Hence, the profit inflation route for extracting larger amounts of supplies from the fixed output of the tropical landmass cannot be followed to a point where accelerating inflation becomes a threat even in the periphery.There has to be an additional route for extracting supplies, apart from profit inflation. Profit inflation can play this role only to a limited extent—other than in exceptional periods such as wartime when the freedom of asset choice is restricted and chaotic developments and massive loss of lives are occurring anyway.

A second factor adds to this. We have so far assumed that the chaos unleashed by profit inflation in the periphery does not spread to the metropolis, and that the metropolis is only concerned about this chaos because it wants to keep an arrangement going and not see a collapse of the periphery's currency. But the currency of the metropolis also is threatened by any tendency toward a collapse of the periphery's currency. This is because if such a collapse makes wealth-holders in the periphery move, say, to holding gold instead of the periphery's currency, then, given that gold supplies are non-augmentable in the short run, the gold price will go up even in terms of the currency of the metropolis. This would induce some wealth-holders to shift from holding the currency of the metropolis to holding gold, which has a low carrying cost. In such a case, the threat of collapse of currency value would no longer remain confined to the periphery alone but would also spread to the metropolis.

It follows that although profit inflation can play a role in extracting supplies for the metropolis out of a given output of tropical goods, this role can only be a limited one. It must not cause anything more than what we called earlier the threshold rate of steady inflation in the periphery (accompanied by a depreciation of its nominal exchange rate). It has to be supplemented by something else, some other means of demand compression in the periphery. We call this "income deflation."

Income deflation achieves the same result as profit inflation but without raising prices. Take a simple example: suppose a certain amount of goods must be squeezed out of the consumption of the workers. (This is called "forced savings" in the literature, though it must be remembered that the benefits of such "savings" squeezed out of the workers in the form of additions to wealth accrue not to them but to the capitalists.) This squeezing out requires a fall in the real wage rate of the workers, but this fall can be effected in two ways: one, which is the way of profit inflation, is by an increase in price relative to the money-wage rate; the other is by a reduction in the money-wage rate relative to the price. This is an income deflation imposed on the workers, and has the advantage from the point of view of capital that it achieves the same end as a profit inflation without in any way threatening the value of money and money-denominated assets.

Income deflation, which, in the example above took the form of a wage deflation (as we were assuming that the universe was peopled exclusively by capitalists and workers), would release tropical products for the metropolis even out of a given and inflexible supply. For this it must be imposed on segments of the population in the periphery that consume such products.

Income deflation can, of course, be imposed on the workers within the metropolis itself, but there are limits to the extent that real income can be squeezed in the face of increasing supply price of tropical products, since capital requires an adequate supply of labor-power of a certain ability for its direct employment. When it comes to the working population of the periphery, it is under no such compulsion to maintain their real living standard, even at a pre-given subsistence level. Hence, income deflation on the working population in the periphery is an essential feature of the arrangement that the metropolis imposes on the periphery.

This arrangement, of keeping the periphery open to trade, keeping the periphery open to capital flows, having some mechanism whereby the production structure of the tropical landmass can be controlled, and imposing income deflation on the working population of the periphery, is capitalism's way of combating the effect of increasing supply price. And this arrangement is an integral part of "imperialism," which entails the subjection of the periphery to a regime that keeps it open to trade and capital flows and allows metropolitan capital to dictate the production pattern on its landmass, while imposing income deflation on its working population.

The nature of this regime, how it has changed over time through the different phases of capitalism, the different mechanisms through which income deflation has been imposed on the working population of the periphery, are matters that we will discuss in detail in the chapters that follow. The point here is to emphasize the theoretical necessity of such a regime. Instead of the conceptualization of capitalism as an isolated capitalist sector, it must be seen as a system that exists within a setting of pre-capitalist producers who were entrapped within certain social relations of their own but are enlisted for its own purposes by capital, which molds these relations and imposes a regime of the sort we have just described upon this setting.

### A Word on Imperialism

We have argued that because capitalism is a preeminently money-using economy, any conceptualization of it as an isolated sector is untenable. This is because a money-using but isolated capitalist sector would be trapped in a state of simple reproduction, that is, a (stationary) state of zero trend rate of growth; it would not be able to accommodate increases in money wages without jeopardizing the value of money; and it would not be able to prevent a collapse of the value of money in the face of increasing supply price. But once we conceptualize capitalism within a setting of pre-capitalist producers who are enlisted to serve its own purposes (so that they no longer remain in their pristine state), these problems disappear.

Encroachments into the markets of pre-capitalist producers enables the capitalist sector to find the exogenous stimulus to break out of the state of simple reproduction and to keep the process of accumulation going in a sustained manner. Additionally, the existence of a group of suppliers of wage goods and inputs to the capitalist sector, located in the midst of vast labor reserves created by the displacement of craft producers owing to the entry of capitalist products (or deindustrialization), makes them price-takers and serves to stabilize the value of money even in the face of metropolitan money-wage or profit margin increases.

These two roles of the pre-capitalist setting within which capitalism is located, however, become less and less significant over time. Once

pre-capitalist craft production dwindles, the scope for capitalism to ener-
gize itself through encroachments upon it also gets exhausted. Likewise,
once the share of primary producers in the total value of output of the
capitalist sector dwindles, precisely because this share is compressible and
has been compressed in the past, the ability of the system to stabilize itself
by compressing this share still further declines.

This does not mean that capitalism has no further reason, on the basis
of these considerations, to control this setting. Whether or not these can
play the role of providing capitalism with exogenous stimulus or stabilizing the value of money in the same manner as done earlier, the question
of capitalism letting go of its control simply does not arise, since any such
letup would plunge the system into a crisis. These mechanisms not being
as efficacious in playing the role they had done before is one thing; their
being dispensable is an altogether different matter.

*The question of imposing a regime upon this pre-capitalist setting to
ward off the threat of increasing supply price stands on an altogether different footing.* It continues to be essential for capitalism, not just as a legacy of
the past but as a requisite for the present as well. In this sense it is central
to the phenomenon of imperialism.[6]

Capitalism has changed so much that many are of the view that the term
*imperialism* has lost its relevance altogether. No doubt, compared to the
colonial era, two fundamental changes are discernible at present: one is the
emergence of countries like India and China into the ranks of economic
powers, with their bourgeoisies integrated into the corpus of global capital. The other is the virtual stagnation or even decline in the real wages of
the workers in the advanced capitalist countries over a period of almost
half a century. This suggests to many that the old dichotomy between the
North and the South, or between "advanced" and "underdeveloped" or
"backward" countries, which the term *imperialism* invoked, is no longer
valid.

While this change in capitalism is certainly of great significance, conceptualizing imperialism in terms of a North-South dichotomy, or of an
advanced-backward country dichotomy, with the former exploiting the
latter, is flawed. Imperialism is a relationship between capitalism and its
setting, central to which is an imposition of a regime upon the setting that

entails income deflation as a means of preventing the threat of increasing supply price. No matter what happens to the bourgeoisies of the South or the workers of the North, this relationship, which existed in the colonial era, persists to this day and the system cannot do without it. But though the content of this relationship remains unchanged, the form of it has changed over time.

# PART 2

# CHAPTER 6

# Periods in Capitalism

The isolated capitalist sector that much of economic theory has been concerned with consists of the capitalists and the workers, with the state ensuring that the rules of the game are followed, though not intervening directly in the economy. Going beyond this isolated capitalist sector to understand the real nature of capitalism entails, therefore, locating it within its setting amid pre-capitalist producers that are enlisted for its own purposes, which thereby destroys their pristine character. But it also means introducing the state as an active participant in economic processes.

Indeed, we cannot introduce the one without also introducing the other. Colonialism, which entailed the subjugation of the pre-capitalist setting within which capitalism emerged, relied on the use of military power by the capitalist state (though on certain occasions, as in India under the rule of the East India Company, the capitalist state may have subcontracted its power to another entity, namely a capitalist enterprise). Even though direct state intervention in "demand management" was a post–Second World War phenomenon, state intervention in economic life through protectionism and through the acquisition of colonies and dependencies, or "economic territory" as Lenin expressed it, has been a feature of capitalism throughout its life. And this intervention goes far beyond what economic theory generally recognizes, namely ensuring that the rules of the game are followed.

The precise manner in which this setting—consisting of the state (or the group of capitalist nation-states existing with a certain relationship among them) and the pre-capitalist universe within which this state enables capitalism to ensconce itself—affects the functioning of capitalism has changed through the history of the system. We shall break up this history into different periods, within each of which the impact of the capitalist setting is analytically invariant, though across periods there are differences. In this chapter, we examine each of these periods briefly, to give a bird's-eye view of our overall argument. In later chapters each of these periods will be discussed at length.

The periodization we follow is: (1) Colonialism prior to the First World War; (2) the interwar years; (3) the post–Second World War years of the "Golden Age of Capitalism"; (4) the era of globalization; and (5) the current conjuncture, which marks the dead end of globalization. The logic of this periodization will become clear as we go along.

## *The Colonial Arrangement and Its Exhaustion*

The colonial period, right until the First World War, though it may not have witnessed as high an economic growth rate as during the quarter century after the Second World War, was marked by the most prolonged boom experienced by the system until now. The colonies of conquest enabled the leading capitalist country of the period, Britain, to sell its goods in their markets as if, in the words of economic historian S. B. Saul, they were "markets on tap."[1] These goods were no longer much in demand in the newly emerging capitalist countries of the time since they were developing their own manufacturing. Britain could therefore keep its own market open to their goods, and yet not face any balance of payments difficulties, because it could exploit the colonial markets. By thus accommodating their ambitions, it could keep them within the international economic system characterized by the gold standard and dominated by itself, instead of having to face a possible revolt by them against itself.

Not only did Britain balance its payments through this triangular trade, whereby it sold its goods to the colonies, while the colonies' goods were sold to the newly emerging capitalist powers, which in turn had a trade surplus vis-à-vis Britain; but it actually made substantial capital exports that sustained this diffusion of capitalism to the newly emerging capitalist countries. These capital exports were financed by the forcible extraction of a surplus without any quid pro quo from the colonies. This extraction was effected through taxes levied on the colonial economy, with the tax revenue simply being siphoned off in the form of an export surplus of commodities.

Both the deindustrialization of the colonial economy that resulted from the sale of metropolitan goods, and the "drain of surplus" from the colonial economy through the taxation system, had the effect of imposing an income deflation on the working population of the colonial economy, which also meant that the impact upon the system of increasing supply price, or even of a fixity of output from the given tropical landmass, could be warded off.

The colonial arrangement was thus an ideal one from the point of view of capitalism. It permitted a diffusion of capitalism to the temperate regions of white settlement; it permitted the maintenance of stability in the value of money in the metropolis and even in the periphery despite the fixity of the tropical landmass; and it kept up the level of aggregate demand for the system as a whole.

But for reasons we shall elaborate in detail later, this arrangement could not last. Colonial markets have obvious limits, so that the arrangement could not have lasted in any event. Besides, Japanese competition after the First World War in the markets of Britain's Asian colonies brought this arrangement to grief. Britain tried for a while to ward off that competition through forming an alliance with the domestic bourgeoisies that were coming up in these colonies (of which the grant of a limited amount of "discriminating protection" to Indian capitalists was an example). However, this did not bring any comfort to the position of Britain. With the onset of the world agricultural crisis in 1926, the entire colonial arrangement upon which the long Victorian and Edwardian boom had been founded collapsed, though colonialism itself continued and was used for financing war expenditure during the Second World War with inordinate ruthlessness, of which the Great Bengal Famine of 1943, exacting a toll of three million lives, was a grim manifestation.

The explanation of the Great Depression that follows from this analysis is completely different from the explanations that usually figure in economic theory, including even in Marxist theory. This is not to say that those explanations lack substance, but rather that an important element of the picture we are concentrating on is missing from those explanations. The chief explanations have been Joseph Schumpeter's,[2] coincidence of the troughs of the three types of business cycles—the Kondratieffs, the Juglars, and the Kitchins; Alvin Hansen's[3] "closing of the frontier"; and Baran and Sweezy's,[4] the rise of monopoly capitalism. Baran and Sweezy's explanation is based on a long tradition of rich theoretical work that has been associated with Kalecki and Steindl, apart from the two authors themselves.

In any of these explanations, however, the role of the exhaustion of the colonial arrangement has not figured. This, in turn, is because the role of colonialism in sustaining the long boom of the long nineteenth century has itself not been adequately recognized. Once we grasp the role of colonialism in sustaining the boom then we are in a position to recognize the importance of the end of this role in precipitating the Depression.

Charles Kindleberger,[5] the most prominent historian of the Great Depression, has written of it coinciding with a period when Britain had lost its leadership role in the capitalist world, while the United States had not yet taken up this role. But behind Britain's losing the leadership role was the exhaustion of the colonial arrangement that had sustained Britain until then.

The logic of our periodization that demarcates the pre–First World War from the interwar years lies not just in a temporal division, nor in a division between a boom period and a slump period. It lies in the fact that the colonial arrangement that had sustained capitalism for so long was getting exhausted without any other arrangement taking over. The Great Depression was a manifestation of this phenomenon.

## The "Golden Age" Years

A new arrangement came into being in the post–Second World War period, but it did so in different ways in the United States and Europe. The Great

Depression came to an end in non-fascist countries, that is, outside of Japan and Germany where militarism had allowed an early recovery, only with the arms buildup on the eve of the Second World War. The brief recovery provided by the New Deal of Franklin Roosevelt in the United States was scuttled by the return to policy orthodoxy that precipitated the 1937 downturn, a kind of depression within a depression. On the eve of the war, while capacity utilization in the consumer goods industries was quite high, the producer goods industries were marked by huge unutilized capacity.[6] The boost to military expenditures for the war improved capacity utilization in that sector as well.

The United States, which had not been as devastated as the European countries and where the balance of class forces had not witnessed as decisive a shift in favor of the working class, persisted with large military expenditures even after the war, both because of its new role as the leader of the capitalist world confronting the "twin threats" of communism and national liberation movements, and also because this appeared to be the easiest mechanism, already in place and not treading on the toes of any capitalists, for maintaining a high level of employment.[7] A return to prewar unemployment levels was obviously unthinkable, because of the threat to capitalism it would have entailed (of which Keynes was acutely aware); hence what some writers have called a "military Keynesianism" came into vogue in the United States, which Marxist writers like Baran, Sweezy, and Magdoff highlighted in several studies.

In Europe, however, the trajectory was different. The continent was devastated. The working class had emerged from the war having made enormous sacrifices, and it was determined not to go back to the prewar years of unemployment and distress. It greatly increased its class strength, of which the defeat of Winston Churchill in the postwar elections in Britain was the clearest sign. The system could not go back to its old ways, and the presence of the Soviet Union next door posed a serious threat to the ruling classes.

It was essential for European capitalism to make concessions, to modify the system in significant ways in order to ward off this threat, and three crucial concessions were made. First, the adoption of state intervention in demand management, which Keynes had long been advocating; second, decolonization, at least at a political level (economic decolonization, entailing a relaxation of control over the resources of the colonies, had to await another round of struggles, often bitter ones, such as the Anglo-French invasion of Egypt in the wake of Nasser's nationalization of the Suez Canal); and third, the introduction of universal adult franchise. In Britain, something close to universal adult franchise had been achieved in 1928 when women won the vote, but even in France universal adult franchise was introduced only in 1945.

The upshot of these changes is that unlike the military Keynesianism of the United States, European Keynesianism took the form of substantial welfare state expenditure under the aegis of Social Democracy. No doubt much of this expenditure was financed through the taxation of workers themselves;[8] nonetheless it entailed a net redistribution of income in an egalitarian direction through fiscal means, which was not just desirable per se but kept up the level of aggregate demand, even after the effects of the postwar reconstruction boom had worn off.

High aggregate demand, which kept down unemployment rates to levels never experienced under capitalism in peacetime, also stimulated high rates of investment and economic growth, and hence high levels of labor productivity growth. This growth was aided by several innovations developed in the interwar period but kept in abeyance because of the depressed economic conditions that were now introduced into the production process. Because of the low unemployment rate—which induced migration from the former colonies and dependencies, such as of Indian, Pakistani, and West Indian workers into Britain, Algerian workers into France, and Turkish workers into Germany—trade unions could enforce high rates of wage increase in the face of high labor productivity growth. The condition of workers, both because of wage increases and welfare state measures, improved significantly—hence the term "Golden Age of Capitalism"—and the point began to be made that "capitalism had changed," that it had turned over a new leaf.[9]

The postwar arrangement, however, had an obvious lacuna in the light of our previous discussion. It contained a substitute for the old colonial arrangement in the matter of finding a market for the products of the capitalist metropolis, and that was the demand generated by the state. Kalecki was to call sales to the state against a fiscal deficit an "export surplus" of the capitalist sector to the state.[10] And even when there was no fiscal deficit but a balanced budget maintained by the state, the multiplier effects of such a balanced budget could keep up aggregate demand. In short, the "market on tap," which the colonial arrangement had provided in the pre–First World War years, was now provided by the capitalist state.

Schumpeter, in an assessment of Keynes's *Economic Consequences of the Peace*, sees it as expressing the position that the stimulus to capitalism provided by the pre–First World War arrangement had come to an end and that capitalism had to obtain a new stimulus which could only come from the state.[11] (Keynes, of course, was not talking about colonialism.) This perception, developed in his later theoretical work, but not taken seriously before the Second World War because of the opposition of finance, not even in the United States, where the switch to the New Deal strategy was far from thorough, can be said to have been realized in the postwar period.

But what the postwar arrangement did not have was any means of imposing income deflation upon the working people of the periphery to prevent the effects of increasing supply price from jeopardizing the value of money. Political decolonization removed from the armory of the capitalist sector the weapon of tax-enforced income deflation that the colonial state had been able to impose.

And yet, interestingly, this did not get in the way of the postwar boom for a long time. Indeed, Arthur Lewis had predicted after the war that there would be a significant increase in raw material prices;[12] and yet the actual price increase was restrained, and there was a resumption of the decline of the terms of trade of primary commodities vis-à-vis manufacturing.[13] How can one explain this phenomenon, which induced a stability in the value of money in the metropolis, even after capitalism had forfeited its capacity to impose income deflation in the periphery because of political decolonization?

Two things happened with decolonization. First, the postcolonial governments that had come everywhere to power on the strength of support from the peasantry and had been committed to improving the lot of the peasantry, introduced land-augmentation measures that, by and large, had been conspicuously absent during the colonial era. We saw that land augmentation required the support of the state. The colonial state had not given this support but had on the contrary squeezed the peasantry through taxes; the postcolonial state did provide this support. Public investment in irrigation increased; public expenditure on research and development into new seeds and new practices increased; public extension services were set up; and the government offered assured remunerative prices to agriculture even as it subsidized inputs for this sector. Because of these measures, there was a substantial increase in agricultural output even on the fixed tropical landmass, which raised domestic absorption of food grains while still making adequate supplies of primary commodities available to the metropolis.

The second factor was the competition between the newly independent countries, each of which was keen on industrializing and hence for importing capital goods for this purpose from the metropolis, by increasing as much as possible their traditional exports. This kept down primary commodity prices for the metropolis, which obtained these commodities in adequate quantities because of the land-augmenting measures being adopted. Thus, India and Sri Lanka competed in the tea market instead of colluding, and India and Bangladesh (then a part of Pakistan) competed in the market for jute, and so on. The effects of decolonization on the availability of raw materials for the metropolis did not manifest themselves for a long time.

But they eventually did, in the early 1970s, when there was a sharp rise in raw material prices. To be sure, there was a speculative element behind this rise. The snapping of the gold-dollar link, which had been a characteristic of the Bretton Woods system, and the subsequent abandonment of the Bretton Woods system itself, deprived the capitalist world of the stable medium of holding wealth that the U.S. dollar had provided under the Bretton Woods system.[14] In the turmoil that immediately followed (until the dollar reestablished its status as the stable medium despite the absence of any explicit gold link), many wealth-holders moved to holding commodities (or rather, claims on commodities), which pushed up commodity prices. But obviously, speculation acted on top of a situation where supply constraints were beginning to manifest themselves.

We can put the matter in exactly the opposite manner. The convertibility of the U.S. dollar to gold at $35 per ounce of gold, as decreed by the Bretton Woods system, became impossible to sustain and had to give way, owing to the desire on the part of, above all, the French government under de Gaulle, to insist on gold payments. This, however, was a result not of bloody-mindedness, as commonly supposed, but because of the inflation that had already made its appearance since the late 1960s. In other words, the Bretton Woods system collapsed because of the emergence of inflation. Though its collapse led, in turn, to an upsurge of inflation, the emergence of inflation can be attributed to the absence of any arrangement underlying the postwar boom for imposing income deflation on the working people of the periphery.[15]

The sudden eruption of a commodity price explosion happened in the context of another phenomenon that was occurring during the so-called Golden Age of capitalism, and this was an enormous concentration of finance in the hands of banks and other financial institutions. There were three sources of such concentration: the first was the persistent U.S. current account deficits that began sometime after the war because of the massive expenditure undertaken by the United States in maintaining a string of military bases across the globe, which ballooned with the Vietnam War (which stoked the inflation that caused the wage explosion of 1968); the second was the savings of the economy during the prolonged boom that were deposited into the banking system; and the third was the first oil shock of 1973, to be followed by another one soon afterward, which suddenly transferred purchasing power from a vast number of oil consumers into the pockets of a few oil producers, who in turn deposited them with metropolitan banks.

Metropolitan banks, therefore, started sitting on vast amounts of finance, which they wanted to lend out. For this, however, it was essential that barriers to capital flows (capital controls), especially financial flows across national boundaries, which had characterized the Bretton Woods system, should be lifted. This happened in Europe in the early 1970s, in Africa and Latin America a decade later, and in India in the 1990s. We thus had the formation of a *globalized* finance capital.

The combination of vast concentrations of finance, on the one hand, with inflation, on the other, both produced under the aegis of the "Golden

Age" regime, was an explosive one. The need to control inflation was particularly acute because of the vast accumulations of finance. And interestingly, the very globalization of finance that came about under the pressure exerted by finance capital to sweep away barriers to capital flows also entailed the reimposition of a regime of income deflation on the working people of the periphery that would control inflation and stabilize the value of money. This was the regime of globalization.

## The Regime of Globalization

Central to the regime of globalization is globalization of capital, and above all, of finance. When finance is globalized while the state remains a nation-state, then the state, willy-nilly, has to act in accordance with the demands of finance; otherwise a financial outflow could cause acute crisis for the economy. Preventing such a capital flight, retaining what is called "investors' confidence," and, for that reason, getting approval from the credit-rating agencies that influence financiers' decisions, becomes the main preoccupations of the state, which essentially means an undermining of the autonomy of the state.

This has major implications for democracy. Democracy requires that alternative visions of society, alternative trajectories of development, should be placed before the people, from which they can choose. But if all political parties have the same policies, namely those approved by finance capital, because as long as they remain trapped within a regime of globalization they cannot do otherwise, then the choice of the people becomes meaningless. No matter whom they elect, the same economic policies will continue to be followed, unless some political formation has the courage to delink from globalization through capital controls. However, few have this courage, because of the transitional difficulties that such delinking would bring in its wake.[16]

This issue of democracy is not one we will follow any further. More pertinent from our point of view is that under such a regime of globalization state intervention in demand management becomes impossible. For instance, boosting aggregate demand on the part of the state requires either running a fiscal deficit or taxing capitalists to finance state spending, given that the capitalists have a higher propensity to save than the workers. Taxing workers, who have a lower propensity to save, and spending the proceeds of such taxation, would not add much to aggregate demand through a balanced budget multiplier.

But finance capital is averse to fiscal deficits for financing larger state expenditure that would boost aggregate demand. It provides all sorts of theoretical justifications for its aversion, all of which are completely invalid. Joan Robinson has called such justifications the "humbug of finance."[17] The real reason for this aversion, however, lies elsewhere, namely in that if the state has to boost demand through its own direct expenditure, then this undermines the social legitimacy of capital, and especially of that segment of capital, specifically finance, which consists of what Keynes had called "functionless investors." Accepting the need for state expenditure for boosting aggregate demand, even when such expenditure is financed by a fiscal deficit, is tantamount to finance accepting its own superfluity, which, of course, it is unwilling to do. And taxing capitalists to enable the state to undertake expenditure that boosts aggregate demand is doubly disagreeable for finance. It not only undermines the social legitimacy of capital, especially finance, but also reduces capitalists' income below what even a fiscal-deficit-financed expenditure of a similar order would have generated.

Keynes, writing in *The Yale Review,* had said: "let finance be primarily national."[18] He was clearly aware that if a nation-state is faced with finance that is international, then it loses its autonomy, including in the matter of intervening to boost aggregate demand and employment. If capitalism had to be saved, he believed, then the levels of unemployment with which it was typically associated had to be reduced through state intervention, but this was not possible unless finance was "national." The contemporary globalization of finance thus undermines the capacity of the state to intervene for boosting aggregate demand and employment.

But globalization of capital does more than that. Since "investors' confidence" becomes an obsession with the state, for which the demands of finance capital have to be acceded to, there is a change in the nature of the state. Instead of being an entity standing above society and apparently looking after the interests of all (despite being a bourgeois state in the sense of ultimately protecting and nurturing the interests of the capitalists through such apparent benevolence toward all), the state now becomes much more exclusively and transparently concerned with promoting the interests of globalized capital, including its domestic component. This means a withdrawal from defending the interests of the peasants, other petty producers, and workers.

Unlike the postcolonial *dirigiste* regime in most countries of the periphery, which, even when they were developing capitalism within their shores, were nonetheless protecting and promoting peasant agriculture, the regime under globalization withdraws from supporting and promoting peasant agriculture and other petty production. It leaves peasants at the mercy of big capital (agribusiness); and its pursuit of "fiscal rectitude," by curtailing the fiscal deficit, usually through a self-denying "fiscal responsibility" legislation that puts a statutory ceiling on it as a proportion of the GDP, entails a rolling back of the support measures for peasants and petty producers that had been introduced in the aftermath of political decolonization.

All this means a loss of income in the periphery for the peasants, petty producers, and workers, who are adversely affected by the growing labor reserves, caused in the main by displaced peasants and petty producers looking for nonexistent jobs elsewhere. The regime of globalization therefore entails the imposition of an income deflation on the working population in the periphery.

What is more, the state in the periphery under neoliberalism (the regime of fiscal austerity, privatization of public services, and the like) mimics to an extent the colonial state, although the element of "drain of surplus" no longer exists as it did before. If metropolitan capital acted in the colonial period through the metropolitan/colonial state for imposing income deflation, globalized capital today, with which the domestic big capital of the periphery is integrated, acts through the neoliberal domestic state to impose similar income deflation. Any tendency for inflation to surface beyond the "threshold" rate immediately calls forth "austerity" and tight money measures whose effect is to counter inflation through imposing an income deflation upon the working population. *In other words, globalization entails not only income deflation in the periphery, but also the setting up of a regime for regulating income deflation in the periphery for protecting the value of money.*

The role of income deflation in bringing an end to the inflation in primary commodity prices in the early 1970s is often not appreciated. Even Paul Krugman is of the view that the inflationary upsurge of that time had been controlled through new sources of raw materials and new lands coming under cultivation.[19] As a matter of fact, there is no evidence of any output expansion in per capita terms, which, if Krugman was right, should have occurred.

On the contrary, if we compare the average annual world per capita cereal output for the triennium 1979–81 with the corresponding figure for the triennium 1999–2001, then we find that this figure *declined* from 355 to 343 kilograms.[20] In other words, cereal output expansion in excess of world population growth did not occur, which means that, since world per capita real income was growing over this period and since the income elasticity of demand for cereals is positive, there should have been a rise in cereal prices relative to the vector of money wages, and a shift in the terms of trade between manufacturing and cereals in favor of the latter (as manufacturing prices are likely to be tied to and move with money wages and even fall relative to money wages because of labor productivity growth). But over this period, we actually find a decline in the terms of trade for cereals vis-à-vis manufacturing in the world economy of the order of 45 percent![21] Clearly, it was income deflation, rather than any output expansion caused by new lands coming into cultivation, that was the reason behind inflation control in the 1970s.

But just as the postwar *dirigiste regimes* had a lacuna, so does the regime of globalization, or more appropriately the neoliberal regime that globalization entails, and this lacuna is the mirror image of the lacuna of the earlier regime. The earlier regime, it may be recalled, had a mechanism for providing markets for the system through state expenditure, but no mechanism for imposing income deflation upon the working population of the periphery. The neoliberal regime under globalization has a mechanism for imposing income deflation upon the working population of the periphery, but no mechanism for providing markets for the system. And it is this lacuna that underlies the current conjuncture in world capitalism, characterized by a dead end for globalization.

No doubt the very burgeoning of finance, or what some have called the "financialization" of economies (parallel to the industrialization that had occurred earlier), becomes a source of demand. The superstructure of finance that is erected over the economy itself boosts aggregate demand. *But this is not a market on tap.* The demand generated by the financial superstructure is similar to the demand generated by the incomes derived from what Baran and Sweezy had called the "costs of circulation." But this does not provide an exogenous stimulus of the sort that pre-capitalist markets earlier and state expenditure in the postwar period had done. The primary exogenous stimulus, if one may call it that, in a neoliberal regime is provided by the formation of occasional "bubbles" in asset prices. Yet this stimulus, too, is not available on tap. "Bubbles" cannot be made to order, which is a major reason why the world capitalist economy continues to languish in a prolonged period of crisis and stagnation.

### The Period of Protracted Crisis

The fact that the neoliberal regime under globalization cannot call on any other exogenous stimulus, such as colonial markets or state expenditure, and that "bubbles," which alone can revive a neoliberal economy, cannot be made to order, is only one of the factors behind the present protracted crisis. This factor is superimposed upon a deeper structural crisis of capitalism that globalization engenders.

World capitalism had for a long time been marked by a segmentation between two *regions.* Labor from the periphery was not allowed to move freely to the metropolis (it still is not), whereas capital from the metropolis, though juridically free to move to the periphery, did not actually do so. It moved only to sectors like plantations and mines and the sectors of trade and services that were associated with the export of primary commodities. But it did not locate manufacturing plants in the periphery, to take advantage of lower wages and produce for the metropolitan market. This segmentation was the cause of real wages in the periphery languishing at some subsistence level while wages in the metropolis kept rising as labor productivity there increased.

The current globalization has brought that segmentation to an end. While labor is still not free to migrate from the periphery to the metropolis (and its desperate and limited defiance of this restraint has given rise to the recent refugee crisis in Europe), capital has shown greater willingness to locate plants in the low-wage economies of the periphery for producing goods that would meet demands in the metropolis. The workers in the metropolis, therefore, now have to compete with the workers in the periphery, because of which, even though their real wages do not fall to the level of real wages in the periphery, they do not rise, either. In fact, Joseph Stiglitz suggests that the real wage rate of a male American worker in 2011 was no higher than in 1968.[22]

At the same time, despite this relocation of activities, the labor reserves in the periphery do not get exhausted. The rate of growth of employment, even in those economies of the periphery that have grown rapidly (if measured carefully to take account of disguised unemployment), has fallen short of the natural rate of growth of the workforce, let alone providing employment to the displaced petty producers who throng the labor market because of the income deflation to which they are subjected. The real wages in the periphery, therefore, do not rise despite this relocation and even the high growth rates generated on account of it. It follows that *the vector of real wages in the world economy today has been more or less stagnant.*

At the same time, the vector of labor productivities, if we take careful account of disguised unemployment, has been rising, which means that the vector of surpluses as a proportion of output has been rising. Since the propensity to consume out of surplus is lower than out of wages, and since this propensity is no higher in economies where the surplus is rising faster than in economies where it is rising more slowly (if anything, faster-growing economies have a larger share of surplus being saved), this implies that *there is an ex ante tendency toward overproduction in the world economy.* The structural crisis of world capitalism arises from this *ex ante* tendency.

This *ex ante* tendency did not manifest itself sooner because of the operation of "bubbles" in the U.S. economy, first the "dot-com bubble," which was followed by the "housing bubble." But with the collapse of the housing bubble, we not only have a persistence of crisis *for this reason* but also the surfacing of an underlying structural crisis arising from the *ex ante* tendency toward overproduction unleashed by globalization.

*Concluding Observations*

World capitalism today is characterized not only by the absence of an exogenous stimulus but also by an *ex ante* tendency toward overproduction. It is this that makes the current crisis both protracted as well as unprecedented, since it is reflective of capitalism having reached a sort of cul-de-sac. Even if it overcomes the current crisis temporarily through the formation of a new "bubble," its collapse will only bring the system back to a crisis. Protectionism, such as what U.S. president Donald Trump was attempting, amounts in effect under these circumstances (that is, in the absence of any significant expansion of state expenditure financed either by a fiscal deficit or by taxes on capitalists) to an export of unemployment to other countries. It can work only if the other countries do not retaliate. If they do, then it gives rise to a competitive "beggar-thy-neighbor" policy that only worsens the crisis by creating further uncertainties and reducing investments further.

Expanding the world market requires a coordinated fiscal stimulus by several major countries acting together, or if each country delinks from globalization by imposing capital controls and then uses its nation-state's newfound freedom from thralldom to finance capital to enlarge state expenditure. Either scenario entails a confrontation with finance capital. It is difficult to visualize the world economy overcoming its current protracted crisis without shaking off the hegemony of finance capital.

# CHAPTER 7

# The Myth of the Agricultural Revolution

lmost every book on the Industrial Revolution in Britain in the
eighteenth century contains a mandatory chapter titled "The
Agricultural Revolution." Other chapters are variously headed
"The Transport Revolution," "The Commercial Revolution," and so on.
That an agricultural revolution took place in the eighteenth century as a
precondition to the transition to factory production in the last quarter of
the century is widely accepted. We argue here that this was scarcely the
case, and that the role usually attributed to the agricultural revolution not
only is a gross exaggeration but also has the effect of obscuring the actual
role played by colonialism.

## *The Demands of Capitalist Industry upon Agriculture*

It is clear that any process of transition to capitalist manufacturing requires
the formation of a proletariat for which there must be a separation of the
small producers from their means of production—that is, the creation
of "free" workers through the proletarianization of peasants and other
petty producers. Such a process of transition also requires, if we abstract
for the time being from the role of colonialism, speeding up the rate of
growth of agricultural output, particularly grain production, to meet the
demands of capitalist industry. In the absence of such a speeding up, there
would be untoward inflation and a squeezing of the living standards of

the population, which, apart from the social consequences, would also adversely affect the market for capitalist industry.

The demands of capitalist industry for agricultural goods arise for several reasons. First, as the workforce shifts out of the primary sector and is increasingly employed in manufacturing and its ancillary activities, the requirement of commodified wage goods, in particular basic food staples, to feed this population rises. Second, the requirements of feed grains for livestock rises fast since in the preindustrial and early industrial era most transportation and traction depended on horse and oxen power. The land has to provide not only increasing food for humans but also more energy in the form of feed for animals. (Fossil fuels as the source of energy started to become important only when the first phase of the Industrial Revolution was over.) Third, as per capita incomes rise, the demand for consuming animal products also rises and requires more output of feed grains. Finally, the raw materials needed by manufacturing have to be met by the primary sector as well.

It is usually taken for granted that the agricultural revolution met all these demands in England over the period 1750 to 1820. However, this claim overlooks some basic facts. First, in the case of England the main raw material of the fastest-growing industry of the Industrial Revolution, raw cotton, was entirely imported, as cotton could not be grown in cold temperate climatic conditions. Second, the output of the basic staple food, corn or wheat, clearly could not have grown at the required rate for providing an elastic supply of bread. Indeed, the main issue on which prolonged agitations took place from the 1790s onward was the rise in the price of bread. Few issues in history relating to political economy have been more discussed and documented than the five decades of agitation over the price of bread in England and the demand for free imports of cheaper corn from the Continent, *misnamed* as the free trade agitation. It is misnamed because the demand was not for generalized free trade but only for freedom to import cheaper corn and other foods as well as raw materials while the same period saw the imposition of high tariffs on Asian textiles.

Yet the obvious inference has escaped many economic historians, namely that if the "agricultural revolution" could not even meet the basic wage-good requirement of the transition to the factory system, then it could hardly have been much of a revolution. To blame the landlords, as is commonly done, for the food shortage, while simultaneously adhering to the idea that an agricultural revolution had indeed occurred, simply will not do. For the whole point of an agricultural revolution is that the capitalist transformation of agriculture leads to a sufficiently large rise in productivity so that the per capita supply of wage-goods rises adequately to meet the increasing demand. The capitalist tenant farmers are supposed to have achieved a large enough rise of productivity, *despite the payment of rent to landlords.*

This rise of productivity did not happen; instead, rapid food price inflation took place. This was because, as we shall see, *per capita grain production, far from rising, fell after the middle of the century and right up to 1820.* Neither land nor labor productivity rose appreciably in England, despite all the enclosures, the transition to larger farm size, to capitalist tenant farming, etc. Even the early eighteenth-century level of per capita grain output, achieved on the basis of the earlier agrarian relations of production, could not be maintained. The result was that though the GDP rose rapidly as did per capita income, there was an erosion of the real incomes of the laboring classes, because of the high rate of food price inflation.

The Industrial Revolution spans a period over much of which Britain was embroiled in the long Napoleonic Wars that lasted from 1793 to 1815. Any involvement in war entails a diversion of resources to war-related industries (shipping, armaments) and induces a war boom that tends to translate into an inflationary shortage of food grains, even when per capita food-grain output is maintained; if per capita output is not maintained, the inflation is steeper. The British case was no exception to this. The country had already become food-deficit by the 1770s, with cereal output per head of population showing a steady decline. Wheat imports, though positive, were restricted by the Corn Laws, which served landlord interests and kept food prices even higher than they would otherwise have been. The war boom from 1793 meant rapid food price inflation from an already high base, and near-starvation for the laboring poor in years of bad harvests of the 1790s.[1]

It is not surprising that the cry for bread and the agitation for free imports of cheaper food grains from abroad became the single most important political economy issue for five decades, from the 1790s to 1846. The landlords put up an obdurate resistance until the mid-nineteenth century, but tariffs finally had to go. The Corn Laws were repealed thirty long years after David Ricardo penned his book *An Essay on the Influence of a Low Price of Corn on the Profits of Stock.*

This prolonged agitation was, at the same time, a telling indicator of the failure of Britain's agriculture in meeting the wage goods needs of capitalist industrialization despite all the enclosures and supposed improvements in the eighteenth century, a failure that intensified in the course of the early nineteenth century. The rising industry of cotton textiles, which was the very embodiment of technical change and the factory system, used raw materials that were entirely imported, as Britain could produce neither raw cotton nor vegetable dyes like indigo. By 1825, the retained imports of all primary products, expressed as a percentage of total domestic primary sector output, had reached 65 percent and this rose to 104 percent by 1855. Britain, in other words, was importing more primary products than it itself produced by that date.[2]

Indeed, it is *prima facie* surprising that an increasingly food-deficit country, with two decades of drain on its resources on account of war-related expenditures, could make the transition, precisely in this period of wartime strains, to the factory system, by investing in a rapidly expanding new industry that produced a consumption good and which, moreover, was based entirely on imported raw materials. Normally, consumption-goods production suffers in wartime, whereas in Britain, it was the fastest-growing industry. How did Britain pay for rising imports of foodstuffs, raw cotton, dyestuffs, and other raw materials, pursue a war (which required increased imports of naval materials like bar iron, timber, hemp, pitch, and tar) and still face no external payments imbalances?

Further, in this period before steam power was harnessed, the main energy source for the expanding transport system was horsepower, for the haulage of barges on canals, for haulage in collieries, for civilian transport, and so on, and horses meant increased animal feed grain consumption. British agriculture was unable to provide that increase except at the expense of a further decline in per capita food grains for human consumption, which was nearly 20 percent lower by 1800 compared to 1750.

### Growth of Grain Production Relative to Population in the Eighteenth Century

The variable that is crucial as an indicator of welfare and a measure of the success of agricultural revolution is the growth of the basic food staple crop in relation to population growth. The older Brownlee series of population for England and Wales was revised by Lee and Schofield, and the latter series and the index derived from it are shown for 1700 to 1800 as the A index column in Table 7.1.[3] Maddison presents some more recent estimates on population for scattered years starting 1700 and ending 1870 from which we calculated the growth rate between 1700 and 1801 and interpolated the intermediate year values on the assumption of steady growth.[4] The Index B column for England and Wales (E+W) has been derived from this series in Table 7.1. The main difference between the two series is the somewhat higher population in the latter series, especially in the earlier years, which reduces the growth rate slightly compared to the first series. The Maddison series for Britain, namely England, Wales, and Scotland (E+W+S), was derived in the same manner by us and is shown as the Index C column.

From Chambers and Mingay, we derive the rise in cereals output in physical terms over the eighteenth century from their discussion that the area under wheat rose by a quarter and yield rose by about one-tenth while the rise in the non-wheat cereals was somewhat faster.[5] This broad picture is confirmed by later research, although some research shows a somewhat higher rise.[6] This gives an increase of 37.5 percent for wheat and 43 percent for all cereals over the period 1700 to 1800. The increase by 43 percent is distributed over the decades of the century in the same proportion as total agricultural output value is distributed in Cole.[7] This is a better procedure than to distribute the increase assuming a constant growth rate. This exercise gives us the index of per capita cereal output shown in the first column of Table 7.2.

We can check that per capita cereal output declined for every population

**TABLE 7.1: Population in million of England and Wales (E+W) and Britain (E+W+S), Constant Prices GDP and Agricultural Output Value in £ million, 1701-1801**

| Year | E + W Lee & Schofield | A Index | E + W Maddison 1700 value | B Index | E + W + S Maddison | C Index | GDP £ millions | Agricultural Output £ millions |
|---|---|---|---|---|---|---|---|---|
| 1695 | 5.18 | 97.90 | 5.604 | 99.5 | - | - | - | - |
| 1701 | 5.29 | 100.0 | 5.632 | 100.0 | 6.673 | 100.0 | 50.0 | 20.0 |
| 1711 | 5.51 | 104.2 | 5.920 | 105.1 | 7.008 | 105.0 | 53.9 | 20.6 |
| 1721 | 5.66 | 107.0 | 6.222 | 110.5 | 7.361 | 110.3 | 57.5 | 24.1 |
| 1731 | 5.59 | 105.7 | 6.541 | 116.1 | 7.731 | 115.85 | 58.7 | 23.6 |
| 1741 | 5.94 | 112.3 | 6.875 | 122.1 | 8.120 | 121.7 | 64.1 | 26.1 |
| 1751 | 6.20 | 117.2 | 7.227 | 128.3 | 8.528 | 127.8 | 70.4 | 28.1 |
| 1761 | 6.62 | 125.1 | 7.596 | 134.9 | 8.957 | 134.2 | 81.9 | 28.9 |
| 1771 | 6.97 | 131.8 | 7.985 | 141.8 | 9.408 | 141.0 | 80.3 | 29.0 |
| 1781 | 7057 | 143.1 | 8.393 | 149.0 | 9.881 | 148.1 | 82.0 | 31.5 |
| 1791 | 8.21 | 155.2 | 8.822 | 156.6 | 10.378 | 155.5 | 104.1 | 33.4 |
| 1801 | 9.16 | 173.2 | 9.277 | 164.7 | 10.902 | 163.4 | 135.8 | 36.2 |

Note: Agricultural output and GDP in million of pounds, population in millions.

Sources: W. A. Cole and Phyllis Deane, *British Economic Growth 1688–1959: Trends and Structure* (Cambridge: Cambridge University Press, 1969); R. D. Lee and R. S. Schofield, "British Population in the Eighteenth Century," in R. Floud and D. McCloskey, eds., *The Economic History of Britain Since 1700* (Cambridge: Cambridge University Press, 1981); Angus Maddison, *The World Economy* (Paris: OECD Development Centre Studies, 2006).

**TABLE 7.2: Estimated Index of Total Cereals Output in Vol. Units; and Indices of Per Capita Cereals Output, 1701–1801 for Britain**

| Year | Cereals Output | PER CAPITA CEREALS | | |
| --- | --- | --- | --- | --- |
| | | A | B | C |
| 1701 | 100.0 | 100.0 | 100.0 | 100.0 |
| 1711 | 101.6 | 97.50 | 96.70 | 96.8 |
| 1721 | 110.9 | 103.6 | 100.4 | 100.5 |
| 1731 | 109.6 | 103.7 | 94.40 | 94.6 |
| 1741 | 116.2 | 103.5 | 95.20 | 95.5 |
| 1751 | 121.5 | 103.7 | 94.70 | 95.0 |
| 1761 | 123.7 | 98.90 | 91.70 | 92.2 |
| 1771 | 123.9 | 89.70 | 87.40 | 87.9 |
| 1781 | 130.6 | 91.30 | 87.70 | 88.2 |
| 1791 | 135.6 | 87.40 | 86.60 | 87.2 |
| 1801 | 143.4 | 82.60 | 86.80 | 87.5 |

Sources: See Table 7.1.

index by varying degrees; the largest decline was by 17.4 percent using the Lee and Schofield index, with the Maddison indices giving around 13 percent decline. The Lee and Schofield population series is the only complete one, and the Maddison population figures are only for individual years at the beginning and end of the century, with values we interpolate by assuming a constant growth rate of population, which was not actually the case. The per capita cereal output, Index A in Table 7.2, using the Lee and Schofield series, should be regarded as the better approximation to the actual trends. This shows that per capita output rose slowly up to the mid-eighteenth century (and this is consistent with the small net export of corn that existed up to 1770). After 1750, however, per capita cereal output starts declining, and despite slight recovery by 1780, the decline resumes in the last two decades coinciding with war, first in North America and then in Europe.

It should be noted that a 17.4 percent decline is quite substantial for per capita cereals output, given that the initial level of availability was low. This is confirmed when we study wheat or corn, the major food staple of the population. We rely on the absolute estimates of wheat area, yield, and output given by Turner, Beckett and Afton for 1750 to 1850, reproduced

**Figure 7.1: Indices of Total Cereal Output and Per Capita Cereals Output, 1700–1800**

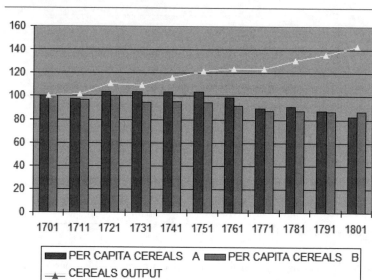

Sources: Table 7.1.

here in Table 7.3.[8] This table also incorporates the rise by 25 percent in area, and of yield by 10 percent that Chambers and Mingay mention over the entire century, to derive the 1700 figure of output. This gives a total rise of output from 33.41 to 45.95 million bushels or by 37.5 percent, whereas population increased by 73.2 percent on the Lee and Schofield figures and by 64.7 percent on the Maddison figures.

The authors are sanguine about per capita output and believe that on the whole English agriculture continued to feed the larger population adequately. They support the Overton position that the agricultural revolution was a reality in the eighteenth century.[9] This conclusion however is contradicted by Overton's own statement:

Population grew at an average of 0.26 per cent per annum from 1700–1750 whereas all the agricultural output indices grew more rapidly (ranging from 0.38 to 0.60 percent per annum): *from 1750–1850 population*

**Figure 7.2: Indices of Population, Total Cereal Output and Per Capita Output 1700–1800**

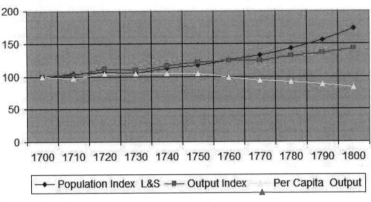

Source: Table 7.1.

*grew at an average of 1.07 percent per annum and the estimates of agricultural output ranged from 0.77 to 0.82 percent per annum.* [10]

On the basis of every revised series of population, it is obvious that per capita agricultural output as well as wheat output declined between 1750 and 1800, and remained stagnant between 1800 and 1820, and it appears from Overton's statement that the subsequent rise was not enough to recover the lost ground, and that on balance per capita output remained lower in 1850 than a century earlier. This is also the finding of recent detailed research with time series data for the period, even after allowing for a possible substantial margin of error.[11] The interesting point is that the decline is concentrated in the second half of the century and later when the maximum "improvements" were taking place with the transition to capitalist agriculture.

From Table 7.4, the annual compound rate of net output growth for wheat over the entire eighteenth century works out to 0.32 percent, with the first half registering 0.31 percent and the second half 0.325 percent. This rise in the growth rate of net output is so insignificant in the second

**TABLE 7.3: Gross Output and Net Output of Corn (Wheat) in England and Wales, 1700–1850**

| Year | Wheat Area (million acre) | Ave Yield (bushel per acre) | Gross Output (million bushel) | Seed (in million bushel) | Net Output (in million bushel) |
|------|---------------------------|------------------------------|-------------------------------|--------------------------|--------------------------------|
| 1700 | 1.752 | 19.07 | 33.41 | 4.21 | 29.20 |
| 1750 | 1.7   | 22.42 | 38.11 | 4.08 | 34.03 |
| 1800 | 2.19  | 20.98 | 45.94 | 5.91 | 40.03 |
| 1820 | 2.55  | 23.60 | 60.18 | 6.89 | 53.29 |
| 1850 | 3.42  | 27.47 | 93.95 | 5.47 | 88.48 |

Source: Turner, Beckett, and Afton, *Farm Production in England, 1700–1917*, chapter 7.

half of the century that it could not cope with the acceleration in the rate of population growth, and so the per capita net output fell.

The annual per capita output in bushels is converted to kilograms for comparison with present-day levels in developing countries in Table 7.4. The initial level of 140 kg. per capita, virtually unchanged between 1700 and 1750, is itself extremely low. If we accept from the writings of contemporaries and those who have investigated diet composition that at least three-fifths of the population relied on wheaten bread (while the remainder consumed other grains), then the per capita figure for the wheat-dependent population is raised to 233 kg. in the mid-eighteenth century. This is still quite low and compares poorly with many Asian and North African developing countries today, such as for example Indonesia and Egypt, whose grain consumption out of domestic output in 2007 was 250 kg. and 358 kg., respectively.[12]

By 1800, per capita wheat output was down to an astonishing low of 112 kg. Owing to cropping pattern and dietary changes, two-thirds of the population is estimated to have become dependent on wheaten bread. This seems too low and is probably obtained by including the Irish population, which subsisted on potatoes but which should not be counted when we are considering the grain output of England and Wales. But even taking this figure to be correct for England and Wales, per capita availability from domestic production for them would have been at most 168 kg. by 1800 and remained unchanged in 1820. So, effectively, the decline would have

**TABLE 7.4: Annual Per Capita Output of Wheat, England and Wales, in Bushels and in Kilograms[13]**

| Year | Net Output (millions of bushels) | Net Output (millions of kilograms) | Population (millions) | Per Capita Output (kilograms) |
|------|------|------|------|------|
| 1700 | 29.20 | 743.530 | 5.29 | 140.55 |
| 1750 | 34.03 | 866.218 | 6.20 | 139.71 |
| 1800 | 40.03 | 1,019.200 | 9.16 | 111.27 |
| 1820 | 53.29 | 1,356.470 | 12.071 | 112.37 |
| 1850 | 88.48 | 2,252.220 | 17.603 | 127.95 |

Source: Net output figures derived earlier divided by population figures from Lee and Schofield, *British Population in the Eighteenth Century.*

been from 233 kg. to 168 kg. for the wheat-dependent population, or by 28 percent. Given the inequality in the distribution of incomes, the quantities affordable by the laboring poor would have been much lower; little wonder, then, that they rioted for cheap bread. It remains to be worked out what the situation for those dependent on rye, oats, potatoes, and the like would have been.

### Net Imports of Grain into England

Domestic production can be augmented by imports, and actual availability is given by domestic output plus net imports. Imports from Ireland supplied nearly one-eighth of Britain's consumption of wheat and wheaten flour by 1800.[14] But imports from Europe were artificially restricted by the Corn Laws, and the absolute quantities imported were kept so low that they had a negligible impact on availability, right up to the 1820s. From Table 7.5, we see that grain was being exported in the first half of the eighteenth century, but by the end of the 1760s net exports became negligible and the direction of the import-export balance was reversed. Net grain imports started and grew slowly but steadily from the beginning of the 1790s. Imports doubled by the decade 1810–19 and doubled again by 1830–39 to 1.3 million quarters, or 16,230 tons. From Figure 7.3, we see that, as domestic per capita output fell, the net imports started rising. However, this chart must be read carefully as the variables are plotted on

**TABLE 7.5: Annual Average Net Imports of Wheat and Wheaten Flour into England, 1720–29 to 1880–89 (in thousand quarters)**

| YEAR | CORN (M − X) |
| --- | --- |
| 1720–29 | −105.5 |
| 1730–39 | −296.7 |
| 1740–49 | −289.3 |
| 1750–59 | −312.8 |
| 1760–69 | −138.5 |
| 1770–79 | −43.1 |
| 1780–89 | −23.4 |
| 1790–99 | 324.5 |
| 1800–09 | 580.9 |
| 1810–19 | 662.9 |
| 1820–29 | 814.7 |
| 1830–39 | 1,298.4 |
| 1840–49 | 1,782.0 |
| 1850–59 | 3,240.0 |
| 1860–69 | 5,844.0 |
| 1870–79 | 9,160.0 |
| 1880–89 | 11,372.00 |

Sources: Mitchell and Deane (1962) and E. J. Hobsbawm (1972).

different axes, and the absolute import figures translate into an amount per capita that was quite trivial and would have raised availability by about one kilogram annually for the wheat-consuming population by 1820.

The failure of the so-called agricultural revolution in the eighteenth century to raise output sufficiently was compounded by the import restrictions on grain. These produced a period of acute stress for the bulk of the population, which was obliged involuntarily to consume less. The rise in rent and profits in agriculture in this period came primarily out of a redistribution of incomes entailed in food price inflation, away from the net food-grain purchasers and toward the food-grain producers and sellers, and, in particular, toward the landlords who skimmed off a larger surplus, as well as toward all employers of wage-paid labor in agriculture, all of whom experienced a profit inflation.

It was only in the 1830s that imports start growing much faster, and they took off after the repeal of the Corn Laws in 1846. From below 2 million quarters at the time of repeal, imports multiplied over the next two decades and reached 12 million quarters by the 1880s.[15]

## Concluding Observations

In eighteenth-century England, there may well have been a revolution

## Figure 7.3: Annual Imports of Corn (Wheat), Average of Decades 1720–1880 (in thousand quarters)

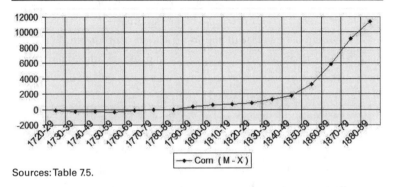

Sources: Table 7.5.

## Figure 7.4: Annual Per Capita Corn (Wheat) Output in Kg. and Corn Imports in 10,000 Quarters, 1700–1850

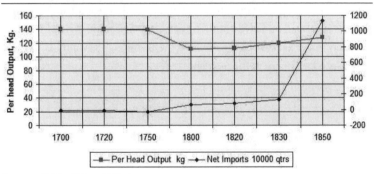

Sources: Tables 7.4 and 7.5.

in the social relations of production, associated with a process of primitive accumulation of capital, of which the Enclosure Movement was the quintessential expression, but the resulting capitalistically organized agriculture showed little success in meeting the challenge of industrialization. Capitalist farming did not raise the productivity of land and labor to the required extent. After 1750, despite all "improvements," yields actually declined, leading to a situation where there was hardly any increase in the net output of the main food-grain crop, wheat. Not surprisingly, there was a substantial decline in per capita output for the population dependent on wheat. Shortage of food constituted a serious bottleneck for the growth of the factory system, which could take place only at the expense of a severe reduction in the living standards of workers, leading to political unrest and a prolonged agitation for unrestricted food imports.

The subsequent increase in import dependence for foodstuffs and raw materials by Britain did not curb the second phase of industrial development after 1815, and further rise in dependence to a point where imports of primary products even exceeded domestic output did not constrain Britain's balance of payments. This was because of Britain's relationship with its tropical colonies of conquest. The trade that Britain carried on with these colonies was of a special nature. Much of it was the unrequited transfer of goods from these colonies, without any quid pro quo, a sheer "draining away" of part of the colonies' economic surplus, which not only financed Britain's current account deficits with the rest of the world but even paid for its capital exports to the temperate regions of European settlement. But appreciating the importance of this relationship requires that we disabuse ourselves of the idea of an "agricultural revolution" in England that prepared the ground for the Industrial Revolution. We discuss this relationship in the next chapter.

# CHAPTER 8

# Capitalism and Colonialism

Of all the different regimes that capitalism has built to overcome the problems it would face if it were indeed a closed and self-contained system, the ideal one from its point of view has been colonialism. Within the term "colonies," one must distinguish between the colonies of settlement, located in the temperate regions, and the colonies of conquest, located mainly in the tropical and semi-tropical regions. To be sure, the colonies of settlement also entailed conquest that drove the original inhabitants of these territories either to extinction or to "reservations." And conquest that allowed mass emigration from Europe to these lands played an enormous role in the economic and social stabilization of metropolitan capitalism (by keeping labor markets tighter than they would otherwise have been) as well as effecting a massive diffusion of capitalism. However, we use the term "colonialism" throughout this book to refer not to the colonies of settlement in the temperate regions but for colonial *possessions,* the tropical and semi-tropical regions acquired through conquest and made into appendages of the metropolitan economy.

Such colonial possessions fulfilled several functions: they provided markets for metropolitan goods (what economic historian S. B. Saul calls "markets on tap") and hence the exogenous stimulus needed for capital accumulation; they provided primary commodities for metropolitan capitalism; they provided these primary commodities gratis, as the counterpart of the economic surplus appropriated by the metropolitan economy; and since siphoning off the surplus kept local absorption of the exportables (or of goods producible on the same landmass as the exportables) restricted, it kept at bay the problem of increasing supply price and the threat it posed to the value of money in the metropolis.

## Two Instruments

The two main instruments used by the imperial powers in their colonies were capturing the colonial markets and appropriating a part of the surplus without any quid pro quo. Capturing colonial markets often required breaking down the natural economy, or the local exchange economy that prevailed earlier, through the forcible introduction of the cash nexus via, for instance, insisting upon cash payments of land revenues to the colonial state. Through these means, which supplanted the earlier exchange economy, to bring in a cash-mediated commodity economy, craft producers who met the local demand for manufactured goods were supplanted to open the way for imports of such goods from the capitalist metropolis.

Likewise, the appropriation of surplus took different forms, depending upon what had existed earlier. In many colonies where plantations were introduced and worked with slaves, it took the form of the surplus appropriated from slave labor (slave rent); in others, such as the already densely populated Asian countries where local empires had existed and surplus extraction had been imposed by earlier rulers, the metropolitan countries that became the new rulers simply took over the apparatus already in place, though giving it their own stamp. In India, the British took over the right to revenue collection that the Mughal emperors had exercised, though in doing so they substituted for the tax on *produce* that had existed earlier a tax on *land*, in the process introducing legally enforceable property rights in land and thereby creating a land market.

These two instruments were independent of each other but additive in their effects. They were independent in the sense that the extraction of surplus by the colonial rulers predated the quest for markets by the metropolis, which really began in the early nineteenth century and proceeded on its own trajectory. They were additive in a way that the following hypothetical example will clarify.

Suppose in a pre-colonial economy there are 100 peasants producing 200 units of agricultural goods (food in this case), of which they give 100 to the emperor. The emperor, whose own demand for food is negligible, uses this surplus to employ 100 artisans for producing manufactures for the imperial household, paying 1 unit of food as the wage per artisan (we abstract, for simplicity, from the raw material requirement of manufacturing). The artisans also produce manufactures for the peasants. Suppose the unit of manufacture is defined as that which one artisan produces. Then food and the manufactured good will be equal in value, since there are no "profits" in either peasant or artisan production and the peasants and the artisans would be expected to have equal per capita (post-tax) earnings (1 unit of food in value). If both peasants and artisans spend their earnings on food and manufactures in the ratio 1:1, then the economy will have 300 artisans, producing 300 manufactured goods, of which 100 will go to the emperor, 50 to the peasants, and 150 to the artisans themselves, which they will consume together with 150 of food made available to them by the peasants (50) and the emperor (100).

Now if the emperor's position is taken by a metropolitan country, then the entire 100 of revenue, instead of being spent locally, will be siphoned out of the country in the form of food, which would displace 100 artisans. In addition, if the peasants now begin to buy the 50 manufactured goods not from the local artisans but from the metropolitan economy, then all the 300 artisans (including those producing for the artisans themselves) will become unemployed. The metropolitan economy would have sold 50 manufactured goods in the colonial market and would have taken out 150 food of which 100 would be without any quid pro quo.

Three points are to be noted about this case. First, in the pre-colonial situation, the Gross *Material* Domestic Product of the economy would have been 500, consisting of 200 food and 300 manufactured goods. This falls to 200 after the colonialization of the economy. The term deindustrialization has been used to describe this situation, since it is the industrial sector that has shrunk by this amount, which, incidentally, shows the complete vacuity of the proposition that "free trade" is always beneficial for the economy. This proposition is based, inter alia, on the assumption that there is full employment of all factors in the post-trade situation, which obviously does not hold, since the displaced artisans have nowhere to go: they simply cannot move into food production as no virgin land exists in the economy to accommodate them. Such "deindustrialization," it should be noted, refers not simply to a decline in the proportion of the workforce employed in industry, but a decline in this proportion that is associated with an overall macroeconomic contraction of the economy. It must therefore be distinguished from the term "deindustrialization" used of late in the context of advanced countries like Britain.[1]

Second, the cause of deindustrialization associated with colonialism is not just the import of metropolitan manufactured goods. Such imports, matched by food exports of equal value, cause in the above example a reduction of only 100 in the local manufacturing sector's output and employment (50 directly and 50 through the "multiplier," that is, the reduced demand for manufactures by the displaced artisans themselves). The further reduction, over and above this, of 200, is caused by the economic surplus of 100 being siphoned off abroad (which displaces 100 artisans directly and another 100 through the multiplier effect). The siphoning off of the economic surplus by the metropolitan power, in other words, not only has the effect of taking away commodities gratis but also of causing the deindustrialization of the economy through an absolute shrinkage in the level of its macroeconomic activity.

Third, as this example clearly shows, taking away 150 units of food by the metropolitan economy *does not create an iota of excess demand pressure either in the colonial economy or anywhere.* Thus, even if food production is subject to "increasing supply price" or is rigidly limited by the absolute fixity of the size of the landmass, no inflationary pressures are generated despite the metropolitan economy taking away 150 units of food. This is because an income deflation has been imposed on the colonial economy through the twin processes of a siphoning away of its surplus, and a displacement of its artisans through competition from imported goods.

Our example is meant to show how the colonial relationship provided markets for metropolitan products, took away primary commodities (food or other commodities that could be grown on the land used for food production) for the requirements of the metropolitan economy, took away primary commodities to a substantial extent gratis, without any quid pro quo, and even while doing so kept completely in abeyance any effect of increasing supply price, that would normally be associated with meeting larger metropolitan requirements of such commodities, and that would normally pose a serious threat to the value of money in the metropolis.

Of the two instruments we have discussed, deindustrialization caused by imports from the metropolis is easier to comprehend, though mainstream economic theory steadfastly refuses to do so to this day, proclaiming instead the virtues of free trade. The siphoning off of the economic surplus, however, the "drain of surplus," is less appreciated and less comprehensible. Let us therefore examine it in greater detail.

## The Drain of Surplus

The reason why the drain of surplus is not easily comprehended is that the balance of payments must always balance. Hence, if any commodities are taken out of a country, then there must be a matching import into that country of some other commodities or services, or alternatively, of IOUs. How then can we talk of "unrequited exports" from the colony?

The simple answer to this question is that there were a whole range of items shown on the debit side of the current account that were either arbitrarily imposed, such as the metropolitan economy making the colony pay for its wars of conquest in some other part of the world, or arose from the colony's being governed by the metropolitan country. In the food example in the last section, when 100 units of food that had originally gone to the emperor were taken out of the colony, its new ruler, the metropolitan country, would offset it in the balance of payments by showing that the colony was importing administrative services from it for its own governance, in which case the colony's balance of payments would be balanced despite its economic surplus being siphoned off.

Conventional accounting obfuscates the drain for two distinct reasons. First, it is incapable of capturing the concept of an economic surplus. Even for the pre-colonial case in the example, conventional accounting would say that taking away 100 units is against the service of governing that the emperor is providing. By conventional national income estimation, the Gross Domestic Product of the country in the pre-colonial situation will be 600 units (including 100 of service rendered by the emperor). And the greater the taxation by the emperor, the greater will be the GDP.

Second, conventional accounting is incapable of grasping that the purpose of colonialism is to extract this surplus; hence, to offset the surplus against the services rendered in the process of extracting it constitutes supreme irony. It is like refusing to recognize the existence of an extortion racket on the grounds that the extortion money that is paid constitutes only the payment for the services of those who have come to collect the extortion money.

There is, as this second point suggests, a *fundamental difference between a country's experience after being colonized and all preceding experience.* Not only is the surplus not spent on domestic goods as was the case earlier, thus giving rise to economic retrogression in the colonial economy, in the sense of a shrinking of the level of macroeconomic activity, but the colonial regime's raison d'être lies in extracting the maximum amount of surplus. It does not simply take away some pre-set magnitude of surplus but *adjusts its demands to whatever is available for it to take.* As we discuss in subsequent chapters, on the basis of the Indian experience, it was not that some given amount was taken away by the colonial regime in the form of an export surplus (as our example suggested). Rather, the amount taken away adjusted to the export surplus that the country was earning, so that it got no credit whatsoever even when its exports surged relative to imports.

The "drain of surplus," in other words, did not just mean a replacement of the old set of surplus extractors by a new set, namely the old imperial regime by the new regime of metropolitan capitalism. It also meant the substitution of capitalist rapacity (rationality) for feudal traditionalism and conventionality. The colony did not witness a continuation of surplus appropriation as it had earlier. Rather, it became an appendage to another economy, the metropolitan economy, which was never the case earlier. It is not surprising that modern mass poverty, as we shall see later, arose for the first time in third world economies only after they were colonized.

## The Triangular Relationship

The role of colonial markets during the "long nineteenth century," which stretches until the outbreak of the First World War, was more complex than what the simple example above would suggest. Britain, as the leading capitalist country, allowed the other newly industrializing countries of the time to enter the British market freely and run current surpluses vis-à-vis itself. This was essential for the preservation of the gold standard, for otherwise countries thwarted in their ambition to industrialize would have withdrawn from it, undermining the arrangement that underlay the long Victorian and Edwardian boom. Because of its colonial possessions Britain could do this, however, and even make capital exports to countries such as the United States, with which it had current deficits.

Britain's colonies such as India had substantial export surpluses with Continental Europe and the United States, and Britain used these export surpluses to settle its own current account deficits with them. and even make capital exports offsetting these with its "drain of surplus" from these colonial countries and also with its sale of goods to these colonial markets.

There are two separate issues to be distinguished here: one is the question of Britain's balance of payments, and the other is the question of the demand for British goods. Let us take the second issue first. The newly industrializing countries, not surprisingly, were lower-cost producers and could outcompete Britain in most industries by the late nineteenth century. (Some economic historians refer to this phenomenon as the "penalty of the early start": Britain, having started early now had equipment that was older and gave lower labor productivity.) For Britain, which was losing its home market to these newly industrializing powers, it was necessary to find alternative markets to maintain its level of aggregate demand without resorting to protectionism—which would have started a spate of "beggar-thy-neighbor" policies and undermined the "long boom." It found these alternative markets in the colonial economies. Hobsbawm describes British exports in the late nineteenth century as being engaged in a "flight to the colonies." Indeed, India and China were absorbing more than half of total British textile exports by the end of the nineteenth century.[2]

The colonized economies (or semi-colonized in the case of China) could not protect themselves. On the contrary, when the colonial government in India, purely for revenue reasons, imposed an import duty on cotton cloth at the end of the century, it simultaneously imposed an equivalent excise duty on domestically produced cloth so as to ensure that the domestic producers did not get any "undue advantage." The colonial and semi-colonial markets were "markets on tap." Thus British goods unable to hold their own in other markets sought increasing refuge in colonial and semi-colonial markets.

Colonies not only absorbed British goods and settled the British balance of payments, but they also provided the commodity form in which Britain could make its capital exports. Since Britain's own goods were not much in demand in the newly-industrializing countries, whereas primary commodities from countries like India were, Britain could use goods obtained from the colonies, through the "drain" and also against British exports to their totally unprotected markets, to make its capital exports to the new industrializers. Or putting it differently, Britain appropriated the export surplus that countries like India were earning vis-à-vis the United States and Continental Europe for financing its capital exports to these regions. India, the biggest British colony, had a key role in this triangular arrangement, which we will examine in subsequent chapters.

The triangular arrangement we have been discussing relates to the heyday of industrial capitalism. But it was not the first triangular arrangement. In the late eighteenth and early nineteenth centuries, Britain was importing a variety of goods from China and had a trade deficit with that country. It had, however, conquered Bengal after the Battle of Plassey, and had started the drain of surplus from that province. It used this drain to finance its deficit with China. For that it was essential that China should be made to have a trade deficit with India. How was this to be ensured?

The solution was found in opium. India was encouraged to *produce* opium and China was encouraged to *consume* opium so that Britain's twin problems of the commodity form in which the surplus could be drained out of Bengal and settling the trade deficit with China could be satisfactorily resolved. When the Chinese emperor objected to this, the Opium Wars were started to open China to opium trade. The colonial relationship in short was not a simple binary relationship between the metropolis and the colony. It was mediated in complex ways, through triangular relationships. We return to these issues in a later chapter.

## Two Contrasting Trajectories

The fact that under capitalism some countries moved ahead in terms of per capita income and standard of living while others not only lagged behind but retrogressed can be explained by this dichotomy between the colonies of settlement and the colonies of conquest. Arthur Lewis mentions a figure of 50 million migrants in the massive emigration of population from Europe to the colonies of settlement in the temperate regions in the "long nineteenth century." This may be on the high side, but there is no doubting that the scale of migration was huge relative to the size of the European population. For Britain, it has been estimated that between the end of the Napoleonic Wars and the First World War, the emigration each year was approximately half the increase in the size of its population.[3]

Emigration on this scale kept the size of the reserve army of labor restricted, that is, it kept the labor market relatively tight, which permitted real wage increases alongside the increase in labor productivity. Since those who emigrated occupied land at the expense of the original inhabitants and set themselves up as farmers with reasonably high per capita incomes, this raised the "reservation wage" in Europe. It is this, rather than the so-called agricultural revolution, that explains why this migration was a "high-wage migration" (on this more later).

Together with the emigration of European labor, there was also a complementary migration of capital from Europe, above all from England, the largest capital exporter of the time. But such capital exports were largely extracted from the tropical colonies and took the commodity form of tropical goods.[4] The surplus extracted from the tropical and semi-tropical colonies was used for capital exports, which led to a diffusion of capitalism into the new settlements. This explains why the colonies retrogressed (via deindustrialization), and the new settlements industrialized (behind tariff walls and by investing beyond their own savings).[5]

This dichotomy between the two segments of the world would have disappeared if—even though capital did not come from the metropolis to the colonies of conquest, except in the spheres of mines, plantations and trade, that is, except to buttress the colonial pattern of international division of labor—labor had been free to move to the metropolis or to the temperate regions where labor from the metropolis was moving. In fact, the nineteenth century witnessed another major stream of labor migration, which was of Indian indentured labor and Chinese "coolie" labor (we are talking here of the post-slavery labor migration).

Here too according to Lewis,[6] about 50 million persons migrated in the "long nineteenth century," but they migrated to tropical or semi-tropical regions. The two streams of migration, one involving a movement from one temperate region (Europe) to other temperate regions (Canada, United States, Australia), and the other involving a movement from one tropical or sub-tropical region (India, China) to other tropical or sub-tropical regions (Fiji, the West Indies), were kept strictly separate. Tropical labor was not allowed to migrate freely to Europe or to the temperate regions where European labor was migrating. Interestingly, that is still the case, and the effort of labor to break the existing restrictions upon such migration has created a veritable crisis and tragedy, the refugee crisis in Europe, with many migrants dying in the process.

Of the two distinct streams of migration, one was a stream of high-wage migration, and the other a stream of low-wage migration. Lewis, while recognizing that a wage difference existed because the two streams were kept strictly separate, attributes it to the fact that there had been an agricultural revolution in England but not in India or elsewhere in the tropics. This, he argues, raised per capita incomes and hence the "reservation wage" in the former compared to the latter.

Quite apart from the fact that there had been hardly any perceptible increase in per capita food-grain or agricultural output in England that could have raised the "reservation wage," Lewis's comparison between the tropics and the temperate regions is fraught with a logical fallacy. If the output produced on an acre of land by an English farmer is to be compared with the output produced on an acre of land by an Indian farmer (to establish that the former's output was higher and hence the "reservation wage" was correspondingly higher), then the comparison must be *for a complete period of production time.* But the English farmer's land would remain fallow during the long winter months, while the Indian farmer would be growing several crops on his land all year-round. Thus, one has to compare not the wheat productivity, nor the productivity of a particular crop, on an identical plot of land by the Indian and the English farmer, but the per capita incomes of the two *over the year as a whole.*[7]

Lewis's argument that the reservation wage of the English emigrant worker was higher than that of the Indian emigrant worker because the productivity of wheat per acre of land of an English farmer was higher than that of the Indian farmer is therefore logically invalid. The Indian farmer did not get any lower income over the year as a whole from an identical plot of land than an English farmer. The annual income is the relevant comparison and on this comparison, the higher wages of the English emigrant workers cannot be explained in the manner that Lewis does.

The reason for the wage difference between the two streams of migration lies elsewhere. Temperate migration was high-wage migration because of the snatching away of land from the indigenous population in the regions to which migration occurred, not because of the high incomes in the regions from which migration occurred. On the other hand, tropical migration was low-wage migration because a vast, destitute reserve army of labor had been created within the tropical colonies on account of the deindustrialization perpetrated on these colonies, owing to the drain of surplus from them, and the displacement of artisans by imports from the metropolis.

Deindustrialization had additional second-order effects on the incomes of the agricultural population, which were already squeezed because of the shift from a tax on produce under the old pre-colonial system to a tax on land under colonialism, making this population come under the grip of money-lenders for paying taxes in bad crop years, money-lenders that gradually acquired land rights. Deindustrialization also raised the pressure of population on land, resulting in a rise in rents and a fall in real wages in the course of the nineteenth century.[8]

The divergent trajectories between the two parts of the world, one experiencing a diffusion of capitalism and higher wages alongside such diffusion, and the other experiencing deindustrialization, an absolute shrinkage of output, and pauperization of vast segments of the pre-capitalist working population, dates back to the nineteenth century, which saw a divergent impact of metropolitan capitalism upon these two parts.

## The Roots of Modern Mass Poverty

The roots of modern mass poverty in the third world go back to the impact of metropolitan capitalism on the tropical and semi-tropical colonies and dependencies. There is a common misconception that the third world has always been afflicted by poverty, because of its low labor productivity that has continued to this day because it has not benefited from the Industrial Revolution as the advanced capitalist world has done. According to this conception, all countries started from a more or less similar situation of economic backwardness, but some, belonging to the metropolis, forged ahead because of their industrial revolution; others belonging to the third world stayed where they were because they could not experience such an industrial revolution.

This conception is flawed in at least three important senses. The first, which has been much discussed following Paul Baran's pioneering work, *The Political Economy of Growth*,[9] is that though it is true that the West first developed capitalism and forged ahead with an Industrial Revolution, countries that did not develop capitalism could nonetheless have done so *in emulation of the West, and ushered in an industrial revolution of their own* as did Japan, the only major Asian country that escaped the tentacles of colonialism. What stood in the way of the backward economies developing their own "capitalism from above" through state initiatives, as in Japan, was colonialism itself, which imposed on them both a pattern of international division of labor in which they remained primary wage goods and raw material producers, and a massive drain of surplus from their economies.[10]

Second, the impact of colonialism was actually to reduce the per capita incomes in the colonized countries and dependencies. This immediately followed from deindustrialization, which marked all these countries, from India to China to Indonesia and others. Indeed, an interesting empirical estimate for India by Shireen Moosvi using the conventional definition of national income, where the colonial government's "services," as indeed of the pre-colonial Mughal emperor Akbar, are counted as part of national income, shows that the real per capita income between 1576 and 1910, underwent an *actual decline.*[11] Hence the picture of all countries starting from a more or less similar situation and some forging ahead while others stayed where they were is wrong: those who forged ahead gave the others a kick backwards.

Third, there is a fundamental difference between the poverty that existed earlier and modern poverty that is associated with capitalism. Modern poverty is not just material deprivation; it involves the insecurity that comes with commodification and the cash nexus. The dissolution of personal relations; the loss of rights, even customary rights, to assets now endowed with a marketable integrated ownership title, allowing its passage into the hands of moneyed interests; linkage to a distant and unknown world market that transmits the effects of events in faraway lands into remote third world villages, visiting destitution on local producers; and the creation of a reserve army of labor so that employment becomes uncertain on a daily basis—all these give a particular poignancy to poverty that did not exist earlier. This modern mass poverty is the legacy of the impact of metropolitan capitalism upon the third world.[12] And as we argue later in this book, this modern mass poverty will not go away as long as the capitalist mode of production remains dominant, even if this mode now spreads to the third world, and a whole range of activities get diffused from the metropolis to the third world along with this spread.

CHAPTER 9

# Colonialism before the First World War

The West European powers appropriated economic surplus from their colonies, and this materially and substantially aided their industrial transition from the eighteenth century onwards as well as the diffusion of capitalism to the regions of new European settlement. In the literature on economic growth, however, we find little awareness of *the existence of such transfers*, let alone their sheer scale, or the specific real and financial mechanisms through which these transfers were effected. Much research still remains to be done in this area. In the case of India, however, for well over a century there has been a rich discussion on transfers, termed the "drain of wealth," initiated by two outstanding writers, Dadabhai Naoroji and R. C. Dutt.[1] In this chapter we confine ourselves to discussing transfers only in the context of India.

With few exceptions the literature on the eighteenth- and nineteenth-century industrial transition in the core countries ignores the drain of wealth, or transfers, from the colonies.[2] The mainstream interpretation posits a purely internal dynamic for the rise of capitalist industrialization, and some authors even suggest that the colonies were a burden on the metropolis, which would have been better off without them.

## Conceptualizing the Drain of Wealth

In the case of India, the concept of "drain" is based on the fact that a substantial part, up to one-third of total rupee tax revenues, was not spent in a normal manner but was used to acquire goods, which were exported and earned gold and foreign exchange from the world. However, these earnings, representing international purchasing power, were never permitted to accrue to the country; they were instead appropriated by the ruling power. The study by Folke Hilgerdt on the pattern of global trade balances and a detailed empirical investigation of Britain's region-wide trade by S.B. Saul tell us that the gold and foreign exchange earned as export surplus by the tropical colonies, and preeminently by India (and treated by Britain as its own earnings), became so large from the last quarter of the nineteenth century that it underpinned the process of the rapid diffusion of capitalism.[3] This took place through Britain's large-scale capital exports, using its colonies' export surplus earnings, that hastened the industrialization of Europe and of regions of new European settlement. The other side of the process was declining per capita food availability and pauperization of the masses in the colonies.

This drain had a twofold dimension. First, there was an *internal dimension*, that is, extraction of economic surplus from producers through rent and taxes. In India, tax extraction in cash by the state was the most important method, with land revenue making up the bulk of taxes for much of the period. Independent producers paid land revenue directly to the state, while cultivating tenants were obliged to pay rent out of their economic surplus to the person designated as the landowner, who in turn paid the land revenue. The government's opium and salt monopolies, whose burden fell on the peasants and workers, were additional important sources of revenue. However, taxation per se did not produce a drain. This arose from its combination with the second, *external dimension,* stressed by Naoroji and Dutt, namely, the designation of a substantial part of the tax revenues as "expenditure abroad" in the budget, that is, the use of this part not in the normal manner within the country, but as reimbursement to the producers for their export surplus with the world, which was kept in London. This export surplus earned specie and sterling, which was entirely siphoned off for its own use by the colonizing power, via manipulated accounting mechanisms that we discuss later.

The use of the state budget in this manner to pay producers of export surplus out of their own tax contribution while the international proceeds of commodity export surplus never gets credited to the country is not found in any sovereign country; it is specific to the colonial system. All producers of export goods were apparently paid. A part of colonial exports was paid for through imports of British manufactures, mainly textiles, but this import arose from keeping the colonial economy trade-liberalized. Goods were absorbed at the expense of displacing local artisan spinners and weavers, whereas the metropolis practiced protection against colonial manufactures for well over a century. After deducting these virtually compulsory imports, the resulting net export surplus earnings were not paid to the producers in a normal manner, because they were paid out of the tax revenue raised within the country, and the overwhelming bulk of such taxes were extracted from the very same producers as rent/land revenue, and indirect taxes, especially from the salt monopoly. This meant that the producers were taxed out of their goods even while appearing to be paid.

To illustrate this proposition, suppose that a peasant-cum-artisan producer in India, in the period of East India Company rule, paid Rs.100 as tax to the state and sold 10 yards of cloth and 2 bags of rice worth in total Rs. 50 to a local trader. This sale would be a normal market transaction and not connected in any way to his tax payment, since the trader would advance his own funds for the purchase, expecting to sell the cloth and rice, and recoup his outlay with a profit. Now, suppose an agent of the Company, not a local trader, bought an additional 10 yards of cloth and 2 bags of rice for export from the peasant-cum-artisan producer by paying him Rs. 50 of the same producer's own money, out of the Rs. 100 total tax taken from him. This means the producer was not paid at all. The producer might have raised questions if the agent of the Company who collected his tax also bought his goods out of that money. But the two agents were different, and the two acts—collecting tax and buying produce—took place at different times by different agents, so the producer did not connect them. Purchase by the Company's agent would appear to the producer as a normal market exchange no different from purchase by the internal trader, but it was qualitatively quite different, since a part of his own tax payment came back to him—a fact he did not know—while his cloth and rice were taken away. In this transaction, the *form* of half of the total tax of Rs. 100 he had paid changed from Rs. 50 cash to 10 yards cloth and 2 bags rice. In effect, he handed over these goods for export completely free to the Company, as the commodity equivalent of Rs. 50 tax, worth, say, £5.0 (at the then current exchange rate of Rs. 10 to £1). The cloth and rice were then exported to England, and sold, say, for £7 after adding freight, insurance, and trader's margin. (Only the rice would be sold and the cloth re-exported because there was an official ban from 1700 on the consumption of Asian textiles in England, on which more later.)

Since the peasants and artisans were the main contributors to the total tax revenue, this meant they were not actually paid; all that happened was that the relevant part of their tax merely changed its form from cash to goods for export. This direct linking of the fiscal system with the trade system is the essence of drain in colonies where the producers were not slaves but nominally free petty producers, namely tax-paying peasants and artisans.

The transfer process at its inception was relatively transparent. The East India Company's trade monopoly granted by the British Parliament began in 1600. The Company had to pay for its import surplus from Asia with silver, arousing the ire of the early mercantilists. The Company acquired tax revenue-collecting rights in Bengal province in 1765, and the substantive drain starts precisely from that date. Some form of drain was already taking place through underpayment for goods using coercion on petty producers, but this was nothing compared to the bonanza after 1765, when the free acquisition of export goods using local taxes started. Bengal's population of about 30 million was nearly four times that of Britain, and the rapacity of the Company, which forcibly trebled revenue collection over the following five years, decimated one-third of that population in the great 1770 famine. Full recovery had not taken place by 1792, and yet the land revenue fixed under the permanent settlement in that year in Bengal exceeded the British government's taxes from land in Britain. In the next eighty years, revenue collections trebled as the Company, using Bengal as its economic base, acquired political control over several other Indian provinces—the Bombay Deccan, Madras, Punjab, and Awadh. Three wars were fought by the Burmese; fertile Lower Burma was occupied by 1856 and the entire country by 1885. Land revenue collection systems were promptly put in place; the very term for the British district administrator was "Collector." Britain saw a steadily increasing and completely costless inflow of tax-financed commodities—textiles (up to the 1840s), rice, salt-peter, indigo, raw cotton, jute—which far exceeded its own requirements; this excess was re-exported to other countries.

The transfer or drain consisted in the fact that Britain's trade deficit with India *did not create any external payment liability for Britain*, as its trade with a sovereign country like France did. Britain's perpetual trade deficit with France had to be settled in the normal way through outflow of specie, borrowing, or a combination of the two. This was true of its deficits with all other sovereign regions and also true of its trade with India up to 1765. After that date, when local tax collection began, the situation changed. On Britain's external account, the cloth and rice import from India now created zero payment liability, since Indian producers had been "paid" already out of their own taxes, that is, effectively not paid at all. This system of getting goods free as the commodity equivalent of the economic surplus extracted as taxes was the essence of the drain, or transfer. It not merely benefited the Company as trader by raising its profit rate to dizzying heights, given that its outlay on purchasing the goods became zero, it also benefited Britain as a country. The growing import surplus of tropical goods created no payment liability, and re-exports of these free goods also bought England goods from other sovereign countries like France, reducing its trade deficit with them.

In England, it was clearly recognized that the apparently negative feature of a trade deficit vis-à-vis India was a net *addition* to England's resources, since locally raised revenues served to acquire goods for import. In England's *Export and Import Report* for the year 1790 it was stated:

> The great excess of the Imports over the Exports in the East India trade, appears as a Balance against us, but *this excess consisting of the produce of the Company's territorial revenues* and of the remittance of fortunes acquired by individuals, instead of being unfavourable is an acquisition of so much *additional wealth* to our public stock.[4]

Had the colony been a sovereign country, its foreign exchange earnings would have accrued entirely to itself, boosting its international purchasing capacity while the local producers of export surplus would have been issued the local currency equivalent of their earnings, not connected in any way to taxes they might or might not pay. The taxes they did pay would have been spent entirely under normal budgetary heads.

The colonizing power always needed to establish property rights in some form over the local population, because this was the necessary condition for surplus extraction and transfer. In India, this was the sovereign right of tax collection, but in the West Indies, plantation slavery meant that the extraction of surplus by British owners took the form mainly of slave-rent, namely the excess of output net of material costs over the bare subsistence of the enslaved workers. In Ireland, English settler landlords took over the land of the local peasantry, and economic surplus was extracted as land rent as well as taxes. ("Land rent" is used here in the sense specified by Adam Smith and Karl Marx, as absolute ground rent, not in the sense in which the term is used by Ricardo.)[5] In all cases, goods were obtained free as the commodity equivalent of the economic surplus appropriated, no matter what the specific form in which this surplus was extracted, whether as slave-rent, land rent, taxes, or a combination of all these.

Tax-financed transfer by the Company was direct and transparent. One-quarter to one-third of the annual net tax revenues was used for purchasing export goods, cotton textiles making up the major part until the 1840s. Thereby the metropolis obtained a vast flow of goods, far in excess of its needs; it retained a part of these within the country and re-exported the remainder to other countries, against the goods it needed from them. Cotton textile imports were entirely re-exported because in 1700, at the insistence of the jealous British woollen industry, Parliament in England had passed a law banning the consumption of imported pure cotton goods from India and Persia, and had enforced the ban in 1721 with heavy fines on those found to violate it. All textiles imported by the Company from India were warehoused in English ports and re-exported, mainly to Europe and the Caribbean. To perfect the spinning jenny and the water frame took seven decades; once cotton yarn could be mechanically spun in England, from 1774, the ban on the consumption of pure cotton goods was lifted but the restriction on the entry of Asian textiles into the British market continued in the form of tariffs, which were raised steeply between 1775 and 1813, with the last tariffs ending only in 1846.[6]

Britain's stringent protectionist policy against Asian textiles, maintained for nearly 150 years, has been ignored completely both in the *Cambridge Economic History of India*[7] (1984) and in the widely read work of historians of Britain's Industrial Revolution and technical change in cotton textiles, and recent authors continue to write in the same blandly amnesic tradition.[8] We have to read earlier works by List, Dutt, Mantoux, and Baran for the true picture regarding Britain's mercantilist policies of discrimination against manufactures from tropical regions, which started even before they became colonies.[9] Economic historian Paul Mantoux's detailed account of machinery in cotton textiles, the driver of the Industrial Revolution in England, makes it clear that the ban on Asian textiles spurred innovation and import substitution to meet pent-up demand. Friedrich List's comments on discrimination against Indian textiles suggest the same. In Mantoux's words regarding the ban on consumption of pure cottons, "The import of pure cottons from whatever source remained forbidden. No protection could be more complete, for it gave the manufacturers a real monopoly of the domestic market."[10]

Under the Navigation Acts dating from the 1650s, every important colonial good, whatever its final destination, had to first come to Britain's ports and then be re-exported. The goods had to be carried only in British ships manned by British officers. There is a misconception that the most important import from colonies was raw materials, but foodstuffs were the most important import all through the eighteenth century and remained so to the mid-nineteenth century when raw cotton imports were growing rapidly.[11]

Phyllis Deane in 1965 in *The First Industrial Revolution* discussed at length how important re-exports were in the eighteenth century, allowing Britain to purchase strategic naval materials from Europe (bar-iron, pitch and tar, timber).[12] This discussion was cut out in her jointly authored book with W. A. Cole in 1969, and re-exports were eliminated from both the import and the export figures, when the authors presented what they called "the volume of British trade."[13] They calculated this by taking *retained imports plus domestic exports*, a concept called "special trade" that is not to be found in any macroeconomics textbook, nor is it ever applied by the international organizations presenting trade data (United Nations, World

Bank, IMF), which always take as the volume of trade the sum of *total imports and total exports* inclusive of re-exports if they are present. This is the correct concept, for re-exports financed imports, whether of final consumer goods or of raw materials, just as a country's domestic exports did.

Calculating from the Deane and Cole data series using the accepted trade concept, namely total imports plus total exports, we find that Britain's total trade-to-GDP ratio had reached 58 percent by the three years centered on 1800 compared to only 36 percent estimated by Deane and Cole using their special trade concept.[14] The confusion was compounded by Simon Kuznets,[15] who reproduced an earlier version of the Deane-Cole figures without mentioning they were not comparable with the trade figures of the other countries he presented.[16] A critique of these trade estimates that have misled many development economists is available in a study by Utsa Patnaik.[17]

### Asymmetry of Production Capacities between the North and the South

A country located in the cold temperate region of Europe that controlled a tropical region sat, in effect, over an inexhaustible gold mine. It was more lucrative than gold, for gold seams might eventually run out, but the surplus-producing and taxable capacity of the peasants and artisans would not, as long as they were not entirely decimated through overexploitation. They could be set to produce more tropical (and sub-tropical) crops like cane sugar, rice, tapioca, and spices, stimulants like coffee, tea, cacao, and tobacco, vegetable oils like groundnut, linseed, and palm oil, drugs like opium, raw materials like indigo, jute, sisal, and cotton, and cut more tropical hardwoods (teak, mahogany, rosewood, ebony) from the forest or from timber plantations, all goods that could never be produced in cold temperate lands.

Northern populations in cold temperate Europe could not then, or for that matter in present times, ever "import-substitute" in these goods, and for that very reason they prized them, developing an increasing appetite for them. Conversely, there was no particular good from temperate lands that the tropical countries wished to import in any substantial way, since they could produce all their traditional requirements. They produced at least two crops a year, while single cropping was imposed by climate in cold temperate lands; the larger countries in the South could produce in winter all of the temperate land crops, in addition to tropical crops in their monsoon season. The Chinese emperor Qianlong, responding to George III, who had sent an envoy to negotiate trade concessions, famously wrote "our Celestial Empire possesses all things in prolific abundance and lacks no product within its own borders."[18]

This important material reality of *asymmetric production capacities*, which explains the historic drive by European countries to subjugate tropical areas and force them to trade at gunpoint, was not only ignored by David Ricardo, but was explicitly assumed away by him.

Ricardo assumed in his model of comparative advantage that "both countries produce both goods"—indeed his assumption was that "all countries produce all goods"—while showing that specialization and exchange according to comparative cost advantage led to mutual benefit. The material fact was ignored that unit cost of production *could not be defined* for tropical goods in the cold temperate European countries where the output of such goods was, and always will be, zero and hence absolute cost was not definable, let alone comparative cost advantage. The supply from domestic sources of a large range of goods was zero at any price, and this continues to be the case at present. Ricardo's theory contained a simple material fallacy, the "converse fallacy of accident," wherein a special case is assumed (both countries produce both goods) and is used to draw an inference (trade is mutually beneficial) that is then improperly applied to cases where the assumption is not true.[19] Since Ricardo's basic assumption was not true, the inference of mutual benefit did not follow. On the contrary, historical evidence shows that the less powerful country, obliged to specialize in export crops, loses out through area diversion (since augmenting cropped area needs state investment, which is not forthcoming), leading to falling domestic food grains output. It also sees a decline of domestic manufacturing output and an increase in unemployment when it is kept compulsorily open to imports of manufactures, since there is little unused land to absorb those thrown out of work.[20]

Compared to the demand for Britain's own goods, tropical goods were demanded by Northern populations, to a greater extent given the permanent non-availability of these goods from domestic sources; and the demand was more income-elastic. Re-exports of a substantial part of its total imports boosted the purchasing power of Britain's domestic exports by 55 percent during the period 1765 to 1821.[21] Four-fifths of goods re-exported by Britain were from tropical regions, and the re-exports went mainly to Continental Europe. The Netherlands' re-exports of imported goods exceeded exports of its domestically produced goods in the eighteenth century .[22] Thus there was a double benefit from the "drain": not only did the metropolis get prized tropical goods free for its own use but also got them free to exchange for temperate land products in which it was deficient.

Asia, West Indies, and Ireland, taken together, accounted for half of all British imports during the period 1784 to 1826. The total transfer, measured by the import surplus into Britain from its tropical colonies in Asia and West Indies (which embodied taxes and slave rent, and hence created no external liability), ranged from 5.3 to 6.1 percent of Britain's GDP from 1801 to 1821.[23] The data in Davis[24] similarly show that the combined deficit of Britain with these colonies ranged from 4 to 6 percent of its GDP during most triennia between 1784–86 and 1824–26.[25]

We can arrive at a rough estimate of the drain from India for the period 1765 to 1836 by using trade data for Britain. The time-series from 1765 to 1822 in Mitchell and Deane and price indices in Imlah,[26] had been used earlier to estimate the import surplus into Britain from Asia as the measure of drain. Using the data from Davis, we bring the estimate up to 1836, after deducting the value of the China trade.[27]

The current value import surplus for 1765 to 1836 is found to total £270.254 million.[28] We can calculate the present value of the drain by bringing forward the estimate of each year's drain at a certain interest rate up to any recent date and then adding up the individual figures. However, we adopt a short-cut procedure that is slightly different. We bring the total drain amount up to the present at 5 percent interest rate *from the midpoint of the period.* And we do so up to a) the time of Independence in 1947 and b) the present year of 2020. *Compounding at a low 5 percent interest rate from the midpoint of the period, which is 1800, and including that year, we find the sum amounts to a) £369.65 billion until Independence; and to b)*

*£12,400 billion until 2020.* We will come back to these figures in the last section. Taking the midpoint of the total drain period as the initial year *understates* the estimate we would get from a proper compounding of each year's figure to the terminal year.[29]

An acute observer, Montgomery Martin, in his 1838 book and while giving evidence to a Select Committee in 1840, deplored the drain on India. Taking the £3 million annual Home Charges as its measure, he applied the prevalent 12 percent interest rate and calculated its total value as £724 million for the three-decade period up to 1833.[30] He pointed out that taking the annual drain, which was slightly in excess of £2 million over the previous fifty years, and applying the same interest rate, gave "the enormous sum" of £8,400 million. "So constant and accumulating a drain even on England would soon impoverish her; how severe then must be its effects on India, where the wages of a labourer is from two pence to three pence a day?"[31]

### *Appropriating the Colonies' Global Exchange Earnings*

In 1833, the East India Company's monopoly of Indian and Chinese trade finally ended, owing to demands from English manufacturers, who, after displacing Indian textiles from European markets, wanted free access to the Indian market. However, the Company continued to rule until the Great Rebellion of 1857–59. India's exports to Britain declined, deindustrializing imports of yarn and cloth from Britain grew fast, and by the late 1840s, India's trade with that country registered a deficit. But Indian exports to the world continued to rise and far exceeded the new deficit with Britain, so that an overall rising merchandise export surplus was always maintained (see Table 9.1[32] and Figure 9.1). This remained a large positive figure even after deducting the import of commodity gold.

The ensuing problem of what Irfan Habib calls "the realization of the tribute" was solved for the time being by promoting India's exports to countries with which Britain ran trade deficits.[33] The drive to expand opium exports to China where the trade was illegal, and to forcibly open up its ports in the Opium Wars, was part of the process of promoting triangular trade patterns. In India, local peasants were coerced under state monopoly into growing opium for a very low price, and the silver *tael*

**TABLE 9.1: India's Merchandise Export Surplus with the World, 1833–1940 in Current Prices in Rs. Crore (1 Crore = 10 million)**

| PERIOD | X - M | PERIOD | X - M |
|---|---|---|---|
| 1833–35 | 3.35 | 1887–89 | 29.14 |
| 1836–38 | 6.82 | 1890–92 | 35.77 |
| 1839–41 | 5.37 | 1893–95 | 35.42 |
| 1842–44 | 6.74 | 1896–98 | 30.85 |
| 1845–47 | 6.37 | 1899–01 | 32.24 |
| 1848–50 | 7.12 | 1902–04 | 52.60 |
| 1851–53 | 8.73 | 1905–07 | 50.00 |
| 1854–56 | 8.81 | 1908–10 | 55.34 |
| 1857–59 | 8.00 | 1911–13 | 73.74 |
| 1860–62 | 16.23 | 1914–16 | 61.90 |
| 1863–65 | 38.08 | 1917–19 | 87.21 |
| 1866–68 | 15.41 | 1920–22 | −14.62 |
| 1869–71 | 23.84 | 1923–25 | 141.23 |
| 1872–74 | 21.56 | 1926–28 | 71.58 |
| 1875–77 | 22.18 | 1929–31 | 51.09 |
| 1878–80 | 23.55 | 1932–34 | 18.57 |
| 1881–83 | 32.38 | 1935–37 | 39.77 |
| 1884–86 | 27.49 | 1938–40 | 35.62 |

Source: K. N. Chaudhuri, "Foreign Trade and Balance of Payments 1757–1947," in D. Kumar, ed. (with the editorial assistance of Meghnad Desai), *The Cambridge Economic History of India, Volume II c.1757–c.1970* (Delhi: Orient Longman, in association with Cambridge University Press, 1984).

proceeds of the Company's opium exports to China (via private shippers) were used to offset Britain's deficits with China.

Gross revenue collections had trebled by the 1820s compared to the 1800s, as the Bombay Deccan and Madras were brought under land revenue settlements and the salt and opium monopolies yielded more revenues. The drain increased, but it was now carried out in a more roundabout manner than the earlier direct merchandise export surplus with Britain, since that direct surplus had turned into a deficit.

A more general solution had to be found to this problem of "realizing" the tribute. The solution came into effect in 1861 after India's governance had passed to the Crown. It was simple and effective: the Secretary of State

**Figure 9.1:India's Merchandise Export Surplus, 1833–1919**

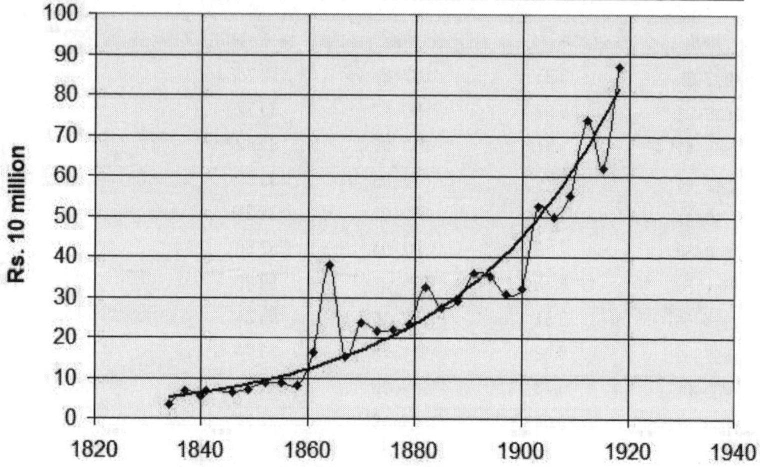

Source: Table 9.1.

for India in Council (a minister of the British government based in London) invited foreign importers of Indian goods to deposit with him gold, sterling, and their own currencies, as payment for their imports from India, against the issue of an official bill of exchange to an equivalent rupee value cashable in India. The exchange rate (rupee relative to sterling, the latter being fixed with respect to gold) at which these Council bills were sold was periodically adjusted carefully to a fraction of a farthing, so that foreign importers would never find it cheaper to send gold as payment directly to Indian exporters, incurring the relevant transport cost, even when that gold might come from Egypt or Australia, compared to using the London Council bill route. The exchange rate was thus administered to vary between "gold points" adjusted to prevent the import of financial gold into India (and also to prevent its export, except when required by the metropolis). Foreign importers of Indian goods tended to prefer Council bills to any other private mode of remittance because they could be certain that the bills would always be honored, since they were issued by a minister of the British government, which meant a sovereign guarantee against default.

The Council bills could be cashed only in rupees and the exporters in

India who received the bills (by post or by telegraph) from foreign importers, on submitting them through the exchange banks, were paid by the
Indian Treasury out of budgetary funds already set aside for the purpose
as expenditure incurred abroad.[34] Exporters in turn paid the producers
from whom they sourced the goods. Thus the essential feature of earlier
drain was retained—producers were apparently paid but not actually paid
for their export surplus because the payment came out of taxes raised in
major part from the very same producers. The export surplus continued
to be merely the commodity form of tax revenues.

However, the scope of this official mechanism was wider than that
under the Company, in that the total export surplus earnings of British
India from the entire world was appropriated. Internal redistribution of
incomes also took place from the producing classes to the trading classes
under this mechanism of transfer, since the export agents took a fairly large
cut out of the producer's price, so that a given value of drain to Britain
entailed an even larger squeeze on producers' incomes.

The total (£428.58 million) of commodity export surplus earnings
over the period 1871 to 1901 was identical with the total expenditure in
England charged to Indian revenues (£428.93), as Table 9.2 shows. It is
important to note that this surplus, defrayed through Council bills, is the
balance of merchandise trade plus the balance of commodity gold flows.
Additional financial gold flows also occurred that belong in the capital
account. Figure 9.2, depicting these two series, makes clear that India's
export surplus earnings fluctuated greatly depending on internal factors
and on world market conditions, but the sterling expenditure by England
using these earnings rose much more steadily. This was because, to deal
with fluctuations of trade, a form of buffer-stock operation with regard to
currency was carried out, of sterling in England and of rupees in India. If
India's net external earnings rose sharply in a particular year, in excess of
spending required by England, then the sterling balances maintained by
the Secretary of State were added to, being drawn down in other years
when the opposite situation prevailed. In such a case of sharp rise in external earnings, at the Indian end there would be an unusually large value of
Council bills tendered and thus excess demand for rupees, so in addition
to the bulk of the planned payment of the bills out of the budget, the paper

**TABLE 9.2: India's Commodity Export Surplus (Value of Council Bills) and Expenditure in England, 1871–1901 (£ million)**

| Period | Council Bills | Expenditure (in England) | Period | Council Bills | Expenditure (in England) |
|---|---|---|---|---|---|
| 1871–72 | 10.310 | 9.851 | 1887–88 | 15.357 | 15.299 |
| 1872–73 | 13.939 | 10.548 | 1888–89 | 14.263 | 14.911 |
| 1873–74 | 13.286 | 10.266 | 1889–90 | 15.475 | 14.790 |
| 1874–75 | 10.842 | 10.605 | 1890–91 | 15.969 | 15.492 |
| 1875–76 | 12.390 | 9.899 | 1891–92 | 16.094 | 15.943 |
| 1876–77 | 12.696 | 13.468 | 1892–93 | 16.532 | 16.242 |
| 1877–78 | 10.134 | 14.008 | 1893–94 | 9.530 | 15.776 |
| 1878–79 | 13.949 | 13.820 | 1894–95 | 16.905 | 15.707 |
| 1879–80 | 15.262 | 14.572 | 1895–96 | 17.664 | 15.560 |
| 1880–81 | 15.240 | 14.451 | 1896–97 | 15.527 | 15.740 |
| 1881–82 | 18.412 | 14.376 | 1897–98 | 8.837 | 16.142 |
| 1882–83 | 15.121 | 14.086 | 1898–99 | 18.692 | 16.325 |
| 1883–84 | 17.600 | 15.003 | 1899–00 | 19.067 | 16.393 |
| 1884–85 | 13.759 | 14.104 | 1900–01 | 13.300 | 17.201 |
| 1885–86 | 10.293 | 13.973 | | | |
| 1886–87 | 12.136 | 14.376 | **TOTAL** | **428.581** | **428.927** |

Sources: *Statistical Abstracts for British India,* various years (Department of Commercial Intelligence and Statistics, India); and R. C. Dutt, *Economic History of India, Vol. II.*

currency reserve (and more rarely the gold standard reserve) at the margin would be drawn down, being replenished in other years of a decline of India's external earnings and hence slackening of demand for rupees.

The new arrangement that operated from 1861 thus retained the basic feature of the earlier direct system under the Company: *the merchandise export surplus continued to be "paid" to its colonized producers out of their own taxes, and hence was not paid for at all.* It continued to be obtained gratis by the metropolis, with the global earnings from it, the gold and foreign exchange, being retained by the metropolis.

A small amount of financial gold as payment by foreigners for India's exports may have evaded this system of economic control and reached India, perhaps through the ports in the princely states. But this is likely to

## Figure 9.2: India's Commodity Export Surplus (Value of Council Bills) and Expenditure in England, 1871–1901

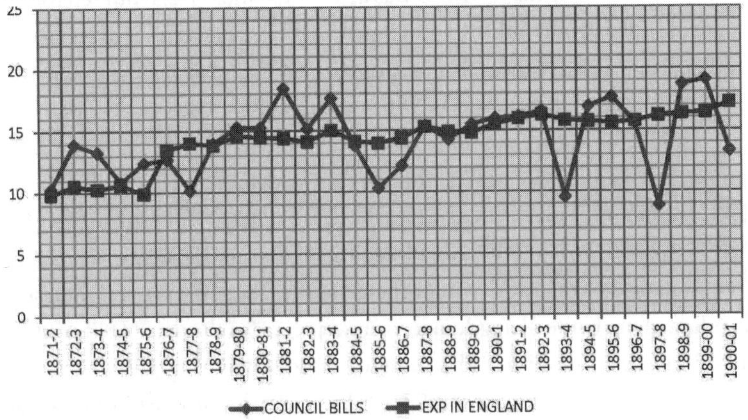

Source: Data series in Table 9.2

have been negligible and is impossible to estimate. The overwhelming bulk of the rest of the world's payments for India's commodity export surplus was successfully intercepted and appropriated by the metropolis and never permitted to reach the colonized producers who had earned it, either as physical gold for financial payment purposes (as opposed to commodity gold, imported like any other good), or as foreign exchange denoted as a net credit for India. Not even the colonial government was credited with any part of India's external earnings against which it could issue rupees, as would happen in a sovereign country. On the contrary, the Secretary of State in London had an official claim on the part of the Indian budget designated as Expenditure in England or sometimes as Expenditure Abroad. Issue of the rupee value of the entire external earnings out of this part of the budget, was not only income-deflating but also made for monetary stringency, lack of liquidity, and hence perpetually high interest rates.

In accounting terms, India's large and rising commodity export surplus was shown as completely offset by the state-administered invisible debits (the tribute) which included all the rupee drain items of the budget, now expressed in sterling on the external account. But the administered, manipulated debits were not necessarily confined to the recurring drain items alone.

For the period 1837–38 to 1900-01, we estimate the drain as £ 596.757 million, by taking the series of "expenditure abroad" in the Indian budget that was paid out; from 1861 this was against Council bills tendered to the value of India's commodity export surplus. This data series is available in both sterling and in rupees from the *Statistical Abstracts for British India*. The midpoint of this period is 1868; cumulating as before at 5 percent interest rate for the seventy-nine years to 1947, and the 152 years to 2020, we obtain the total value of the drain by these dates as £28.17 billion and £992.14 billon, respectively. Adding these estimates to our estimate for the earlier period 1765 to 1836, we obtain the figures in Table 9.3.

For an idea of the relative importance of the drain, the Gross Domestic Product of the United Kingdom in current prices for the dates 1836, 1900, and 1947 are also given. The value of the drain during 1765 to 1900, cumulated to 1947, gives us £397.8 billion, nearly thirty-eight times the 1947 GDP of the UK. Since nominal values are used here, with no adjustment for price change, the value of the drain up to 1900 would be a much higher multiple of the UK's 1947 GDP when this is expressed in constant 1900 prices. Cumulated up to 2020, the drain amounts to £13.39 *trillion,* over four times the UK's estimated GDP for that year.

Over most of the period, the exchange rate of the U.S. dollar against sterling was, at best, £1= $4.84. Thus, the drain for 1765 to 1900 cumulated to 1947 in dollar terms is $1.925 trillion, and cumulated up to 2020, $ 64.82 trillion. The former figure is greater than the combined 1947 GDP of the United Kingdom, the United States, and Canada. The latter figure is similarly much higher than the combined 2020 GDP of these countries.

## *Imposition of Sterling Indebtedness*

Our estimates are minimal estimates, and they are by no means a full measure of the actual sums coming from India for Britain's benefit. Over a run of years, the total of invisible demands was always pitched higher than India's ability to meet the total through foreign exchange earnings, no matter how fast the latter might grow, so indebtedness to Britain was enforced. India's huge external earnings not only magically disappeared into the yawning maw of the Secretary of State's account in London, but

**TABLE 9.3: Estimated Value of Drain from India, 1765–1900**

| Period | Absolute Value of Drain (£ million) | CUMULATIVE VALUE AT 5 PERCENT INTEREST | |
| --- | --- | --- | --- |
| | | Up to 1947 (£ Billion) | Up to 2020 (£ Billion) |
| 1765–1836 | 270.2537 | 369.6476 | 12399.9 |
| 1837–1900 | 596.757 | 28.1677 | 992.135 |
| **1765–1900** | **867.011** | **397.8153** | **13392.035** |

| GDP OF UK IN £ MILLION | |
| --- | --- |
| 1836 | 592 |
| 1900 | 1,963 |
| 1947 | 10,544 |

the country was shown to be in perpetual deficit. Had its own gold and foreign exchange earnings from export surplus actually been credited to it, even partially if not wholly, then given the large size of these earnings, India could have imported technology to build up a modern industrial structure much earlier than Japan did after its 1868 Meiji revolution, or exported capital itself and not been obliged to borrow. The Indian railways could have been built several times over from India's own exceptionally high external earnings during the raw cotton boom of the 1860s and 1870s (see Table 9.1 and Figure 9.1). Between 1860 and 1876, commodity export surplus earnings totaled £135 million, whereas railway and irrigation investment was only £26 million. But since all of India's gold and forex earnings was appropriated by Britain using the method discussed earlier, borrowing from the London money market was thrust on India for building railways, at an interest rate guaranteed to foreign private lenders by the colonial government, regardless of the actual profitability of the railways.

While India's entire external earnings went directly into the Secretary of State's account in London, they were offset in accounting terms by administering a large number of arbitrary invisible liabilities denominated in sterling. These included all the annual drain items charged to the Indian

budget under Expenditure in England and were expressed both in sterling and in rupees. These were also known as the Home Charges and had
military expenses and interest on debt as the main components. There is a
misconception that Home Charges were on account of the foreign administrators' recompense in sterling for pensions, leave allowances, and the
like. But all these administrative charges added together, based on budgetary data from 1861 to 1934, amounted on average to only 12.7 percent of
the Home Charges.

Interest payments in sterling constituted the largest item, over half of
Home Charges, not because there was much investment inflow (the entire
subcontinent had received hardly one-tenth of total British foreign investment by 1913) but because practically every large extraneous expense
was partly or wholly charged to the Indian revenues and their excess over
India's export surplus earnings was recorded as increase in India's sterling debt. These extra expenses comprised the costs arising from Britain's
many imperial wars of conquest outside Indian borders; the sterling cost
of suppressing the Great Rebellion of 1857 in India; indemnifying the
East India Company as governance passed to the Crown and guaranteeing a return from the Indian budget to its shareholders; the cost of telegraph lines—the Red Sea line and the Mauritius to Cape Town line; the
cost of maintaining British legations in a number of countries; the cost of
importing monetary gold in the 1890s for the reserve requirements of the
gold exchange standard, most of this gold being later absorbed by Britain
against issue of securities; and many such items.

These costs, always in excess of India's fast-rising foreign earnings,
were shown as a cumulating debt that India owed. There was a quantum jump by nine times in sterling debt between 1856 and 1861 alone,
from £4 million to £35 million against the cost of suppressing the Great
Rebellion. Sterling debt rose again in the 1870s, doubling to £70 million,
and exceeded rupee debt in the mid-1880s, again registering a quantum
jump from 1891 as monetary gold was imported by the government for
reserve requirements. By 1901, total sterling debt stood at £135 million,
over one-fifth of British India's GDP and eight times its annual export surplus earnings.

From the turn of the century, four-fifths of the monetary gold,

## Figure 9.3: India's Sterling Debt, 1837–38 to 1901–02

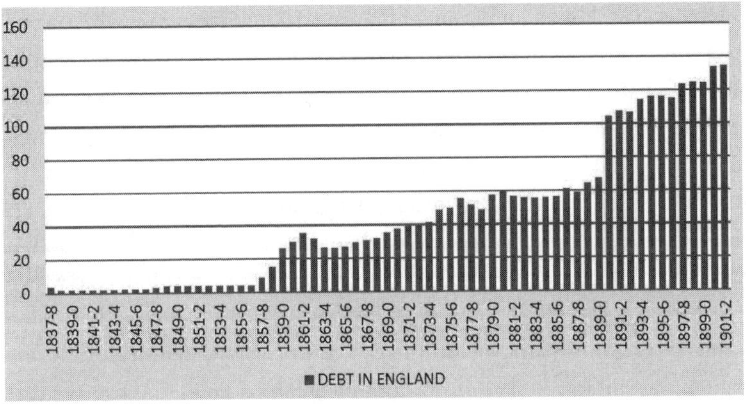

Source: *Statistical Abstracts for British India,* various years (Department of Commercial Intelligence and Statistics, India).

imported at great Indian expense for backing its currency, was physically shifted to London against issue of British government securities by suitably amending the provisions on reserve requirements. Inflow of this "Indian gold" over several years, eagerly awaited by private investment firms in London, was the basis for extending loans to these firms at a low interest rate, namely pumping cheap liquidity into the London money market.[35] India, meanwhile, continued to pay interest on the debt incurred for importing the gold. Figure 9.3 traces the movement of sterling debt from 1837 to 1902.

Because the government in Britain controlled the nature and amount of invisible liabilities it chose to heap on India, it could adjust these liabilities to the annual fluctuations (that it could not control) of export surplus earnings; and second, it did not confine total liabilities to the actual total of external earnings but imposed indebtedness whenever it needed extra funds. The adjustment was always carried out in a non-symmetric manner.

When India's export surplus earnings rose to an unusual extent, additional demands were promptly added to the normal drain items, in order to siphon off these earnings. In 1919, export surplus earnings reached a peak of £114 million. War materials worth £67 million imported from

India were not paid for by Britain constituting a forced contribution.[36] Additionally, munificent "gifts"from India were presented by the British to themselves. For example, an additional £100 million (a very large sum, exceeding India's entire annual budget and amounting to 3 percent of Britain's national income at that time) was transferred as a "gift" from India to Britain during the First World War, a gift no ordinary Indian knew about, followed by another £45 million "gift" the next year, both by increasing India's debt burden.[37] On the other hand, if India's export earnings fell, owing, say, to world recessionary conditions, the sum demanded as sterling tribute was never lowered, and any gap between tribute and actual earnings was covered by (enforced) borrowing by India. Even during the Great Depression years, when India's export earnings fell drastically, the tribute was not lowered, so in addition to enforced debt, the large distress outflow of financial gold was also mandated.

Such manipulation of invisible liabilities by government ensured that, over any given run of years, India's current account was always made to remain in deficit no matter how large its merchandise surplus became, excepting the two years of import surge after the First World War when there was a commodity trade deficit. (Gold outflow during the Depression years was non-commodity or financial gold as explained in the next chapter.)

Both Naoroji and Dutt were acutely aware that when monies raised from producers in India were not spent in their entirety within the country under normal budgetary heads it meant a severe squeeze on the producers' incomes. Dutt supported and quoted an influential administrator, George Wingate, writing in the 1830s: "The tribute paid to Great Britain is by far the most objectionable feature in our existing policy. Taxes spent in the country from which they are raised are totally different in their effects from taxes raised in one country and spent in another. . . . As regards its effects on national production, the whole amount might as well be thrown into the sea as transferred to another country."[38]

They were right, for surplus budgets to an unimaginably large extent were being operated with a strongly deflationary impact on mass purchasing power. (The budgets appeared to be balanced only by including the drain items on the expenditure side.) Such income deflation was the necessary economic mechanism of imperialism since there was no overt use of force to promote export crops save in the early years of indigo and opium cultivation. Income deflation reduced the producers' consumption of basic staple food grains and achieved both the diversion of cultivated land area to non-grain export crops, and the export of food grains. The steady decline in per capita food grain absorption in British India was an expression of this income deflation.[39] What needed to be added to Wingate's remarks is that for the colonial rulers, the taxation revenues in the Indian budget explicitly set aside as Expenditure in England were not "thrown into the sea" but were embodied in vast volumes of goods that were completely free for Britain, which imported them far in excess of its domestic needs for re-exporting the balance to other countries.

While the pre-British rulers, including invaders, had raised taxes, they had become a permanent part of the domiciled population, spending all public funds within the country. There was no tax-financed export drive producing a drain, hence no income-deflating impact on producers as under British rule. Naoroji and Dutt pointed out that the very existence of the large number of specific heads of spending *outside* the country, which constituted the drain items in the budget, arose from India being a colony, run for the sole benefit of the metropolis. Home Charges were not the cost of administering India, for the regular salaries of British civil and military personnel serving in India were paid from the domestic expenditure part of the budget. The sterling charges were for furlough, leave, and pension allowances and averaged only 12.7 percent during 1861 to 1934. The major part, over 77 percent of Home Charges, comprised interest payments on debt arising mainly from military spending abroad and current military expenditures, while 10 percent went on purchase of government stores. The cost of colonial wars of conquest outside India was always put partly or mainly on the Indian revenues.[40] This parasitic pattern was to be disastrously repeated as late as 1941 to 1946 when the enormous burden of financing Allied war spending in South Asia was put on the Indian revenues through a forced loan, raised through a rapid profit inflation that resulted in three million civilians starving to death, a matter we discuss in a later chapter.

We have talked of the metropolitan economy appropriating a part of the surplus of the colony gratis, which constitutes the drain. But since a part, however small, of these drain items were expenditures for specific purposes, whose recipients were specific economic agents in the metropolis being compensated for specific services rendered, the question arises: can we legitimately talk of the metropolis extracting a "drain" from the colony?

This question can be answered on two levels. First, how the proceeds of the drain are distributed is irrelevant to the fact of the drain, just as how the proceeds of an extortion racket are distributed and how the different agents involved are compensated for their services is irrelevant for identifying the fact of extortion. Colonial drain was analogous to extortion; and the claim of the metropolitan country that it was providing "governance" was analogous to the claim of the extortionist that it provided "protection."

Second, even if local administrative functions had been transferred in entirety to Indians, this, while desirable on independent grounds, would not have reduced the drain by one iota, as long as political control was retained by Britain, so that it continued to link the internal budget with external earnings. As we have seen, the whole of India's external earnings was intercepted in London and appropriated by Britain, while its rupee equivalent was "paid" to producers in India who had earned the export surplus, out of taxes raised from the very same producers. Whatever specific invisible liabilities were detailed on the debit side to justify this appropriation affected neither the actual existence of this drain nor its value. Even if, hypothetically, no sterling leave and furlough allowances or pensions for British administrators and soldiers were charged to the revenues (these in any case accounted for only one-eighth of the Home Charges), these particular charges could have been substituted by any other items the rulers' ingenuity could devise—say by the cost of maintaining some of the Queen Empress's many palaces in Britain, on the argument that she ruled India.

# CHAPTER 10

# Further on Colonial Transfers and Their Implications

J. K. Galbraith, in his review of Keynes's *Collected Writings*, wrote impatiently that Keynes "became concerned with the trivial intricacies of currency and banking in India. . . . On this he wrote a monograph, *Indian Currency and Finance. . .* Any scholar of moderate capacity could have learned all that was useful to know about the subject in about three months, perhaps less."[1]

Galbraith could not have been more wrong. Appropriating from India (and smaller colonies) year after year before the First World War, at least £ 40–50 million in gold and foreign exchange earnings for imperial ends, was not a "trivial" matter. The smooth functioning of the international gold standard depended on it and also Britain's position as the world capitalist leader, with the pound sterling being considered "as good as gold" and with the dollar as yet not in the picture. The question for imperialist rulers was one of devising the most efficient monetary and exchange rate system for maximizing and appropriating India's external earnings. This question engaged some of the best English minds of the time. Not only did Keynes study the Indian financial system, which he found "intricate and highly artificial,"[2] he gave lecture courses to students in Cambridge on the subject for a number of years and gave evidence to or was a member of a number of official Commissions on Indian finance and currency (the Chamberlain, Babington–Smith, and Hilton Young commissions, and for a time the Indian Fiscal Commission).

**TABLE 10.1: Depreciation of Rupee against Sterling, 1871–1901**

| PERIOD | RS. PER POUND | PERIOD | RS. PER POUND |
|--------|---------------|--------|---------------|
| 1871–72 | 10.378 | 1886–87 | 13.793 |
| 1872–73 | 10.549 | 1887–88 | 14.286 |
| 1873–74 | 10.738 | 1888–89 | 14.724 |
| 1874–75 | 10.726 | 1889–90 | 14.545 |
| 1875–76 | 11.098 | 1890–91 | 13.333 |
| 1876–77 | 11.707 | 1891–92 | 14.371 |
| 1877–78 | 11.566 | 1892–93 | 16.107 |
| 1878–79 | 12.152 | 1893–94 | 16.552 |
| 1879–80 | 12.000 | 1894–95 | 18.321 |
| 1880–81 | 12.000 | 1895–96 | 17.647 |
| 1881–82 | 12.075 | 1896–97 | 16.667 |
| 1882–83 | 12.308 | 1897–98 | 15.686 |
| 1883–84 | 12.308 | 1898–99 | 15.000 |
| 1884–85 | 12.427 | 1899–00 | 15.000 |
| 1885–86 | 13.187 | 1900–01 | 15.000 |

Source: *Statistical Abstracts* and R. C. Dutt, *Economic History of India.*

The reason that there were so many commissions at short intervals on Indian financial matters was that the prolonged global decline of the price of silver relative to gold during the quarter-century after 1871, hence rupee depreciation (as the rupee was a silver currency), created specific problems of maintaining the transfer to Britain. Later on, the sharp appreciation of the Indian rupee during the First World War created converse problems of appropriating external earnings. The steep fall in the price of silver, especially from the 1880s, made Indian goods cheaper in gold standard countries, and exports grew considerably, as did the exports of Japan, which also had a silver currency. But unlike Japan, India was subject to the drain, entailing a downwardly inflexible sterling demand on exchange earnings. When the rupee depreciated, more rupee taxes had to be raised from the local producers to meet this sterling demand.

Suppose that in a given year in the 1870s, as usual, India's entire commodity export surplus earnings of £15 million was taken by Britain, while Council bills to an equivalent rupee value were issued that charged the sum to the Indian revenues. This meant that at the initial exchange rate of £ 1 = Rs.10, under Expenditure in England, Rs.150 million had to be set aside in the budget to pay out against Council bills tendered in India. When the rupee depreciated to £1 = Rs.18, the same £15 million drain now required Rs.270 million to be paid out from the budget, requiring additional revenues of Rs.120 million. The idea of reducing sterling demands on the revenues was never entertained by the rulers. On the contrary, sterling demands rose by one-third over the three decades. To finance this when the rupee was depreciating meant either raising much higher tax revenues in India despite the population being already overtaxed or a larger share of the total budget had to go as drain items under Expenditure in England, exercising a corresponding compression on other normal expenditures. Table 10.1 shows the depreciation of the rupee, slow during the 1870s but speeding up from the middle of the 1880s. For an entire century before that the rupee-sterling exchange rate had been steady at roughly Rs.10 to £1.

So unprecedented was rapid rupee depreciation that it found an echo in English literature of the time. In Oscar Wilde's comedy *The Importance of Being Earnest,* first staged in 1895, Cecily's tutor decides that the violent fall of the rupee was not a subject fit for her sensitive ears. The matter was far from being a joke for Indian taxpayers, however. Table 10.2 shows the additional burden of taxation arising from the combination of rupee depreciation and higher sterling demands on the revenues. It compares actual rupee payments against Council bills and the hypothetical payments, taking as constant the exchange rate that prevailed in 1871-72. This extra burden of taxation amounted to Rs.141 crores, or more than £100 million. Indian public opinion seems to have always agitated for the wrong objective, for rupee depreciation and more exports, seemingly unaware that the higher India's export surplus earnings were, the greater the benefit to England, and the greater the tax burden on India's working masses to defray these higher earnings out of the budget. The producers stood to benefit from a higher rupee, which would have obviated some of the increased tax burden on them. The Herschell Committee's recommendation of closing the mints to free coinage of silver was implemented and did succeed in improving

**TABLE 10.2: Actual Payments against Council Bills and Estimated Payments with Constant 1871–2 Exchange Rate[3]**

| PERIOD | COUNCIL BILLS CONSTANT RS. CRORE | COUNCIL BILLS ACTUAL RS. CRORE | PERIOD | 3-YEAR TOTALS | |
|---|---|---|---|---|---|
| | | | | COUNCIL BILLS CONSTANT RS. CRORE | COUNCIL BILLS ACTUAL RS. CRORE |
| 1871–72 to 1875–76 | 76.139 | 79.913 | 1871–73 | 38.953 | 39.671 |
| 1876–77 to 1880–81 | 69.724 | 80.137 | 1874–76 | 37.186 | 40.242 |
| OVER DECADE | 132.787 | 145.187 | 1877–79 | 40.832 | 46.986 |
| DIFFERENCE | | 12.4 | 1880–82 | 50.626 | 59.131 |
| 1881–82 to 1885–86 | 78.036 | 93.176 | 1883–85 | 43.226 | 52.333 |
| 1886–87 to 1890–91 | 75.967 | 103.478 | 1886–88 | 43.334 | 59.679 |
| OVER DECADE | 154.003 | 196.654 | 1889–91 | 49.335 | 66.928 |
| DIFFERENCE | | 42.651 | 1892–94 | 44.591 | 73.374 |
| 1891–92 to 1895–96 | 79.625 | 127.675 | 1895–97 | 43.617 | 70.913 |
| 1896–97 to 1900–01 | 78.275 | 116.33 | 1898–00 | 52.99 | 76.589 |
| OVER DECADE | 157.9 | 244.005 | | | |
| DIFFERENCE | | 86.105 | | | |
| | | | | | |
| TOTAL | 444.69 | 585.846 | TOTAL | 444.69 | 585.846 |
| DIFFERENCE | | 141.156 | DIFFERENCE | | 141.156 |

Source: *Statistical Abstracts* and R. C. Dutt, *Economic History of India*.

the exchange rate from its nadir of Rs.18 to Rs.15, still a long way below the initial Rs.10.4 (see Table 10.1).

Total central government revenue collections were increased steeply, doubling from Rs.158 crore in 1871 to Rs.317 crore three decades later. Land revenue rose by one-third, but the bulk of increased revenues came from heavier indirect taxes on necessities, including a new tax on salt, even though the government's salt monopoly meant that its price was already at least seven times greater than it would have been without monopoly. The doubling of total revenues more than met the additional demand by Britain charged to India at the depreciating rupee, amounting to Rs.141 crore, as Table 10.2 shows. With such increasing exactions, the 1890s saw deeper agrarian distress and an unusually high incidence of famines.

The only people who did benefit from more exports were the interme-
diaries (*dalals*) of the export-import trade, who took a large cut as commis-
sion/profit from the amounts paid out to the peasants and artisans from the
latter's taxes. Many Indian business houses had started life as trading agents
of the Company in the infamous opium trade to China. They were inclined
to bring the *dalal* viewpoint to the issue of the exchange rate while ignoring the interests of peasant producers. The business leaders, both British
and Indian, and professionals were vociferous in opposing any income tax
affecting their own interests, while they supported further indirect taxes on
necessities like salt, bearing adversely on the poor. Dadabhai Naoroji, in his
usual insightful manner, had noticed and regretted this class bias, which was
captured by historian S. Bhattacharya: "The members of the British Indian
Association urged the Government to increase the salt tax and to reduce or
abolish the Income Tax. The Bengal Chamber of Commerce was also of the
opinion that the Income Tax might be got rid of by increasing the salt duty."[4]

## Macroeconomics of the Drain of Wealth

The essence of the internal-cum-external drain as conceptualized by
Naoroji and Dutt can be captured by suitably modifying the identity linking the budgetary balance, the external balance, and the savings-investment
balance for both colony and metropolis. This has been shown earlier for
both colony and metropolis; here we briefly recapitulate the part dealing
with the colony.[5] The drain can be measured either by looking at that part
of the colony's rupee budget which was set aside for spending outside the
country, or, alternatively, by looking at its commodity export surplus, since
these earnings covered the items of spending outside the country (assuming that India's external indebtedness never increased). Either measure
would do as a minimal approximation to the actual drain.

In a sovereign country, the familiar identity is expressed as follows:

$$( S - I ) = ( G - T ) + NX \ldots (1)$$

where S and I refer to private savings and investment, G is government
expenditure, T is taxes and other forms of revenue so that ( G – T ) is the

budget deficit. NX is the current account surplus on the balance of payments. In a sovereign economy, if there is a balance between private savings and private investment, then a budgetary surplus would be reflected in a current account surplus, and likewise a current account deficit would accompany a budgetary deficit. Given a balanced budget, a current account deficit would be reflected in an excess of private investment over savings. Likewise, a deficit budget, with a balanced current account, is accompanied by an excess of private savings over private investment.

In a colony, the budget appears to be balanced as part of the policy of "sound finance," so that $(G - T) = 0$. But actually, the budget was kept in large surplus every year, since only a part of tax revenue was spent in a normal manner, and this exercised a strongly deflationary impact. Total public spending G was divided by government itself into two parts, which we can denote as GD, the part spent domestically, and as GA, the part spent abroad. GA constituted the total of drain items. These were administratively imposed like the bulk of the "Home Charges," 87 percent of which comprised military expenses and interest charges on a sterling debt; the size of both was decided by the British government. Thus, the budget, though apparently balanced, was perpetually in surplus when we consider heads of normal internal spending, leaving out the drain items (GA).

$$T = G = (GD + GA)$$
$$(T - GD) > 0 \ldots (2)$$

This division of the budget was reflected in a corresponding division of Net Exports NX into two parts: we define NX1 as the colony's total earnings from the world, including Britain, on account of its commodity export surplus taking merchandise, commodity gold, and normal invisible items like freight, insurance, and commission on trade. It is a large positive figure. NX2 is the balance of invisible items charged to the colony that arise from its colonial status. It is a large negative figure that includes all the drain items GA of the internal budget, now expressed in sterling. (In many years −NX2 would include additional items over and above the usual drain items, but let us for the moment concentrate on the simpler picture.) Since all the colony's global export surplus earnings, NX1, are siphoned off by imposing an equivalent value of invisible liabilities, NX2, it follows that

$$NX = ( NX1 + NX2 ) = 0$$
$$\text{since } NX1 = -NX2 - NX2 = GA \dots (3)$$

The commodity export surplus grew especially fast from the early 1890s onward, aided by the depreciation of silver relative to gold, which greatly increased the GA requirement in rupee terms to meet the same level of downwardly inflexible sterling demands as before. Hence, it meant increased taxation, T, on producers. When the limit of tax extraction was reached (or when large scale import of monetary gold took place), the adjustment to increased demands by the metropolis was made through enforced borrowing thrust on India. Thus, NX became negative and –NX2 = GA became larger than (T – GD) when such enforced borrowing took place.

The above framework enables us to see that though while foreigners made payment in full for their import surplus from India, namely NX1, net invisibles equaling at least this amount, namely –NX2, were demanded by the metropolis leaving India's current account NX in deficit on average. Looking at the UN data on trade surplus in the next section and the estimates of balance of payments,[6] we see that no matter how fast the commodity trade surplus grew—India posted the second-largest and rising *merchandise* export surplus in the world for decades, so that even after deducting net import of *commodity gold*, the commodity trade surplus increased fast—invisible demands administered by the metropolis and imposed on India grew even faster. The current account was made to remain in deficit and India was forced to borrow, increasing future interest burdens.

Payments made by foreigners took the form of official bills of exchange (Council bills including telegraphic transfers). This sum must be identically equal to the commodity export surplus of India with the world (balance of merchandise plus balance of commodity gold) plus normal trade-associated invisibles like freight, insurance, and commission. We use the term NX1 for this sum and define it as exports *f.o.b.* minus imports *c.i.f.* The producers of export surplus were paid out of taxes minus GD; so in the absence of any increase in debt, NX1 would be equal to –NX2 which in turn would equal GA. But when the total of the invisible demands on India, –NX2, was pitched higher than NX1, then the difference would constitute additional borrowing, which would equal –NX2 –NX1.

The drain can be approximated at a minimal level, if we leave aside borrowing, by taking either the total of budgetary expenditures set aside for spending abroad, namely GA, or, equivalently, NX1, the actual exchange earnings that made possible this spending abroad on the GA items. But since there was some borrowing, we may approximate the drain at a more accurate (and higher) level, by taking the sum of NX1 and additional long-term borrowing, which would give us –NX2, the actual total of invisible liabilities imposed on India. This always exceeded its commodity export surplus earnings no matter how large the latter might be and kept an entire people as perpetually indebted to Britain as any bonded laborer to his landlord-cum-creditor.

In all this, gold movements play an important if problematic part. India was a large net importer of gold for the period before the Great Depression. It is standard practice by authors to treat all net gold flows as *commodity gold* and put them in the trade account along with other goods. But this is not a correct procedure, for all gold flows could not have been solely commodity gold. Under the gold standard, the accepted means of settling imbalance in international payments was gold flows, today termed *financial gold*, as distinct from commodity gold. Further, gold was imported by the colonial government for the reserve requirements of India's gold exchange standard, and this definitely constituted monetary gold, a subset of financial gold. India's merchandise export surplus has tended to be substantially underestimated in the literature by treating all financial gold inflow at par with merchandise imports, and conversely, the current account deficit during the Depression years has been severely underestimated, by treating distress financial gold outflow as commodity gold exports.[7] The official trade statistics collected at that time could have made the distinction between commodity gold and non-commodity gold but they did not make the distinction explicitly. As a rule of thumb, gold imported or exported by government always constituted financial gold, and not commodity gold.

*Britain's Capital Exports and the Diffusion of Capitalism*

Returning to the inapposite remarks by Galbraith on the "trivial" nature of Indian finance, they indicated he was unfamiliar with the work of Hilgerdt or Saul on the international pattern of trade and payments.[8] Unfortunately, he was not exceptional in this respect. There is to this day little recognition in the literature that the large capital exports from Britain, especially during the last three decades of the nineteenth century, that speeded up the construction of roads, railways, and factories in Continental Europe, the United States, and Canada depended crucially on Britain's ability to siphon off India's gold and foreign exchange earnings, as it did the earnings of other smaller colonies. These earnings not only offset the deficits that Britain was running on its current account with these regions, but it helped to offset additional deficits owing to its capital exports to these same regions.

In his valuable study, Saul did not talk explicitly of "drain" from India, for he appears to have had little knowledge of the tax-financed nature of its export surplus.[9] His main concern was tracing Britain's balance of payments with different regions of the world from the 1880s to the First World War, and this showed a striking picture. Britain incurred large and rising current account deficits with the European Continent, North America, and regions of recent European settlement, while it posted a huge and rising current account surplus only with its tropical colonies, preeminently with India. Further, Britain exported capital, entailing capital account deficits, to the greatest extent to those very same newly industrializing regions of European settlement, with which it ran current account deficits. The two deficits added up to mounting balance of payments deficits with these regions.

Saul estimated that in 1880 Britain's deficit with the United States plus Continental Europe was over £70 million, and pointed out that the £25 million credit that Britain showed vis-à-vis India, which was India's entire commodity export surplus that year, meant that "Britain settled more than one-third of her deficits with Europe and the US through India."[10] By 1910, the balance of payments deficit that Britain had with Europe, the United States, and Canada combined had reached £120 million. That year

India's global commodity export surplus was a massive £57.8 million but a slightly larger sum, £60 million, was shown by Britain as owed to it by India.[11]

Saul says: "The key to Britain's whole payments pattern lay in India, financing as she probably did more than two-fifths of Britain's total deficits."[12] The total amount £60 million (comprising its managed trade surplus of £19 million that year plus £41 million invisible liabilities politically imposed by Britain and shown as its total credit with India in 1910) was pitched a little higher than India's actual export surplus of £57.8 million vis-à-vis the rest of the world in that year . The balance, £2.2 million, would have been either a drawing down of the Secretary of State's balances or shown in the accounts as addition to India's debt to Britain, or a combination of the two.

India's merchandise trade grew remarkably fast during 1901 to 1913, with total trade doubling from £148 million to £300 million, at over 6 percent per annum; the average annual commodity export surplus was £ 25.7 million, 60 percent higher than in the earlier decade. The industrializing countries were expanding their demand for foodstuffs and raw materials from tropical regions. As usual, these fast-rising earnings were appropriated by Britain via a corresponding rise in the annual issue of Council bills.[13] While shipping shortage constrained trade during the first two years of the war, India's trade grew even faster during 1914 to 1919 with total trade value nearly doubling again over the five years (see Figure 10.1).

The rupee appreciated rapidly against sterling during the war years, from Rs.15 to Rs.9.5 per £1, as shortage of shipping led to import compression while the belligerent powers demanded Indian jute for the millions of sandbags used in trench warfare. Silver rupees started to be melted down as their market value in terms of gold soon exceeded the official exchange rate. Merchandise export surplus earnings averaged £63 million during 1915–19, reaching an unprecedented £114 million in 1919 (see Figure 10.2). These earnings, even after deducting commodity gold imports, were far in excess of the annual expenditures charged to India under the usual drain items. Repaying at least part of India's managed sterling debt out of its record earnings would have benefited Indians by reducing interest burdens, but no matter how large its external earnings,

## Figure 10.1: Total Merchandise Trade of India, 1900–1920

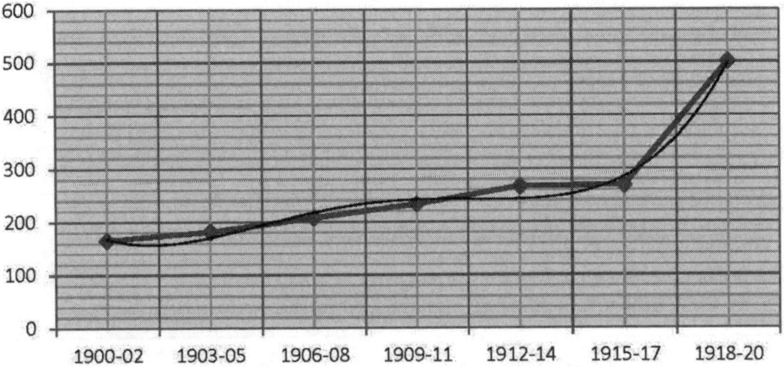

Source: United Nations Historical Data (1962). Rupee-based trade data for 1914–1919 are from the Statistical Abstracts, converted to sterling, using exchange rates available in U.S. Financial Statistics. The last figure is a two-year average.

they were always appropriated and an entire subject population was kept perpetually indebted.

Saul's study documented the important "balancing role" that India played in the multilateral trade system centered on Britain during the period of the gold standard, but he does not seem to have been aware of the linking of trade with taxes that made for the drain. A balancing role, whereby a country uses its surplus external earnings from one region to offset its deficits with other regions, is normal and legitimate if such earnings are obtained under normal trade conditions. But Britain did not have a legitimate surplus with India; it could link taxes with trade solely owing to the direct political control it exercised. Without such control, it could not have appropriated India's entire net global external earnings to balance its own deficits, for this was only possible by imposing manipulated invisible items on India's external account while charging these to the Indian budget. The detailed 1962 United Nations trade data matrix for different countries shows that Saul's conclusion was correct, that in the pre–First World War period India's earnings paid for two-fifths of Britain's deficits. Saul certainly realized that Britain treated Indian export earnings as its own since he pointed out that in effect Britain used Indian goods, which

**Figure 10.2: Merchandise Export Surplus of India, 1901–1919**

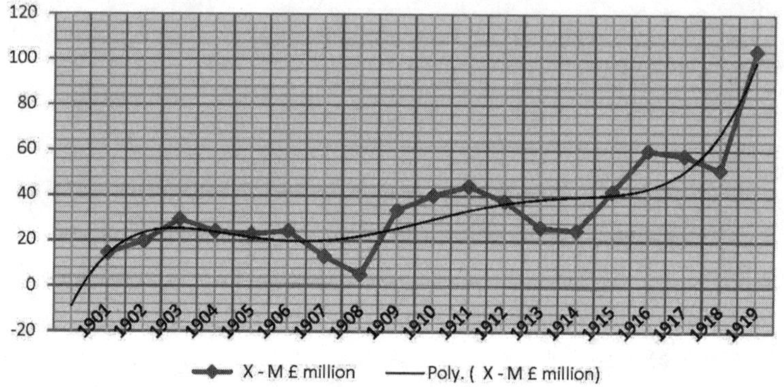

Source: United Nations Historical Data (1962).

were largely duty-free on the Continent and North America, to jump the tariff barriers that Britain's own export goods faced.

India's role, however, was not limited to offsetting Britain's current account deficits. "But this was by no means all, for it was mainly through India that the British balance of payments found the flexibility essential for a great capital exporting country."[14] Saul went on to say: "The importance of India's trade to the pattern of world trade balances can hardly be exaggerated."[15]

In fact, Britain would not have been a capital exporting country at all, great or otherwise, if it did not have complete control over colonial exchange earnings, since with the rest of the world it ran current account deficits of such a magnitude that it would have needed to borrow capital. The present-day world capitalist leader, the United States, also has been running large current account deficits with the world, but without access to colonial transfers in the old form that Britain had enjoyed. Not surprisingly, the United States is not an exporter of capital but is the world's largest debtor.

*The Interwar Period: Changing Magnitude of the Drain*

Folke Hilgerdt prepared a study for the League of Nations for 1928 of the merchandise exports and imports of the major trading countries and regions of the world.[16] Figure 10.3 shows the network of world trade, summarizing the pattern of multilateral trade by depicting flows between the major regions and countries, though not all countries. The data for India are not given separately but included in the broad region labelled "Tropics." The arrows point *toward* the country/region with the *trade deficits*, and point *away* from the countries/regions with the *trade surpluses*. Saul adopted the opposite convention while depicting the network for 1913 in a similar form, but with arrows pointing toward the trade surplus countries.[17]

The figures in million U.S. dollars from the Hilgerdt network diagram are shown in Table 10.3.[18] (Note that surplus of country A with B is different from deficit of B with A, as the export f.o.b. from country A to B is a smaller figure, than import c.i.f. of the same goods by B from A.) Only two regions posted overall merchandise trade surpluses with the world, namely the United States and the Tropics, of $880 million, and $690 million, respectively. The notable feature is that all arrows but one pointed toward the United Kingdom, indicating its heavy trade deficit, totalling $1,680 mn. (the largest in the world for a single country) with only one arrow that pointed away, toward the Tropics with which the UK had a trade surplus of $210 million. The United States had surpluses totalling $1,830 mn. with every region of the world except the Tropics, against which it ran a massive deficit of $950 million. The Tropics, in turn, had trade surpluses with every region in the world totalling $1,040 mn. except UK, with which it had a deficit of $350 million. The deficit with the UK was the result of most of the Tropics, India being the largest component, being part of the British Empire with compulsory free trade.

The UK had trade deficits with every region other than the Tropics, the largest deficits being with Continental Europe and the United States, continuing the prewar pattern. Europe, other than Germany and the UK, ran large overall deficits on merchandise trade. The trade of the temperate regions of recent settlement was balanced, with the surpluses earned from Europe being almost the same as the deficits incurred with the Tropics and the United States.

The data, in current dollars, available from the later (1962) United Nations historical study of merchandise trade series for different countries

**TABLE 10.3: Merchandise Trade Balances of Major Regions and Countries in 1928 (USD million)**

| Trade Balance of: | Trade Balance with → U.S. | Tropics | UK | Germany | Rest of Europe | Temperate Recent Settled Regions | Total Positive Balance | Total Negative Balance | Overall Balance |
|---|---|---|---|---|---|---|---|---|---|
| U.S.A | 0 | -950 | 610 | 190 | 430 | 600 | 1,830 | -950 | 880 |
| Tropics | 640 | 0 | -350 | 180 | 190 | 30 | 1,040 | -350 | 690 |
| UK | -670 | 210 | 0 | -100 | -810 | -100 | 210 | -1,680 | -1,470 |
| Germany | -280 | -280 | 80 | 0 | 390 | -330 | 470 | -890 | -420 |
| Rest of Europe | -620 | -330 | 480 | -550 | 0 | -660 | 480 | -2,160 | -1,680 |
| Temperate Recent Settled Regions | 690 | -130 | 80 | 250 | 460 | 0 | 790 | -800 | -10 |

**Figure 10.3: The Multilateral Trade Network in 1928**

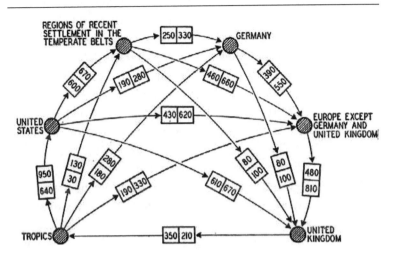

from 1900 to 1960 gives the sources and destination imports and exports for selected years.[19] Analyzing these data in Table 10.4, we separate India's trade with the United Kingdom and its trade with the rest of the world. A comparison of 1928 with 1900 shows the large rise in the Indian subcontinent's merchandise trade balance with the rest of the world (excluding the UK) from $151 million to $497 million. After deducting its negative balance with the UK, India's overall merchandise trade balance more than trebled from $114 million to $392 million, with its rising earnings being appropriated by the United Kingdom (after allowing for the balance of commodity gold). Indian SC refers to the Indian Sub-Continent comprising today's India, Pakistan, Bangladesh, and Sri Lanka.

*Rise and Decline of India's Trade in the Interwar Period*

As in other primary product exporting regions, India's trade showed a roller-coaster pattern of rapid growth up to 1928 followed by collapse after that up to 1933, with a slow recovery thereafter. Looking at country-wide annual data on exports and imports, we find that India posted the second-highest merchandise export surplus globally from 1900 to 1928 (though it lagged far behind the United States, with Argentina just below India). Export earnings by India from the rest of the world scaled their highest level of the post–First World War period, by 1925 at $1.4 billion (or £282.86 million), while export surplus reached $450 million or £92.57 million.

While it grew rapidly, trade also became more volatile during the two decades following 1914, and the use of Council Bills came to be regularly supplemented by, and in many years entirely supplanted by direct sale or purchase of sterling for rupees by the Secretary of State. For example, the spike in India's merchandise export surplus earnings to a two-year total of £158 million during 1918 and 1919, and restriction on private gold imports, meant that the rupee value of the commodity export surplus at the official exchange rate exceeded the entire central government revenues, while even at the appreciated market exchange rate it was over three quarters of the revenues, so Council Bills no longer sufficed as the sole means of payment to producers. A part of India's exports of strategic war materials was taken by Britain without any payment at all, a little over one third of export surplus was paid out from the budget through Council Bills, while the rupee equivalent of the remainder was raised by selling sterling to private buyers.

We use mainly data from the *Statistical Abstracts for British India* to arrive at the value of the commodity export surplus, namely the transfer for the period 1900 to 1921, at £479 million. This estimate of the drain is an underestimate since the financial stratagems used by Britain to avoid entirely or postpone indefinitely its payments due to Indian producers could not be taken into account. A question may arise, if revenues became insufficient to pay out rupees against export surplus, why did the government not resort to even higher taxation as it had done so often in the past? The answer is that taxes had been raised by over half already from 1914 to 1918, including a further tax on salt, the perennial favorite; and from late 1918 the global influenza pandemic intervened to devastate India.

Demobilized soldiers returning from war theaters in Europe and Mesopotamia caused the pandemic to spread rapidly, claiming between 13 to 15 million lives during 1918–19, about a quarter of the estimated

**TABLE 10.4: Indian Subcontinent's Trade Balance with the UK and Rest of World (USD Millions)**

|  | Indian S.C. Exports To ROW Excluding UK | Indian S.C. Imports To ROW Excluding UK | Inidan S.C. Trade Balance With ROW Excluding UK | Trade Balance with UK | Available for Financing UK Deficits with ROW |
|---|---|---|---|---|---|
| 1900 | 256 | 105 | **151** | −37 | 114 |
| 1913 | 662 | 248 | **414** | −138 | 276 |
| 1928 | 1,057 | 560 | **497** | −105 | 392 |

Note: Indian subcontinent (S.C.) refers to today's India, Pakistan, Bangladesh, and Sri Lanka. ROW refers to "rest of world" (excluding UK).

global tally of 50 to 60 million deaths and the highest for any country. The entire increase in population since the 1911 Census was wiped out, and British India, excluding Afghanistan and Burma, actually showed an absolute decline of population in the 1921 census compared to 1911. But there was no sparing the people even under such dire conditions. Imperialists did not believe in tempering the wind to the shorn lamb. The colonial government decided to give £100 million as a "gift" to Britain to support its war needs by increasing Indian sterling debt to that extent, and this was followed by another "gift" of £45 million to Britain the next year.[20]

Wartime restrictions on imports led to a post-war import surge and India saw a rare two years of trade deficit during 1920 and 1921, which was met by the Secretary of State selling rupees to purchase sterling from the public. In the next triennium, 1922 to 1924, however, India's merchandise export surplus bounced back to Rs.141 crore or £89 million annual average, reaching its highest level in 1925 at £125 million. As primary product prices started falling from that year, volume increases compensated to some extent for the price fall until 1928. Thereafter, the collapse of primary product prices from 1929 caused the export surplus to decline to below Rs.11 crore or £8 million by 1932. There was acute agrarian distress with farm debts rising fast, and a loss of mortgaged assets including land, both soon leading to pauperization of the peasantry. The employment problem was exacerbated with the colonial government cutting all productive expenditure in the domestic part of the budget, to implement the dogmatic balanced-budget deflationary policies advised by the Treasury in Britain to maintain the system of fixed exchange rates. (The implications of this for the Great Depression are discussed later.)

Only two years into the Depression, the 1931 Census recorded 38 percent of rural workers as dependent mainly on wages compared to 26 percent in 1921. Millions of small producers liquidated what little assets they had in the struggle to survive, and every year from 1932 to 1938 saw a torrent of distress gold flowing out of the country to Britain. Trying to cope with reduced trade and domestic unemployment, Britain intensified its invisible tribute demands on India even as the latter's commodity export surplus earnings declined drastically.

Using the balance of payments estimate by Banerjee, modified by separating financial gold from commodity gold on the basis of data from the *Statistical Abstract for India 1920 to 1940*, we find that during the period 1922 to 1938 the total commodity export surplus was £827 million. The total invisible liabilities heaped on India were £1209 million producing an exceptionally large current account deficit of £382 million. This deficit was balanced in the capital account by financial gold outflow of £260 million and addition to debt of £122 million. India accounted for nearly two-fifths of gold inflows into Britain during this period.

Kindelberger,[21] quoting a study by Triantis,[22] points out that while six countries mainly in Latin America saw the steepest fall in their exchange earnings, India was put in the group of countries with moderately severe decline by 60 to 75 percent in external earnings. Our data show, however, that India suffered a 94 percent decline in merchandise export surplus between the peak in 1925 and the trough in 1932, and even compared to 1929 there was over 85 percent decline by 1932. All these countries saw large outflows of financial gold. While other countries devalued their currencies, the Indian rupee was kept tied to sterling and there was no rupee devaluation until sterling itself was devalued.

The balance of payments estimates for India incorrectly classified its large distress gold outflow as exports in the current account, thus treating it as commodity gold and thereby suggesting a rosy and wholly unrealistic picture for the 1930s. As in a mirror image, in British studies these same financial gold inflows from India and other colonies were incorrectly recorded as imports in the current account, as in Mitchell and Deane[23] and by other scholars using this data source. Thereby, the current account was fallaciously inferred by many authors to be in much larger deficit, to the extent of these gold inflows, than was the case. In fact, the financial gold inflows from colonies in many years completely offset Britain's true current account deficit and contributed to its faster recovery compared to other industrial countries.

We can now summarize our estimate of the drain, made over four sub-periods, covering the period 1765 to 1938; see Table 10.5. (The period 1765 to 1900 was depicted in chapter 9.) The interest rate used for compounding remains 5 percent, and two terminal dates are considered—the first up to Independence in 1947 and the second up to 2020. For comparison, the GDP of India and the United Kingdom are also given for selected years. By 1947, the compounded value of the drain was 38 times the GDP of the UK that year, and 78 times India's GDP. The exchange rate against the dollar over the entire period may be taken as roughly, £1 = $4.84. In dollar terms, the absolute value of drain from 1765 to 1938 amounted to $10.5 billion. The compounded value to 1947 works out at $1.95 trillion

### TABLE 10.5: Estimated Value of Drain from India, 1765–1938

| Period | Absolute Value of Drain (£ Million) | COMPOUNDED VALUE AT 5 PERCENT | |
|---|---|---|---|
| | | up to 1947 (£ Billion) | up to 2020 (£ Billion) |
| 1765–1836 | 270.254 | 369.648 | 12399.9 |
| 1837–1900 | 596.757 | 28.168 | 992.4 |
| **1765–1900** | **867.011** | **397.816** | **13392.3** |
| 1901–1921 | 270.254 | 3.06 | 102.58 |
| 1922–1938 | 596.757 | 1.25 | 42.00 |
| **1765–1938** | **867.011** | **402.126** | **13536.88** |
| GDP IN £ BILLION | | | |
| | **UK** | **INDIA** | |
| 1836 | 0.592 | N/A | |
| 1900 | 1.963 | 0.645 | |
| 1947 | 10.544 | 5.186 | |
| 2020 | 3071 | 3157 | |

Source: Authors' calculations from previously cited data and sources.

## Figure 10.4: British India's Per Capita National Income 1900–1946 in Rupees in Constant 1949 Prices (three-year averages)

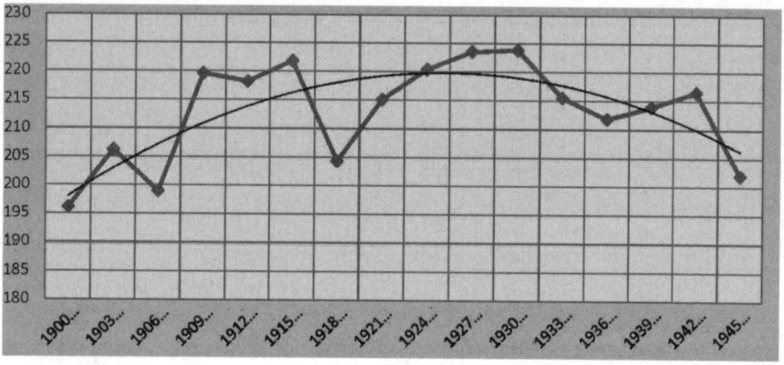

Source: S. Sivasubramonian, *National Income of India* (Delhi: Oxford University Press, 2000).

and up to 2020, at $65.64 trillion, the latter figure being three times the GDP of the United States that year. In Table 10.5, GDP figures are in current prices as are the series used for computing the drain.

The impact of this sustained drain of all net external earnings, combined with expansion of the reserve army of labor owing to displacement of domestic manufacturing production, was stagnation of per capita income. The definitive estimate of the whole of India's national income by S. Sivasubramonian was adjusted for British India by applying its share of population in total population, while for obtaining per capita annual income the population for each year was obtained by interpolation from the decennial population totals. There was a 12 percent rise in real per capita income over the period 1900–05 to 1927–31, and decline thereafter with a net gain of less than 5 percent over nearly half a century, taking 1942–47 as the terminal period (see Figure 10.4).[24] Per capita annual food grain absorption, which is an important index of the compression of mass internal demand, declined sharply over the same period.

# PART 3

# CHAPTER 11

# The Unraveling of the Colonial Arrangement

By the term "colonial arrangement," we mean the entire network of relationships that prevailed in the latter half of the nineteenth century. These involved Britain, the late industrializers of Continental Europe and the temperate regions of European settlement, and the colonies of conquest located mainly in the tropical and semi-tropical regions.

What this relationship entailed, to recapitulate in brief, was that Britain kept its own market open to the new industrializers, while finding a market for its own goods in the colonial economies (and also China) at the expense of the local craftsmen there. It substantially "drained away" the economic surplus of these colonies, using these funds for settling its current account deficits with, and also making capital exports to, the new industrializers. The commodity-form these capital exports took was of the products that constituted the colonies' exports. So, the colonies played three roles: first, providing a market for the leading capitalist economy's goods and indirectly for the goods of the metropolitan capitalist world; second, providing the surplus for capital exports and for a diffusion of capitalism; and, third, providing an appropriate commodity-form that could make all this possible.

This colonial arrangement unraveled after the First World War. Not that all these roles simultaneously ceased to be played by the colonies, but some did. In particular, the role of the tropical colonies as a source of surplus extraction did not diminish, though there was a problem in finding the commodity-form it should take after the world agricultural crisis, when agricultural prices collapsed and gold became for a number of years the form of surplus extraction. In fact, the role of surplus extraction actually increased during the Second World War, compared to what it had been earlier, when colonial surplus was required for war finance. So large was the surplus extracted during the war years that three million people died in the 1943–44 Bengal famine. But the role of the colonies in providing a market for British goods diminished after the First World War.

There were several reasons for this. An obvious one is the inherent limits of the colonial markets. To understand these limits, let us go back to the simple example given in chapter 8. The process of deindustrialization in the colony occurs through two means: one is through the "drain" of surplus itself, which takes the commodity-form of primary goods, and the other is the substitution of imported metropolitan manufactures for those produced by local craftsmen. The drain of surplus does not create any demand for metropolitan manufactures; rather, it destroys the demand for the products of the local craftsmen, which had arisen earlier because of the spending of the surplus internally by the Emperor and his nobility and tax-gatherers, who, taken together, had constituted the landlord class. A market for metropolitan manufactures arises *only to the extent that primary producers' incomes in the colony are left with the producers themselves (or with those, such as merchants and residual landlords, living off them) and not "drained" away.*

There is, therefore, an inherent contradiction between the "source-of-surplus extraction" role of the colonies and their "market-provider" role. The greater the surplus extracted from the colony, the smaller is its role as a market for metropolitan goods.

One can appreciate the contradiction between these two roles of the colony and still visualize the contradiction as occurring only within a particular slice of time. In a colonial economy growing at say 5 percent per annum, if we take a year, for example, we can say that if a larger share of output is taken away as drain then the market for metropolitan manufactured goods is correspondingly smaller. Nonetheless, the market for metropolitan goods would still be growing at more than 5 percent per annum as long as local craft production has not been completely eliminated, and exactly at 5 percent per annum when it has been completely eliminated. It may, therefore, be thought that though the drain of surplus constricts the market for metropolitan goods in the colony, this market can nonetheless continue to grow over time and hence continue providing a stimulus to capital accumulation in the metropolis.[1]

The drain, however, affects not only the size of the market for metropolitan manufactured goods in a given slice of time, but also the growth rate of the colonial economy and hence the growth rate in the size of the market for metropolitan goods. Since the bulk of the economic surplus, other than what was spent for maintaining the colonial administration locally and the residual amount that was left to the local landlord class, was drained out and not invested in expanding the productive base of the colonial economy, the growth rate of that economy was near zero, if not negative. It could be negative, leaving aside the statistical impact of deindustrialization, since irrigation works and other assets inherited from earlier were not always maintained.

In India, all public investment projects had to fulfill a narrow "rate of return criterion." Because over large tracts of the country, notably Bengal, the revenues obtained by the colonial administration were permanently fixed, the rate of return on any investment project was nil for the colonial state and no "land-augmenting" investment was undertaken in such tracts. Even in other parts, where revenue settlement was not permanent but revised periodically, say once every thirty years, the rate of return criterion ruled out any productive investment in agriculture. Because agriculture was the cornerstone of the economy, this meant overall economic stagnation. The role of agriculture can be gauged from the fact that even when "discriminating protection" for domestic manufacturers in a few industries was introduced in India in the interwar period, investment in these industries, after an initial burst, tended to peter out.[2] This was because the home market, whose size was determined by the size of agricultural output, was more or less stagnant due to the stagnation of agriculture, and protection only brought to the local producers a larger share of this stagnant market. In the entire period of colonial rule in India, no major investment projects were undertaken other than in the "canal colonies" of Punjab. And even investment in railways, where the government guaranteed a 5 percent rate of return, did not have any linkage effects on domestic industry, and was undertaken mainly for extracting raw materials from the colony so that its growth-enhancing role was negligible.[3]

The drain of surplus from the colonial economies, therefore, not only adversely affected the size of the market that metropolitan goods could access, but also kept these economies virtually stagnant. Once this market was exhausted, no further stimulus could be derived by the metropolis from the colonial market for sustaining capital accumulation. To be sure, if the process of colonialization could extend to newer areas, then this stimulus could be kept going longer, but once the process of colonialization was complete, this stimulus had to get exhausted. Something of the sort seems to have happened after the First World War.

The emergence of Japan as a new capitalist power in Asia that launched a relentless drive to capture Britain's Asian markets was the other major factor that made the earlier colonial arrangement no longer effective. Japan had been the one Asian country not forced to join the ranks of colonies and semi-colonies of the metropolitan powers, and, though it had been subjected to unequal treaties by these powers, the Japanese state after the Meiji Restoration had both sufficient will and sufficient elbow room to push through a program of capitalist industrialization and launch an aggressive drive for export markets. (Many have disputed the claim that Japanese industrialization was export-led, but this is an issue that need not detain us here.)

Japan's case has often been cited, notably by Paul Baran, as an illustration of how countries in the periphery, had they not been victims of imperialist annexation, could have embarked on an industrialization drive in emulation of the metropolitan countries and promoted by their states.[4] While this argument is valid within the context it was made in, it should not be forgotten that capitalist industrialization, if it is to be transformative and not of the "enclave" variety, necessarily requires imperialist annexations or to be "accommodated" within a world of imperialist annexations, as Japan was to exemplify. (To what extent recent examples like South Korea and China disprove this generalization will be discussed later.) Hence the idea that the entire third world could have developed

Japan-style capitalist industrialization if only it had not been colonized cannot withstand scrutiny.

Britain sought to counter Japan's relentless drive to penetrate its Asian markets by enlisting the support of the local bourgeoisies in its colonies, which had come up in the interstices of colonialism but whose ambitions had been kept in check by the very structures of colonialism. The introduction of "discriminating protection" in India referred to above, which permitted a limited break from the colonial pattern of international division of labor and used the "infant industries" argument in its own justification, was one instance of such forging of an alliance. The "Buy Empire" campaign that was launched in the colonies was another. A system of "imperial preferences" in matters of tariff was instituted that sought to keep out "outsiders" like Japan from the Asian colonial markets of Britain. But though these measures, including at a later date the imposition of quantitative trade restrictions on Japanese imports into these markets, for instance through the so-called Indo-Japanese protocol of the 1930s, did little to revive Britain's fading prospects in the Asian colonial markets, they strengthened Japan's resolve to go imperialist itself. While Britain's concerted effort to keep Japan from encroaching upon the markets of its empire bore little fruit for Britain, it persuaded even larger segments of the Japanese ruling class that Japan may as well also acquire a larger empire for itself.

### The Return to the Gold Standard

The loss of colonial markets also explains the balance of payments problems of Britain in the interwar period. The most significant event of the period, of course, was Britain's return to the gold standard in 1925 at prewar parity. But even the discussion of this event has invariably made no reference to the loss of colonial markets, to the fact that the unsustainability of Britain's return to the gold standard at prewar parity arose precisely because the colonial arrangement was no longer working in the interwar period.

This is hardly surprising.[5] Indeed, the colonial arrangement does not even figure in discussions of the sustainability of the prewar gold standard.

But in view of our extensive discussion of the role of the colonial arrangement in sustaining the gold standard, based on the work of S. B. Saul, the breakdown of that arrangement has to be accorded a centrality in any explanation of Britain's balance of payments problems in the interwar period.

Discussion on the unsustainability of the prewar parity when Britain returned to the gold standard has focused mainly upon the relative price levels in the United States and Britain. Since the United States had maintained its prewar parity on the gold standard, and since British prices at prewar parity were nearly 6 percent higher than the corresponding prices in the United States (some opponents of return at prewar parity claimed that they were 10 percent higher, while several proponents of return at prewar parity thought they were 2.5 percent higher), return at prewar parity would have entailed an overvaluation of the pound sterling. Keynes, who was opposed to a return to the gold standard, wanted the floating exchange rate to continue.

We argue, however, that while the exhaustion of Britain's colonial markets and their growing penetration by Japan manifested themselves through the unsustainability of the prewar parity at which Britain returned to the gold standard, *they would have manifested themselves anyway, nullifying whatever policy Britain followed for improving its balance of payments.*

Floating the exchange rate would not have overcome Britain's difficulties. The loss of markets to Japan could not have been negated this way, since the Japanese would have retaliated. And if Britain's loss of markets to Japan was compensated by a capture of markets from other competitors, then they too would have retaliated. Hence, *there was no equilibrium exchange rate of the pound sterling at which the British balance of payments could have stabilized.* Even if the current balance could, in principle, have improved with exchange rate depreciation *in the absence of retaliation*, there were limits to which competitors would have allowed Britain to encroach on their markets.

The fear expressed by A. C. Pigou that with the system of floating exchange rates, there would be a continuous depreciation of this rate, or "debasement of the currency," which would be damaging to the financial health of the British economy, was an implicit recognition of this fact.

Because of this apprehension Pigou wanted a return to the gold standard, which would at least fix the exchange rate. But even a fixed exchange rate, no matter what the parity, would have scarcely helped.

Let us briefly see what a fixed exchange rate would have implied. Introducing such fixity through a return to the gold standard, no matter what the parity, would necessarily have immediately required, at given money wages and prices, an adequate amount of capital inflows to manage the balance of payments, for which the interest rate had to be raised.

But if the balance of payments was to be sustained through a better current balance rather than through capital inflows, then the current balance had to be improved. If the parity at which Britain returned to the gold standard had been low enough to bring about an improvement in the current balance without any lowering of the domestic price level, then this would have required a lowering of money wages, and hence real wages. This is because the higher sterling value of imported inputs at the new exchange rate would have had to be accommodated at the given price level only through a money wage (and hence real wage) cut. Besides, if the current balance did improve, then a competitor like Japan would have retaliated by going off the gold standard and depreciating its currency, as indeed it did later.

On the other hand, if the parity had been high, as it actually was when Britain returned to the gold standard, then the domestic price level had to be brought down through a lowering of money wages. This too would have entailed a real wage cut;[6] and if successful in improving the current balance, it would also have invited retaliation. In other words, whether Britain adopted a floating rate as Keynes had suggested or a fixed rate as Pigou had suggested, along with a lowering of money wages and prices, there would necessarily have been a real wage cut. And it would have been ineffective to boot, as Britain's competitors would have retaliated if it showed signs of improving Britain's current balance.

Indeed, both the proponents and opponents of a return to the gold standard wanted a reduction in dollar terms of the British wage rate, which meant, in effect, a reduction in the real wage rate. However, while the proponents wanted it through a reduction in the money wage rate (their estimates of the requisite cut were small), the opponents wanted it through a reduction in the British exchange rate rather than through a reduction in British money wage rate. Among their arguments for doing so could be a belief in the "money illusion" on the part of the workers, that is, they would react sharply to a cut in money wages (which in fact they did), but not to a cut in real wages due to an exchange rate depreciation. Indeed, we have no means of knowing how they would have reacted to such a cut.

In short, how a cut in British real wages could be effected was the point of the debate, but a cut in real wages was not being opposed by any side. And a cut had become necessary because the British balance of payments were no longer sustainable, owing, *inter alia*, to the loss of colonial markets.

But whether Britain went back to the gold standard at the prewar parity, or at some other parity, or continued with a floating exchange rate, as suggested by Keynes, its balance of payments could not have been stabilized. Any improvement in its current balance, no matter how it was achieved, even if through a reduction in the domestic level of activity caused by the fall in real wages, would have meant a deterioration in the current balance of one or the other of its competitors. Such a deterioration in their current balance would necessarily have meant a fall in the level of activity in their economy, since government expenditure to sustain the level of activity had not yet come to be in vogue. In response to this, the competitors would have retaliated, either by lowering their own exchange rate if it had been floating earlier or by moving to a floating rate if they had been on the gold standard.

*The crucial advantage of the colonial markets had been that the colonies could not retaliate.* The colonies provided a sanctuary to which Britain could export as much as it liked to avoid any balance of payments difficulties, which in turn helped the entire capitalist world to run account surpluses vis-à-vis Britain. The loss of this sanctuary necessarily meant difficulties for Britain no matter what exchange rate regime it adopted, and no matter what parity it adopted in the event of returning to the gold standard.

Hence, the structural problems facing Britain owing to the collapse of the colonial arrangement that had sustained it earlier should not be reduced to a question of what the appropriate gold-pound-sterling parity was. Whatever the parity, Britain faced a problem.

This unsustainability of the prewar parity led to an attempt at wage deflation to make the exchange rate stick, which in turn resulted in the 1926 General Strike in Britain. The return to gold at prewar parity was the demand of the City, which wanted London to remain the financial center of the capitalist world. Crucial to its ambition was the need to ensure that the pound sterling was "as good as gold," namely that wealth-holders who put their trust in sterling would never have any cause to rue their decision, since sterling would never depreciate in value vis-à-vis gold (or other currencies under a gold standard arrangement). The unsustainability of the prewar parity owing to the unraveling of the colonial arrangement, which sharpened the conflict between British finance capital and the British working class, must not, however, mislead us into thinking that some other parity would have been sustainable.

The gold standard became unsustainable because the exhaustion of the colonial and semi-colonial markets meant that no "outside" space was available to which British goods could retreat. Now the different capitalist powers were locked in a zero-sum game where none of them could improve its current balance without someone else's current balance worsening.

The implications of capitalist powers getting locked in a zero-sum game were mentioned in passing by Keynes in *The General Theory*. Referring to the "economic causes of war, namely the pressure of population, and the competitive struggle for markets," he writes:

> It is the second factor that probably played a predominant part in the nineteenth century, and might again, that is germane to this discussion. . . . Under the system of domestic laissez-faire and international gold standard such as was orthodox in the latter half of the nineteenth century there was no means open to a government whereby to mitigate economic distress at home except through the competitive struggle for markets. For all measures helpful to a state of chronic or intermittent underemployment were ruled out, except measures to improve the balance of trade on income account.[7]

Keynes was wrong on his facts. There were no major wars in Europe between the Crimean War and the First World War, other than the wars for

German and Italian unification, and this was precisely because there were no competitive struggles for markets as the colonial and semi-colonial markets were available and "on tap." But with the exhaustion of colonial and semi-colonial markets, we get into the situation described by Keynes, and a competitive struggle for markets comes on the agenda. Britain was caught in this struggle in the interwar period and, no matter what instruments it used, it would have faced retaliation and been unsuccessful in overcoming its balance of payments difficulties.[8]

The unraveling of the colonial arrangement that sharpened the contradiction between British finance capital and the British working class has important theoretical implications. Colonialism, or more generally imperialism, has been widely seen as blunting the intensity of class conflict in advanced capitalist countries. This has always been explained, following Lenin, through the fact that the super-profits earned by monopoly capital are used to "bribe" a "labor aristocracy," a thin upper stratum of the working class (which includes trade union leaders).

Michal Kalecki's theory of distribution made possible a widening of the discussion from mere monopoly super-profits, which appear to be confined to only a certain segment of the capitalists, to the entire issue of the terms of trade between manufacturing and primary commodities. Since the manufacturing sector as a whole follows "markup" pricing, a rise in money wages can be "passed on" without any reduction in the capitalists' profit margins; it can cause a rise in real wages through the terms of trade between manufacturing and primary commodities being tilted against the latter. The functioning of the price system, in short, was such that a rise in workers' share in the gross value of output could be accommodated without a decline in capitalists' share through a squeeze on the share of the primary commodity producers. It is not some category of "super-profits" but the very *modus operandi* of the system that accommodates workers at the expense of primary commodity producers, and imperialism is the entire arrangement that makes this possible.

But whether we take the Leninist conception of "super-profits" being used to "bribe" a "labor aristocracy" or the notion derived from Kalecki of an arrangement where a rise in money wages gives rise to a higher wage share by turning the terms of trade against primary commodity producers, the role of imperialism in stabilizing capitalism through accommodating workers has been seen entirely in terms of its *distributive* implications. But as our discussion of the colonial arrangement shows, the role of imperialism in stabilizing the system by placating the working class has to be seen not in merely distributive terms but in more comprehensive terms, namely its implications for employment, growth, exchange rate, confidence in the leading currency, and so on. The return to gold at prewar parity did not per se mean any increase in capitalists' share or primary producers' share; nonetheless, it led to an attempt to reduce the workers' share. The colonial prop that contributes toward blunting working-class resistance consists, in other words, in much more than merely providing super-profits or enabling higher wages.

### Agricultural Crisis

Apart from the loss of Britain's Asian markets, another factor that undermined the colonial arrangement was the agricultural crisis that set in during the 1920s. The war years had raised agricultural prices; in the postwar period these prices kept declining, so that fixing a precise date for the onset of the agricultural crisis becomes difficult. But whatever the precise date, the agricultural crisis added further to Britain's balance of payments problems.

Britain, we have seen, had managed its balance of payments by using the export surplus of the colonies, which it appropriated gratis against arbitrarily-imposed items of expenditure that figured both in the colonial government's budget and on the debit side of the current account of the balance of payments of the colony (since they had to be spent abroad). But the export items of the colonies that yielded this surplus consisted mainly of primary commodities, especially agricultural goods. With the fall in agricultural prices, there was a fall in the export surplus of colonies, which was now not enough to meet Britain's balance of payments requirements.

This, to be sure, meant that the colonies had to borrow more in order to defray their drain-related expenditure, which in turn added to their future payment obligations. But this was of little assistance to the British balance of payments. Let us say that India has to pay 100 pounds to Britain on account of drain-related payments but has no export surplus with which to pay it. Then, India borrows 100 pounds and pays Britain. But if Britain has to settle its deficit with the United States, then it will ideally need either dollars or gold for this purpose. If it has neither, then there will be an excess supply of pounds and an excess demand for gold or dollars, which would threaten the pound sterling's exchange rate. Being on the gold standard where the currency is supposed to be convertible into gold, Britain will then have to adopt domestic recessionary policies to maintain its exchange rate.

Thus, both the loss of colonial markets and the world agricultural crisis made the earlier colonial arrangement untenable. Britain could no longer play its customary role as the leader of world capitalism. Its level of activity could not be sustained in the face of the growing balance of payments difficulties it faced. And this, in turn, affected the entire capitalist world. The Great Depression of the 1930s had its roots in this unraveling of the colonial arrangement.

One implication of the agricultural crisis, as we have just seen, was the inability of the colonies to meet their drain-related expenditures, and hence they got into debt. Soon, however, Britain demanded that they should repay their debt through gold. As a result, colonies like India had to ship gold to Britain. Put differently, the form of the drain, which could no longer be agricultural goods (exported to the newly-industrializing world but used to settle Britain's deficits with that world), now became gold, because of the sharp drop in the prices of such goods. This may have brought some relief to the British balance of payments, but it accentuated greatly the impact of the Great Depression on the colonial economies.

As we have seen, meeting the drain-related expenditures meant having a budget surplus that corresponded to the export surplus on the balance of payments of the colony. During the Great Depression, when there was a deficiency of aggregate demand, the need was to boost aggregate demand through a fiscal deficit. In the colonies, however, loan repayment at this very juncture meant an *increase* in the size of the fiscal surplus. This had the opposite effect to what was required, namely a contractionary effect on the colonial economy caught in the throes of the Great Depression.

This effect was over and above the effect of the price crash of agricultural goods. Since the drain-related expenditure was fixed in pounds sterling, it was also fixed in nominal terms in local currency at any given exchange rate. To meet this expenditure, adequate tax revenue had to be raised, which in the context of a fall in agricultural prices meant a larger effective tax burden on the peasantry. The large-scale indebtedness of the peasantry all over the third world during the Depression years was not just because of the shift in the terms of trade between manufacturing and primary products in favor of the former, but also because the cash payment obligations of the peasantry, including for tax payments, remained unchanged even as their money incomes fell because of the decline in agricultural prices. Loan repayment by government added to this.

The unraveling of the colonial arrangement, in short, had a destabilizing effect on world capitalism, which not only brought the long Victorian and Edwardian booms to an end but plunged the world economy into the Great Depression. We shall discuss this in the next chapter.

# CHAPTER 12

# A Perspective on the Great Depression

The Great Depression of the 1930s has been variously explained. But curiously, among these explanations the role of the unraveling of the colonial arrangement that had sustained the long boom of "the long nineteenth century" does not even figure. This is a lacuna we attempt to overcome in the present chapter.

## Alternative Explanations of the Depression

The number of explanations advanced for the Great Depression underscores as much the importance of the event in the history of capitalism as the richness of the theoretical attempts to capture its dynamics. Joseph Schumpeter had explained the Great Depression in terms of the fact that the troughs of all the three business cycles, the Kondratieff, the Juglar, and the Kitchin, had coincided. Alvin Hansen, a prominent economist in the Keynesian tradition, had seen it as the consequence of the "closing of the frontier." Nicholas Kaldor, another Keynesian, who had sought to theorize technological progress, had seen it as arising from a shift in the "technological progress function," that is, a drying up of the stream of innovations. Baran and Sweezy attributed the Great Depression to the emergence of monopoly capitalism, which brought with it a stagnationist tendency. And Charles Kindleberger saw in it a period of transition where Britain had lost its capacity to exercise the leadership role over the capitalist world, while the United States, which was to succeed Britain as the leader, was not yet ready to take on this role.

In addition to these, there is the monetarist explanation by Milton Friedman, which sees money supply changes as the underlying factor behind the Great Depression. But Friedman's explanation, already critiqued by Kindleberger, is not only based on a flawed theory (which is true of monetarism in all its versions), but also a flawed epistemology (which is specific to Friedman). So we shall not be concerned with it in what follows.

Taking the other explanations, no doubt there are elements of truth in most of them. An event like the Great Depression, which represents the breakdown of an entire order, and hence involves the simultaneous malfunctioning of several of the interrelated parts that constituted that order, permits, not implausibly, the identification of any one of those particular parts as the source that caused the breakdown of the whole. Our concern here is not with the question of which of these is the better explanation but whether they constitute, all taken together, an exhaustive account of the breakdown, or have missed some key element. Let us therefore look at these explanations, at least the prominent ones, from this perspective.

Even if one accepts Schumpeter's explanation as valid for understanding the depth of the crisis, it still leaves open the question of why the Depression lasted so long. As is well known, the liberal capitalist world, as distinct from the fascist countries, came out of it only with war preparations in the late 1930s.[1] The fascist countries had come out of it earlier because of arming themselves to perpetrate the war. To this question of why the Depression lasted so long, Schumpeter's answer was a political one, namely the hostility toward business that had surfaced during the 1930s, especially in the United States. This answer was challenged by Arthur Smithies many years ago, and we need not repeat his arguments here.[2]

There is, however, a theoretical problem with Schumpeter's explanation. The "circular flow," which represented the state of equilibrium in his analysis around which cyclical fluctuations occurred, was a Walrasian equilibrium with full employment. Even his cycles were primarily price cycles rather than employment cycles, as Oskar Lange pointed out in a review of his opus long ago.[3] Schumpeter, in short, did not recognize the possibility of a deficiency in aggregate demand. Thus, not only is there an empirical problem in explaining through his analysis the massive unemployment that was the hallmark of the Great Depression, but the theoretical premise of his overall argument is flawed, as the Kaleckian-Keynesian revolution in macroeconomics pointed out. Indeed, this latter tradition saw capitalism generally as a demand-constrained system.

From within the Keynesian tradition, Alvin Hansen's explanation of the Depression as arising from a closing of the frontier, which, according to him, dampened the investment drive that had long sustained a capitalist boom, is the most noteworthy. What we argued earlier, that the loss of colonial markets for British imperialism played a crucial role in precipitating the crisis, is in no way incompatible with the "closing of the frontier" argument.

The "colonial arrangement" included as part of the total picture the pushing of the frontier through emigration of labor from Europe to the temperate regions of new settlement and the complementary export of capital from Europe, financed by the drain from the tropical colonies. The unraveling of the colonial arrangement, owing to two factors, namely the loss of colonial markets and the world agricultural crisis causing a price crash for agricultural goods that made the colonial drain insufficient for balancing the British balance of payments, have already been discussed by us. The "closing of the frontier" emphasized by Hansen can be seen as the third component in the unraveling of the colonial arrangement.

But in view of the fact that the "closing of the frontier" argument is usually silent about the role of the colonies, a few further words on this role are in order. It may be thought that since Europe was exporting capital to the new regions of European settlement, and even using the surplus from the colonies for this purpose, it is the investment opportunity available in these regions that kept the system going. In short, the colonies were quite unimportant when it came to finding the stimulus for growth; this stimulus lay in the pushing of the frontier.

This, however, is a flawed conception. The goods demanded by the new regions of European settlement were *not* the goods produced by Britain, the leading capital exporter. Therefore, the stimulus for investment in

Britain came not from the demand from the new regions, because the new regions had little appetite for British goods. Likewise, if there was demand for tropical products in these new regions, and capital exports from Britain simply amounted to taking the credit for tropical goods that were exported, which were not goods of its own, then the need of a market for British goods cannot be said to have been solved by the pushing of the frontier. Thus Britain cannot be said to have sustained its own boom, upon which in turn the entire capitalist world depended because of their encroachment upon the British market, by the mere pushing of the frontier without any reference to colonialism.

Britain's markets, and hence investment stimulus, came from its ability to export at will to tropical colonies like India and semi-colonies like China. And since Britain provided a market to other capitalist countries, their investment stimulus was maintained through the penetration of the British market by their manufactured goods, so that they too indirectly derived their investment stimulus from encroachment on the tropical colonies. In other words, to focus on the closing of the frontier as *the* cause of the crisis is to miss the point, at least as far as Britain was concerned and hence all those countries benefitting from the availability of the British market; the real stimulus here came from colonialism. The United States had a merchandise trade surplus with the U.K., in 1928 of $610 million, as Hilkgerdt's estimates quoted in chapter 10 show, and Europe of $560 million; any loss of the U.K. market therefore would have caused a recessionary impact on the entire capitalist world. The loss of colonial markets thus started a process, as far as Britain was concerned, and, through its second-order effects on other countries, that led to the Great Depression.

But, of course, the closing of the frontier would have played an important role in precipitating a crisis in the U.S. economy, which in turn would also have had its own second-order effect on other countries, including Britain itself. We thus have a complex picture, where all three elements constituting the collapse of the colonial arrangement played a role. To emphasize the closing of the frontier alone as the cause of the crisis, without bringing in the entire colonial arrangement and its unraveling after the First World War into the picture, will simply not do.

### The Theory of Monopoly Capitalism

The transition to monopoly capitalism as the cause of the crisis, which Baran and Sweezy have theorized, is a powerful argument that needs a longer discussion. This explanation, which belongs to the Kaleckian tradition, figured prominently in the work of Josef Steindl, and Baran and Sweezy followed his lead.

One of the major arguments that they derived from Steindl was that innovations, which were always seen in the Keynesian and Kaleckian traditions as stimulating investment, did not do so under monopoly capitalism. This is because an oligopolistic firm, introducing, say, a new process, and *undertaking additional investment, in addition to what the overall growth of the market would have warranted anyway,* would have to find room for the additional products generated by such extra investment. And it would have to do so at the expense of its rivals. Snatching markets away from the rivals, however, is not easy under oligopolistic conditions, *even when these rivals have introduced no new processes*: any price cutting to sell more by the innovator might lead to a price war, to everyone's detriment. And any extra sales effort, which is also typically matched by such effort by rivals, can alter market shares, if at all, only over a prolonged period of time. Hence, in oligopolistic conditions, innovations only alter the *form* that investment, which would have occurred anyway, takes; they do not add to the *magnitude* of investment.

If this is one implication of the transition to monopoly capitalism, the other implication, which is equally profound, is that it entails a shift in income distribution from the workers, the petty producers, and the small capitalists (who tend to get squeezed out by the large oligopolistic firms) toward these oligopolistic firms. Since the propensity to consume (to use a Keynesian term) at the margin is greater for the losers from this income distribution shift than for the gainers, this, *ceteris paribus*, generates a tendency toward a shrinking of demand and hence overproduction. This tendency, of course, is *ex ante*, which can be kept in check if the level of investment, or of autonomous demand generally, increases for some other reason arising from the transition to monopoly capitalism. But as we have just discussed, precisely the opposite happens because of this transition, through a reduction in the effect of innovations upon the magnitude of investment.

The transition to monopoly capitalism, therefore, is associated with a tendency toward overproduction and hence stagnation. What is more, when monopoly capitalism comes into being, it is not just a once-and-for-all shift in income distribution in favor of the oligopolists that occurs at the moment of its genesis, but a continuous shift that characterizes it, a tendency toward "an increasing share of the economic surplus." Hence, this tendency toward stagnation is continuously strengthened.

What may keep this tendency from getting realized, according to them, that is, what may prevent the *ex ante* tendency toward overproduction from becoming *ex post* overproduction, is (other than state expenditure and sales effort) the emergence of "epoch-making innovations." Unlike the usual run of innovations, they argue, these innovations cause additional investment to be undertaken, whose product does not have to be accommodated at the expense of the rivals *through price cuts*. This is precisely because they are "epoch-making."

Automobiles constituted an "epoch-making" innovation at the beginning of the twentieth century and kept up aggregate demand despite the onset of monopoly capitalism. In other words, the boost to aggregate demand caused by the introduction and spread of automobiles kept at bay the stagnationist tendency that monopoly capitalism brings in its wake. But, with the end of the automobile boom and in the absence of any new stimulus such as what state expenditure was to provide after the Second World War, this stagnationist tendency, together with its second-order effects, asserted itself through the Great Depression.

Of course non-military state expenditure was increased during the New Deal, with the United States becoming the first country to adopt what one may call "Keynesian policies" independent of militarism. But the opposition of big business to state activism in "demand management" made the Roosevelt administration withdraw quickly from its activist stance. The recovery that the New Deal brought about was accordingly short-lived, and the United States plunged once more into a recession in 1937 owing to the withdrawal of the fiscal stimulus. Final recovery was only to come as the country prepared for the Second World War in response to the fascist threat.

Baran and Sweezy do not consider colonial markets as an exogenous stimulus of note, so that their discussion is limited to innovations and state expenditure as the only possible ways of overcoming *ex ante* overproduction. That they do not consider colonial markets as an exogenous stimulus is not because they are unaware of the historical significance of the colonies but because of a theoretical proposition they subscribe to, which derives from Kalecki but misses an important fact about colonialism. And this proposition goes as follows.

Consider the macroeconomic identity Y=C+I+G+X-M. Let C = C(Y); let G be a given magnitude and let $I_t = D_{t-1}$ where D refers to investment decisions. Investment decisions taken in the previous period, in other words, cause investment expenditure in the current period, so that the investment expenditure in the current period can be taken to be a given sum. The only way that aggregate demand can be raised in this case (except through larger government expenditure) is *through a larger export surplus, not larger exports as such*.

Colonial markets, it follows, would have played a role in boosting aggregate demand in the capitalist metropolis, only if *export surpluses* were made to such markets from the metropolis, a proposition explicitly advanced by Kalecki.[4] But because historically export surpluses from the metropolis to the colonies were nonexistent, and the direction of the export surplus was the very opposite of it, as we have seen, the role of colonial markets does not have much significance according to this reasoning.

But the role of colonial markets lay not in boosting aggregate demand in this general sense, but rather in providing an exogenous stimulus for investment. Investment expenditure, in other words, did not depend only upon the profit-rate or the rate of capacity utilization and the like, which had prevailed in the previous period (we say "previous period" because of Kalecki's assumption of a time lag between investment decisions and investment expenditure). It was directly stimulated by the availability of the colonial market that was "on tap," that is, *where sales were more or less guaranteed*. A metropolitan economy that had access to colonial markets could never fall into a state of simple reproduction, as Kalecki had argued that a capitalist economy would in the absence of stimuli arising from government expenditure and innovations.

Once we recognize that colonial markets play this role, that they are on a par with government expenditure in providing an exogenous stimulus (the role of innovations in providing an exogenous stimulus is less persuasive), then a stagnationist tendency can in principle be overcome through encroachments into the colonial market. And if it was not in the interwar period, because of which the Great Depression occurred, then the reason must lie in the unraveling of the colonial arrangement, which is what we have been arguing. The point is that the Baran-Sweezy argument, notwithstanding its obvious importance, has to be located within a larger picture relating to the metropolis-colony relationship.

### Leadership of the Capitalist World

Charles Kindleberger's *The World in Depression* is an impressively detailed and specific study, where he puts forward the idea that capitalism requires for its stable functioning a world leader, and the Great Depression happened because it was a period when the system lacked such a leader.[5] It was an expression of the fact that Britain, the declining power, was unable, and the United States, the newly emerging power, was unwilling to assume the role of a world leader. As he put it:

> ... the 1929 depression was so wide, so deep and so long because the international economic system was rendered unstable by British inability and United States unwillingness to assume responsibility for stabilising it in three particulars: (a) maintaining a relatively open market for distress goods; (b) providing counter-cyclical long-term lending; and (c) discounting in crisis.... The world economic system was unstable unless some country stabilised it, as Britain had done in the nineteenth century and up to 1913. In 1929, the British couldn't and the United States wouldn't. When every country turned to protect its national private interest, the world public interest went down the drain, and with it the private interests of all.[6]

Kindleberger's observations can scarcely be disputed, but they are incomplete. How can a leader keep its own markets open to others unless it has some mechanism whereby the entry of other countries' goods into its market does not entail an increase in its own domestic unemployment? And if it allows access to its market to other countries in order to alleviate their distress, then its indebtedness must increase. How can a leader afford to keep getting increasingly mired in debt? In short, the leadership role in the capitalist world can be exercised by a country not because it is benevolent or full of goodwill as Kindleberger's remarks may be misconstrued to mean, but because it has *power*. And this power must have at least two components: first, an ability to generate an "exogenous" market for its goods (from outside its own domestic capitalist economy proper) so that it does not sink into deeper Depression while trying to save other distressed economies; and second, it must have an ability to absorb other countries' goods, either without getting into greater debt itself, or with the capacity to withstand the burden of greater debt in case it does get into greater debt.

The leadership role, in other words, has to do with how a country is positioned within the world economy and of the balance of class forces within it. Britain could play this role at the time it did because colonialism allowed Britain to possess the requisite power for this role in both the senses mentioned above. Because of the existence of the colonial market "on tap" it could keep its own market open to the entry of goods from other metropolitan capitalist countries, without experiencing a net contraction of aggregate demand for its goods. Likewise, it could enlarge the purchasing power available to the newly industrializing countries through capital exports because it drained away the surplus of the colonies to finance such capital exports. Britain's leadership role was thus made possible because its colonial possessions gave it the power to play this role. And when the markets provided by colonies got exhausted or encroached upon, either by another newly emerging power, such as Japan, or by the emerging domestic bourgeoisies in the colonies themselves, Britain ceased to be able to play this role any longer.

The "unwillingness" of the United States likewise arose not only because it had no such extensive colonial possessions to give it a market "on tap" but also because the other possible source of external demand ("external" to the capitalist sector proper), namely state expenditure, could not be used. The "unwillingness" of the United States to play the leadership role of the capitalist world, in other words, really meant the U.S. state's inability to overcome the opposition of U.S. finance capital to larger state intervention for generating aggregate demand.

The New Deal intervention we saw was brief for this reason. Once there was some recovery under the New Deal, fiscal "rectitude" was once again asserted, which brought the economy back to a recession in 1937. Just prior to the rearmament effort for the war, while the consumption goods sector in the United States was working at a reasonable rate of capacity utilization, the investment goods sector was still experiencing massive unutilized capacity.

What appears at first sight as the world capitalist system's failure to make a transition from Britain to the United States as its leader turns out on closer inspection to be the *system's failure to make a transition from colonial markets as the external prop for its stability to state expenditure as the external prop.* To be sure, associated with any change in the external prop is an entire change in the characteristics of the system, including on the question of who plays the leadership role. But simply focusing on the absence of a leader without recognizing that the problem really was the absence, as yet, of an external prop to take the place of the colonial prop, is misleading.

## Finance Capital and State Intervention

U.S. finance capital, we suggested above, was opposed to U.S. state intervention for boosting aggregate demand. But it is not just U.S. finance capital; opposition to state intervention to boost aggregate demand is a common trait of finance capital, which is why when Keynes originally suggested "public works" financed by a fiscal deficit to alleviate unemployment in Britain in 1929, through a position articulated by Lloyd George, the leader of the Liberal Party to which he belonged, the British Treasury, under the influence of the City of London, had turned it down. And even after Keynes had written his *General Theory*, the opposition by British financial interests to his position contained in it continued. This is why his opus was less influential, including even in academic circles, in his own country than in the United States.

Why finance capital should be so systematically opposed to state intervention to enlarge aggregate demand remains an intriguing question. Before exploring it, however, we should clarify a preliminary point. Larger state expenditure that is financed through taxes on workers, though it would be acceptable to finance capital, would not obviously give rise to much net expansion in aggregate demand because the workers consume a substantial part of their incomes. This would amount, therefore, to a mere substitution of state demand for workers' demand, with little net increase in aggregate demand. A net increase can come about if larger state expenditure is financed either through a tax on the rich (who have a high propensity to save) or through a fiscal deficit, which means not taxing anyone.

Now, a tax on the rich to finance larger state expenditure does not make them any worse off than before the government embarked on such a program. Let us consider concretely a tax on profits and let us assume for simplicity that all wages and half of post-tax profits are consumed and the shares of wages and profits in total income are half and half. Then a government expenditure of $100 financed by a tax on profits will raise income by $200: the wage bill by $100 and pretax profits by $100. But since this increase in pretax profits will be taxed away, *post-tax profits and capitalists' wealth will be left exactly where they had been.* Employment and output would have increased without the capitalists, despite paying more taxes than before, being any worse off than before.

Even so, one can understand finance capital being opposed to larger taxes on the capitalists, and more generally upon the rich, despite their not being worse off through paying such larger taxes. But why should it be opposed to a larger fiscal deficit, which does not entail any larger tax payments by anyone and, on the contrary, *increases capitalists' post-tax profits and wealth?* In the above example, $100 of additional government expenditure financed by a fiscal deficit will raise income by $400, and profits by $200. Capitalists' consumption will rise by $100, and wealth (through larger savings held in the form of claims on the government) by $100. Why should finance capital be opposed to such spending financed by a larger fiscal deficit?

Keynes's answer to this question, which would be echoed by many economists even today, was that finance capital was unaware of the actual implications of a fiscal deficit. Its opposition to fiscal deficits was based on a wrong understanding. In fact, the theory of the multiplier, developed in Keynes's pupil Richard Kahn's original article on the subject, was an early attempt, even prior to the publication of the *General Theory*, to eliminate the basic misunderstanding upon which the opposition of the "Treasury View" in 1929, to the proposal to finance a program of public works through a fiscal deficit, was based.[7]

The opposition to fiscal deficits was based on the argument that government borrowing "crowds out" private investment, because there is a fixed pool of savings in the economy (leaving aside foreign borrowings and lendings) from which, if the government takes more, less is left for private investment. In such a case, the increase in employment caused by public works would be offset by the decrease in employment caused by the reduction in private investment, so that there would be little net expansion of employment.

The fallacy in this argument arose from the fact that savings, far from constituting a "fixed pool," depend upon income and would increase through an increase in income and employment. At any interest rate, therefore, a fiscal deficit would generate an exactly equal amount of excess private savings over private investment (in a closed economy) and thereby finance itself, through an expansion in income (and employment), without causing any crowding out. This proposition was just a corollary to investment (in a closed economy) generating an amount of savings exactly equal to itself at any interest rate, by causing a rise in income that is exactly such as to make this happen..

Keynes's presumption, however, turned out to be wrong. The opposition of finance capital to fiscal deficits, even in the midst of crises where a fiscal deficit will raise not just income and employment but the magnitude of profits as well, continues unabated. This is evident in that all over the world, with the exception of the United States, governments have adopted "fiscal responsibility" legislation limiting the magnitude of the fiscal deficit to 3 percent of the GDP, which is reminiscent of the "balanced budgets" earlier. So, instead of correct theory overcoming the hostility of finance to fiscal deficits, this hostility has trumped correct theory by bringing back the pre-Keynesian concept of the "crowding out" effect.

Michal Kalecki was closer to the mark when he suggested that the opposition of finance to fiscal deficits, or more generally to any direct state intervention through fiscal means for increasing the level of activity in the economy, arises because such intervention undermines the social power of capital, and with it, in particular, of that segment of capital which consists of finance, controlled by "functionless investors," to use Keynes's phrase.[8] It makes the level of activity in the economy independent of the "state of confidence" of the capitalists, and thereby strikes at the base of the social power of capital.

It opens the possibility for the question to be raised: If the state can directly increase investment, then why do we need capitalists? And once it does, then the next government may widen state intervention even further by encroaching on the domain of the capitalists. This fear of state intervention among the capitalists, however, does not arise under fascism because under fascism they have direct control over state power. Under fascism, as Kalecki put it, "there is no next government."

The matter may be put in a somewhat different way. Consider a slave system. Within the system, it is obvious that the slaves' interest lies in keeping the slave owner happy, for otherwise he is likely to whip the slaves. But if one looks at the system from "outside," then it is equally obvious that the slaves' interest lies in overthrowing the system. These two positions are what one may call positions of "epistemic interiority" and "epistemic exteriority." For slavery as a system to continue, it is important that epistemic exteriority must be prevented, that is, there must be an "epistemic closure." Indeed, all systems based on class antagonism require an epistemic closure in this sense for their survival and continuity, which includes capitalism as well.

Fiscal intervention by the government to raise employment directly breaks this "epistemic closure." This is felt spontaneously by capitalists, including above all the financiers, which is why they oppose such intervention (and why they are less averse to government intervention through monetary policy, since it operates, after all, through capitalists' investment decisions). Except in a period of great weakness of finance capital, when its hegemony is socially challenged and it is forced to make concessions, it strongly and successfully opposes direct state intervention in demand management, as it did in the 1930s.

## Concluding Observations

The Great Depression was a period when world capitalism was between external props. The prop of the colonial arrangement had gone, which is not to say that colonialism had become obsolete, but rather that there was no new prop, such as what direct state intervention in demand management could provide.

Indeed, colonialism and state intervention in demand management are the only two possible external props that capitalism can use. Schumpeter attributes to Keynes's *The Economic Consequences of the Peace* an understanding precisely of this kind (though of course neither Keynes nor Schumpeter mentioned colonialism), namely that the pre–First World War conditions under which capitalism had thrived had passed and that capitalism would now need a new basis for a boom, which could only be provided by the state. He then suggests that the intellectual agenda that was to be carried to completion in the *General Theory* had already been sketched out in *The Economic Consequences of the Peace*. Whether this reading of *The Economic Consequences of the Peace* is correct is beside the point; the fact of capitalism in the interwar period, having run out of props, without which it cannot grow, is undeniable.

That capitalism had run out of leaders, as Kindleberger suggests, was merely a manifestation of the more basic fact that it had run out of props. The Great Depression was so deep and prolonged because of this basic fact.

# CHAPTER 13

# Public Policy and the Great Famine in Bengal, 1943–44

As we have seen, the mechanism of the drain of wealth up to the Depression turned on Britain's appropriating every year India's entire global external earnings of gold and sterling from commodity export surplus, while using rupee budgetary revenues to recompense the producers for their net exports. The appropriation took place against regular administered invisible demands on India that were detailed both in sterling on India's external account and in rupees in the budget under "expenditure abroad." The total of these invisible demands, however, included non-recurring items as well, and thereby the total was always pitched higher than India's external earnings over a run of years, no matter how fast the latter might grow, so that the current account was kept in deficit. As India's external earnings declined sharply during the Depression, Britain's invisible demands, far from declining, rose further as it sought to moderate its own crisis at the colonies' expense. This produced exceptionally enlarged current account deficits for India from 1925–26 to 1938–39, and these forced substantial and unprecedented outflows of financial gold to Britain, in addition to India's incurring fresh debt to finance them.

The war years saw enhanced levels of extracting resources from India, but through an entirely different mechanism, that of a "profit inflation," whose theoretical and practical meanings we explore in this chapter. While it was taking India's global foreign exchange earnings, which had always been the object over the entire period of colonial rule, two factors now produced an altered situation. First, these earnings had declined with no prospect of recovering to earlier heights in a changed world slowly recovering from the Depression. Second, with the outbreak of war, Allied troops and air personnel poured into Eastern India, and the immensely enhanced war expenditure required for their operations was now charged directly to the Indian budget against a promise of repayment after the war ended, whenever that might be. In effect, a forced loan was taken from India, which was declared a combatant nation without consulting its people. Its people were also not consulted over the decision to put the burden of the Allies' war spending on the Indian budget.

There are several dimensions of this decision to make Indians bear the brunt of war financing that are not generally known. The first is the astonishing scale of financing in relation to the size of the normal budget—over the period 1939 to 1943, there was a nearly eight-fold expansion of budgetary expenditure. The second is the mechanism by which three-quarters of this expansion was effected, through deficit financing and monetizing the deficit, producing a much more rapid inflation than in other countries. The wholesale price index rose 70 percent in Britain over the war period, while it rose 300 percent in India as a whole, and to a greater extent in Eastern India. The great famine of 1943–44, in which three million civilians belonging to the poorest rural classes starved to death in Bengal, was a result of this exceptionally rapid food price inflation. The third is that these measures leading to rapid inflation were not accidental but quite deliberate, representing the policy of "profit inflation" for meeting the abnormal spending required in wartime, a policy that had been put forward at a theoretical level by John Maynard Keynes and was implemented in practice in India. The same policy of profit inflation had been proposed for Britain by Keynes, but it was not implemented, owing to strong opposition from the trade unions, and was substituted by enhanced progressive taxation. In view of his expertise on India, Keynes himself had been given special charge of Indian monetary affairs, in addition to his general advisory role, when he was appointed in 1940 as adviser (along with Lord Catto) to Britain's Chancellor of the Exchequer.

### Profit Inflation as a Means of Raising Resources

The policy of *profit inflation* was deliberately followed by the British and colonial governments with a specific purpose: to raise resources from the Indian population by curtailing mass consumption in order to finance the Allies' war in Asia with Japan. Keynesian demand-management policies are usually associated with raising employment and incomes, but Keynes also discussed the exact opposite, measures for curtailing mass incomes. He considered these necessary to raise resources for financing wartime spending in both *A Treatise on Money* referring to the First World War, and in *How to Pay for the War*, regarding the Second World War.[1]

Keynes had been closely associated with Indian affairs from an early period of his life. He served for two years in the India Office in London, leaving it when twenty-five years of age, and used the experience he gained there to publish *Indian Currency and Finance* five years later.[2] He gave evidence to, or was a member of, successive commissions set up to deliberate on Indian finance and currency: the Chamberlain, Babington-Smith, and Hilton Young commissions, and for a while the Indian Fiscal Commission. He wrote articles on India and reviewed books on the Indian economy for the *Economic Journal*, which he edited (such as T. Morison's *The Economic Transition in India* that discussed the drain of wealth). Keynes also lectured at Cambridge for many years on Indian monetary affairs.

In 1940, in view of the unusual financial situation arising from war, the British government appointed two economic advisers to the Chancellor of the Exchequer, an ex-banker, Lord Catto, and J. M. Keynes, with *Indian monetary matters specifically entrusted to Keynes given his expertise in the area*. Keynes was the most influential figure at the Bretton Woods Conference in 1944, where the repayment of sterling owed by Britain to India was discussed by him with the Indian delegation. Keynes's four-decades-long India connection, his interest in the Indian monetary system, and his part in policies followed in India during the Second World War have been neglected by his biographers, who appear to have had little interest in, or understanding of, the financial and monetary mechanisms underpinning colonial rule that concerned Keynes.

The term "profit inflation" was coined by Keynes to describe a situation where output prices rise faster than money wages because of an excess of demand over inelastic supplies. Profit inflation redistributes incomes from wages to profits and ensures substantial reductions in the consumption of wage-earners. It can be applied equally to a situation, where in addition to wage-earners, a large part of the working population comprises self-employed petty producers like artisans, fisher folk, and small peasants who have to buy food staples from the market since they produce either no food at all or not enough to meet their needs.

Profit inflation was a deliberate policy adopted in India for war financing. Without a deliberate policy of curtailing mass consumption, over £1,600 million of extra resources could not have been extracted from Indians during the war, with the bulk of this burden falling on the population of Bengal since Allied forces were located in and operated from that province. The state policy was to redistribute incomes away from the mass of the working population, toward capitalists and companies, by inducing a rapid profit inflation. The colonial state directly spent, in every war year after 1941, a multiple of its normal revenues by printing money, an extreme measure of profit inflation.

In *A Treatise on Money: The Applied Theory of Money*, referring to the First World War, Keynes had written:

> The war inevitably involved in all countries an immense diversion of resources to forms of production which, since they did not add to the volume of liquid consumption goods purchasable and consumable by income earners, had just the same effect as an increase in investment in fixed capital would have in ordinary times. The investment thus required was, especially after the initial period, on such a scale that it exceeded the maximum possible amount of voluntary saving which one could expect, even allowing for the cessation of most other kinds of investment including the replacement of wastage. *Thus forced transferences of purchasing power in some shape or form were a necessary condition of investment in the material of war on the desired scale.* The means of effecting this transference *with the minimum of social friction and disturbance* was the question for solution.[3]

He then went on to discuss the three different methods through which such "forced transferences of purchasing power" could be achieved: first, by reducing money wages while keeping prices steady; second, by letting prices rise more than money wages so as to reduce real wages; and third, by taxing earnings. Taking up the third course, he wrote that "the rich were too few," and therefore "the taxation would have had to be aimed directly at the relatively poor, since it was above all their consumption, in view of its aggregate magnitude, which had somehow or other to be reduced."[4] But the additional taxation of wage-earners would have to be substantial, it would meet trade union resistance, and it would be difficult for the government to implement.

"It was a choice, therefore, between the remaining alternatives—between lowering money wages and letting prices rise…. it would be natural—and sensible—to prefer the latter."[5] Keynes argued that it would be as difficult to enforce the required 25 percent money wage cut as to impose heavier taxes: *"I conclude therefore that to allow prices to rise by permitting a profit inflation, is in time of war, both inevitable and wise."*[6]

Keynes was positing money illusion on the part of workers; they would oppose money-wage cuts for given prices but they would not, to the same extent, oppose inflation without a matching money-wage increase, even though the second course lowered their real wages to exactly the same degree as the first. However, a profit inflation cutting real wages and raising profits would not by itself serve fully the aim of financing war spending, if all profits were retained by capitalists; taxation of profits was essential:

It is expedient to use entrepreneurs as collecting agents. But let them be agents and not principals. Having adopted for quite good reasons a policy which pours the booty into their laps, let us be sure that they hand it over as taxes and that they are not able to obtain a claim over the future income of the community by being allowed to "lend" to the State what has thus accrued to them. *To let prices rise relatively to earnings and then tax entrepreneurs to the utmost is the right procedure for "virtuous" war finance.* For high taxation of profits and of incomes above the exemption limit is not a substitute for profit inflation but an adjunct of it.[7]

Keynes's reasoning is clear. There had to be a substantial decline in the real consumption of the ordinary mass of the population, and this could best be achieved without working-class political opposition, not through additional taxation, but by a profit inflation, by following policies that raised output prices without raising wage incomes at all, or to the same extent. This would redistribute incomes away from wages to profits, which should then be taxed.

Keynes's views on raising resources for war spending in Britain were amplified in newspaper articles in 1939 and 1940 and in *How to Pay for the War*, where he repeated the necessity of reducing mass consumption through an engineered inflation and also discussed the methods of taxation and deferred payments.[8] As an influential adviser both to the British Chancellor of the Exchequer and to the Prime Minister, in view of his long association with Indian fiancial affairs, Keynes "had special authority in discussion of Indian financial questions." [9] And this is how he came to implement his ideas on profit inflation as the means of raising finance to serve the Allies' military spending in India.

## War Financing through Profit Inflation in India

India's export earnings recovered slowly from the mid-1930s as the developed world, especially the United States, started following expansionary policies. Total budget spending from 1937–38 to 1939–40 averaged Rs.888 million, while the average annual deficit was only Rs.13.3 million. (With the exchange rate averaging about Rs13.5 to £1, the initial budget size was about £66 million.) During 1939–40, gold worth Rs.347 million was transferred from India to London, and the Reserve Bank of India (RBI) was credited with equivalent blocked sterling marking, in effect a forced loan.

After December 1941, when the United States entered the war against Japan, Allied forces poured into Bengal, and war spending grew by leaps and bounds. The category "recoverable expenditure" had been created under an agreement signed by the colonial government with Britain, specifying that the major costs of provisioning and operating Allied forces in India would be met through Indian resources until the end of the war. It represented a forced loan from India to Britain of unspecified value. The Reserve Bank of India would be credited with the sterling equivalent of the rupees spent by the government. However, the account would be frozen, no sterling would be made available for actual spending, and the account would be activated only at the end of the war, whenever that might be. The remaining war spending was to be borne entirely by India. It was the "recoverable war expenditures" that became a death warrant for three million persons in Bengal.

The movement of Allied troops and air forces into Eastern India grew rapidly from early 1942; construction of airstrips, barracks, and war-related industries was undertaken at a feverish pace. Private investment and output grew fast for munitions, chemicals, uniforms, bandages, and the like. The troops and supporting personnel had to be fed, clothed, and transported at public expense. A war boom of unprecedented proportions resulted as total spending by the central government exploded to reach Rs.667 crore by fiscal 1942–43, or *a 7.5-fold increase in expenditure over the Rs.88.8 crore annual average for the triennium 1937–40, merely three years after the end of the triennium* (see Table 13.1). Increased taxation had only doubled the revenues by 1942–43, and the government's deficit on its own account had ballooned from near zero to Rs.112.2 crore in 1942–3. However, over the same period a more than four times larger sum was additionally spent every year under "recoverable expenditure" for the Allied forces, comprising additional deficit financing and amounting to 2.2 times the normal pre-1940–41 annual budget. The total deficit summed over the three years from 1940–41 to 1942–43 reached Rs.704 crore, or Rs.235 crore annual average (see Table 13.1). Eighty-one percent of the total deficit was on account of the "recoverable war expenditures" undertaken for the Allied forces, while nineteen percent was on account of the central government's own spending.

This exploding deficit was entirely met by printing money, which was justified by treating Britain's sterling-denominated entries with the Reserve Bank of India as assets. That this was not only specious but disingenuous reasoning is clear enough. Assets or "reserves," as the term itself indicates, are meant to be actually there to be drawn upon in case of need, while these sterling reserves were a paper fiction; they did not actually

**TABLE 13.1: Central Government Total Outlay, Revenues and Deficits 1937–1946 in Rupees Crore (one crore = 10 million)**

| Year | [1] Total Gov't Outlay (4 + 6) | [2] Percent 3 to 1 | [3] Revenue | [4] Expenditure | [5] Budget Deficit (3 – 4) | [6] Recoverable Expenditure (Deficit) | [7] Total Deficit (5 + 6) | [8] Merchandise Surplus |
|---|---|---|---|---|---|---|---|---|
| 1937–38 | 86.61 | 100 | 86.61 | 86.61 | 0 | 0 | 0 | 43.0 |
| 1938–39 | 85.15 | 99.3 | 84.52 | 85.16 | –0.63 | 0 | –0.63 | 78.0 |
| 1939–40 | 98.57 | 95.9 | 94.57 | 94.57 | 0 | –4.00 | –4.00 | 80.0 |
| 1940–41 | 167.18 | 64.4 | 107.65 | 114.18 | –6.53 | –53.00 | –59.53 | 53.6 |
| 1941–42 | 341.26 | 39.4 | 134.57 | 147.26 | –12.69 | –194.00 | –206.69 | 80.1 |
| 1942–43 | 667.04 | 26.5 | 176.88 | 289.05 | –112.17 | –325.48 | –437.65 | 86.7 |
| 1943–44 | 857.17 | 29.4 | 252.00 | 441.85 | –189.78 | –377.87 | –567.65 | 96.3 |
| 1944–45 | 970.38 | 34.6 | 335.57 | 496.71 | –161.14 | –410.84 | –571.98 | 28.0 |
| 1945–46 | 894.20 | 40.3 | 360.67 | 484.57 | –123.90 | –374.54 | –498.44 | 27.0 |
| TOTAL | 4,167.56 | 39.2 | 1,633.04 | 2,239.96 | –606.84 | 1,739.73 | –2,346.60 | 572.70 |

Source: *Report on Currency and Finance 1946-47*, (Bombay: Reserve Bank of india, 1947), Table 15.[10]

exist since not a penny could be drawn. Nor was there any certainty of their being paid out in future, as promised, after the war ended. The non-existent, so-called reserves were an accounting device for extracting massive resources from the Indian people.

During the Depression years, administrators trained in classical theories of sound finance and balanced budgets had actually cut domestic spending as revenues had fallen, thus intensifying the adverse effects of depression. Such conservative officials in India did not decide on the opposite course of monetizing massive deficits every year amounting to a multiple of the entire normal budget. Indian monetary policy was now being directed solely from London, and all caution was thrown to the winds to serve metropolitan interests at the expense of the Indian people. The Reserve Bank of India, set up in 1935, served as a pliant tool and implemented the fiction that mere paper entries of sterling sums were the same as actual reserves. Corresponding to the suddenly expanding level of wartime activity, it expanded the money supply nearly sevenfold (Table 13.2).

The reckless deficit spending undertaken for the Allies grew fastest between 1940–41 and 1942–43. The 1940–41 outlay was already 69 percent higher than the previous year; the next year, it more than doubled, and nearly doubled again the following year. Over two years government outlays expanded at 98 percent per annum (Table 13.1). By 1942–43, total outlays reached a level equaling 35 percent of the initial, 1939–40, national income of British India, and they reached 51 percent of it as outlays peaked at Rs.970 crore in 1944–45.[11] Keynes cautioned against excessive spending, but solely in the interest of limiting Britain's postwar indebtedness. He showed no interest in the extent of adverse impact on the Indian population—after all, the whole point was precisely to reduce their consumption.

The unprecedented explosion of public expenditure, combined with the private investment boom generated, through multiplier effects that were strong for a poor population, a sudden and immensely increased demand for food, clothing, and other necessities on the part of the rising numbers employed in the war industries, in addition to the demands of the Allied personnel. While multiplier effects that raise demand call forth

**Figure 13.1: Central Government Total Outlays, Revenues and Deficits, 1938–39 to 1945–46, in Rs. Crore (one crore = 10 million)**

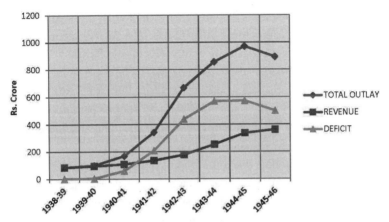

Source: Table 13.1.

increased output, where most of the demand was for primary products and expanded with such rapidity in a matter of months, the adjustment was bound to be through rise in prices rather than output increase. Agricultural output could not possibly grow fast, and in Bengal rice output had been in absolute decline for three decades owing to land and resource diversion to export crops. Nowhere in the world were such irresponsible monetary policies followed during the war as in India, and arguably nowhere else was inflation as rapid.

The personnel required for producing essential materials and war goods were protected from price rise to a large extent through a system of food procurement and rationing which was rapidly put in place by the government.[12] The urban population in one way or another had access to food, though it did have to take large cuts in real consumption. The burden of financing the mountainous extra public outlays was passed on to the unprotected mass of the rural population, which was severely affected, other than a small minority of landlords and moneylenders who benefited by foreclosing on the mortgaged assets of the majority struggling to survive.

Most of the government provisioning for the troops, supporting personnel, and the new urban public distribution system was sourced from the surrounding hinterland of the towns in Bengal. Prices of all necessities started rising: the price of rice per maund (a maund equalled 82 lbs) in Calcutta quadrupled from Rs 6 in January 1942 to Rs 24 in April 1943 and nearly doubled again to Rs. 40 by October the same year. Small towns saw the price per maund rising to between Rs 60 and Rs.100.[13] For comparison, in 1940 the per capita income was Rs.5.33 per month. While prices trebled in India as a whole by 1943 (see Table 13.2), the inflation was much sharper and compressed within a shorter period in Bengal where the bulk of the increased government spending and sourcing of food from rural areas actually took place.

Not an iota of sterling due to India as recoverable war expenditure was made available for food imports. India had again developed a merchandise export surplus, which, had it been a free country, could have paid for food imports. But these earnings continued to be entirely appropriated by Britain: from 1939–40 to 1943–44 India's merchandise export surplus totaled Rs. 397 crore or about £290 million (Table 13.1) and a sum in excess of this was paid by the RBI to Britain as "debt repayment."[14]

As rice prices doubled, quadrupled, and rose sixfold, the laborers, artisans, fisherfolk, and poor peasantry in Bengal did not know what had hit them. Food stocks physically disappeared, as the government bought up available supplies through contractors for urban distribution and as traders held on to stocks anticipating further price rises. Many thousands of rural families, already at the margin of subsistence, sank first into dearth, then into hunger, followed by starvation and finally by death. Many of those who survived and migrated in search of food to the cities, in their weakened state, succumbed to disease. The final death toll during 1943–44 has been placed conservatively, after reviewing the evidence, at between 2.7 to 3.1 million by A. K. Sen,[15] while some authors writing at that time cite up to 3.5 million, taking into account secondary effects of higher morbidity. The sample survey carried out by Mahalanobis, Mukherjee, and Ghosh from the Indian Statistical Institute, on the after-effects of the famine, found that among the survivors, half a million families had been reduced to utter destitution.[16]

**TABLE 13.2: Index of Money Supply,  Wholesale Price Index, and Total Deficit, 1940–1946**

| Year | Index of Money Supply | Wholesale Price Index | Total Deficit (Rs. Crore) |
|------|----------------------|----------------------|---------------------------|
| 1940 | 100.0 | 100 | 4.00 |
| 1941 | 126.5 | 141 | 59.53 |
| 1942 | 215.1 | 187 | 206.69 |
| 1943 | 357.7 | 311 | 437.65 |
| 1944 | 486.5 | 302 | 567.65 |
| 1945 | 607.3 | 292 | 571.98 |
| 1946 | 686.8 | 328 | 498.44 |

Source: *Report on Currency and Finance 1946–47* and *1947–48* (Bombay: Reserve Bank of India, 1948).

British rule in India had started with the massive famine in Bengal in 1770, which decimated 10 million people or one-third of the population of the province, the rapacity of the East India Company in trebling taxes over five years being a major reason for the high toll. British rule in India ended with a massive famine, yet again in Bengal, which was made to bear the brunt of resource extraction for the war.

Amartya K. Sen, in *Poverty and Famines*, had rightly concluded: "The 1943 famine can indeed be described as a 'boom famine' related to powerful inflationary pressures initiated by public expenditure expansion" and had traced "failure of exchange entitlements" to such inflationary pressures.[17] Utsa Patnaik had earlier identified the famine as the result of an engineered profit inflation as described by Keynes in his *Treatise on Money* but did not know then that Keynes was personally charged with advising on Indian monetary matters from 1940, this information becoming available in A. Chandavarkar's *Keynes and India*.[18] The digitization of the Reserve Bank of India records has made it easier to access the detailed data presented in Table 13.1,[19] and the publication of a definitive study of India's national income has enabled us to relate deficit financing to GDP.[20]

Even though deficit financing continued at a high level until 1946, prices ceased to rise after 1943 (see Table 13.2). This was owing to the severe compression of mass demand throughout the country and the three million excess deaths, which together outweighed the continued increase in demand from organized labor employed in war-related activities, whose wages were indexed, however inadequately, to inflation. In an advanced country with unionized labor and wage indexation, a wage-price spiral would have taken place, and the inflation might have acclererated. But in India, even at its height, the organized labor force, at one million. was very small relative to total labor force; and the mass of unorganized labor, along with petty producers, simply suffered absolute immiserization.

Profit inflation saw its inception when the colonial government agreed to meet Allied war spending to an unlimited extent from the Indian budget, incurred deficits each war year to the tune of a multiple of the entire prewar budget, and monetized the deficits, printing money using the fiction that mere paper entries of sterling sums owed could be treated at par with actual reserves. The resulting inflationary war boom meant that the enormous excess of government deficit plus private investment over voluntary savings was brought to equality through the *forced savings* entailed in the inflation. The real income decline was so inequitably concentrated on the poorest and most vulnerable segments of the population, and the inflation was so rapid that it physically eliminated millions through starvation.

Utsa Patnaik wrote over a quarter-century ago: "Such a savage and rapid compression of the real income and consumption of the most vulnerable sections of a population as a direct result of financing expenditures far in excess of voluntary savings can find few parallels in the modern world."[21] Bengal's population was especially vulnerable because its per capita absorption of foodgrains had fallen to the largest extent, by 38 percent in the interwar period, compared to 29 percent average for British India.[22] During this period there was absolute decline in rice output in Bengal while exported commercial crops continued to grow.

The civilian mortality alone during the two years of famine in Bengal was over six times the total war-related deaths of armed forces personnel and civilians, estimated at less than half a million, in Britain during the entire war period. The age structure of the population in India shows that 37 percent comprised children, defined as those aged fourteen years and less. Even if we assume that child death count in total famine mortality was a lower proportion than this, at least twice as many children died from starvation during the two years, compared to the below half a million total war-related deaths in Britain over the entire war period.

While no previous author to our knowledge has linked Keynes directly to the great famine in Bengal, after putting together all the facts we have cited, there is no doubt that Keynes himself, charged with advising on Indian monetary policy, was fully aware of and directly involved in Indian fiscal and monetary developments during the war. The profit inflation resulted in forced consumption decline, hence forced savings of such a drastic magnitude that it killed three million people through starvation. Wholesale prices rose by 70 percent in England comparing 1944 to 1935, while the rise was over 300 percent in India as a whole and even higher in Bengal.[23] Keynes's advice that after "pouring the booty" into the laps of capitalists they should be taxed, was also implemented faithfully. Direct taxes in India, including the corporation tax, rose more than tenfold, and their share in total tax revenues rose from below one-quarter to seven-tenths (see Table 13.3); this, however, contributed a negligible share, below 7 percent of total additional expenditure, which relied on massive deficit financing.

**TABLE 13.3: Total Tax Revenue and Income Tax (in Rupees Crore), and Percentage Share of Income Tax in Total Taxes, 1938–1945 (one Crore = 10 million)**

| PERIOD | [A] Total Tax Revenue | [B] Income Tax | [A] / [B] Income Tax/ Total (%) | Index Total Tax Revenue | Index Income Tax Revenue |
|---|---|---|---|---|---|
| 1938–39 | 73.8 | 17.3 | 23.4 | 100 | 100 |
| 1939–40 | 81.9 | 19.4 | 23.7 | 111 | 112 |
| 1940–41 | 79.7 | 25.9 | 32.5 | 108 | 150 |
| 1941–42 | 103.3 | 44.1 | 42.7 | 140 | 255 |
| 1942–43 | 134.5 | 85.8 | 63.8 | 182 | 496 |
| 1943–44 | 199.2 | 138.0 | 69.3 | 270 | 798 |
| 1944–45 | 261.1 | 182.6 | 69.9 | 354 | 1055 |
| (Budget) Total | 933.5 | 513.1 | 55.0 | | |

Source: P. S. Lokanathan (1946), 38.

*Contrasting Keynesian Wartime Policies in India and in Britain*

In articles published in British newspapers in late 1939, and in *How to Pay for the War*, Keynes repeated his earlier observations on the absolute necessity of reducing mass consumption in Britain. However, his initial proposals of raising resources through profit inflation and compulsory savings met with a reception from the trade unions that was "frosty" according to Keynes biographer Robert Skidelsky. Labor leaders, especially Aneurin Bevan, certainly did not suffer from money illusion and strongly opposed inflation as a means of war finance. Facing strong trade union opposition, Keynes was obliged to give up profit inflation and advocate additional taxes to control *ex ante* demand. Keynes was not in favor of rationing of essentials even in wartime, and his views on this coincided with those of right-wing economist F. von Hayek, who commended Keynes's position. Wiser counsel from other members of government prevailed and rationing of all essential commodities was introduced. In order to ensure working class support, not only was the socially divisive and highly regressive measure of inflation given up as an explicit method of war financing by Keynes, but he reformulated "compulsory savings" as the better-sounding "deferred incomes." Additional taxation of £250 million was considered enough in the 1941 budget to cover the inflationary gap.[24]

Keynes worked out a preliminary estimate of national income for Britain and a detailed plan to distribute the proposed increased tax burden equitably over its population. He estimated Britain's net national income, at market prices, at £6229 million in 1940.[25] Families earning below £5 per week were to be exempt, while graded taxation was to be imposed on higher income groups. Given a total population of 47.5 million, this meant a per capita annual income of £131.14, while in India in 1940 per capita income was Rs.64 (or £4.27).[26] The average income of the Briton was 31 times that of the Indian, and the additional taxes in Britain's 1941 budget amounted to £5.26 per capita, or 4 percent of average income. The monetized deficit financing per capita in British India in 1942–43, however, amounted to 20 percent of the Indian's per capita income.

Keynes's idea of *deferred income* was precisely what was entailed in the agreement signed by the British government with the colonial state, which put the onus of footing the war bill on India, with a mere undertaking to repay after the end of the war, except that the deferred income was to apply to an entire people, not particular classes that could afford to pay. The amount was astronomical relative to paying capacity; the method used was deliberate rapid inflation, highly regressive in hurting most the already poor among the peasantry and all rural net food purchasers; and there was no specific deadline by which repayment would take place, if at all. India was Britain's largest creditor: its sterling debt to Egypt was far smaller.

As far back as 1867, a noted administrator in India, W. W. Hunter, had identified the classes in Bengal that were entirely dependent on purchasing food from the market and were therefore the most vulnerable in the event of food price inflation. These classes comprised laborers, artisans, and fishermen. In his remarkable little book titled *A Famine Warning System for Bengal,* Hunter had given the estimated numbers belonging to these classes for the different districts of Bengal Province, the prevailing price of rice, and the extent of rise in this price that should serve as a warning trigger for government to intervene to prevent a famine arising from further inflation.[27] Hunter's book is significant in showing that administrators did not think of famine as arising from decline in food availability alone, as in a drought, but clearly specified what A. K. Sen was later to term "failure of exchange entitlements" of net food purchasers as a cause of famine, and advocated a warning system to prevent inflation beyond a point deemed to be safe.[28]

Exactly the opposite policy was followed during wartime, and the measures to promote rapid inflation detailed so far were quite deliberate: administrators were not so obtuse as to be unaware of the adverse impact of inflation on the population, a much higher fraction of which had become pauperized and landless after the Depression years and was more vulnerable than ever before. As the actual deaths mounted, the thrust of policy continued to be to suck food grains away from the famished rural population, and available food supplies with Britain were directed not to India but to other countries in Europe.[29] The rulers cared little for what today would be termed "collateral damage," of deaths from rapid inflation and its impact on production, since it was clear to them that the days of British rule, and hence of tax collection in India, were numbered.

Was there an economic alternative to the imposition of the enormous burden of war financing on India and the resultant extinguishing of 3 million lives? Indeed, there was. The total deficit of Rs.606 crore between 1940–41 and 1945–46 (see column 5 of Table 13.1), arising from the government of India's own excess budgetary spending, and the inflation this entailed, was absorbable through reduced consumption by the population. It was the additional war expenditure imposed on India from 1940–41 onward, the "recoverable expenditure," entailing forced savings nearly three times higher and totalling Rs.1740 crore by 1945–46, that led to the extreme compression of rural consumption in Bengal and claimed three million lives. This was an impossible sum demanded of a people already overtaxed, drained for two centuries of exchange earnings, and pushed into under-nutrition. But it would not have been an impossible sum for the metropolitan population, which had a per capita income thirty times that of the Indian population. The sum of Rs.1740 crore or £1276 million spent from 1940–41 to 1945–46 could have been raised by additional annual taxation in Britain of £4.5 per capita, and if the United States had also chipped in, then the per capita burden of this expenditure on the combined population of the two countries would have been only £1. Along with this, crediting India with its own external earnings from the world, which instead were entirely appropriated by Britain, even as famine raged, would have been the more humane solution.

At Bretton Woods, 1944 and later, Britain argued for cancelling part of its debt and for postponing repayment of the rest beyond the end of the war, citing lack of capacity to pay. According to Skidelsky, the intention Keynes expressed from the beginning was to get at least one-third of Britain's total sterling debt to other countries written off and another one-third paid in future installments. Keynes took a strong position against that of the Indian delegation and scuttled its request for partial trilateral convertibility involving the United States, which could have made some dollar funds available immediately to India for badly needed food imports, since only the United States had goods to export. Keynes insisted that it was a bilateral matter between India and Britain, even though India had financed Allied forces, not Britain's alone. The Indian delegation, including its British finance member, pressed Britain to honor its commitment of repaying sterling debt, citing the extreme suffering the population had gone through. The illogical response was that the suffering was in the past. It was even suggested by a member of the British delegation that writing off sterling debt be made a condition for Indian independence, but this was not supported, fortunately, by Keynes.[30]

On the issue of sterling balances, the creditor nation, India, was in a weaker position than the debtor imperialist country that, using its political position, had unilaterally taken a forced loan of gargantuan proportions and when the time came for repayment, was implacable in trying to reduce its obligation drastically. With not a penny of sterling funds owed to India released, and with India's own wartime earnings from export surplus entirely taken over by Britain, very little food imports could take place: by 1946, per capita grain availability had dropped further to 137 kg. in India. By April 1946, Keynes was prematurely dead from a long-standing heart problem. The policies that followed in India to raise wartime resources were thus in sharp contrast to those followed in Britain. An equitably distributed tax burden over classes at different levels of income was worked out, while part of extra taxes were to be repaid after the war ended. But no such considerations existed when it came to a colonized population with one-thirtieth of the per head income of the Briton.

Sterling balances owed to India under interim agreements were divided into two accounts in 1947, the first containing only £65 million that could be spent, while the second was frozen. In 1948, the balances in the two accounts were £80.6 million and £1,033.2 million respectively; the 30 percent sterling devaluation against the dollar in 1949 greatly reduced purchasing capacity of both balances, even as the second remained frozen until the 1950s, a decade after the famine, when the inflation caused by the Korean War had reduced real values further. Whatever was paid up was divided between India and Pakistan in proportion to their populations. India's share of the depleted sterling balances helped it to launch the ambitious Second Five-Year Plan for development by providing a buffer against balance of payments worries for two to three years. The small fraction of sterling balances that Pakistan received is not likely to have been spent for the benefit of its eastern region, which later became Bangladesh, from where the majority of the famine victims had hailed. Even in this very limited sense, no compensation was received for the enforced sacrifice of millions of lives.

The policies followed were of demand management, which are always opaque to the general population, and remain opaque to this day, even to the educated elite. The extreme compression of mass demand to raise forced savings that led to three million civilian deaths could be successfully camouflaged as a simple famine and continue to be attributed fallaciously to natural phenomena like cyclone, or to food shortage, or to speculation and hoarding, or to not importing food in time, or a combination of these factors.

# PART 4

# CHAPTER 14

# Postwar Dirigisme and Its Contradictions

Capitalism emerged from the war facing a serious threat to its survival. The socialist bloc had expanded greatly through the Red Army's march across Eastern Europe; and though the left lost the Greek civil war, partly no doubt as a consequence of the Yalta agreement that prevented adequate Soviet support for the revolution, a "Soviet threat" nonetheless loomed large over Western Europe, where in any case the Soviet Union enjoyed much goodwill because of its epic struggle against Nazi Germany. The working class in Western Europe, which had made enormous sacrifices during the war, was determined not to go back to the prewar years of Depression and unemployment. An expression of this determination was the defeat of the Winston Churchill–led Conservative Party in the postwar British elections.

It was also clear that the old imperialist powers of Europe could no longer hold on to their colonial possessions in the face of the postwar upsurge of national liberation struggles. Many of these struggles were led by the Communists, but whether they were or not, they almost invariably enjoyed the support of the Soviet Union.

## The Restructuring of Capitalism

Capitalism's response to this threat to its survival was twofold. One was to start the cold war against the Soviet Union; the other was to restructure itself in several ways, as a means of rolling back the socialist challenge, by making concessions that it otherwise would have recoiled from. There were at least three major spheres where such concessions were made.

The *first concession* was the institution of electoral democracy based on universal adult suffrage, which, even in France, the country of the classic bourgeois revolution, occurred only in 1945. Many believe these days that electoral democracy with universal adult suffrage is a "natural" accompaniment of capitalism. This, however, is untrue; its realization occurred predominantly in the postwar years and only after long years of struggle. (Even in Britain, women had got the vote only in 1928, and still some property-based restrictions on suffrage had remained.)

The *second concession* made by capitalism was political decolonization. In East and South East Asia where the United States had become the preeminent power after the defeat of Japan, it sought to place itself in the position occupied earlier by the old colonial powers and thereby prolong imperial occupation. But this policy, which had disastrous consequences in Korea and Vietnam, could not succeed; the process of political decolonization could not be halted, though in many instances, such as West Africa, it still remains incomplete in crucial ways to this day, as French troops continue to remain stationed there.

Yet more important and contentious than political decolonization was the process of economic decolonization, that is, former colonies' acquiring control over their own natural resources, which metropolitan capital had seized during the colonial era. Economic decolonization was bitterly fought by the metropolitan powers, with coups against third world leaders, like Mossadegh in Iran and Arbenz in Guatemala, who dared to nationalize their country's resources. There was a full-fledged invasion of Egypt by a joint Anglo-French force when Nasser nationalized the Suez Canal. The Soviet Union's role was particularly important in making economic decolonization possible. Toward this end it helped to build up the public sector in many third world countries for developing and processing their natural resources, the control over which was snatched back from metropolitan capital.

The *third concession* that capitalism had to make was the institution of state intervention in demand management, as had been advocated by

Keynesianism. State intervention through monetary policy had always been there, as was the use of the fiscal instrument for stimulating demand *by inducing capitalists to spend more.* What Keynesianism had advocated, however, went further, namely the direct intervention by the state, *through its own spending,* to maintain aggregate demand close to full employment output. This got instituted in the postwar period.

It may appear odd at first sight to call the maintenance of a high level of aggregate demand through state intervention in this manner, which keeps up employment, output *and profits,* a concession on the part of capital. It represents after all a "Pareto-improvement" compared to a state of large-scale involuntary unemployment, in the sense that nobody is worse off through such improvement, while some, if not all, are better off, which includes the profit-earners. Then why should capitalists object to such intervention in the first place?

Even capitalists, in other words, benefit from an increase in state expenditure that is meant to increase aggregate demand, by getting larger profits. If the increase in state expenditure is financed by a fiscal deficit, then the rise in profits caused by it is obvious. But even if the increase in state expenditure is financed entirely through taxes on profits, there need not be a fall in post-tax profits compared to the initial situation if the workers consume their entire income. In this case, moreover, since capacity utilization improves, so does private investment over time, and hence profits. Why, then, should capitalists object to state intervention in demand management through fiscal means, that is, through enlarged state expenditure?

The opposition of capitalists to state intervention through fiscal means for raising employment, certainly as long as unemployment remains greater than the "inflationary barrier," appears at first sight to be inexplicable. And yet, there can be little doubt about the reality of such opposition, which has manifested itself time and again. There was the opposition to Lloyd George's 1929 plan of fiscal-deficit-funded state-run public works for overcoming mass unemployment, which predated the "Keynesian Revolution." And in the 1930s, when Roosevelt's New Deal had started a recovery in the United States, it was soon abandoned under the pressure of financial interests precisely because of its success, plunging that country once again into a recession in 1937.

In chapter 12, we argued that this opposition is not of an economic but of an epistemic character. Direct state intervention in demand management, which bypasses the capitalists, undermines the social legitimacy of the system. The capitalists' class instinct therefore tells them to oppose such intervention, to project an intellectual position that helps to enforce an "epistemic closure," where there is no scope for looking beyond the capitalists to generate a recovery. This way, there is no chink left for questioning the social legitimacy of the system.

In the immediate postwar period capitalism, faced with a threat to its survival, had little choice before it. It had to put up with Keynesian demand management through state expenditure, both in the United States and in Europe, because of which the postwar era saw capitalism achieve high rates of employment that were, over a comparable period of time, quite unprecedented in its entire history. Such state intervention in demand management required, to start with, an appropriate international monetary arrangement, one the Bretton Woods system provided.

## The Bretton Woods System

The presumption behind state intervention in demand management was that the pursuit of private rationality by economic agents produced in the aggregate an outcome that was not only socially irrational but also inimical to private interests, which a situation of involuntary unemployment evidently was. The state was seen, therefore, not as an entity having some specific interest of its own and entering the fray to achieve it, but as the promoter of the social interest. It effected an intrusion of social rationality into a sphere characterized by the pervasive, and futile, pursuit of private rationality. An obvious necessary condition for this to happen was that the state must have the autonomy to pursue policies it considered appropriate.

The state that is supposed to pursue such policies, however, happens to be a nation-state. For it to have such autonomy, not only must it not be a prisoner of finance capital, but it also should be able to pursue policies that are not necessarily to the liking of finance capital. For this it is necessary that cross-border flows of finance must be restricted, for, if finance is international and can move across national boundaries at will, then the nation-state's writ cannot run against it, as it would simply quit the country en masse, precipitating a crisis. Keynes, we saw earlier, had expressed this idea in an article in *The Yale Review* in 1933, even before *The General Theory* had been written, where he had said, ". . . above all, let finance be primarily national."[1]

The Bretton Woods system that was set up in 1944 gave expression to this idea. It was a regime where controls were imposed by the nation-states over cross-border capital flows, including above all the cross-border flows of finance, so that the state could intervene in demand management to push economies closer to full employment.

But even if demand could be "managed" by the state, there still remained a problem relating to the balance of payments. Moving close to full employment could still be thwarted by the emergence of a current account deficit on the balance of payments that was unsustainable. Of course, since the deficits of all countries taken together must add up to zero, if the surplus countries could expand their domestic demand, if not through an increase in domestic employment (for they are likely to be close to full employment anyway) then at least through an increase in domestic consumption at that given level of employment, then the deficit countries could automatically get rid of their deficits without having to curtail their domestic activity.

The Bretton Woods arrangement, however, could not institute such adjustment on the part of surplus countries. The United States, then a surplus country, opposed any provision that would force adjustment upon surplus countries to get rid of their surpluses. Under the Bretton Woods system, therefore, it was only the deficit countries that were obliged to carry out adjustment. And they were allowed a whole range of instruments for this purpose, from exchange rate depreciations to tariffs and quantitative restrictions. Exchange rate depreciations, of course, would be of no avail if they were followed by retaliation by other countries. To prevent such retaliation and hence to curtail the absolute rights of countries to undertake depreciations, the Bretton Woods system insisted that these could be effected only with the permission of the IMF. It was, in short, a fixed nominal exchange rate system with capital and trade controls (and hence a system of multiple effective exchange rates) where the nominal rate could be adjusted with the permission of the IMF. And within this system, nation-states could undertake demand management measures.

Though Keynes was no means the sole or even the principal author of this arrangement (the U.S. representative at Bretton Woods, Harry White, had a powerful role), an inkling of its theoretical underpinnings can be obtained from certain remarks of Keynes in *The General Theory*. Holding that a "competitive struggle for markets" as a cause of wars "probably played a predominant part in the nineteenth century," he wrote that under the system of domestic laissez faire and an international gold standard, which prevailed, there were no means available to governments other than a competitive struggle to reduce domestic unemployment.

Keynes, as we have seen, was factually wrong. The latter half of the nineteenth century was a period remarkably free of wars over markets (since Britain kept its markets open to its rivals and yet kept up its aggregate demand and managed to balance its payments through the control it exercised over its colonies). Indeed, between the Crimean War and the First World War, the only wars between European powers were over the German and Italian unifications, and these were not, primarily, struggles for markets. But what concerns us here is his theoretical position, namely that a regime of balanced budgets and fixed exchange rates leaves no scope for any *internal* mechanism for increasing employment. What the Bretton Woods system did was to negate both. Budgets did not have to be balanced, for which control over financial flows was necessary, and exchange rates became subject to adjustment.

## Contradictions of the Dirigiste Arrangement

Colonialism had been ideal from the point of view of capitalism, because not only did the colonies provide a market via the replacement of local craft production, but also because *the same act of destruction released raw materials for capitalist use.* The act of finding a market, in short, was simultaneously an act of income deflation in the colonies through the destruction of local crafts (supplemented, of course, by income deflation through the "drain" effected by the taxation system). Inflationary pressures were thus kept at bay in the metropolis even while metropolitan capitalism got itself a market. The two requirements of capitalism, for finding markets and for imposing an income deflation in the outlying regions to ward off the threat of increasing supply price, were both achieved at one stroke.

But when state expenditure creates a market, it does not thereby release any raw materials in the way that the market obtained through the destruction of colonial crafts had done. The two moments, of finding a market and of obtaining supplies of raw materials, which are subject to increasing supply price, are now no longer woven into each other. If state expenditure provides the market, then it is necessary in some other way to impose income deflation on the third world raw material users, so that increasing supply price does not come into play, threatening the value of money in the metropolis. But within the postwar dirigiste arrangement, there was no such "other way," which left the system perennially vulnerable to inflation.

This vulnerability was quite distinct from the vulnerability to inflation arising from the high level of employment, which Joan Robinson's "inflationary barrier" had emphasized and which actually went back to Marx's proposition that the existence of a certain reserve army of labor was an essential condition for the viability of capitalism.

Marx's proposition has been usually interpreted to mean that if the reserve army fell below a certain relative size vis-à-vis the active army, then the trade unions would become strong enough to demand and obtain *real wages* relative to labor productivity, which would squeeze the rate of profit to levels that would threaten the survival of the system. (This is not the only reason for the existence of a reserve army according to Marx; the imposition of work-discipline, which capitalism achieves through coercion upon the workers, becomes impossible in the absence of a reserve army into whose ranks the workers from the active army can be pushed as punishment for "indiscipline.")

Marx's argument actually related proximately to money-wage movements, but, since in his schema money-wage and real wage movements always went together, as he was talking about a commodity money system, the argument can be interpreted as referring to either. If we talk, however, of a paper money or credit money system, then a fall in the relative size of the reserve army of labor would raise money wages, exactly as Marx had argued, though instead of increasing real wages, higher money wages would get "passed on" in the form of higher prices. Marx's proposition about the system depending upon the existence of a minimum relative size of the reserve army of labor therefore has a wider validity beyond the commodity-money world that he was specifically talking about, which Joan Robinson's 1956 concept of an "inflationary barrier" brought out later.[2]

But even if a reserve army of adequate size is maintained and there is stability in money wages, as the economy grows it would require larger and larger amounts of raw materials, a part of which has to come from the tropical landmass. Since the supply price of this part is increasing, it would jeopardize the value of money in the metropolis either directly or indirectly, via jeopardizing the value of money in the periphery, which would then control its exports to the metropolis. *Even with given money wages all around, therefore, there would be a threat to the value of money.* Because of this, the imposition of income deflation on input producers and input users in the periphery becomes necessary, even if the state through its expenditure provides adequate markets for the capitalist products in the metropolis. *The postwar dirigiste arrangement did not have any mechanism for imposing such income deflation.*

## The Consequences of the Absence of Drain

Deindustrialization had not been the only mechanism for income deflation in the periphery. The drain of surplus was also an important mechanism for achieving the same end, so that the value of money in the metropolis did not get undermined by the phenomenon of increasing supply price. Political decolonization, which brought the drain to an end, removed *ipso facto* a powerful instrument of income deflation. To be sure, other ways of surplus transfer from the periphery continued, such as through unequal exchange,[3] or through payment for intellectual property rights to metropolitan capital. However, the politically imposed transfers, such as through the colonial taxation system, came to an end, which regenerated the possibility of inflation and hence the threat to the value of money.

There is yet an additional powerful implication of the elimination of the colonial drain. In the colonial period Britain, the leading capitalist country, kept its own market open for the newly industrializing countries of that time. Had it not done so, the system of the gold standard would have been difficult to sustain because of the struggles for markets among the rival capitalist countries, and the world capitalist economy would have run into a crisis much earlier than it did. In fact, keeping its market open for encroachment by newly industrializing countries is an important hallmark of a world capitalist leader at all times.

Britain, however, managed to avoid getting into any balance of payments problems because of the drain from the colonies. Suppose it did not have access to the drain, then it would have got into debt with countries running a current account surplus vis-à-vis itself. The drain, in other words, prevented an outpouring of IOUs by Britain.

In the post–Second World War period, since political decolonization forecloses the possibility of a drain, the leading capitalist country of this time, the United States, which had to keep its markets open to others as part of its leadership role, has increasingly gone into debt. (This "openness" was being revoked under Donald Trump, an issue we discuss later.) In the absence of the drain, in other words, the world has had to hold on to a continuous outpouring of IOUs by the United States, making it, paradoxically, the most indebted country in the world. The most powerful capitalist country in the world being the most highly indebted represents an unprecedented situation in the history of world capitalism. But this only reflects another unprecedented situation, namely that we have for the first time the leading capitalist country not having access (to a degree that covers its current account deficit on the balance of payments) to a drain of surplus from an empire.

This has two obvious implications. The first is the fragility it lends to the global financial system. This is an obvious and much discussed point and need not be labored any further. The second is that the *IOUs of the leading country provide the base for an enormous growth of a financial superstructure.*

While this growth in the financial superstructure has been a remarkable fact in the postwar period, and some have even coined a new term, "financialization," to describe it, what is often not appreciated is that *financialization owes not a little to the phenomenon of the absence of the drain of surplus from the periphery into the leading capitalist power.*

To be sure, even if there had been a drain of surplus from the periphery, it still might not have sufficed to prevent a rise in the outpouring of IOUs from the leading capitalist power, so that some "financialization" might still have been inevitable. But financialization certainly would not have proceeded at the pace it has if the leading capitalist country had access to a substantial drain of surplus from the periphery. *Financialization, in short, is the other side of the coin to the absence of a substantial "drain of surplus" from the periphery to the metropolis as had occurred in the colonial period.*

With the outpouring of IOUs from the leading capitalist country to the rest of the world, the question arises: How is the value of the leading country's currency, not just vis-à-vis the currencies of other capitalist countries, but also with respect to the world of commodities, preserved?

The Bretton Woods system sought to resolve this problem in a purely formal way by officially decreeing the U.S. dollar to be "as good as gold" and by fixing its price in terms of gold at $35 per ounce of gold. Such a system, however, could remain viable only if there was no rush to actually convert dollars into gold, but it obviously could not survive if there was such a rush. Since the printing of dollars was unrelated to the magnitude of gold that actually happened to be in the possession of the central bank of the leading capitalist country, gold convertibility of the dollar could clearly not be sustained, if ever it was seriously challenged.

The presumption behind the Bretton Woods arrangement was that it would not be challenged because of an implicit understanding between the major capitalist countries, that is, the sheer power relationship between the advanced countries will keep the system going. But clearly if the outpouring of dollars reached massive proportions (an issue we will examine later), the system could not last. This is precisely what happened in the early 1970s, leading first to the suspension of dollar convertibility in 1971, and then the abandonment of the Bretton Woods arrangement altogether in 1973.

To sum up, the basic weakness of the postwar dirigiste arrangement lay in that it sought to erect an international monetary system without the underpinning of colonialism, as the gold standard had. The absence of the colonial prop manifested itself in two ways: first, the absence of any mechanism for income deflation meant that inflation arising from increasing supply price and threatening the value of money could not be kept at bay; and second, the absence of colonial drain meant that the debt of the leading capitalist country piled up, causing a massive expansion in the financial superstructure and making the system particularly vulnerable and fragile. The collapse of the Bretton Woods system and with it of Keynesian demand management was the inevitable result, which only underscored that *capitalism could not function without either a direct colonial prop or some arrangement that could produce a similar effect as a colonial prop.*

Putting it differently, two of the concessions that postwar capitalism had given, namely political decolonization on the one hand and Keynesian demand management on the other, were mutually contradictory. This would become clear only over time. During the time the contradiction did not erupt (for reasons we shall discuss later), the system functioned exceedingly well, to produce what has been called the "Golden Age of Capitalism." But this "Golden Age" was essentially an aberration, something that was intrinsically incapable of being sustained.

## Contradictions of Third World Dirigisme

Dirigiste regimes also came into existence in most third world countries in the wake of decolonization. Though these regimes differed from one another in important ways, as we shall see, they all had one point in common, namely to use the state, including a public sector, against the domination by metropolitan capital that had been their legacy. Public sector enterprises were started to develop and process natural resources, to develop infrastructure, and to plug gaps in the production structure, especially with regard to basic and producer goods industries. Since the domestic capitalist class had been relatively weak and underdeveloped to start with, with little interest in undertaking any research and development, the public sector also became the means for developing whatever limited technological self-reliance that third world countries managed to achieve.

Breaking out of the colonial pattern of international division of labor, through embarking on a process of industrialization, required protecting the home market from the entry of metropolitan products. The dirigiste regimes therefore set up tariff barriers and quantitative trade restrictions, behind which "import-substituting" industrialization could proceed. But since the technology for such industrialization remained largely in the hands of metropolitan capital, collaboration with such capital became necessary for the domestic bourgeoisie, so that joint ventures involving domestic and foreign capital became the order of the day, and came up behind tariff walls. Thus, protectionism necessarily also meant protecting metropolitan capital that had jumped the protectionist walls to locate production units within the country through joint ventures.

Protectionism, however, only enabled domestic producers, whether in the public or in the private sector, to capture a larger chunk of the home market; it could not by itself give rise to larger growth over time. The dynamics of the system depended upon the rate at which the home market itself was expanding, especially since breaking into export markets for units that developed under the dirigiste regime behind protectionist walls was extremely difficult (unless metropolitan capital permitted it, which, except in the case of a few countries in East Asia in that period, close to the United States and supportive of its war against the Vietnamese, was scarcely on the cards).

One very important factor affecting the growth of the home market was the rate of growth of agriculture. And while all over the third world the growth rate of agriculture picked up compared to the colonial period, there were major constraints upon this growth arising from the degree of land concentration.

We must distinguish here between three distinct cases. The first is where the Communists had led the anti-colonial struggle; decolonization here was followed by radical land redistribution (followed in most cases by the formation of cooperatives and collectives). The second case is where the land had been substantially taken over by colonialists earlier, as in the case of the Japanese colonies; here, the U.S. occupation forces at the end of the war carried out land redistribution at the expense of the Japanese landlords. The third case is where neither of the above two situations obtained; decolonization in these remaining cases was not followed by any radical land redistribution so that the rural power structure did not change sufficiently to encourage investment by smaller peasants. (Zimbabwe was one important exception to this, though it carried out land redistribution not immediately following decolonization but at a much later date.)

The reason for this pusillanimity in carrying out land redistribution is what Lenin had noted in the case of Russia much earlier.[4] Where the bourgeoisie comes late to the historical scene, it is afraid that any attack on landed property may rebound into an attack on bourgeois property, and thus makes common cause with the landed interests in defending private property, even though this entails arresting the democratic revolution in the country. Therefore, the dirigiste regimes that came up in countries where the bourgeoisie, or proto-bourgeois elements, had played a leading role in the anti-colonial struggle invariably eschewed any radical land redistribution.

This is not to say that in this third group of countries, which constituted the majority of the countries of the third world, the nature of landownership remained completely unchanged. Many feudal or semi-feudal landlords, those who were not interested in turning to capitalist farming in the new situation, sold their land to rich tenants who now came to constitute a proto-capitalist *kulak* class. A tendency toward capitalist agriculture containing an admixture of landlord and peasant capitalism emerged in these countries. But, while the composition of the top landowning group thus underwent a change, the extent of land concentration did not diminish; a vast mass of pauperized peasants and agricultural laborers with little or no land continued to exist as before, despite decolonization.

At the same time, agriculture was protected and promoted in various ways under the dirigiste regime by the new post-colonial state: through subsidized inputs; tariffs and quantitative trade restrictions; provision of cheap credit; provision of assured remunerative prices; public investment in irrigation and infrastructure; research and development under the aegis of the government for developing better seeds and better agricultural practices; and public extension services for disseminating information about better practices. The main beneficiaries of these measures no doubt were the better-off peasants and landlords turning to capitalist farming; but compared to the colonial period, agricultural growth picked up.

What was striking about the new third world dirigiste regime is that though it did not break land concentration and allowed the eviction of tenants for the resumption of land for capitalist farming by the earlier landlords (which constitutes one kind of primitive accumulation of capital), it did insulate agriculture from encroachment by domestic and foreign monopoly capitalists, and thereby prevented primitive accumulation of the other, classic kind.

Though the growth rate of agriculture picked up in these countries, it nonetheless limited the growth of the domestic market, especially because of the unequal distribution of income that accompanied such growth across the agriculture-dependent population. The constraint upon industrialization arising from this source continued to plague the dirigiste regime.

The other major source of the growth of the domestic market was the growth of state expenditure, which created greater employment opportunities in the traditional bureaucracy, in the "development bureaucracy," and in the public sector, for large numbers of middle-class youth. Michal Kalecki had coined the term "intermediate regimes" to describe this phenomenon.[5] He saw the urban middle class and the rich peasants who had a similar "intermediate" social position to this middle class in the countryside as constituting the main social support–base for regimes that were characterized by a policy mix of state capitalism (public sector) and non-alignment (in foreign policy), and which obtained aid from both the Soviet Union and the advanced capitalist countries, using the former to drive a better bargain with the latter. What Kalecki's analysis misses, even if we go along with his characterization, is the contradictions of these regimes.

The basic contradiction of such regimes, notwithstanding their substantial achievements , is that the growth in state expenditure, which is the main source of the dynamics of the system (given the inadequate stimulus from agricultural growth owing to the absence of land redistribution), cannot be sustained because the state gets gradually engulfed in a fiscal crisis. This is because the competing claims upon the state budget from the bourgeois and proto-bourgeois elements, and from the emerging rural capitalists drawn from the ranks of both landlords and rich peasants, cannot be reconciled, except either through inflation at the expense of the workers, agricultural laborers, and middle-class employees, or through a curtailment of state spending, or, typically, a mixture of the two.[6]

The dirigiste regimes that came up in the postwar years had much to their credit. They sustained rates of economic growth which were quite unprecedented, both in the advanced and in the underdeveloped countries, by their respective historical standards. But they represented essentially a passing phase, a transitional arrangement that could not be sustained for long. They represented an attempt to control capitalism, but "controlled capitalism" could not withstand the "spontaneity" of this mode of production.

# CHAPTER 15

# The Long Postwar Boom

The postwar economic regimes in advanced capitalist economies that involved state intervention in demand management overcame one particular problem that had arisen with the end of the prop of colonialism, namely the problem of deficiency of aggregate demand, of which the Great Depression had been a clear manifestation. However, they did not contain any mechanisms for overcoming the other problem, namely the tendency toward inflation that could arise in the event of demand outrunning raw material availability, and also, more generally, because of increasing supply price. And, of course, demand stimulation by the state to raise employment also opened up the possibility that the reserve army of labor could dwindle to a point where inflation could arise from the side of the labor market, as Joan Robinson's idea of an "inflationary barrier" had anticipated.

If, despite these obvious hurdles that could stifle a state expenditure-stimulated boom, postwar capitalism nonetheless enjoyed a prolonged boom more pronounced than any boom ever experienced in its entire history over a comparable period of time, which has made many call this period the "Golden Age of Capitalism," then the reasons for it need careful investigation. This is what we do in the present chapter. But first, let us look briefly at the nature of the boom itself. The facts about this boom are well known, though the interpretations differ; we will therefore focus more on interpretations, and, more generally, the theoretical perspectives.

## State Intervention in Demand Management

State intervention in demand management through larger government expenditure took the form of military spending in the United States, which is why some have called this policy "military Keynesianism."[1] The United States came out of the Great Depression essentially through larger military expenditure in the run-up to the Second World War. Germany and Japan, which had begun the militarization drive earlier, had overcome the Depression earlier as well, Japan being the first country to do so. The finance minister in the early 1930s, Takahashi, had been murdered for wanting a halt to further militarization once the "slack" associated with the Depression had been exhausted. The liberal capitalist countries, notably the United States, had followed suit only in the late 1930s.

The United States continued with a large military budget even after the war for a number of reasons: first, because it was a convenient way of preventing a slide back into recession, which, in the new context of the socialist challenge, would also have been politically inexpedient; second, because military expenditure has the "advantage" that it does not entail encroaching upon the sphere of activity of private capital and hence does not arouse any opposition on that count; and third, because military expenditure neither increases the standard of living of the workers, which would strengthen their bargaining strength vis-à-vis the capitalists, generating anger among the latter, nor adds to capacity as investment does. If it did add to capacity, then it would create problems of capacity utilization in the future, and require that the state, if it is to avoid such unutilized capacity and hence the onset of a recession, must keep increasing its investment expenditure and piling up capacity in a meaningless spiral, as the Russian economist Mikhail Tugan-Baranovsky had visualized.[2]

But it was not just a question of keeping up the level of aggregate demand. The share of government expenditure increased as a proportion of GDP in the United States during the 1950s and 1960s. This increase, which was part and parcel of an increase in the share of economic surplus in the GDP, has been interpreted differently by different authors.

Baran and Sweezy, following their own earlier separate works that had argued along similar lines, suggested that there was an *ex ante* tendency for the share of surplus to increase, because the rate of growth of labor productivity tended to exceed the rate of growth of real wages, which meant that there was also an *ex ante* tendency toward overproduction, since wage-earners' propensity to consume was higher than of those to whom the surplus accrued. Overproduction, however, was kept in check by growing government expenditure, especially military expenditure.[3]

Nicholas Kaldor, reviewing Baran's book, contested this claim of a tendency for the share of economic surplus to rise on the grounds that there was no sign of any secular increase in the share of post-tax profits in GDP.[4] If there had been an *ex ante* tendency for the surplus to increase, and its effect by way of generating overproduction had been kept at bay through state expenditure *financed by a fiscal deficit*, then we would have certainly seen the share of (post-tax) profits in GDP increasing over time. Since there was no sign of this, Kaldor would have had a point in claiming that Baran's premise of a rise in the share of surplus was wrong, provided the overproduction-offsetting expenditure had been financed by a fiscal deficit.

But from an observed *ex post* constancy in the share of (post-tax) profits in GDP, we cannot reject the claim of an increase in the *ex ante* share of surplus, as Kaldor does, for two obvious reasons. First, if growing government expenditure is financed by a tax on profits, then all three phenomena can simultaneously occur, namely a rise in the *ex ante* share of surplus, growing government expenditure (which means a rise in the observed *ex post* share of surplus), and a constancy in the ratio of post-tax profits in GDP. An observed constancy in the share of post-tax profits therefore does not constitute a refutation of Baran and Sweezy's argument.

Second, since surplus also includes the post-tax wages of "unproductive workers," apart from total post-tax profits and all tax revenues accruing to the state, an increase in such wages, associated for instance with a rise in the costs of circulation, could reflect a rise in the share of surplus (both *ex ante* and *ex post*), even if neither the share of government tax revenue nor the share of post-tax profits in GDP increase over time. Since Baran and Sweezy's argument also focused on a rise in costs of circulation and on growing government expenditure relative to GDP financed not by a growing ratio of fiscal deficit but by growing taxes, including on capitalists, they were clearly immune to Kaldor's criticism for this reason as well.

Nonetheless, a question does remain over Baran and Sweezy's argument. Suppose there is no tendency for the share of surplus to rise *ex ante* but the government increases its expenditure relative to GDP by taxing workers, with the tax share on profits remaining unchanged and the distribution of income between pretax wages and pretax profits remaining unchanged. In this case, there would have been no increase in the *ex ante* share of surplus, but only an increase in the *ex post* share of surplus. We cannot infer from an observed increase in the *ex post* share of surplus that there is also an increase in the *ex ante* share as well. The latter has to be independently and separately established.

One may think that looking at the ratio of pretax profits to pretax wages in GDP would be an obvious way of establishing an *ex ante* tendency for the share of surplus in GDP to rise. Even this, however, is inadequate: at any given level of capacity utilization, if the government raises its expenditure and finances it by taxing profits, and if the capitalists squeeze wages in order to make up for the higher taxes they have to pay, then there would be a higher share of pretax profits (at the expense of pretax wages) in output, but it would not have been caused by any *ex ante* tendency for the share of surplus to rise as Baran and Sweezy had envisaged. Hence, the Baran-Sweezy argument requires a more careful marshalling of evidence than just looking at a few ratios.

But no matter what view we have on the question of an increase in the *ex ante* share of surplus, there can be little doubt that capitalism in the period of postwar *dirigisme* saw an increase in the *ex post* share of surplus in output in the United States and in the capitalist world as a whole. In other words, whether the increase in the share of government expenditure in output and of the costs of circulation warded off a tendency toward overproduction that was immanent in an increase in the *ex ante* share of surplus, it did occur, so that the share of post-tax wages of the productive workers in total output declined over time.

This assertion would appear to go against the "profit-squeeze" hypothesis that has been put forward by many, including Glyn and Sutcliffe in the context of British capitalism. Quite apart from the statistical issues that have been raised with regard to this hypothesis, namely whether to take depreciation and stock appreciation as part of profit, it should be remembered that we are not discussing the share of wages compared to that of profits, but the share of wages compared to the surplus, much of which accrues to the state.[5] As Turner, Jackson, and Wilkinson argued in the context of British capitalism, taxation was a major instrument for squeezing wages; they had even talked of a "wage-tax spiral."[6] Much of the welfare state expenditure undertaken in Europe was financed by taxes on the workers themselves, though obviously not all of that expense was so financed, for then it would have had little demand-stimulating effect, which it undoubtedly had.[7]

Even if the tax revenue raised from the workers and the capitalists is in exactly the same ratio as the one in which pretax income is distributed among them,  and the value of the balanced budget multiplier is unity, larger government expenditure raises the share of *ex post* surplus in total output. When there is unutilized capacity and unemployment in the economy, it does so via output adjustment. And if the increase in government expenditure relative to base output persists even after "involuntary unemployment" has been overcome, then despite balancing its budget through taxes raised in this manner, the government would be unleashing a process of inflation in terms of the wage unit.

In other words, even the process of overcoming involuntary unemployment through government expenditure financed by equivalent taxation may entail an increase in the share of surplus in total output in the economy. Whether larger government expenditure takes the form of military spending as in the United States, or of welfare state spending under the aegis of Social Democracy as in Europe,[8] as long as this enhanced expenditure is met  through taxing productive workers to a greater extent than before, it would still entail a rise in the *ex post* share of economic surplus in total output.[9] In other words, the postwar dirigiste regimes, while keeping the advanced capitalist economies close to full employment (but never at actual full employment, since a capitalist economy can never function without a reserve army of labor), effected, at the same time, an increase in the *ex post* share of economic surplus in GDP.

This now raises an important question: If the unemployment rate is low and yet the share of surplus in output is increasing, then why did the workers not press for higher wages in order to fight against their declining share?

## The Question of Working-Class Resistance

Two answers can be given to this question. The first is that inflation below a certain threshold would go unnoticed by the workers, in the sense of not being anticipated and hence not entering into the money-wage bargain.[10] This is simply the "money illusion" argument of Keynes in a different guise. Some hypothesis of this sort also underlies the Phillips Curve, which states that workers *never* anticipate inflation. The first argument says that they do not anticipate inflation below a certain threshold, but it amounts to saying that as long as inflation remains below that threshold the Phillips Curve remains valid. And for a long period when the postwar dirigiste regime was in operation, the rate of inflation, though positive and eroding the share of post-tax wages, was not too high, which makes this hypothesis regarding why workers did not jack up money-wage demands to fight against a declining share of post-tax wages in output a plausible one. Workers fighting against a declining wage share would have meant accelerating inflation.

The second answer is that the United States, to an extent, exported its inflation to other capitalist countries. Traditionally the United States had been a current account surplus economy, which was one reason why it prevented the Bretton Woods system from having any provision for making the surplus countries undertake measures to overcome their current account surpluses. But during the 1950s it set up a string of bases across the world to encircle the Soviet Union in the name of warding off its challenge to capitalism, a challenge that did not exist at all, since having lost 20 million people in the war, the Soviet Union was in no mood to spread socialism beyond what had been achieved by the end of the war, and was criticized on this score by Mao's China.

The cost of maintaining this string of bases meant that in the course of the 1950s the United States became a current account deficit economy. Expenditure on these bases was met through the budget, and corresponding to the fiscal deficit there developed a current account deficit. The United States simply printed money to meet these deficits, and since under the Bretton Woods system the dollar was "as good as gold," other countries were obliged to hold on to these dollars.

To be sure, behind the *formal* acceptance of the dollar to be "as good as gold" there was the *real* acceptance of the fact that the U.S. bases against the Soviet Union were meant to serve not just U.S. interests but the interests of the entire capitalist world. The other capitalist countries accepted the outpouring of dollars not because of a piece of paper signed at Bretton Woods declaring the dollar to be "as good as gold" but because the United States was the undisputed leader of the capitalist world. And they accepted for the same reason the outflow of dollars from the United States even when some of these printed dollars were being used for taking over European factories and other assets.

There was some breast-beating in Europe over this, specifically over the unwisdom of lending to a country (which is what holding on to its currency means) so that it can use the loans to buy up the assets of the lending country. But little could be done about it. As a result, the torrent of dollars from the United States continued, and these were held by European banks, which wanted to invest them abroad but were prevented from doing so because of the Bretton Woods system that allowed all sovereign countries the right to control capital flows into or out of their economies.

In the absence of the ability of the United States to run these current deficits, it would have to squeeze domestic absorption via a higher rate of inflation compared to what actually occurred for maintaining its overseas bases. Its own rate of inflation, therefore, was moderated because of its ability to run current deficits, which meant, in turn, that elsewhere the pressure of demand, and hence the rate of inflation, was higher than it would *ceteris paribus* have been otherwise. The United States thus exported to an extent its inflation to other countries.

To summarize the picture that obtained during the so-called Golden Age, U.S. militarism kept up demand both within the country and elsewhere. It kept up demand elsewhere in two distinct ways: one was by virtue of the fact that a high level of demand within the United States props up other economies; the other was because the United States ran a current account deficit, which meant that other countries, forced to run a corresponding current account surplus, found their aggregate demand to be even higher than their domestic circumstances warranted. They too used government expenditure to boost their domestic economies, and in

Europe's case through substantial welfare expenditure under the aegis of social democracy. But their domestic boost to aggregate demand was bolstered by U.S. militarism.

Since this meant high levels of employment and capacity utilization, it called forth significant private investment and hence high rates of economic growth. As a direct consequence of economic growth, as the Kaldor-Verdoorn law suggests (that there is a positive relationship between economic growth and growth of labor productivity, with causation running from the former to the latter), and because several innovations that had not been introduced during the Depression could now be introduced in boom conditions, advanced capitalist economies witnessed high rates of labor productivity growth. And in a situation of low unemployment and hence strong bargaining power of trade unions, that meant high rates of real wage growth. With unemployment low and real wages growing rapidly, the working class in the advanced capitalist countries witnessed an improvement in its living standards that was quite unparalleled in the history of capitalism.

Even so, the share of post-tax wages in total output was declining during this period, with a corresponding increase in the share of economic surplus. This would normally be expected to cause strong money-wage demands, leading to accelerating inflation, but inflation remained both low and non-accelerating, with no signs of any wage explosion until 1968 (on which more later), because the lowness of this inflation rate prevented its being taken into reckoning. Besides, it always takes time for workers to take stock of their cumulative losses. Put differently, the significant absolute improvement in the conditions of the workers prevented them from becoming agitated over their loss of shares in relative terms. This was a situation that was bound to come to an end sooner or later, as it actually did. But while it lasted, it kept the "Golden Age" going.

But what about the other source of inflationary pressures, namely primary commodity prices? Let us turn to this issue now.

### Terms of Trade vis-à-vis Primary Commodities

Many economists, notably W. Arthur Lewis,[11] had predicted after the

Second World War that there would be a rapid increase in raw material prices in the years to come. But far from this happening, raw material prices after the Korean War boom fell relative to manufactured goods prices, and that too when the overall rate of inflation was low. Between 1952 and 1971, there was a 23 percent drop in the prices of all primary commodities relative to manufactures; if we take non-oil primary commodities the drop was 26 percent.

Also remarkable is that almost the entire drop in the terms of trade of primary commodities vis-à-vis manufactures occurred prior to the notable acceleration in inflation that happened in the advanced capitalist countries with the wage explosion of 1968, which one would expect to turn the terms of trade against primary commodities. Paradoxically, in the period 1967–72, there was hardly any movement in the terms of trade in either direction, but in the period 1951–67, there had been a secular movement in favor of manufactures while the fact of the protracted boom, together with the rapid growth of labor productivity in manufacturing, would have suggested the opposite, as economists like Lewis had also anticipated.

The terms of trade movement is not difficult to explain. Economic surplus as a proportion of gross value added in the advanced countries increased during the 1950s and '60s. Capitalists producing manufactured goods typically charge a price that is a mark up over the unit prime cost. The state further imposes an indirect tax mark up on this price. The rise in the profit-cum-indirect tax margin, which raises the share of surplus in the gross value of output, is likely to entail a decline not only in the share of predirect-tax wages in gross value of output but also in the share of primary commodity producers. And despite this decline for primary producers the share of pretax wages in gross value added too can still go down, as indeed happened.[12] Hence, the adverse terms of trade movement for primary producers is also a part of the rise in the share of surplus.

But the real question is, how did this happen while the rate of inflation remained relatively low? This is contrary to what would be expected since the phenomenon of increasing supply price in primary production, if nothing else, should have caused an acceleration of inflation owing to the persistence of the boom. Even over 1960–73, toward the latter part of which inflation had become quite pronounced, the average inflation rate for twenty-one OECD countries was just 4 percent. In particular when income deflation through the mechanisms of the colonial period could no longer be imposed upon the third world, how is it that the phenomenon of increasing supply price did not make itself felt through a primary commodity price explosion?

Two reasons can be adduced for it. One, we have seen that the phenomenon of increasing supply price could be countered, in the case of commodities produced by the tropical landmass, through land-augmenting measures,[13] of which irrigation is the most important (both for its own sake and also for making other land-augmenting measures such as high-yielding seed varieties effective). The colonial administration had undertaken very few land-augmenting measures in the third world. In fact, the Canal Colonies of Punjab were the only major irrigation project undertaken anywhere in the British Empire during the entire colonial period. *The post-colonial dirigiste regimes that arose in the third world, however, made it a point to undertake land-augmenting measures.* Corresponding to the growing demand in the metropolis for the products of the tropical landmass, there was also a growing supply through land-augmenting measures, which therefore kept the phenomenon of increasing supply price (which occurs only when there is little or no land-augmentation) in abeyance.

Put differently, metropolitan capitalism imposes income deflation on the outlying regions for obtaining supplies of products of the tropical landmass at non-increasing prices relative to money wages not because such income deflation is *inevitable* in any sense, but because *it is capitalism's way of obtaining supplies.* Capitalism does not want an activist state intervening to raise production via land-augmentation, even within peripheral economies. Under British colonial rule, all government investment had to fetch a minimum rate of return, and the colonial administration always advanced the argument that there was no certainty that investment in land-augmentation would fetch this rate of return.

The reason for income deflation on the producers in the periphery, in other words, was not natural or geographical; it was social. And with the coming into being of post-colonial regimes, this social compulsion disappeared to a great extent. The post-colonial *dirigiste regimes* had no compunctions about using fiscal resources, including fiscal deficits, to undertake irrigation investment, and more generally to undertaking land augmentation. Per capita agricultural output increased like never before, and this meant that inflation arising from this source was kept in check.

The second reason is that all over the third world the effort on the part of the new regimes was to industrialize, for which these countries required as much foreign exchange as they could possibly lay their hands on. Hence the pressure to sell products of the tropical landmass made many of these countries fight against one another to boost sales. The new producing countries, moreover, were at an advantage since they could initiate price competition and snatch away markets from the existing large producers among such tropical countries who dominated the market but could not engage in price competition without being large-scale losers. Hence, price competition to expand market shares became the order of the day, with new or small sellers taking the lead in cutting prices. Sri Lanka expanded its market shares in the tea market at the expense of India, while Bangladesh did the same in the case of jute textiles. And they did so through price competition.

This increased competition among third world countries was also a factor keeping down the rate of inflation, despite the phenomenon of increasing supply price. The initiation of land augmentation within most third world countries, and the intense competition among them for pushing out more and more primary product exports to obtain the foreign exchange required for industrialization, were the two factors that kept primary commodity prices under control, even in the midst of such a large boom.

This, however, could only provide a temporary palliative. The third world dirigiste regimes got embroiled in fiscal crises over time, since the emerging capitalist and landlord-capitalist strata used the budget as a means of primitive accumulation of capital that included rampant and growing tax evasion. The state therefore could continue the government investment-led growth process only through larger recourse to indirect taxation or deficit financing, both of which imposed an inflationary squeeze on the working people that was politically inexpedient within a framework of parliamentary democracy. Under the circumstances, it cut back on the tempo of public investment, pushing dirigisme into a dead end and holding back on land augmentation.

The Golden Age conjuncture was necessarily a transient one. It could last only as long as the workers in the metropolis did not take note of the rising share of economic surplus in the GDP and did not jack up their money-wage claims to get back lost ground, and also as long as land augmentation could continue in the third world with the dirigiste regime not getting enmeshed in a fiscal crisis. Both of these denouements were bound to occur sooner or later, as indeed they did. But before that happened, capitalism enjoyed a Golden Age not because of itself but despite itself. This was so because dirigisme, both in the metropolis and in the third world, though an essential factor underlying the boom, was anathema for capitalism.

### A Perspective on Imperialism

Political decolonization was followed by economic decolonization against which the metropolitan countries fought bitterly, to the point of staging coups d'état against third world governments that dared to take control over their own national resources. The coups against Mossadegh in Iran and Arbenz in Guatemala were among the earliest such efforts, to be followed, prominently, by the coup against Allende in Chile. The fact of military interventions against third world governments in the course of this protracted fight has given the impression that imperialism was a powerful reality in the 1950s and '60s, and apparently no longer is a reality.

Precisely the opposite is correct. Once imperialism is seen as an arrangement for imposing income deflation on the third world population in order to get their primary commodities without running into the problem of increasing supply price, it is clear that this arrangement had fallen through after political decolonization. The period of the 1950s and '60s, far from being the heyday of imperialism in a new guise, represents rather a loosening of the imperialist knot, when imperialism could not impose its will on the third world. Imperialism's aggressiveness in that period reflects its frustration at this inability. As we shall argue in a later chapter, metropolitan capital is in a much stronger position today to impose its will on third world states and third world petty producers than in the Golden Age years. Indeed, in the sense of not having to resort to so many coups, imperialism appears "invisible."

CHAPTER 16

# The End of Postwar Dirigisme

The unraveling of the colonial arrangement, which preceded the various measures of political and economic decolonization, and which, in our view, was a major reason for the Great Depression, had meant that markets were no longer available "on tap" from this source for metropolitan capitalism. Political, and subsequently economic decolonization, meant two further things: first, the drain of resources that had characterized the colonial period and had acquired immense proportions during the Second World War and inflicted upon Bengal a famine that killed three million people was no longer available. This meant that commodities were no longer available gratis to the leading capitalist power, so that playing the leadership role by running a current account deficit with other emerging powers got it deeper and deeper into debt. This is what happened to the postwar leader, the United States.

Second, the income deflation that the drain and the process of deindustrialization had imposed on the colonies and semi-colonies of the third world to prevent the effects of increasing supply price from manifesting themselves in the form of a destabilization of the value of money could now no longer be imposed, which made the system additionally vulnerable.

While state intervention in demand management, which Keynes had advocated and which became a reality after the Second World War, could overcome the problem of deficiency of demand that the unraveling of the colonial arrangement had thrown up, the other two problems mentioned above could not be overcome. The postwar dirigiste regime in the metropolitan capitalist countries remained vulnerable on these two counts. It also remained vulnerable to the possibility of a money-wage explosion, since the share of surplus in GDP was increasing in metropolitan countries during the long boom, even as the unemployment rate came down greatly, to around 2 percent in Britain in the mid-1960s and around 4 percent officially in the United States in the Kennedy years, which greatly strengthened the bargaining position of the workers.

These vulnerabilities did not become apparent immediately. They took time to manifest themselves, giving a false impression that they did not exist at all. But when they did appear, it spelled the end of the postwar boom, the so-called Golden Age of Capitalism, and of the dirigiste regime itself, which was no longer sustainable in the new situation. Let us look at how the different contradictions of the postwar regime played out.

### Inflation and the Wage Explosion

Throughout the 1950s and '60s, the workers, especially the "productive workers," were losing ground because of the increase in the share of surplus (including costs of circulation) in GDP in the advanced capitalist countries. This was because, apart from the rise in the costs of circulation, there was a significant increase everywhere in the ratio of government expenditure to GDP. Whether this warded off an independently given tendency toward overproduction or was a *sui generis* phenomenon, an issue we touched upon earlier, need not enter the discussion here. But its obvious manifestation was that prices rose more rapidly than unit labor costs (taking post direct-tax wages), that is, post–direct tax real wages rose less than labor productivity.

This did not, however, disrupt the boom, and that is because the rate of inflation, itself being small, did not attract notice from the workers, especially since (post–direct tax) real wages were rising rapidly anyway, even if less rapidly than labor productivity. Rapid labor productivity growth was stimulated both by high GDP growth and also by the use of the backlog of un-introduced innovations from the interwar period when the conditions of depression had thwarted their introduction.

The rate of inflation began increasing in the mid-1960s. The reason was that the United States had become a current account deficit country from its earlier status of being a surplus country. The primary reason for this turnaround was the expenditure it incurred in maintaining military bases all over the world. This basically meant that other countries, taken together, were forced to run a current surplus with the United States, which meant, on the one hand, a boost to their aggregate demand coming from this external source, and, on the other, accumulating dollar reserves as payment for this current surplus.

The running of a current account deficit by the United States provided a boost to the process of diffusion of capitalism to other countries, notably in East Asia, which was exactly analogous to the way that Britain's running of a persistent current deficit with capitalist rivals like Germany and the United States had done in the period before the First World War. The only difference was that Britain's deficit with rival powers was more than offset by its drain from the colonies. Britain, far from becoming externally indebted, actually became the world's largest creditor nation at that time, whereas in the case of the United States there was no such drain income, and its current account deficit entailed accumulating external debt (which was paid for under the Bretton Woods system by the export of U.S. dollars).

Running a current account deficit for facilitating a diffusion of capitalism and thereby satisfying the aspirations of the bourgeoisies in other emerging countries is a hallmark of the leader of the capitalist world. A deficit is the instrument through which the leader holds together the capitalist world and keeps the system of its international payments arrangement intact, by accommodating its rival powers. The U.S. deficit played this role.

With the heating up of the Vietnam War the U.S. fiscal deficit, and consequently its current account deficit, began to widen further, which created excess demand pressures, not just in the United States but in other capitalist countries as well, which had to run correspondingly wider current account surpluses.[1] This meant a boost to the rate of inflation globally, that is, a further increase in the level of prices relative to post–direct tax wages in the advanced capitalist world. This increase proved to be the proverbial last straw on the camel's back; the rate of inflation exceeded the threshold rate above which it is incorporated into wage demands. In consequence there was a worldwide money-wage explosion in 1968, which further pushed up the inflation rate. This was the first instance of the bursting forth of a contradiction that underlay the long boom but had until then remained dormant.

Sweezy and Magdoff, following a line of argumentation that goes back to Hyman Minsky and even earlier to Irving Fisher, argue that an increase in inflation is endemic to a situation of Keynesian demand management.[2] The aim of demand management is to prolong the boom and to prevent a crisis that would cause substantial unemployment. However, the longer the boom lasts, the fragility of the economy, including financial fragility, which Minsky emphasized, keeps increasing, and hence the depth of the crisis that would follow the collapse of the boom also keeps increasing. Preventing a collapse of the boom therefore acquired greater and greater urgency over time, but it amounted, in effect, to continuing to support an increasingly fragile economy through state intervention.

Such support, needless to say, must also take the form of preventing a drop in the inflation rate, for any such drop would push the economy toward a debt deflation of the sort that Irving Fisher had discussed, which would have serious recessionary consequences. So, the only direction in which the inflation rate can move realistically, in a capitalist economy where state intervention is supposed to maintain a high level of employment, is upward. (Steady inflation is at best an exceptional case.)

Whether an increase in the inflation rate was inevitable in an economy where the state was committed to propping up the level of activity despite growing financial fragility, which Sweezy and Magdoff suggested, or whether it arose because growing military expenditure, which necessarily leads to war, and eventually did actually precipitate one (in Vietnam), required even greater growth in such expenditure, is an issue that need not detain us here. On the basis of what we have suggested about a threshold level of inflation beyond which it becomes incorporated into the wage-bargain, even an erratic jump in inflation would push it beyond this threshold, precipitating accelerating inflation. The system, in short, was foredoomed to an inflationary crisis for any of these reasons.

Put differently, the concept of an "inflationary barrier" advanced by Joan Robinson cannot be identified with some particular level of unemployment. (Likewise, the idea of a unique "non-accelerating inflation rate of unemployment" is a chimera.) A given level of unemployment at which inflation has not been accelerating may suddenly witness accelerating inflation if there is an increase in workers' consciousness and militancy. Indeed, whether inflation accelerates at a given rate of unemployment depends upon a host of factors, including the movements in the terms of trade, the past history of inflation, erratic jumps in aggregate demand, the learning process of the workers, and so on. The idea that a capitalist economy can be stabilized at a high rate of employment forever through state intervention in aggregate demand alone is false.

This became apparent in the advanced capitalist economies in the course of the long boom. The postwar dirigiste regime in the metropolitan world did experience an increase in the rate of inflation in the latter half of the 1960s. This caused a money-wage explosion, both as a response to it, and also for making up the loss in the share of the workers over the preceding period, which in turn led to a further acceleration in inflation. This was serious enough, but it also made the system unviable for another reason, to which we now turn.

### The Collapse of the Bretton Woods System

The Bretton Woods system was based on a contradiction. The dollar was declared to be as "good as gold" and convertible into gold at $35 per ounce. Since the specificity of gold arises from the idea that it is never expected to, and never does, fall in value relative to the world of commodities in a secular sense, which is what gives meaning to the term "as good as gold," the dollar being declared as good as gold required that its value should not fall in a secular sense vis-à-vis the world of commodities. If it ever did, then the dollar would cease to be "as good as gold," in which case it would be impossible to maintain its convertibility into gold. In other words, the Bretton Woods system required for its viability that there should be no secular inflation in commodity prices in terms of the dollar. At the same time, it had no mechanism to ensure that there was no secular inflation in commodity prices in terms of the dollar. *The contradiction in the Bretton Woods system consisted in institutionalizing something that it had no means of realizing.*

The worldwide wage explosion in 1968 was thus the first blow to the Bretton Woods system. The creditors of the United States, who were sitting on a mountain of dollars that had accumulated ever since dollars started pouring out of the country as it became a current deficit country, now insisted on converting dollars into gold, which was not tenable. The gold-dollar link that had been the lynchpin of Bretton Woods was abandoned in 1971 and the system itself in 1973.

There is a misconception about the events leading to the collapse of the Bretton Woods system. Since President de Gaulle of France had taken a lead in demanding gold in lieu of dollars, the crisis of the system has often been attributed to de Gaulle's bloody-mindedness arising from the American takeover of European firms through dollars printed back home. There was no doubt much angst in Europe at the time over the "American challenge," and the Bretton Woods system that sanctified the dollar as being "as good as gold" was seen as an instrument of American hegemony. But the contradiction of the system was deeper and had structural roots: crucial elements of the colonial system that had worked to Britain's advantage were not available to the United States. It lacked, to be more specific, any mechanism for keeping the inflation rate under control. And it is this lacuna that manifested itself in the late 1960s and early '70s. It was not de Gaulle's bloody-mindedness but the basic contradictions of the Bretton Woods system that led to its collapse.

### Terms of Trade Movements

The collapse of the Bretton Woods system in 1973 suddenly left the world capitalist economy without a stable medium of holding wealth. The dollar (and dollar-denominated assets) had played this role earlier, but with currencies on a float and their respective values subject to great uncertainty, the world's wealth-holders were suddenly left without any reliable medium for holding their wealth. There was a rush to holding commodities, which contributed to the sudden upsurge in primary commodity prices in 1973.

No doubt an excess demand pressure was beginning to be felt, but the massive jump in the net barter terms of trade cannot be explained merely by "normal" excess demand without bringing in the panic shift to commodities that followed the collapse of Bretton Woods.

The net barter terms of trade between manufacturing and primary products that had moved against the primary commodities between 1950 and 1972 jumped by nearly 25 percent in their favor in 1973, and whether we include oil in primary commodities makes little difference to this movement. Soon enough, this rush to commodities subsided, even though there was a marginal increase, by about 9 percent, in the terms of trade of non-oil primary commodities between 1973 and 1974. In the case of oil, however, the story was completely different. The formation of OPEC and the decision to jack up oil prices by enforcing output cuts among members shifted the terms of trade between primary commodities including oil and manufactured goods by about 104 percent in favor of the former between 1973 and 1974.

The oil price hike was followed by a period of rapid inflation in the advanced countries. The inflation rate for the twenty-one OECD countries as a whole was 8.5 percent for 1973–80, and 8.8 and 8.6 percent for 1980 and 1981, respectively, compared to a mere 4 percent for the entire period of 1960 to 1973.

The inflation that continued in the late 1970s despite a reduction in the level of activity that occurred after 1973, which is often referred to as the "second slump" (the first being the slump of the 1930s), has been much discussed, with the term "stagflation" used to describe the phenomenon. But there is nothing remarkable about it. The inflationary upsurge was sustained by its own momentum, with inflation causing money wage demands, which then fed into inflation, and so on. This inflation was finally brought under control only with a change in economic regime, with dirigisme and the commitment to high levels of employment becoming things of the past, and a new regime of "neoliberalism" being introduced in the advanced countries with the triumph of Thatcherism in Britain and of Reaganomics in the United States.

There is a difference between the 1973–75 slump and what followed in the Reagan-Thatcher period. The 1973–75 slump occurred when the massive oil shock resulted in a shift in global income distribution from the bulk of the population in the advanced capitalist countries that were oil consumers to the OPEC countries, which held much of their enhanced incomes in the form of bank deposits with metropolitan banks. The "marginal propensity to consume" (to use a Keynesian term) by those from whom income distribution shifted was higher than the marginal propensity to consume of those in whose favor income distribution shifted. *The oil price hike in short had a demand-depressing effect on the global economy.*

To offset this effect what was needed was an increase in state expenditures at the global level. But since there was no coordination among capitalist states in this regard at the global level, since each state was making its own decision about how to cope with the oil shock and the resulting inflation, each took the decision to restrain or contract state expenditure in the wake of this shock. Individual capitalist states, instead of taking needed counter-recessionary measures, took measures on the contrary that either did nothing to offset the recession or actually compounded it.

The 1973–75 crisis can thus be seen as the consequence of the kneejerk reaction of the dirigiste regime to the upsurge of inflation. The paradigm still remained the Phillips Curve, only with the proviso that it had "shifted"; that is, the presumption was that after a certain time things would "settle down," and there would once again be a revival of state intervention in demand management to achieve high levels of employment, perhaps not so high as had been experienced during the Golden Age, but sufficiently high nonetheless.

Some even thought of a "prices and incomes policy" with which countries could recapture the low levels of unemployment they had experienced during the "Golden Age" years. Such policies were tried for a while but without success. It was clear that a going back to the days of the postwar *dirigiste regimes* was no longer possible. An altogether new regime then began to emerge.

But capitalism is not a planned system; so the new regime did not emerge in a planned manner. It emerged as a consequence of the balance of class forces then existing. In particular, finance capital, which had been forced to make concessions after the war and had to willy-nilly accept the Keynesian demand management it had opposed in the prewar period, now asserted its will, both because Keynesianism was discredited by the inflation and also because finance capital had become greatly strengthened during the Golden Age years. It had become "international," precisely what Keynes had not wanted it to be, anticipating rightly that such internationalization would undermine the autonomy of the nation-state to pursue demand management policies, though he did entertain the hope that the opposition of finance to state intervention in demand management would disappear when the correct theory was presented to it, since he attributed such opposition to a basic misconception. International finance capital backed the Reagan-Thatcher agenda, and the outcome was the end of the dirigiste regimes. Let us turn now to a discussion of the process of "internationalization" or "globalization" of finance.

### The Process of Globalization of Finance

The end of the colonial arrangement meant that the leading capitalist country, which in an earlier epoch had offset its current deficit with rival powers through a drain from the colonies, now had to increase its debt. In the case of the new leader, the United States, debt took the form of exporting dollars. And as the U.S. current balance, which was positive to start with (otherwise the United States could not have become the world capitalist leader) became negative, the deficit started widening, with the ratio of dollar deposits in metropolitan banks (toward which the exported dollars gravitated) to the GDP in the metropolis increasing. And with it, there was increased pressure to open the entire world to unrestricted financial flows in search of profitable investment opportunities, which the Bretton Woods system had allowed countries to put up barriers against.

This pressure in a sense had to succeed. Since under Bretton Woods the surplus countries had been under no obligation to undertake any adjustments, which had to be carried out exclusively by the current-deficit countries, the latter, before undertaking the journey of deflation-cum-currency devaluation, were keen to have at least some short-term financing to give them some breathing space. The increased liquidity in the international financial markets caused by the large-scale dollar outflows from the United States, which had been the progenitor of the Eurodollar market, made it possible for the deficit countries to arrange short-term funding through "hot money" flows to meet immediate balance of payments difficulties. Britain, which was in balance of payments difficulties toward the end of the 1960s, was a major recipient of such flows.

The process of globalization of finance can be said to have begun with such flows. Once the flows started, governments had to be careful not to upset the "confidence of the investors," a euphemism for speculators' confidence, for then the balance of payments could suddenly plunge into a crisis. And since such "confidence" required keeping the economy open to financial flows, economies increasingly became open to such flows, moving away from the capital controls that the Bretton Woods system had allowed them to institute. This happened in Europe toward the end of the '60s, in Africa and Latin America, where IMF "conditionalities" were used for such "opening up," in the '80s, and in India in the '90s. Whether the currency acquired full convertibility, which in many of these third world countries it did not, the economy got caught in the vortex of globalized financial flows.

When the oil shocks happened in 1973 and 1980, there was a further swelling of dollar deposits with the metropolitan banks, and several countries, especially in the third world, got saddled with balance of payments problems. The metropolitan banks were involved in the recycling of petrodollars, but they needed an agency to act as a monitor for them and the IMF took on this role. It not only acted as a conduit for such recycling through its own "Oil Facility" and "Extended Facility" loans, but it also facilitated borrowing by third world countries once they had accepted the "discipline" of IMF "conditionalities." All this meant a change in the role of the IMF, from merely being an occasional lender to countries undergoing balance of payments stress and advising them to undertake "stabilization," to becoming an instrument of international finance capital to get countries to undertake "structural adjustment," which would open them up to unrestricted global flows in goods, services, and capital, including above all finance. It was ironic that an institution with whose founding John Maynard Keynes had been associated in his capacity as a founder of the Bretton Woods system, who had wanted to "let finance be national," now became an instrument for opening up economies to "reforms" so that finance ceased to be national.

Opening economies to global financial flows entailed a change in the relative weights of the nation-state and the-now globalized finance capital. To prevent finance from flowing out en masse, the state had to be careful not to upset the "confidence of the investors," which meant kowtowing to the demands of finance. Finance, in turn, which had had to yield ground in the immediate postwar years because of the socialist threat and working-class restiveness in the advanced countries, was now in a position to establish its supreme hegemony, of which the adoption of neoliberal policies was an obvious manifestation.

This hegemony, and the associated neoliberal policies did not suddenly appear fully formed on one fine day. The crisis of the dirigiste regime caused by inflation, against which it had no bulwark in the post-colonial era, was exploited by international or globalized finance capital, which was in the process of being formed within the Bretton Woods system to launch an attack against this regime and replace it with the neoliberal regime, whose characteristics and implications we will examine in the next chapter. But before proceeding further we must distinguish between the account of the transition from dirigisme to neoliberalism that we have given above and accounts given by others. In particular, we shall take up certain comments by Paul Krugman for underscoring the *sui generis* nature of our analysis.

### *The Pitfalls of a Ricardian Reading of the Transition*

Paul Krugman, of course, is not concerned with the transition between regimes. His concern is with the phenomenon of inflation, why it occurred in the late '60s and early '70s, and why it subsided subsequently, and he has provided a Ricardian interpretation.[3] While we have emphasized the vulnerability of metropolitan capitalism because the colonial prop was no longer available to it, and while its market-providing role was taken over by the state that now carried out "demand management," its inflation-restraining role could no longer be fulfilled, so that it was only a matter of time before the system would run aground, Krugman takes an altogether different track, which is essentially Ricardian in nature.

The inflation in the early '70s, he argues, was because of a resource crisis, that is, excess demand pressures with regard to resource availability.

The crisis was overcome, according to him, through supply adjustments such as oil strikes in the North Sea and the Gulf of Mexico, and the entry of new land into cultivation. This is essentially a Ricardian explanation (though without bringing in the question of "diminishing returns" and secular shifts in terms of trade).

The inadequacy of this explanation is evident from the fact that the crisis of resource shortage of the 1970s was not universally overcome through supply adjustment. In the case of the most vital primary commodity for instance, food grains, it was overcome through a severe compression of demand, and this was achieved through the imposition of an income deflation upon large masses of the population of the world. *Globalization of finance, which was responsible for ushering in the neoliberal regime, played the role of imposing this income deflation.*

An income deflation, it is often not recognized, has an effect analogous to that of what Keynes had called a profit inflation in eliminating excess demand. While profit inflation does so by raising prices relative to money incomes, an income deflation does so by squeezing money incomes relative to prices. Hence "inflation control" can always be achieved through an income deflation that brings about the same effect as profit inflation would have done, but in a different way. But whereas the two have the same consequence by way of eliminating excess demand, an income deflation is preferred by finance capital since it does not cause a fall in the real value of financial assets. The hegemony of finance in the world economy therefore meant a switch to income deflation, which was imposed through the neoliberal regime that the world moved into with the collapse of dirigisme.

The methods of income deflation, especially in the third world, were obvious: cuts in subsidies; cuts in transfer payments to the poor; cuts in government expenditure that reduced both welfare spending and employment; privatization of essential services, which, though it raises the effective price paid by the poor, is not captured by typical price indices; the reduction in private demand for other goods owing to the privatization of essential services; and so on. In short, the entire gamut of measures that constitute neoliberal policies have this one overwhelming characteristic, of squeezing the demand for goods on the part of the working people from the income side rather than from the price side. And it is this squeeze rather than any supply adjustment that ended the 1970s inflation in primary commodity prices.

Because of this income deflation, the supply side also suffers. In other words, income deflation, while squeezing the demand side, also squeezes the supply side, since the victims of such deflation include the peasants and petty producers as well. But the squeeze on the demand side is greater than any squeeze on the supply side, which, after all, is how it overcomes the problem of excess demand.

According to the Food and Agricultural Organization (FAO), the average annual world cereal output during the triennium 1979–81 was 1,573 million tons for a population (for the midyear of the triennium) of 4,435 million. For the triennium 1999–2001, the cereal output had increased to 2,084 million tons for a world population (again for the midyear 2000) of 6,071 million. This represents a *decline* in per capita cereal output of the world, from 355 kilograms in 1980 to 343 kilograms in 2000. In other words, far from there being a supply adjustment, there was actually a decline in the per capita cereal output of the world. Since the income elasticity of demand for cereals is certainly positive *if we take both direct and indirect demand for cereals* (the latter through processed foods and through feed for animals whose products are then consumed), that is, if we take the final demand for cereals as well as the input demand in the Leontief (input-output) sense, there should have been an excess demand for cereals causing a rise in their prices relative to the vector of money wages and money incomes.

This should also have caused a shift in the terms of trade between cereals and manufactured goods in favor of the former, since manufactured goods prices are typically fixed on a prime cost-plus basis, and the rate of growth of labor productivity was much higher in manufacturing than in cereal production. Ironically, we find a decline in the terms of trade for cereals vis-à-vis manufacturing in the world economy that was as high as 45 percent over these two decades.[4] In other words, excess demand pressures that would have arisen in the cereal markets were nullified without causing any profit inflation through the imposition of an income deflation, which was so sharp that the terms of trade actually moved in a direction opposite to what one would have expected.

## An Echo of Colonialism

The colonial regime, as we have seen, imposed income deflation upon the working people of the colonies and semi-colonies of the third world. The income deflation that neoliberalism has imposed is a replication of this colonial phenomenon. The mechanisms through which income deflation is imposed in the two periods are obviously different: in the colonial period the mechanism was a mix of drain and deindustrialization. In the neoliberal era the mechanism is through public expenditure cuts, some degree of deindustrialization in the sense of traditional activities being replaced by those under the aegis of multinational corporations, such as Walmart replacing a host of retail traders, and also a winding up of the institutional support system by the state that had been developed for peasant agriculture and other petty producers like handloom weavers, which lowers their incomes. At any rate, colonial-style drain of surplus is no longer possible, though some transfers from the third world to the metropolitan countries continue. But income deflation is imposed nonetheless.

We shall look at the implications of the neoliberal regime in detail in the next chapter. But two points about it need to be noted here. First, the dirigiste period had seen an attempt to build an alternative structure, under the influence of Keynesian ideas, *which was an alternative to the colonial structure*, with state intervention boosting aggregate demand. This, however, suffered from a major lacuna: there was nothing to replace the inflation-controlling role of the colonial regime, which is why inflation flared up in the early 1970s. Neoliberalism entails a partial rectification of this, by instituting income deflation, as in the colonial times, but in a new form, so that a mechanism for inflation control of the sort that had existed earlier is re-created. Neoliberalism, in short, represents a reassertion of imperialism.

But precisely because this reassertion occurs without any necessary armed intervention, through the "peaceful" operation of the market, it is not recognized as such. We have seen that many who recognize imperialism as a phenomenon during the dirigiste period because of the several instances of armed intervention against third world governments attempting economic decolonization, do not do so in the current period when such instances of armed intervention have become comparatively more scarce (except in specific regions).[5] This is an error. The earlier interventions occurred because imperialism was being challenged and was generally in retreat. The absence of such interventions today testifies to the triumph of imperialism: income deflation can be imposed on third world populations through governments compelled to do so by the logic of being caught in the web of neoliberalism.

Second, because neoliberalism represents the hegemony of international finance capital, which frowns upon state intervention in demand management, it has no mechanism for stimulating demand in the metropolitan capitalist economy. Colonial markets are now clearly inadequate, and the state is no longer allowed to stimulate demand directly. The only means through which demand can be stimulated in metropolitan capitalism today is through the formation of asset price bubbles.

To put it differently, the colonial arrangement constituted an ideal situation for capitalism. The failure of Keynesianism, which fulfilled one role of colonialism but not the others, showed that capitalism could not function for any length of time in its absence. Neoliberalism fulfills the role of colonialism that Keynesianism could not, but in the process it fails to fulfill the role that Keynesianism had done.

Neoliberalism tries to re-create some features of colonialism, namely income deflation on the working people of the third world, with a view to stabilizing capitalism, and does succeed in this regard. In the process, it exposes capitalism to another kind of structural crisis arising from the side of demand, which we will soon examine.

# PART 5

# CHAPTER 17

# The Neoliberal Regime

Neoliberalism is usually presented in terms of a state versus market dichotomy. Ironically, this is often accepted even by its critics who see the core of neoliberalism as consisting in "liberalization, privatization, and globalization," with the first of the three being interpreted as a "retreat of the state." This, however, is totally misleading. Neoliberalism entails not a retreat or a withdrawal of the state, not a shift from a regime of state intervention to a regime of "leaving things to the market," which is the way that neoliberalism would like to present itself, but rather as *a change in the nature of state intervention*. Underlying it is a change in the nature of the state itself, which in turn reflects a change in the nature of the classes and the correlation between them. A better way of approaching neoliberalism is not through its symptoms but through its class character.

The essence of neoliberalism consists in a dual change that comes about in a capitalist economy: a change in the class configuration and an accompanying change in the nature of the state and its *modus operandi*. Lenin had discussed in his *Imperialism*, following the lead of Hobson and Hilferding, how within each metropolitan country a financial oligarchy comes up with the emergence of monopoly, which presides over a mass of finance capital that represents a fusion between industrial and bank capital, and which wants as large an economic territory as possible to steal a march over its rivals. Contemporary globalization implies, in contrast, that within each country, not just in metropolitan countries but in others as well, there is a financial oligarchy, or what we would prefer to call a corporate-financial oligarchy, *which is globalized, in the sense of going all over the world in quest of gains instead of seeking an exclusive economic territory of its own.*

There are at least three differences between the oligarchy discussed by Lenin and the oligarchy today. First, it is not a specific nation-based, and nation-state aided entity engaged in a rivalry with other similar nation-based and nation-state aided entities, but a globalized entity whose "national" character recedes to the background. As this happens for all such entities, instead of a rivalry among them, we have a certain fusion of these different entities into a common being. This common being is what we have called international finance capital.

Second, international finance capital contributes toward a muting of "inter-imperialist rivalry," which had been the focus of Lenin's attention. International finance capital is averse to a world partitioned into different spheres of influence, for that impedes its free movement across the globe.

Third, free movement is not just for setting up industries, let alone for promoting some "national interest" against the "national interest" of others. It does, of course, set up industries if they can be profitably run in some locations. But, above all, its quest for gain takes the form of seeking speculative gains. Speculation occupies center stage in the current era of globalization. This does not mean that we cannot distinguish capital-in-production from capital-as-finance, the latter obviously roaming all over the world in search of speculative gains. What it means is that there is no Chinese wall separating the two. The multinational corporations that are supposedly the custodians of capital-in-production also engage in speculative activities, as do the dealers in capital-as-finance. And the dealers in capital-as-finance also engage in financing productive activities as do the custodians of capital-in-production.

Within each capitalist economy, the distinction between the corporate-financial oligarchy and the rest, consisting of smaller capitalists, petty producers, peasants, and craftsmen, becomes sharper, with the former getting globalized in its operations and hence getting integrated into international finance capital.

The specificity of this development would become clear if we contrast it with what had happened in a number of third world countries in the immediate aftermath of decolonization. The bourgeoisie in these countries, including the big bourgeoisie, which had been thwarted in its ambitions in the colonial period, had demanded and obtained from the new post-colonial state protection against metropolitan capital. Not only were these economies cordoned off from free capital flows, but they were protected against the free flows of goods and services, so that the big bourgeoisie could carve out for itself a space where it could fulfill its ambition *without worrying about any encroachment by metropolitan capital.* Third world dirigisme had been a weapon used by the local big bourgeoisie against metropolitan capital. But the use of this weapon had also benefited a host of petty producers, peasants, and craftsmen who had also been protected from encroachment by metropolitan capital.

The dirigiste regime had thus been a carryover of the anti-colonial struggle. And the big bourgeoisie engaged in manufacturing (called the "national bourgeoisie" in contrast to the "comprador bourgeoisie" engaged in colonial trade), which had been a part of the anti-colonial struggle and in leadership of it in countries where the Communists or similar left formations were not leading it, continued even after decolonization to remain in the camp of the working people against metropolitan capital, though with its own motivations and ambitions.

What we find under neoliberalism is a shift in its position. It now makes common cause with metropolitan capital to "open up" the world for free flows of capital and of goods and services, *to the detriment of vast sections of peasants and petty producers, and even small capitalists.* The hiatus that existed earlier between the "national economy" and metropolitan capital now shifts its location to within the country, between international finance capital with which the domestic big bourgeoisie gets integrated and the rest of the economy, which suffers in terms of output and employment because of the "opening up" to free flows of capital and goods and services.

The second change that occurs is the change in the nature of state intervention. Since the nation-state cannot afford to offend international finance capital (for fear of creating a financial crisis through capital outflows in the event of its doing so), the state intervenes almost exclusively at the behest of such globalized capital. Instead of appearing to stand above classes and playing the role of a detached and benevolent umpire, which the bourgeois state had traditionally tried to do, it now intervenes in the interests of globalized capital in general and its local counterpart, the domestic corporate-financial oligarchy, under the pretense that the interests of this oligarchy is coterminous with the interests of the nation. A notion of "development" is adopted for this purpose, so that anyone opposed to such intervention in favor of the corporate-financial oligarchy is branded as "anti-development" and hence *ipso facto* "anti-national."

Rudolf Hilferding noted how in the era of finance capital the nation's interests are proclaimed to be identical with the interests of finance capital, whereby, he concluded, a glorification of the "national idea" had become the ideology of finance capital.[1] But Hilferding's perception referred to the era of nation-based finance capital. What happens in the current era of globalization is that the promotion of the interests of international finance capital, including of metropolitan capital, which constitutes its largest component, gets justified by a glorification of the "national idea" within the third world, in a remarkable inversion of the logic of anti-colonialism.

How this ideological inversion manages to acquire domestic support is a matter we shall come to later. But the point to note here is that within the neoliberal regime where the state intervenes in favor of globalized capital, *it simultaneously withdraws the support it had extended to peasants, petty producers, craftsmen, and small capitalists*, plunging these classes, especially the peasants and petty producers, into a deep crisis, as they cannot withstand the encroachment by the domestic corporate-financial oligarchy, and of international capital generally.

The essence of globalization lies in this basic change that comes about, of which the privatization of essential services; the handing over of publicly owned assets to big private capital, whether to the domestic corporate-financial oligarchy or to metropolitan capital; the running down of price-support schemes for the peasantry that had been erected earlier; the cutbacks in public investment caused by the curbing of the fiscal deficit (to within 3 percent of GDP and no longer zero as under the gold standard) while taxes on the rich cannot be raised, for that too undermines the "confidence of the investors"; and the opening of the economy to free flows of goods and services and capital (though absolute freedom has not yet been accorded to the last of these in all countries) are just manifestations.

## Implications of Neoliberalism

This basic shift in class configuration and the policy changes it gives rise to have profound implications. An implication that has received much attention is the shift of capital from the high-wage economies of the advanced capitalist world to the low-wage economies of the Global South. This constitutes a sharp contrast with historical experience. Throughout the period before the current globalization, capital flows from the Global North were essentially toward other countries within the North, to the temperate regions of European settlement to which migration was occurring on a massive scale. The migration of capital was complementary to the migration of European labor.[2] Capital that came to the South went to spheres like minerals, plantations, and trade, which complemented the colonial-style division of labor.[3]

But capital movement from the North to the South to produce the same goods as were being produced in the North and with the same technology, but at the lower Southern wages to meet the world market, which would have boosted the profitability of the production of such goods, never really occurred. Had it occurred, the distinction between developed and underdeveloped countries would have disappeared, since the massive labor reserves generated in the South owing to deindustrialization and surplus drain would have got absorbed until the relative sizes of the reserve army of labor, and the real wage rates, got more or less equalized in the two segments of the world. But this did not occur, and why it did not has been a big question before development economists till now.[4]

Even in the postwar dirigiste period when capital movements from the North to the South for setting up manufacturing industries in the latter occurred, that is, when capital movements did finally detach themselves from merely buttressing the colonial-style division of labor, this was more for tariff-jumping than for servicing the global market while taking advantage of the low third world wages. Since third world governments after decolonization were breaking away from the colonial division of labor and protecting domestic markets from imports, metropolitan capital could no longer access these markets while locating production in advanced countries. Thus it had to produce locally for accessing these markets. The market capital was accessing through such local production, however, was not the global market but only the local market.

The current globalization broke with this. There was a genuine shift of activities from the North to the South for meeting global demand while taking advantage of the lower Southern wages. China was the major beneficiary of this shift of manufacturing activities, and India was the major beneficiary of a shift of service sector activities.

Such a shift meant, first, a massive diffusion of capitalism from North to South. To be sure, there was capitalism developing within the dirigiste regimes that had come up in the third world after decolonization; but that capitalism had been hemmed in by the need of the regime to protect petty production, to impose controls of various kinds, and to preserve a generally egalitarian orientation that had been the legacy of the anti-colonial struggle. This hemming in could be justified by referring to the tendency of Northern capital to stay in the North, that is, the tendency of Northern capital to promote an international dichotomy between the developed and the underdeveloped countries. Now, however, full-blown capitalism finally got a chance to develop in the South. Export orientation, until then not considered an adequate strategy for development, since it could only refurbish the colonial division of labor without allowing third world countries to break out of it, now became the instrument for development, and metropolitan capital, till then considered a hindrance to third world development, now became a facilitator, welcomed with open arms.

Second, this new strategy meant an acceleration in GDP growth rates in the third world. True, this did not occur uniformly, but was mainly concentrated in East, Southeast, and South Asia; and true also that an acceleration in third world growth rates compared to the colonial past had already occurred in the dirigiste period. But that acceleration occurred not under the auspices of metropolitan capital, but in opposition to it, through protection, import-substituting industrialization with public investment playing a major role, and the stimulation of agricultural growth. It had occurred, in other words, not as part of an export-oriented strategy but in explicit contrast to the "openness" of the colonial period. The acceleration in the current period is of a different nature, based as it is on the "spontaneous" diffusion of activities from the North to the South as distinct from the enforced diffusion of such activities under dirigisme; the latter had involved activities being snatched away by the South from the North, which is what import-substitution entailed.

Third, both of the above traits entailed a flourishing urban middle class. The outsourcing of activities from North to South, the acceleration of growth as a consequence of it, the diffusion of capitalism to the South with the army of employees in the sphere of finance and commodity circulation it invariably creates, brought in its wake a flourishing urban middle class that constituted the chief social support base for globalization in the third world.

The importance of the urban middle class was underscored by Kalecki in his remarks on the "intermediate regimes" where he had described this class, together with the well-to-do peasants, as the backbone of the dirigiste regime.[5] Though one may differ from Kalecki's calling this class the ruling class, the social importance of the urban middle class in the third world cannot be underestimated. But just as it had supported the dirigiste regime, which it saw as opening up employment opportunities for itself, with *dirigisme* running into a dead end, it switched to supporting neoliberalism and the regime of globalization as it opened up new employment opportunities for this class.

While all this was one set of implications of globalization, there was another important set, which is less appreciated. Let us turn to it.

### *The Crisis of Traditional Petty Production*

The dirigiste regime had in various ways supported, protected, and promoted petty production, especially peasant agriculture, even in countries where the Communists had not led the anti-colonial struggle and where consequently there had been no thoroughgoing land reforms. In these countries, landlord capitalism had grown alongside peasant capitalism and had even carried out a process of "internal" primitive accumulation of capital, with landlords ousting tenants to use land for capitalist farming, though big capital from outside was not generally involved. The regime of protection and promotion of peasant agriculture therefore had conferred uneven benefits on the peasantry, with the rich peasants and landlords being its main beneficiaries. Nonetheless, it had not been without benefit for the mass of petty producers.

The promotion of peasant agriculture had taken a variety of forms: tariff protection and quantitative trade restrictions to insulate the sector from world market price fluctuations, which, as is well known, are very wide in the case of primary commodities; provision of a range of subsidized inputs; research and development in state agencies for evolving better production practices; public investment in irrigation and other facilities of benefit to petty production; procurement of produce at assured prices by public agencies; dissemination of better practices through a wide public extension network developed for the purpose; and so on. One consequence of all this was an acceleration of agricultural growth that had the effect of preventing the phenomenon of increasing supply price from manifesting itself, and hence letting the "Golden Age of Capitalism" have a prolonged run.

With neoliberalism, however, all these measures of protection and promotion are progressively withdrawn and the agriculture sector (and more generally petty production) becomes open to encroachment by big capital, including metropolitan capital, from outside, and hence to the classical form of "primitive accumulation of capital." Subsidized inputs are eliminated in the name of fiscal rectitude; public procurement at assured remunerative prices is eliminated as unwarranted interference in the functioning of the market, an elimination institutionalized under the WTO (though in the case of food crops the elimination of procurement is still not institutionalized as has happened for cash crops); public extension services are eliminated with peasants and petty producers now made to enter into a direct relationship with multinational agribusiness and multinational retail giants like Walmart; public investment in irrigation and other such overheads is wound down along with public investment in general; and quantitative trade restrictions are removed, with tariffs set inordinately low, lower even than the "tariff bounds" allowed by the WTO. This makes domestic prices move in sync with the fluctuating world prices in the case of cash crops at least, and catches the peasants in a debt trap, as in colonial times.

And on top of all this, the pressure for land acquisition to meet the various demands of the bourgeoisie and the urban middle class, such as housing, real estate, infrastructure (which often camouflages the demand for land for real estate purposes), and industrialization, leads to the dispossession of the peasants and the diversion of agricultural land for other uses.

Therefore, a twofold process of primitive accumulation of capital occurs under neoliberalism. There is primitive accumulation in a flow sense, where the average real incomes of the peasants and petty producers are squeezed, and there is primitive accumulation of capital in a stock sense, where they are simply deprived of their assets, either without any payment (this is true especially where the assets belong to the tribal population) or at throwaway prices. The point is that the unleashing of primitive accumulation of capital, or "accumulation through encroachment" (as one of us has called the conjoint processes of primitive accumulation at the expense of petty producers and similar accumulation at the expense of the state, through privatization of public assets), is an important feature of neoliberalism.[6] The suicides of 300,000 peasants in India over the two and a half decades after 1990 is indicative of the virulence of the process.

But that is by no means all. When traditional petty producers are dispossessed, or when they get squeezed enough to want to move out of agriculture or other traditional occupations in search of work in urban areas, they do not find adequate work and swell the ranks of the labor reserves. Indeed, the distinction between an active army of labor and a reserve army as usually understood ceases to be applicable. Employment rationing takes a form where instead of some being fully employed and others fully unemployed, most are employed only part of the time, owing to the proliferation of casual employment, part-time employment, intermittent employment, "petty entrepreneurship" (a euphemism for disguised unemployment), and so on. Nonetheless, whatever the form of the labor reserves, displaced peasants and petty producers join the ranks of these reserves, because not enough jobs are created to absorb them together with the natural increase in the workforce, even in economies that are growing rapidly.

This is because under neoliberalism the restrictions on the pace of technological-cum-structural change are removed, which means that the rate of growth of labor productivity accelerates. Since the rate of growth of employment in the capitalist sector is the difference between the rate of growth of output and the *ex ante* rate of growth of labor productivity (that is, correcting for the effect of a rise in disguised unemployment), if this difference falls below the sum of the natural rate of growth of the workforce and the rate of growth of job-seekers from the petty production sector, then the relative size of the labor reserves must increase. This is exactly what is happening.

A pervasive belief, derived from the experience of Europe, is that while petty producers are dispossessed by the encroachment of capitalism, they get reabsorbed in the role of proletarians at a later date, so that their sufferings are only for a transitional period. That is, the process of primitive accumulation of capital brings only temporary suffering, except to a small segment of the dispossessed who remain trapped within the ranks of the reserve army of labor and experience prolonged suffering.

This belief, however, is a misconception. The reason why the dispossessed and pauperized petty producers in Europe did not just linger on as a vast unemployed and underemployed mass was not because they were absorbed as proletarians into the expanding capitalist sector, but because they emigrated in large numbers to the temperate regions of European settlement. Capitalism does not, in short, have an immanent tendency to absorb the bulk of the petty producers it displaces. And since for the people of third world countries such emigration possibilities do not exist, there is nothing to restrain the growth of unemployment and poverty as a consequence of primitive accumulation. Indeed, unemployment and poverty do increase secularly under the neoliberal dispensation in the third world.

The *ex ante* rate of growth of labor productivity under neoliberalism is high in the third world for at least three reasons. First, the desire to imitate metropolitan lifestyles on the part of the bourgeoisie and the urban middle class implies a shift in product mix and technology to bridge the gap between what exists in the third world and what is available in the metropolis; this is employment-displacing. Second, the desire to continuously alter this lifestyle in sync with the changes taking place in the metropolis implies a pace of technological-cum-structural change that is typically employment-displacing. And third, a shift in income distribution away from the workers, peasants, and petty producers toward the bourgeoisie and the urban middle class entails a change in the consumption basket; the change in the product mix in accordance with this change in the consumption basket is also employment-displacing.

For all these reasons, neoliberalism, though ushering in primitive accumulation of capital, does not create enough jobs, even in economies experiencing high rates of GDP growth, to absorb those displaced into the active army of labor. This, however, raises an important question: Is not creating enough jobs a necessary characteristic of the neoliberal regime, or is it only a happenstance, something that just happens to arise only because of certain parameter values? *Our argument is that it is a necessary characteristic of the neoliberal economy.* Let us see why.

### Reading Market Signals in a Neoliberal Regime

Let us suppose that a producer in the petty production economy, in which we include tenants and laborers, was earning on average an amount $x$ per period, and the process of primitive accumulation of capital in the flow sense reduced it to $y$ (where $y < x$). If such a person migrates to the capitalist sector and *does get absorbed* into the active army of labor at a per capita real income $z$ that is higher than $x$, then there would be an increase in the average per capita real income of the working people *as a whole* compared to the original situation. This would raise the average per capita demand for food grains, which, if per capita food grains output is not rising, would cause excess demand in the food grains market, and hence inflation. Controlling such inflation would require cutting back on aggregate demand, and on employment and output, causing precisely a denouement of not enough jobs in the economy to absorb the total number of job-seekers, consisting of both displaced petty producers and the natural increase in the workforce that we have been talking about.

Put differently, the rate of growth of employment, $g_e$ in the capitalist sector, is given by the following:

$$g_e = \text{Min.}[(g - g_p), f(g_r)] \cdots$$

where g is the rate of growth of output in the capitalist sector, $g_p$ is the rate of growth in labor productivity in this sector, $g_f$ the rate of growth of food grains output in the economy, and $f(g_f)$ the rate of growth of employment in the capitalist sector that any $g_f$ can sustain without giving rise to excess demand pressures in the food grains market. For the rate of growth of employment to absorb displaced producers from the pre-capitalist sector, not only should the rate of growth of labor demand, the first term within square brackets, exceed the natural rate of growth in the workforce, but so must the second term. For that to happen the rate of growth of food grain output must exceed the rate of population growth, so as to allow an increase in per capita real income compared to the original  situation (since z > x).[7]

An objection might be raised on the grounds that a country does not have to meet its food grains requirement out of its own production; it can always import food grains. But the world as a whole cannot do so; nor can large economies, for their going to the international market will push up world food grain prices, posing a threat to the value of money. Hence, they will have to be more or less "self-sufficient" in food grains.

Raising per capita food grain output, however, requires land augmentation measures on the part of the state. Land augmentation must occur not just for providing food grains for the domestic market but also, above all, for meeting export demand from the metropolis, for which land has to be diverted from food grain production. Measures of land augmentation, though they played an important role under dirigisme, are eschewed under neoliberalism because of the change in the nature of the state, which we discussed above. Emphasis shifts instead toward keeping down domestic absorption of food grains (which are both exports and export-substitutes) through income deflation measures directed against the working people.

An additional factor works in the same direction of preventing land augmentation. The process of primitive accumulation of capital directed against peasant agriculture has the effect of *reducing* this sector's, as well as the overall demand for food grains, even before any shift of displaced petty producers to towns has occurred. *And this provides a market signal that leads to a curtailment of state efforts toward land augmentation.* A rise in the cost of essential services, like healthcare, for example, on account of privatization, which is a powerful instrument for unleashing primitive accumulation, causes a decline in food grain demand, as agriculturists and others are forced to skimp on food intake to meet hospital bills for illnesses.

The market signals under a neoliberal regime, in other words, point always in a direction opposite to what social rationality would demand. And since under this regime, the state, which in the Keynesian perception stood as the promoter of social rationality, is reduced to act in accordance with the dictates of private rationality, we get perverse results, and one such result is state withdrawal from land augmentation even in countries afflicted by hunger.

In fact, in a neoliberal economy, an excess supply of food grains on account of a reduction in purchasing power in the hands of the working people causes a withdrawal of the state from land-augmentation measures and hence a lowering of the growth rate of food grain production. But an excess demand for food grains, such as would occur if the displaced petty producers get absorbed into the active army of labor, causes not the opposite, that is, a vigorous pursuit of land augmentation, but rather a lowering of aggregate demand through monetary stringency and fiscal austerity in order to ward off inflation by accentuating unemployment.

The state's withdrawal from land augmentation because of this perverse reading of signals implies that the rate of growth of food grain production under neoliberalism scarcely exceeds the rate of population growth, even as the *level* of per capita food grain consumption is lower than in the original situation (when the average income in the petty production economy was $x$). In addition agricultural exports increase under this regime, either food grain exports or exports of non-food grains toward which land has to be diverted from food grains, so that a neoliberal regime is invariably associated with a decline, compared to the original situation, in per capita *availability* of food grains (defined as net production minus net exports plus net decumulation of stocks) and a rate of growth of per capita availability that is zero or less. Because of this, the displaced petty producers, upon whom a process of primitive accumulation of capital is inflicted, can never get absorbed into the active army of labor. What is more, let alone getting absorbed at the income level $z$, their average per capita income remains even lower than $x$. This is because of the fall in per capita food grain availability, compared to the original situation.[8]

As $x$ itself represents an increase over $y$, to which the average per capita real income had shrunk as a result of primitive accumulation, an increase back to $x$ itself would cause an excess demand for food grains because of the reduced per capita food grains availability, and hence inflationary pressures. Such pressures, if they arise, would necessitate contractionary policies because of which an increase in the average per capita income to $x$ becomes impossible in the petty production sector. Thus the decline in per capita food grains availability implies that the per capita real incomes can neither increase from $y$ to $z$ nor even recover from $y$ to $x$.

It follows, therefore, that under the neoliberal regime, there is a decline in the average material living condition of the working people taken as a whole, compared to the original pre-neoliberal level, no matter how high the GDP growth rate happens to be. All this has an implication for poverty.

## The Question of Poverty

When petty producers remain in their traditional occupations accepting lower incomes, the worsening of their living standards is obvious. But even when they migrate to cities in search of jobs, the non-availability of jobs implies a worsening of their living standards, since they never get on average the income $x$ they were getting earlier. Not only do they experience a reduction in real incomes compared to the original situation, but this has the effect of pulling down the real wages of even the organized full-time workers, since an increase in the relative size of labor reserves always has this effect.

As a result, a congruence develops under neoliberal capitalism between the interests of the workers and those of the peasants and petty producers. The process of primitive accumulation directed against the latter, which worsens their condition, also worsens the condition of the workers in general, including even the organized, unionized workers, whose bargaining strength drops as a consequence. This phenomenon, of displacement of traditional petty producers who migrate to cities but are not absorbed into the active army of labor, or do not migrate but linger on at lower living standards in their traditional habitat, results in an increase in the relative size of absolute poverty.

This, indeed, is what has been happening, even in economies experiencing rapid GDP growth. It is significant that the per capita cereal output for the world as a whole for triennium 2015–17 (average annual output divided by 2016 population) was 344.9 kilograms, distinctly lower than the 355 kg. for 1979–81 (calculated similarly by dividing the triennium average by the mid-triennium population). Even in India, which has been one of the high-growth economies, the percentage of rural population that does not have access to 2,200 calories per person per day (the official norm for defining poverty) has increased from 58 percent in 1993–94, shortly after neoliberal policies were introduced in 1991, to 68 percent in 2011–12. For urban India, where the calorie norm is 2,100 per person per day, the corresponding figures are 57 percent and 65 percent, respectively.

Since a growth in absolute poverty is assiduously denied by the defenders of neoliberalism, it is important to clarify exactly what we are arguing. There is no doubt that there has been a great improvement in the lives of the people of the third world after decolonization: better infrastructure; modern medicine, greater awareness of hygiene, and other developments have increased human longevity and reduced infant and maternal mortality rates. In other words, to talk of an increase in the magnitude of poverty must not be taken to mean that people today are worse off compared to, say, half a century ago. *What it means is something specific, namely that per capita command over a particular basket of essential goods, including above all food grains, has become less than it was prior to the introduction of the neoliberal regime.*[9]

The association of neoliberal capitalism with an increase in poverty arises not out of any conspiracy or diabolical intent; it is simply a part of its *modus operandi*, whereby a process of primitive accumulation of capital is unleashed while there is a dogged effort to restrain inflation. This is achieved without interfering too much with the functioning of the market by curtailing government spending, including on land augmentation.[10] This provides the setting for income deflation. If the rate of growth of labor demand (that is, $g - g_p$), is spontaneously low, then there is spontaneous income deflation anyway; otherwise, anti-inflationary measures ensure such income deflation.

The decline in per capita world cereal output in the aftermath of the inflation of the 1970s and in per capita world cereal absorption is merely a reflection of the *modus operandi* of neoliberalism, which is missed by Krugman and others who do not see its role in imposing income deflation.

An important corollary follows from the above, where we talked about exports to the metropolis as a constant element in the background. The same phenomenon, however, can arise because of sales for the consumption of the bourgeoisie and the middle class domestically, consumption that is both direct and indirect (through processed foods and feed grains for animal products). Any acceleration in the growth of the non-agricultural sector is likely to increase this "export demand" as well. Since this would lead to a reduction in the per capita absorption of food grains by the rest of society, that is, by the non-bourgeois and non-middle-class sections, and hence to an increase in absolute poverty, the following necessarily holds : *An acceleration in the growth rate of an economy located on the tropical landmass, unless it is accompanied by appropriate measures of land augmentation, which under neoliberal conditions it scarcely is, will cause greater absolute poverty in the same economy.*

This is because the demand on the landmass, either for itself (for building golf courses, luxury villas, and the like) or its products, will increase with the rise in GDP, which under neoliberalism would be met through imposing even harsher income deflation on the working people and hence engendering greater poverty. It is not only the demand of the metropolis that underlies the growth in poverty in the third world country, but its own growth (since it is unaccompanied by land augmentation). The higher this growth, the greater is the magnitude of absolute poverty.

The fact that the logic of capitalism produces wealth at one pole and poverty at another has been underscored by Marx. He was referring primarily to the growth of the reserve army of labor and his proposition is of a general character. It can be given precision if we take into account the income deflation that becomes necessary under capitalism if inflation arising from increasing supply price for products grown on the fixed tropical landmass is to be avoided, which it must be for preserving the value of money.

While much has been written on the growth-enhancing effects in the third world of globalization, which leads to an outsourcing of activities from the North to the South, the other aspect of globalization, of exercising income deflation and growing absolute poverty, has scarcely received notice. We return to this theme in the next chapter.

CHAPTER 18

# *Inequality and* Ex Ante *Overproduction*

What is striking about the current globalization is that for the first time in the history of capitalism there has been a de-segmentation of the world economy. Throughout the history of capitalism till now, labor from the South had been barred from migrating freely to the North. It still is. There were, as Arthur Lewis has argued, two great streams of migration in the long nineteenth century, stretching up to the First World War, after the forced migration of the slave trade had come to an end, transporting about twenty million persons from Africa to the Americas.[1]

One stream of migration was from some tropical and semi-tropical regions of the world to other tropical and semi-tropical regions, which took low-wage coolie or indentured labor to work on mines, plantations, or other sites in destinations like the West Indies, Fiji, East Africa, and the Western Pacific from countries like China and India where deindustrialization under the colonial or semi-colonial regimes had created massive labor reserves. The other was a high-wage migration from temperate regions to other temperate regions, essentially from Europe to Canada, the United States, Australia, New Zealand, and South Africa where it was possible for the migrants to set themselves up as farmers by snatching land away from the local inhabitants. The high-wage nature of this migration was not because an "Agricultural Revolution" had happened in Europe, but because of this ability to snatch land away from the local inhabitants. *Note that these two streams were kept strictly separate, so that low-wage labor from the tropics could not compete with the high-wage labor of the temperate regions to bid down the latter's wage.*

This separation, exercised through coercion, was complemented by another separation. Capital from the North did not move freely to the South, even though it was juridically free to do so. Much of it went initially from Britain to Europe and subsequently from Britain and Europe to the temperate regions of European settlement, nourished substantially by the drain from the tropical and semi-tropical colonies. The capital that did come from the North to the South went into sectors like mines and plantations, essentially to buttress the colonial pattern of international division of labor, but not to break this pattern by shifting the location of manufacturing industries from high-wage to low-wage lands.

Since labor from the South could not move freely to the North, and since capital from the North did not move to the South except to specific pockets of activity that colonialism promoted, the world economy became in effect a segmented one. Capital generated from within the South itself was small and could not get going because it faced barriers imposed by "free trade" and "laissez-faire" within its own country, and protectionism over much of the metropolis, not to mention other invisible barriers such as racial discrimination.[2]

Within this segmented world, real wages in the North could increase through workers' struggles along with labor productivity, not necessarily in tandem, as the latter increased because of economic growth accompanied by technological progress while real wages in the South, where the massive labor reserves of the world created by colonial drain and deindustrialization continued to be concentrated, notwithstanding the emigration just discussed, remained more or less tied to a subsistence level.[3] The genesis of the division between the advanced and the underdeveloped countries lay in this segmentation of the world economy. Why capital from the North did not move to the South to take advantage of its low wages for producing the same goods with the same technology as used in the North remains, as we have seen, a moot question. But the fact remains that it did not; and that is why the world got divided into two segments.

This geographical segmentation appears to have ended with the current globalization. Even though labor mobility from the tropical and semi-tropical regions of the world to the temperate regions is still restricted, and attempts to flout such restrictions are countered these days in extremely inhumane ways, as the fate of the refugees from the South in both Europe and the United States shows, capital is now more willing to locate plants in the South to take advantage of its lower wages. To be sure, not all southern countries have been recipients of capital relocation from the North, but many have been, and even this fact has important implications. The de-segmentation in other words arises because of capital's greater willingness to locate activities in the South, to take advantage of its lower wages, for meeting the global market.

The first implication of this willingness to relocate activities from the North to the South is the linking of the wages prevailing in the two segments. They do not get equalized because of the mobility of capital, in the manner depicted in economics textbooks. But clearly the difference between wages cannot keep growing as it had done historically, for any difference above a certain threshold would certainly entail greater movement of capital from the North to the South.

While northern wages, therefore, can no longer move too far out of line with southern wages, the latter scarcely manage to rise above the subsistence level (not a biological but a historical one) to which they have been tied for long. This is because despite the relocation of activities from the North to take advantage of the South's low wages, the relative size of the labor reserves in the South scarcely diminishes. As discussed in the last chapter, the process of primitive accumulation of capital that the neoliberal policies under globalization unleash, together with the natural rate of population growth, and hence workforce growth, ensure that labor supplies grow at a rate that is even higher than the growth of labor demand, even in countries that emerge as the favored destinations for northern capital. Matters are of course worse for the other countries. In the event of wages rising in the South, income deflationary policies that cause contraction in employment are unleashed in the name of fighting inflation; these ensure that wages in the South do not increase, so that the demand for goods produced under increasing supply price remains restricted, without posing any threat to the value of money anywhere in the system.

These two processes, namely, the linking of northern wages to those in the South, and the continued tying of southern wages to a barely increasing subsistence level, imply that the vector of real wages across the world remains more or less constant.[4] But since the vector of labor productivities keeps increasing, the proportion of surplus in output within each country keeps increasing, which is the fundamental reason for the rise in income inequality that has been observed during the period of globalization.

## *The Rise in Income Inequality*

Let us look more closely at this question of income inequality. The above argument would explain why within each country there is an increase in the share of surplus in output. But then it may be asked, how do we link a rise in the share of surplus, which is a macro phenomenon, with an increase in income inequality? Before answering this question, however, we should clarify one particular point.

The proposition about a rise in the share of the surplus refers to *ex ante* surplus, that is, that with any given output there is a rise in labor productivity for given wages, so that if that output continued to be produced it would yield a higher surplus. Yet that output may not continue to be produced, and the surplus that would have been generated had that output been produced may not actually be generated. For that amount of surplus to be produced, an amount of expenditure (at base prices) exactly equal to it has to be undertaken; if it is, then that surplus gets *realized*.

A simple way in which this realization can occur is if the larger expenditure corresponding to the larger surplus from a given output is incurred on this output itself; then the output remains unchanged and simply more of it is taken by the surplus earners while less is left for the wage earners. But if this larger expenditure is incurred on goods other than the bundle in terms of which, as it were, the *ex ante* additional surplus accrues, then there will be more complex patterns of adjustment, which we need not enter here. But it must always be the case that after all adjustments have been made, assuming all wages of "productive workers" are consumed, *the ex post or "realized" surplus must equal the sum of investment, net exports, government consumption, capitalists' consumption, and the consumption of the "unproductive workers."*

If investment plus capitalists' consumption plus consumption by unproductive workers plus net exports and government consumption remains unchanged despite the increase in the share of surplus, then the amount of *ex post* surplus will remain the same as before, but the rise in the share of the surplus in output will manifest itself in terms of a *reduction in output* compared to the initial situation. This is when an overproduction crisis arises because of a rise in the share of surplus, a matter we discuss in the next section.

What is striking is this: no matter what adjustment takes place, a rise in the *ex ante* share of the surplus manifests itself as a rise in the *ex post* share of the surplus. Let us illustrate this point by taking two examples, one where there is no change in the absolute amount of *ex post* surplus, and one in which there is.

Let us for convenience assume that all surplus takes the form of profits, that is, we ignore the existence of "unproductive workers," of taxation and government expenditure, and of foreign trade. Suppose in the initial situation 100 units of wage goods were being produced of which 50 was the wage-bill and 50 profits, and the latter in turn was spent, directly or indirectly, on investment goods (we assume zero capitalists' consumption). In the investment goods sector, the wage bill was 50 and profits 50 (these profits are also obviously spent, directly or indirectly, on investment goods). The total surplus was thus 100. Now, suppose because of an increase in labor productivity in the wage goods sector with given real wages, the *ex ante* surplus of the sector rises to 60, but total investment remains unchanged. If investment remains unchanged, then the realized surplus remains unchanged. All that happens is that the output of the wage goods sector falls by one-sixth, from 100 to 83.33, so that 50 surplus, as before, is generated out of this *smaller output*. But in this case, total surplus would be 100, as before, out of an output of 183.33 (instead of the 200 earlier), so that the *share of surplus in total output* would have risen.

Let us now move to the opposite case where *ex ante* and *ex post* surplus are always equal, that is, let us assume a "non-crisis normal." The demand for investment goods here increases as a result of the amount of surplus in the wage goods sector being 60 instead of 50. Since in the investment goods sector there has been no increase in labor productivity the share of surplus in that sector remains unchanged. There will thus be an increase in the investment sector's output (to 120), wage bill (to 60), and surplus (to 60), which is assumed to be spent on investment because we are assuming a "non-crisis normal." In the new situation, therefore, total surplus will be 120 (that is, 60+60), and total output 220 (that is, 100+120); the share of surplus in the total economy would have increased from 50 percent (100 out of an output of 200) to 54.5 percent (120 out of 220).

It follows that no matter what adjustment occurs, an increase in the share of *ex ante* surplus in output manifests itself as an increase in the share of *ex post* surplus in output. Now, if the surplus accrues to, say, the top 10 percent of the population who own property in the form of capital stock, then the rise in the share of surplus would have manifested itself as a rise in the share of the top 10 percent in total income. Hence, *an observed increase in income inequality between households can be explained by a rise in the ex ante share of surplus in output arising from a rise in labor productivity at given real wages, not necessarily across the board but in some originating sector.*

The fact that there has been such an increase in inequality of income distribution in most countries has been established by Thomas Piketty and several other researchers.[5] Piketty's own explanation for this phenomenon, however, is theoretically flawed. He explains the increase in income inequality through a neoclassical growth model in which an excess of the rate of profits over the natural rate of growth causes capital deepening during a traverse to the steady state. Capital deepening, in a situation of the elasticity of substitution between capital and labor being greater than unity, raises the share of profits in output which, according to him, underlies the growing income inequality. His explanation invokes two inequalities: $r > n$, and $\varepsilon > 1$, where $r$, $n$, and $\varepsilon$ refer, respectively, to the rate of profit, the natural rate of growth, and the elasticity of substitution.

But even within its own terms, $r > n$ need not entail capital deepening, since, as Pasinetti had shown, in a steady state $n = s_c \cdot r$, where $s_c$ denotes capitalists' propensity to save and is less than 1.[6] And there is no reason why $\varepsilon$ should be greater than 1. Besides, on this reasoning, the increase in income inequality should automatically come to an end when a steady state has been reached and this is so even assuming $s_c = 1$.

Above all, the neoclassical growth model assumes full employment at all times and thus Say's Law, which, as we have seen, has no validity in a money-using economy. The full employment assumption on which Piketty's explanation rests is not only empirically flawed but is logically untenable for a capitalist economy, which is preeminently money-using. Piketty's valuable empirical results have to be theoretically explained in a manner different from his own.[7] The explanation we have provided above in terms of a rise in the share of surplus within each country, because the country-wise vector of labor productivities has increased while the country-wise vector of real wages has not, under the regime of globalization, is meant to fill this gap.

### Ex Ante Tendency Toward Overproduction

We have talked so far of a rise in the share of surplus within each country. One cannot logically infer from this that there would be a rise in the share of surplus in the world economy as a whole when there is a change in the distribution of world output across countries (which, after all, is ultimately the reason why the share of surplus in each country is rising). But a sufficient condition for the share of surplus in world output to rise when this share is rising within each country is that the post-relocation share of surplus in countries to which such relocation is occurring must be greater than or equal to the pre-relocation share of surplus in the countries from which such relocation is occurring. Since the share of surplus is rising everywhere, this condition is automatically satisfied if the post-relocation share of surplus in countries to which relocation occurs is higher than the post-relocation share of the surplus in countries from which relocation occurs.

Now, there can be little doubt that the so-called newly emerging countries like India, China, and Brazil have larger shares of surplus in their output at present than the advanced capitalist countries had in the base period. Just to take an illustrative figure, the top 1 percent of the population in the United States had 11 percent of total income in the year 1978 compared to 13 percent for China and over 22 percent for India in 2014. It follows that the rise in the share of surplus within countries in the period of globalization, and on account of globalization, has also increased the overall share of surplus in world output.

An increase in the share of surplus in world output has the effect of giving rise to *ex ante* overproduction for reasons discussed by Kalecki and that informed the argument advanced by Baran and Sweezy in the case of the United States in *Monopoly Capital*.[8] The reason is that the proportion of income consumed by surplus earners is generally less than the proportion of income consumed by wage-earners in any period. So, any redistribution of income from wages to surplus in any period has the effect of reducing consumption in that period, and, for any given level of investment, the level of aggregate demand in that period. Since the actual investment in any period is determined by investment decisions taken in the past, its level can be assumed to be a given entity in the period in question. A shift from wages to surplus thus has the effect of reducing the level of aggregate demand in the period in question.

But it is not just that a situation of *ex ante* overproduction develops in the period in question. Unless it is countered, it gives rise to a reduction in capacity utilization in the period and this affects the investment decisions taken in that period that will fructify as actual investment in subsequent period(s). Hence, investment in the next period falls relative to what it would have been, which then affects what happens in the period after the next one. It follows that even a once-and-for-all shift from wages to surplus that occurs in any period has the effect of lowering the profile of investment and output in all subsequent periods compared to what it otherwise would have been. If, to start with, the economy was experiencing steady growth, then the rise in the share of surplus will push it toward lower growth.

The lowering of the profile of output occurs for two distinct reasons: one is the reduction in the value of the Keynesian multiplier because of the reduction in the economy's "propensity to consume" owing to the shift from wages to surplus; the other is the lowering of the investment profile that occurs because investment is sensitive to the level of capacity utilization. (Kalecki had taken investment to be sensitive not to the level of capacity utilization but to the rate of profit, and since in the period when a shift occurs from wages to surplus there is no change in the rate of profit, as the actual investment remains unchanged, his argument was that the lowering of the output profile occurred because of a fall in the profile of consumption alone. Josef Steindl took investment to be sensitive to capacity utilization and adduced both the reasons for a lowering of the output profile.)

If we are talking not of a once-and-for-all shift from wages to surplus but a shift that keeps occurring over time, that is, a series of shifts, which is what our argument has emphasized, then the economy moves toward lower and lower growth since labor productivity *keeps increasing* while real wages remain more or less constant.

Any such tendency toward overproduction and stagnation arising from a shift from wages to surplus is an *ex ante* tendency, which need not actually manifest itself if there are some countervailing factors. Now, for a long period, right until the First World War, capitalism had two important characteristics: one was the segmentation of the world economy that enabled workers to obtain higher wages as labor productivity increased in the advanced capitalist world, so that the tendency for a movement from wages to surplus was kept in check.

To be sure, there was a shift, not from the wage-earners but from the raw material producers to the surplus earners. This is manifest, on the one hand, from the admittedly debatable statistical finding that the share of wages in national income in the advanced capitalist countries remained more or less constant in the last quarter of the nineteenth century and stretching right until the Second World War, and, on the other hand, from the secular decline in the terms of trade for primary commodities vis-à-vis manufacturing over the same period. This shift in distribution too could have created an *ex ante* tendency toward overproduction and hence stagnation; indeed, it has been argued that it did.[9]

But here the second characteristic becomes relevant, namely the availability of the colonial and semi-colonial markets "on tap." True, the provision of such a counter to this tendency required that newer and newer markets had to be accessed, through further and further encroachments into the economies of the colonies and semi-colonies. But there was no barrier to doing so, which is why the long boom of the long nineteenth century could be sustained despite a rise in what Kalecki calls the "degree of monopoly," which should have increased the share of oligopoly profits in the total value of output, including raw material costs, and hence entailed an *ex ante* tendency toward overproduction and stagnation.

In the post–Second World War period of dirigisme, there was again a counter to any tendency toward *ex ante* overproduction and stagnation in the advanced capitalist world that was provided by state intervention in demand management. The market provided by state spending was again a market "on tap" within this regime. Since the state was committed to maintaining high levels of employment, as large-scale unemployment would have undermined the social legitimacy of the system in the face of the socialist challenge, it actually set up a market on tap. Whether or not there was any such *ex ante* tendency toward overproduction and stagnation within the postwar dirigiste regime in the United States, as argued by Baran and Sweezy, is a matter of debate, as we have seen in chapter 15. But even if there was such a tendency, it remained only *ex ante* because of state intervention, which made the postwar boom, the so-called Golden Age of Capitalism, possible.

What is true about the contemporary phase of neoliberal capitalism is that capitalism is subject *both* to an *ex ante* tendency toward overproduction and stagnation *and* a lack of any counter in the form of a market on tap to which it can turn for preventing this tendency from being realized. The two main counters, which were also the two main exogenous stimuli (on this more later), that served capitalism historically are no longer available to it. Encroachments into the pre-capitalist sphere that colonialism and semi-colonialism had permitted would no longer suffice for the purpose of countering the *ex ante* tendency toward overproduction and stagnation. And finance capital can now effectively prevent state intervention in demand management, which it had always opposed but had to accept perforce in the postwar context of a socialist threat. Hence encroachments into the pre-capitalist sector, though they occur, cannot solve the system's problem, nor can state intervention, as is evident from the fact that in the midst of the post-2008 recession, the emphasis everywhere, after an initial period of dithering, has been on "austerity" and fiscal rectitude (until the current pandemic that has forced some relaxation).

## The Role of Bubbles

The question must arise: If neoliberal capitalism entails a tendency toward stagnation and if the two basic counters that capitalism has historically had against any stagnationist tendency by way of having markets on tap are no longer available to it in this phase, then how do we explain that prior to the 2008 financial crisis, it experienced quite impressive growth rates? We should be clear that the growth rate of the advanced capitalist countries (OECD) in the period 1973–2008 was roughly half of the growth rate during say 1951 to 1973. In other words, there is scarcely any doubt that neoliberal capitalism has on average seen lower growth rates in the advanced capitalist countries, but this growth rate has not necessarily been *slowing down*, as our argument would suggest.

The answer to this question, which many have given, is that two factors have replaced the role that the state had played through its demand management, after it ceased to play that role under pressure from globalized finance capital. One is burgeoning debt, which boosted workers' (and not only workers') consumption despite the stagnation in real wages, and the other is asset price bubbles.

Debt alone can play only a transient role in boosting aggregate demand, since there would be a reluctance both on the part of borrowers to go on borrowing more and more relative to the size of their incomes and assets, and on the part of the lenders to go on lending more and more relative to the size of the assets and incomes of the borrowers. Asset price bubbles enter here: they increase both the borrowers' and the lenders' willingness to increase debt and hence boost consumption and aggregate demand. And to the extent that the bubble occurs in financial assets, it also reduces the cost of borrowing and thereby may have some stimulating role on investment as well. The artificial boost to the value of assets that is provided by an asset price bubble thus raises aggregate demand both through larger consumption and, possibly, larger investment.

There can be little doubt that the growth process under neoliberal capitalism has been heavily dependent upon the formation of asset price bubbles, especially in the United States, which has boosted demand in that country and hence for world capitalism as a whole. The growth phase of the 1990s was related to the "dot-com bubble" in the United States, while the growth phase of the current century prior to 2008 was linked to the housing bubble in the same country.

It is ironic that in the aftermath of the collapse of the housing bubble there has been much criticism of the U.S. Federal Reserve for its "irresponsibility" in promoting and sustaining the bubble. Alan Greenspan's lowering of interest rates after the collapse of the dot-com bubble to generate the housing bubble has come in for particularly severe criticism. What is missed in this criticism is that in the absence of the housing bubble, there would have been no boom in the wake of the post-dot-com slowdown.

Bubbles, in other words, constitute the very mechanism through which growth is generated under neoliberal capitalism, even though each bubble inevitably collapses, bringing a crisis in its wake. To criticize a Greenspan for promoting a bubble is thus to blame an individual for the flaws of the system, and indeed to subscribe to the pious belief that even in the absence of the bubble the system would exhibit respectable growth. When "subprime lending" is castigated, the point missed is that in the absence of the lending that appears in retrospect as "subprime," there would have been no economic boom in the system.

If the economy is to avoid sliding into stagnation, it becomes necessary to prolong the boom by lowering the interest rate, whose *modus operandi* in a neoliberal capitalist economy is through promoting the formation of a new bubble (though this may not in fact occur). The logic of the system requires that for growth to happen "subprime lending" must not appear as subprime. If it does appear subprime and is therefore curtailed, then growth gets eliminated.

The question would arise: If bubbles can play the role under neoliberal capitalism of being a stimulus for growth, which was played by the colonial arrangement before the First World War and by state intervention after the Second World War, then why do we see neoliberalism as being specially afflicted by a problem in this regard? The answer is that bubbles as a stimulus differ from the previous stimuli in two crucial ways.

First, they are not an exogenous stimulus like making inroads into precapitalist markets under the colonial arrangement or getting the state to intervene in demand management. An exogenous stimulus implies that in addition to the multiplier-accelerator mechanism, or the occurrence of investment in expectation of growth in the market because growth has been occurring in the past, there is an additional amount of investment that occurs in every period stimulated by this exogenous element. Colonial markets and state intervention are exogenous in this sense; bubbles are not. They may get formed or they may not get formed; there is no investment that occurs in every period because of a bubble, since such a bubble may not exist at all. The positive trend to the system that colonialism or state intervention provide because they give a floor to investment even in the event of a collapse of the boom, is not provided by a bubble.

Second, state intervention and colonial markets were not just exogenous in the sense that they provided a positive trend to the system; they provided *markets on tap*, which prevented the boom from collapsing. They did not just provide a floor in the event of the boom collapsing; they actually prevented the boom from collapsing since they plugged any deficiency in aggregate demand that might cause the boom to collapse. Bubbles obviously are not such markets on tap.

Neoliberal capitalism differs from all previous phases of capitalism, other than the interwar years of Depression. In a fundamental respect it lacks a prop of the sort that these previous phases, which were characterized by long booms, had a prop that is both an exogenous stimulus and a market on tap. It is, therefore, inherently prone to stagnation as capitalism had been in the interwar period, similarly lacking a prop. And this proneness to stagnation is greatly magnified by the shift from wages to surplus that it causes in the world economy.

We mentioned earlier that colonialism was the ideal arrangement for capitalism. It provided a prop for aggregate demand, while at the same time ensuring that income deflation occurred to prevent any threat to the value of money anywhere in the system. Post–Second World War dirigisme provided a prop all right, but it did not have any mechanism to prevent inflation and hence a threat to the value of money. Neoliberal capitalism ensures that there is no threat to the value of money by imposing income deflation on the third world, but it lacks any prop for sustaining growth. Growth under this arrangement is essentially driven by the formation of bubbles, but they occur neither with any predictable regularity nor can they be made to occur. The neoliberal phase brings capitalism to an impasse, which we discuss in the next chapter.

CHAPTER 19

# *Capitalism at an Impasse*

W e argued in the previous chapter that the post-2008 crisis of capitalism, which persists to this day, is not just a sequel to the collapse of a housing bubble in the United States. It is a manifestation of a deeper problem. And this deeper problem consists in the fact that, as in the interwar period of the Great Depression, capitalism today lacks even an exogenous stimulus that could provide a floor to downturns and ensure a positive growth trend, let alone a "market on tap" that could prevent a downturn.

The colonial arrangement, which played a crucial role as an exogenous stimulus, more or less exhausted its capacity to play this role by the First World War, while state intervention in demand management, which acted as an exogenous stimulus after the Second World War, cannot serve this purpose any longer because of the opposition of globalized finance capital, an opposition whose effectiveness has increased many-fold because of this globalization itself. In the absence of an exogenous stimulus, growth phases occur only when there is the formation of a bubble; these bubbles are neither truly exogenous nor provide a market on tap. And this problem of the absence of an exogenous stimulus is compounded by the existence of a tendency toward overproduction that is also engendered by the globalization of capital.

We are therefore in a period of protracted stagnation of world capitalism, which would be punctuated, within the prevailing regime, by bouts of revival caused by the formation of occasional asset-price bubbles, but these bouts of revival would collapse as the bubble collapses. Neoliberal capitalism, though it has a mechanism for dealing with inflation and hence the threat to the value of money, has absolutely no mechanism to stimulate growth other than asset-price bubbles And this infirmity exists within a context marked by an *ex ante* tendency toward overproduction, the like of which had never characterized world capitalism earlier.

The absence of an external prop for stimulating growth is a characteristic that the current phase of capitalism shares with capitalism of the interwar period. But there is one important difference between the two periods. In the interwar period, the way forward for capitalism had been clear to many in the wake of the Keynesian Revolution, and that way forward was the introduction of state intervention in demand management. Pursuing this way forward required only the overcoming of the opposition of finance capital, *which itself was nation-based,* to such state intervention. Today, the way forward for capitalism is not clear. To revert back to a regime of state intervention would require instituting controls over cross-border capital flows. Since the state remains a nation-state, for it to play an active role it must detach the national economy from global capital flows to assert itself against the will of international finance capital. It requires, in other words, *a retreat from globalization,* since the main feature of the current globalization is the globalization of capital flows, including above all finance.

There is another possibility, namely to have a surrogate global state, in the form of a coordination among the major nation-states, which fights and overcomes the opposition of globalized finance capital to a stimulation of the world economy through a coordinated fiscal effort. The idea would be to replicate on a global scale, through several powerful nation-states acting together in a concerted manner against the opposition of globalized finance capital, what individual nation-states had done after the Second World War in terms of overcoming the opposition of their respective national finance capitals. The outcome now would be a coordinated fiscal stimulus for the global economy.

As yet, however, there is little discussion of this possibility. In the interwar years, at least, there had been many voices, including that of Keynes, recommending a coordinated fiscal stimulus by major nation-states.[1] Today, there is hardly any voice advocating such a course of action. So dominant is the influence of international finance capital that most economists still swear by "sound finance" as the virtuous path for a nation-state to follow.

The structural crisis of capitalism consists not just in the inability of the system to generate sustained growth, other than through occasional bubbles, and hence its inability to overcome large-scale unemployment, which together with the wage-stagnation caused by the globalization of capital implies a squeeze on workers' earnings even in advanced countries. The structural crisis consists also in the absence of any clear idea of a way forward. The reason is that any way forward requires overcoming the hegemony of international finance capital, whether through a national withdrawal from globalization or through a coordinated international onslaught upon this hegemony. There is, however, no awareness as yet in bourgeois circles of even the need to overcome this hegemony, let alone any attempt actually to overcome it.

What is noteworthy is that the liberal bourgeois establishment, to which Keynes had belonged and which would be expected to visualize ways of overcoming the structural crisis of capitalism *in order to save the system*, does not recognize the structural crisis. While Keynes in his time had been worried that "the world will not much longer tolerate the unemployment, which, apart from brief intervals of excitement, is associated," and in his opinion "inevitably associated with present-day capitalistic individualism," liberal thinking in our time seems not even to recognize the existence of a serious problem of unemployment which will "not much longer" be tolerated.[2] The overcoming of the structural crisis of capitalism seems particularly difficult in this context, and therein lies the impasse of capitalism.

In case we have given the impression that this is only an intellectual failure, we must correct ourselves, since it has deep material roots. The transcendence of the current conjuncture requires overcoming the hegemony of international finance capital, but overcoming it is scarcely possible within the confines of the capitalist system, that is, through measures that would not recursively lead to a transcendence of the system.

Retreat from the current globalization to activate the state of a particular nation to undertake measures for overcoming the crisis obviously requires a change in the class basis of the state, that is, the formation of an alternative class alliance in opposition to the domestic big bourgeoisie that is itself a part of globalized capital. Hence, it already represents a step toward the transcendence of the capitalist system. But even if we consider the possibility of coordinated action on the part of major nation-states to overcome the opposition of international finance capital to a global fiscal stimulus, this too would require an activation of other social classes to counter its hegemony.

What is more, any such fiscal stimulation would, in the absence of income deflation of the sort exercised by neoliberalism today, revive inflation and undermine the value of money. And if income deflation is to be imposed on third world working people, then it would mean fiscal stimulation in one part of the world and fiscal contraction in another. This would be an impossibility unless the coordinating nation-states also launched a coordinated imperialist offensive, which, given advanced country diversity, is not going to be easy. Therefore, international finance capital in the face of such inflation will once again reassert its hegemony.

Of course, the prospects of inflation even in the event of a coordinated fiscal stimulus can be kept at bay if the petty producers in the third world, instead of being subject to income deflation, are on the contrary supported and protected by this new regime led by a set of coordinated nation-states. That would be a regime of *global dirigisme*. It would mean preventing the process of primitive accumulation of capital unleashed by neoliberalism, in which case it would not just be a matter of overcoming the opposition of international finance capital to fiscal stimulation, but putting serious restrictions on the *modus operandi* of capital itself. Such a global dirigiste regime, if at all it comes about, cannot be a lasting phenomenon. In view of the "spontaneity" of capitalism, it will either have to strengthen these restrictions more and more and move beyond capitalism, or loosen them over time, lapsing back to a situation of hegemony of international finance capital.

Putting the matter differently, international finance capital represents *the highest level of development of capitalism*. There are no shoots of any higher development that can be discerned anywhere within the system.

So overcoming its hegemony seems an impossible project within the confines of capitalism, which is why liberal intellectuals have preferred not even to take cognizance of the problem that confronts capitalism today. The current impasse of capitalism can thus be more accurately defined. The system cannot move forward without overcoming the hegemony of international finance capital, but at the same time this hegemony cannot be overcome without unleashing a process of transcendence of capitalism itself.

## The Rise of Fascist Tendencies

The paralysis of the liberal bourgeois establishment is curiously combined at the present juncture with a certain stasis of the left as well. This stasis has two obvious causes. One is the collapse of the Soviet Union and Eastern European socialism, and the turn of several third world socialist countries toward greater integration into the capitalist world economy, including inviting foreign capitalists into these countries and promoting local capitalists, which has increased their domestic income and wealth inequalities to a point where it has become a matter of debate whether they should still be called socialist. This has created a widespread impression that socialism is unworkable, and even those left forces that had been critical of the earlier socialist regimes have also suffered as a consequence.

The second cause is the decline in the strength of the working class. The rise in unemployment during the crisis is an obvious reason for it. But, in addition, the very fact of globalization and relocation of activities to lower-wage economies has undermined the strength of trade unions, with the threat of outsourcing hanging over their heads like the sword of Damocles. Besides, privatization, which is an important feature of neoliberal capitalism, also tends to weaken trade unions. Indeed, all over the world the extent of unionization is greater in the public sector than in the private sector, with the ratio of unionized workers to the total in the United States being 33 and 7 percent respectively (the public sector here includes education). This weakening of trade unions, and of working-class power in general, has had a debilitating effect on the left.

In addition to these causes, however, there is a deeper cause for left stasis, and that has to do with its sheer ambivalence toward the current globalization. Although this globalization is occurring under the auspices of international finance capital and has been a universal source of dissatisfaction within the left, its being globalization of a sort nonetheless has received a cautious welcome, at least in the sense that any de-linking from it, which is the first of the two ways out of the current predicament, is frowned upon as a retreat to "nationalism."

This is a point we discuss at greater length in the final chapter of this book. The point to note here is that for significant sections of the left, at least in the advanced countries, any retreat from this finance-dominated globalization is seen as a reactionary step, a reversal to "nationalism." While this sentiment is understandable because of the two world wars that have been fought on European soil, it contributes to the phenomenon of left stasis. The left often finds itself in the company of the liberal bourgeois establishment in opposing regimes that wish to de-link from the process of globalization.

At the same time, the left has not pursued the alternative possibility mentioned earlier, of a coordinated fiscal stimulus by several advanced countries. What is remarkable is that despite the debt crisis engulfing several European countries, all of whom have been coerced into undertaking "austerity" measures, no serious demand was raised for a coordinated expansion of the economies of the European Union, which would have improved the conditions of the indebted countries. Attention was focused on what should be done to alleviate the problems of particular countries but not on any overall measures for recovery, which reflects perhaps an unwillingness on the part of the left to get caught in the domain of "transitional demands."

Given the liberal bourgeoisie's paralysis and the left's caution and ambivalence on globalization, it is right-wing forces that are emerging globally and claiming to be the harbingers of a new and better order. They have been labeled as "populist," but this is a grossly inappropriate description. The term "populism," also used for progressive regimes, serves to provide ideological respectability to the neoliberal opposition to genuine pro-people economic measures by categorizing such measures along with the racist, xenophobic, and divisive policies of the emerging right. It would be more appropriate to call the emerging right-wing forces "neo-fascist." But it must be understood that they are quite a heterogeneous bunch. that we cannot expect a repetition of the 1930s-style fascism in today's context; that a fascist state must be distinguished from a fascist movement even when it occupies state power; and that even the fascist movement changes its character, especially vis-à-vis big capital, in the course of its journey to power.

Apart from a general muscular inhumaneness, there are at least four basic features that fascist movements typically display and that the currently emerging right-wing movements are displaying in varying degrees, with the *Hindutva* movement in India perhaps being the closest to fascism, though we do not yet have a fascist state anywhere in the world. The first is the targeting and vilification of some hapless minority group as being responsible for the crisis-induced plight of the majority. This is a trait that almost all the current crop of right-wing movements share. They claim that it is not the "system" that is responsible for the plight of the majority but the "Other": Mexican immigrants, Muslim immigrants, and Chinese workers "stealing jobs" in the case of the United States; Muslims and the *dalits* in India; the immigrants in European countries, though the identity of the culpable "immigrant" varies from one country to another; and so on.

The second feature is support for international finance capital, and, in turn, obtaining its support, which typically becomes more open and vocal as the movement comes closer to power. This is because the fascist movement can never aspire to power without the support of the big bourgeoisie whom therefore it begins to woo as it becomes stronger. To be sure there are differences between a Trump and a Modi on economic policy, with the former moving headlong toward protectionism while the latter apotheosizes neoliberalism in all its aspects. But there is never any confrontation with *globalized finance* or any proposal for controlling its free cross-border flows *by any of these political movements*, not even by Trump with his protectionist rhetoric and measures.

The third feature is the supplementing of authoritarianism from the top with an unleashing of fascist gangs in the streets to terrorize opponents. Fascism is basically different from mere authoritarianism, insofar as it constitutes a mass movement that is based on the petty bourgeoisie, within which the urban salariat has to be included, that draws in the lumpen proletariat, and even sections of the working class in certain circumstances. Being a movement gives fascism a mass character, which Palmiro Togliatti underscored when he had talked of its having both a "class nature" and a "mass nature."[3] This motley mass uses strong-arm methods promoted by the leaders of the fascist movement against its opponents, which include the left, the liberal intelligentsia, and targeted minority groups. When fascist elements come to power but a fascist state has not yet been established, these street gangs are not necessarily dissolved since they play a major role in suppressing opponents and facilitating the journey toward a fascist state, though whether a fascist state will at all be reached in today's situation as it did in the 1930s remains a moot point. (When it was reached in Germany, the SA had been destroyed, both for enlisting the support of finance capital, and also for absorbing the instruments of the earlier bourgeois state, such as the armed forces, into the new fascist state.)

The fourth feature of fascism is the promotion of unreason. The obliteration of the dividing line between history and mythology, a contempt and total disregard for any evidence that goes against fascist ideological beliefs, and an extreme hostility toward the intelligentsia characterize the fascist movement, which itself after all is based upon unreason.

Movements characterized by these features exist in all modern societies, but usually as fringe phenomena. They move center stage in periods of crisis when the liberal bourgeois establishment appears helpless or unconcerned about the crisis and when the left for reasons of its own is not in a position to project an alternative. Where the left does project an alternative, such as in the United States under Bernie Sanders or in Britain under Jeremy Corbyn, it cuts the ground from under the feet of the fascists by taking away chunks of their mass support. But when it does not offer an alternative, the fascist movement gets strengthened, cashing in on the people's anger, but deflecting it away from the system, toward some hapless minority group. Precisely for this reason, fascist movements get adopted by finance capital, both to keep at bay any potential challenge from the left, and also to introduce a divisive discourse that makes any united mass action on quotidian material issues that much more difficult. By adopting the fascists, by forming an alliance, as Kalecki put it, between itself and the "fascist upstarts," big capital, which might otherwise have been at the receiving end of mass anger, uses it against the trade unions and the working class to enfeeble them further.

Neoliberalism provides a fertile ground for the growth of fascism. While it unleashes crisis and stagnation upon the economy, it undermines the liberal bourgeois establishment's capacity to deal with the crisis and also weakens the left through the assault of globalization upon the nationally organized working class. At the same time, the global mobility of capital makes it easy to carry out propaganda such as the "Chinese are stealing our jobs" or the "Mexicans are stealing our jobs." Neoliberalism thus creates conditions propitious for fascism.

There is an additional point. The ideological justification for capitalism, at least in the recent period, has been that it benefits everyone. The postwar regime's high levels of employment, together with welfare expenditure (though a good deal of that was financed by Social Security taxation, at the expense of the working class itself), had provided some credence to this claim. But under neoliberal capitalism, when welfare expenditure is wound down and inequalities are on the increase, the ideological justification still centers around the claim that capitalism can provide high growth and high employment. Indeed, the winding down of welfare expenditure and other such "populist measures" is even lauded as being essential for this. A period of stagnation and crisis therefore makes neoliberal capitalism particularly vulnerable, since it directly negates the claims made in justification of the system. The discourse shift provided by fascism becomes a welcome phenomenon for the  big bourgeoisie (constituting a part of international finance capital) in this context.

## The Infirmity of Contemporary Fascism

The basic difference between the fascism of the 1930s and contemporary fascism (or neo-fascism) is that, unlike then, contemporary fascist movements, even if they come to power, can do little to overcome the crisis afflicting their respective countries. Japan, it may be recalled, was the first country to have come out of the Great Depression through state military spending financed by borrowing, the earliest version of what one may call "military Keynesianism." Germany followed suit shortly thereafter when the Nazis came to power and started rearming the country. There was a brief period between the end of the Depression and the start of the war in these countries during which the fascists succeeded in placing their economies in a better position than the liberal capitalist ones.

In contemporary conditions, however, larger state spending, no matter for what purpose, which would have to be financed either by taxes on the rich or by a fiscal deficit to be able to enlarge activity, would be frowned upon by globalized finance, which would oppose both these means of financing. And since no fascist movement anywhere is proposing controls over cross-border financial flows, this opposition would be decisive in preventing any expansion in domestic aggregate demand through state spending, which would therefore prevent any overcoming of the crisis.

What fascist movements can do under these circumstances is greater protectionism, as indeed Trump is doing. But such "beggar thy neighbor" policies, if pursued by all capitalist countries, as they inevitably would be, since no country will be willing merely to turn the other cheek, would not improve the condition of any one of them. On the contrary, such policies are likely to worsen the conditions for all through a further shrinking of global aggregate demand, as the so-called "animal spirits" of the capitalists dry up in the face of aggressive universal protectionism.

We have argued that overcoming the current crisis, whether within the confines of a single economy or globally, requires overcoming the hegemony of international finance capital. No nation-state, not even one where the fascists are in power, can overcome the crisis unless it is willing to overcome this hegemony. And a hallmark of contemporary fascism is that, far from trying to overcome this hegemony, it is on the contrary keen to enlist the support of international finance capital for its accession to, and stay in, power.

This fact has an important implication. Earlier fascism had proceeded from rearmament to war, and had burned itself out through war, though at great cost to mankind. Contemporary fascism, just as it cannot overcome the crisis through rearmament, or use the slack of the crisis to effect rearmament (if it rearms at the expense of the workers' consumption, then it will not have overcome the crisis, and, unless it abrogates electoral democracy altogether, it will have to pay a heavy electoral price), also would not burn itself out through war. It is therefore likely to be around for a long time, which means that it will succeed in bringing about a more gradual, more "peaceful" and less coercive fascification of the society and the polity, with even the political formations of the liberal bourgeois establishment emulating the fascist ones in expressing themselves against persecuted minority groups. With fascist and liberal political formations competing against one another electorally, and with the crisis showing no signs of abating, which keeps alive popular discontent, liberal political formations would find themselves being forced increasingly to echo the same right-wing, racist, anti-immigrant, anti-Muslim rhetoric that the fascists would be spewing out. Contemporary fascism, though it may not engulf the world in the kind of devastation that earlier fascism had done, will nonetheless cause great damage to the social fabric of the capitalist countries.

This enjoins a historic task upon the left. It alone is in a position to prevent this damage to the social fabric by pursuing policies that can take these countries out of their current crisis, policies that would contest the hegemony of international finance capital, and in the process bring about a transcendence of capitalism. Since overcoming the hegemony of international finance capital will unleash a process of transcendence of capitalism, none of the other political formations is equal to the task. Precisely for this reason however the left alone can take on this task. We are once again, in other words, facing a choice between socialism and barbarism, but in a different way from what Rosa Luxemburg had visualized in her specific context.[4]

### U.S. Response to the Crisis

What has been said above may appear to be contradicted by the U.S. case. The United States under President Trump has not only protected itself against imports but has also enlarged the fiscal deficit. It has done so not just by giving large tax concessions to the corporations but even enlarging government expenditure. And yet it has imposed no capital controls. Finance is certainly not flowing out of the country because of its "deviant" behavior. Our argument that without overcoming the hegemony of international finance capital, there is no way of overcoming the crisis, whether for an individual country or for the world economy as a whole, appears to be contradicted by the U.S. experience.

Before we discuss this issue, it should be noted that for the United States the two measures, protection against imports and fiscal stimulation of domestic demand, have to go together, for otherwise any such stimulation will leak out in the form of larger imports, creating employment elsewhere while the United States itself experiences increased external indebtedness without much increase in domestic employment. It makes sense, therefore, for the United States, while providing a fiscal stimulus to its domestic economy, to ensure that the impact of this stimulus does not simply leak out abroad. In short, it represents a consistent policy move.

There is an obvious reason why this move has not led to any financial outflows, but rather has been accompanied by substantial financial inflows. This is the unique position of the United States, which no other country enjoys, namely that among the world's wealth-holders its currency is considered to be "as good as gold" even when, unlike under the Bretton Woods system, there is no formal convertibility between the dollar and gold at a fixed price. Dollar, and dollar-denominated assets, therefore become a stable medium for holding wealth. This makes the United States immune to financial outflows in the event of an increase in its fiscal deficit, unlike any other country, since no wealth-holder thereby loses confidence in its currency, or expects other wealth-holders to be doing so.

When other countries retaliate against U.S. imports through their own protectionist measures, not only will the level of activity in the United States suffer on this account, but even that of the capitalist world as a whole by sapping the capitalists' state of confidence. Hence, the apparent success of the United States in putting in place an expansionary policy without any controls over cross-border financial flows is misleading; this "success" lasts only as long as others do nothing to expand their level of activity.

The current pandemic will ensure that it cannot be for long. All countries at present are caught in its grip and experiencing massive unemployment and reductions in output because of the lockdowns associated with it. But when the pandemic subsides, it will be difficult for them even to return to their pre-pandemic level of activity, let alone expand that level. This is because during the pandemic-caused lockdown households and firms have been afflicted with income loss and have reduced their net worth to maintain essential expenditures, through borrowing or running down cash holdings. When the pandemic subsides, they will try to build up their net worth by keeping down expenditures, so that these expenditures will not recover to pre-pandemic levels any time soon. The shock of the pandemic therefore, even after the pandemic itself is over, will further aggravate the protracted crisis of capitalism. And in this context, other countries will be even less willing to accept without retaliating against Trump's unilateral policies for U.S. recovery.

The very fact that the United States is adopting such policies is indicative of the degree to which it has abandoned any leadership role. Until recently, the United States, like Britain earlier, had left its own market open to other advanced capitalist countries and run a current account deficit vis-à-vis them, which, as we have seen, is what the leadership role demands. Under Trump, however, the United States is attempting to go it alone. But "going it alone," which after all is what we would like the third world countries to do by de-linking from neoliberal globalization, cannot work in a world of free global financial flows.

It would not be enough for other countries merely to retaliate against U.S. imports for their recovery. They would also have to adopt fiscally expansionary policies. But if fiscal expansion for increasing activity is to be fruitful and not have its effect nullified by interest rate increases to prevent financial outflows, then interest rates have to be made non-competitive across countries, and this can only happen if they are detached from considerations of cross-border financial flows, that is, if capital controls are put in place. Keynes's remark that finance must be "primarily national" (if policies for larger employment are to be put in place) has a greater element of truth than is commonly imagined. Putting such controls in place, however, requires overcoming the hegemony of international finance capital, which cannot be done within the confines of capitalism today, unlike what Keynes had imagined.

One set of countries that will particularly feel the adverse effects of protectionism in the United States are the "newly emerging economies" of the third world. For them, the phase of high growth is over, and along with it the massive diffusion of activities from the advanced capitalist countries of the world that has occurred into their economies. The working people in these economies, who had been squeezed during the period of high growth because of the unleashing of primitive accumulation of capital, are not going to get any relief because of the end of this high growth. They are, on the contrary, going to get further squeezed in the new situation because of the reduced employment opportunities as a consequence of the slowing down of growth. There is, in short, no symmetry in this matter. And they are going to be joined by segments of the middle class which had done well earlier but will now find their prospects bleak. We shall take up these issues in the last chapter.

# PART 6

CHAPTER 20

# *Capitalism in History*

Almost the whole of economics, whether in its classical or in its neoclassical version, analyzes capitalism as a closed self-contained entity, and this is true even of the Marxist tradition, in which the analysis of capitalist dynamics typically refers to a conceptual universe consisting of the capitalists, the workers, and the state that hovers in the background to enforce property relations and what is often called "rules of the game." But once we see capitalism as it really has been, ensconced within a milieu that was pre-capitalist to start with but is then molded by capitalism for its own purposes, leaving it neither in its pristine form nor assimilated into the capitalist sector (as Rosa Luxemburg had visualized), then the dynamics of capitalism appear in an altogether different light. What is more, many of the propositions commonly advanced about capitalism appear in a different light when we move from a perception of capitalism as an isolated system to a perception of capitalism as enveloped within a world that is not itself capitalist but which it subjugates.

Lest we are accused of not taking cognizance of Marx's brilliant analysis of the relation between the capitalist and the pre-capitalist sectors in his discussion of "primitive accumulation of capital," we should clarify that our argument, advanced in chapter 17, has been that the process of primitive accumulation of capital is not confined to some "pre-history" of capitalism; rather, it occurs throughout its history (a view which, we argue below, Marx himself was coming to). Primitive accumulation accompanies the process of "normal" accumulation of capital, analyzed by Marx through his two-department schemes in Volume II of *Capital*. Any analysis of the real history of capitalism cannot ignore the *continuous* process of primitive accumulation of capital that occurs throughout its life. A cognizance of this fact has important implications.

### Capitalism and the Production of Poverty

The first implication of a change in the perception of capitalism, the recognition that it is enmeshed in a pre-capitalist milieu that it molds to its own requirements, is in regard to capitalism's production of poverty. In talking of capitalism's "production of poverty" we are not just saying that "poverty" under capitalism is altogether different from "poverty" in all pre-capitalist societies since it is accompanied by an essential element of *insecurity* induced by participation in the market. This is no doubt true and important, but we have something additional in mind.

When Marx wrote of capitalism producing wealth at one pole and poverty at another, he was, as the context makes clear, referring to the "reserve army of labor." Marx's remark is generally interpreted as meaning that since the expanded reproduction of capital is accompanied by an increase in the absolute size though not necessarily the relative size (compared to the active army of labor), of the reserve army of labor, which is the main repository of poverty in its capitalist incarnation, accumulation is marked by an increase in poverty.

Interpreted in this manner, Marx's remark is both true and unexceptionable. Who can deny that capitalism cannot function without a reserve army of labor (though this may nowadays be called by some other name, like NAIRU), or that the absolute size of this reserve must increase over time as the workforce increases, or that poverty is typically associated with unemployment? Goodwin's formalization of Marx was just one way of clarifying the underlying logic of the argument.[1]

But once we see capitalism within its global setting, the proposition about the production of poverty takes on a very different meaning. The vast labor reserves created in countries like India, China, Indonesia, and Bangladesh through deindustrialization (and surplus drain in the case of colonies) *is also a product of capitalism.* And capitalism, through such drain and deindustrialization, is the progenitor of modern mass poverty in these countries. Hence capitalism's production of poverty must be interpreted in a global setting.[2]

But these labor reserves are not just something that got created and happened to persist over time. Their existence and perpetuation are essential to the logic of capitalism. And this is so because products of the tropical landmass are subject to increasing supply price; land-augmenting measures, which could keep increasing supply price at bay, typically require state intervention and are eschewed under capitalism for this reason, for capitalists do not want an activist state except when it directly promotes their own interests. If, owing to capital accumulation, a growing metropolitan demand for products of this tropical landmass has to be met without causing inflation, which would destabilize the value of money within the system, then coercion has to be exercised directly or indirectly to ensure that the local demand for such products, that is, the demand within countries of the tropical (and semi-tropical) landmass, which more or less coincides with the third world, is correspondingly adjusted *downward.* This requires what we have called income deflation in the third world economies.

The existence of vast labor reserves in the third world is one way of imposing income deflation on its working people, whereby their absorption of such goods is squeezed. If perchance labor reserves begin to get exhausted, creating larger incomes for the working people, then their demand for goods with increasing supply price would increase, destabilizing the value of money within the system and hence the system itself. To prevent destabilization, measures of "inflation control" would be adopted and these would re-create the labor reserves. Hence the labor reserves are not just an accidental historical legacy of deindustrialization of the colonial times; they are part of the logic of the system itself.

The poverty produced by income deflation is distinct from the poverty produced by the existence of a reserve army of labor in the metropolis, with which typically Marx's remark about the production of wealth at one pole and poverty at another has been associated. Put differently, the growth of wealth at one pole through capital accumulation must be accompanied, *independently of what happens to the reserve army in the metropolis,* by an appropriate squeeze on the *absolute* amount of products subject to increasing supply price that is absorbed by the people of this tropical landmass. Since these goods must enter in some minimal amount into any basket, the access to which must be a benchmark for defining poverty, it follows that *there must be growing absolute poverty in the third world accompanying capital accumulation, and hence the growth of wealth, in the metropolis.*

It follows as well that capitalism's production of poverty must be seen as a phenomenon occurring at the global level, and not just locally within the metropolis through an increase in the absolute size of the domestic reserve army. And when we adopt this global perspective, we would find an increase in absolute poverty occurring alongside capital accumulation, at least in terms of the deprivation of goods subject to increasing supply price. Focusing attention solely upon the metropolis and interpreting Marx's proposition solely in terms of the absolute size of the reserve army of labor within the metropolis (for which Marx must be held responsible) makes it easy to show that the magnitude of poverty produced by capitalism is relatively small. It makes it easy as well to present capitalism in a more favorable light, as a more benign system than it actually is. Such a benign picture of capitalism, however, turns out to be a misleading one once we look at its global or imperial character.

### Capitalism and Its Socially "Progressive" Character

The second implication of seeing capitalism in its global setting has to do with the nature of the proletariat. Pre-capitalist societies consisted of communities to which one belonged by birth, not out of choice. They were highly oppressive, stratified, and stultifying. Capitalism was credited with breaking these communities through the process of primitive accumulation of capital, which took, for example, the form of "enclosures" in England. Those driven out from the villages came to the newly emerging bourgeois cities and towns and joined the ranks of the proletariat. These workers, though recruited from persons of diverse origins who barely knew one another to start with, and were in a situation of competition, forged over time a new community through "combinations" leading to trade union and political actions.

Marx, in *The Poverty of Philosophy*, talks of the bemusement of bourgeois economists that the workers pay significant amounts from their meager wages to keep these combinations going, even though they were scarcely effective in obtaining wage increases. This is because, he argues, even though combinations at the outset are formed for obtaining wage increases, the workers soon begin to value them for their own sake: keeping combinations going becomes more important for them than wage increases. They transcend their individual interests, in other words, to form a new community. Capitalism thus destroys the old community in order to form, despite itself and against its own wishes, a new community that will eventually destroy it.

While this picture Marx drew has validity for metropolitan capitalism, where, because of the mass emigration to the temperate regions, the reserve army of labor relative to the active army remained small, and powerful combinations or trade unions could come up uniting the workers in a new community (to which socialist politics was brought from "outside"), it is less pertinent in the economies of the periphery. This is because the process of primitive accumulation of capital is not followed by any significant absorption of the displaced petty producers and agricultural laborers into the active army of labor, whose growth remains limited. They swell the labor reserves and what is more, employment rationing takes a form in which the distinction between an active and a reserve army largely disappears, with almost everyone being employed for part of the time and unemployed for the rest. Casual employment, intermittent employment, part-time employment, and short-term "contract employment" proliferate, which makes any trade union action, any formation of a new community, that much more difficult. And to the extent that the existence of labor reserves causes a reversion to domestic production through the old "putting out" system, the problem gets further compounded.

The limited job opportunities in the capitalist sector also act as a damper on out-migration from the traditional petty production sectors, despite these sectors facing primitive accumulation of capital in "flow terms," that is, through an income squeeze. The affected petty producers linger on in their traditional callings despite the squeeze on their incomes, which also means that the old community does not get destroyed. Capitalism in the third world therefore not only does not lead to the creation of a new community with anything like the vigor it had displayed in the metropolis; but it does not also lead to a destruction of the old community with anything like the vigor it had displayed in the metropolis. Thus, the revolutionary potential that Marx had associated with capitalism, looking at it exclusively as a metropolitan phenomenon, is singularly absent when we look at it in the context of the third world and as a global phenomenon. Its metropolitan vigor then appears both non-replicable and a product of specific circumstances like the massive emigration to the temperate lands of settlement, rather than of any necessary inner logic of the system.

The third implication is related to this. Bourgeois revolutions that were the progenitors of capitalism had inscribed on their banner slogans like "liberty," "equality," and "fraternity," and advanced these ideas against feudal values and the feudal ideology, no matter how betrayed they might have been by the reality of capitalist development. In the third world, not only is the old community not destroyed, but the imposition of primitive accumulation first under colonialism and then by the domestic bourgeoisie linked to international finance capital occurs on the basis of an alliance with the landlord class, whose concentrated land ownership is not destroyed as they are "incentivized" to become capitalist landlords. This means the perpetuation of the ideological apparatus of the feudal order, and even several of its social institutions, such as the caste system. In addition, capitalism also brought, through colonialism, new institutions and ideologies of inequality such as racism and apartheid.

Some authors in India have suggested that colonialism, because of institutions like equality before the law, made a dent in the caste system. But the increased pressure of population on land, owing to the displacement of artisans through deindustrialization in the colonial period, impoverished the agricultural laborers, among whom the *dalits* preponderate, to a greater extent than any other section. And concepts like equality before the law remained only on paper. Until independence *dalits*, even in the neighborhood of the capital city Delhi, were not socially allowed to own any land.

Capitalism in the periphery, in other words, does not, through its own immanent tendencies, bring about in ideological terms or in terms of social institutions the kind of revolutionary transformation that is typically associated with it, at least in the metropolitan context.

This is not to say that ideological transformations are not effected in the third world, but these are the result of the anti-colonial struggle, of the struggle *against* metropolitan capitalism. To be sure, these ideas, which, at least in their modern form are new to the third world (though their own versions of such ideas may have existed earlier), arise because of the bourgeois ideology prevalent in the metropolis. And this, despite being severely challenged and even overwhelmed, both occasionally and for longer stretches of time, by anti-Semitism, racism, anti-minorityism, anti-Islamism, and patriarchy maintains its formal adherence to a certain notion of equality. But the institution of this notion of equality in the third world is the product not of capitalist encroachment or capitalist development but of a struggle against such encroachment and development.

The upshot of our argument is that when we look at capitalism in its global setting, its revolutionary potential, so prominent in the metropolis and highlighted in most writings emanating from the metropolis, appears singularly exaggerated. And this brings us to our fourth point.

In Marxist discussions there is usually a distinction drawn between a phase of capitalism when it was historically progressive and a phase when it becomes historically obsolete. While this is in conformity with the philosophical conception underlying Marxism, a demarcation between the two phases in historical terms is problematical. Following Lenin, the line is usually drawn between the pre-monopoly phase and the monopoly phase. The latter, which Lenin characterized as "moribund capitalism," is identified as the period when capitalism becomes historically obsolete, as it enmeshes mankind in imperialist wars for repartitioning a world that has already been partitioned.

But whether there is such a clear distinction between the two phases has been debated. Anwar Shaikh has rejected this distinction.[3] And Kalecki too sees not just perfect competition of the neoclassical economists but even the free competition of the classical economists as being historically inaccurate. He sees collusion among capitalists for fixing prices as a phenomenon that goes back all the way, in which case an analytical distinction between the two phases of capitalism, as distinct from empirical demarcations that would have little theoretical sanction, becomes unsustainable. Interestingly, even Adam Smith, the doyen of classical economics, had talked of capitalists being always and everywhere in collusion.

Once we look at capitalism as a global phenomenon, the basis for such a distinction in historical terms becomes even shakier. Capitalism from the very beginning was imperialist—Lenin's "imperialism" being only one particular phase of this long history. Not only has its ability to develop the productive forces not been visibly impaired at any point in its earlier history (notwithstanding theoretical prognostications by many authors, notably Josef Steindl), but all such development has been accompanied by a ruthless and continuous process of primitive accumulation of capital at the expense of the working people of the third world. This distinction between a progressive and an obsolete phase cannot be drawn with any conviction in the history of capitalism, and certainly not if one looks at it from the point of view of its interactions with the working people of the third world.

Indeed, if we are to talk of a period when capitalism becomes historically obsolete then that period can be said to begin now, when we have seen that capitalism has run into an impasse from which there is no clear way out.

## Marx on Imperialism

Marx was acutely aware of the phenomenon of imperialism, and in a series of articles in the *New York Daily Tribune* on India, he wrote with remarkable insight on the role of British colonialism in breaking up the traditional Indian society.[4] Marx's views here have been much discussed, and we need not enter that debate. What is remarkable is that in all his writings, for which he did considerable research, there is very little about the impact of imperialism on *the metropolitan economy*. What imperialism did to the colonies is discussed with great acuity and sympathy for the colonized, but how the metropolis benefited from imperialism is scarcely discussed, especially in his *magnum opus*. There are stray references here and there in *Capital,* and in Volume III, in particular, there is a mention of colonial trade as a counteracting tendency to the falling tendency of the rate of profit. But beyond that, there is not much on what role the colonies played in the dynamics of capitalism, or even whether they were necessary at all in this dynamic.

Marx's views on the subject, however, underwent a change, perhaps as he found the prospects of a European revolution on which he had pinned great hopes receding. On February 19, 1881, he wrote an important letter to Nikolai Danielson, the Narodnik economist, in which he talked about the Indians "gratuitously and annually" sending over to England a sum amounting to more than the income of the 60 million agricultural and industrial laborers of India.[5]

This is the first time that Marx writes about the "drain," which he would have known perhaps from the work of the pioneer author on the subject, Dadabhai Naoroji, whom he never appears to have met but shared a common friend with, Henry Hyndman, the British socialist author. Given the scale of the "drain" that Marx mentions, and his awareness of the squeeze it imposed upon the Indian people (resulting in a series of disastrous famines), he could not have believed that this unrequited transfer played only a trifling role in the development of the British economy. He could not, in other words, have believed that the dynamics of the British economy, the nature of its accumulation process, could be understood only by looking at its internal processes. And if the drain was important for Britain and hence for metropolitan capitalism, then surely the closed isolated universe analyzed in *Capital,* though invaluable for understanding how surplus value was extracted under the system and how and why it was realized and capitalized, could not constitute the whole story for Marx. That story could be gleaned only when metropolitan capitalism was analyzed in its global setting.

Marx died a couple of years after this letter to Danielson. So he could not develop his thinking in the direction of an analytical incorporation of imperialism into his schema, but a shift in the trend of his thought is clear from another instance. While earlier in his *Tribune* articles he had seen the development of Indian railways as part of the "regeneration" process of India under colonial rule that would follow the process of "destruction" of its old structure, even remarking that producer goods industries would develop in India in the wake of the railways, in the Danielson letter he talks of the railways as being "useless to the Hindoos." Marx clearly had developed by 1881 much skepticism over the limited regeneration of the colonial economy, which he had earlier believed possible as a spontaneous effect of imperialism.

There is no reason today, when we have much greater information about the interaction between the metropolis on the one hand and the colonies and semi-colonies on the other, why we should continue to look at capitalism and its dynamics as if it constitutes a closed, isolated system. And yet almost fourteen decades after Marx's letter to Danielson, Marxist analyses of capitalism continue to proceed as if it was a closed isolated system. This has to be given up. Capitalism has to be seen in its global setting and analyzed within a broader framework than the one in which the analysis of *Capital* had been located.

A point needs clarification: Marxist theory should be seen at two levels. In contrast to all liberal thought, Marx saw capitalism as a "spontaneous system" driven by its own immanent tendencies, where the individual economic agents, though they appear to be the subjects of the process, are coerced into acting in particular ways by the fact of competition. The capitalist accumulates not out of his or her own volition, but because of being engaged in a Darwinian struggle where not accumulating would mean falling by the wayside. Marx even referred to the capitalist, the supposed hero in the dramatis personae of the system, as "capital personified": the immanent tendencies of capital work themselves out through the behavior of capitalists and other human agents, who are forced by the system to act in particular ways and therefore constitute alienated beings.

Within this overall perspective, where Marx differs fundamentally from Smith and the entire liberal tradition that sees the individual as acting out of his or her own volition, he locates his profound analysis of the extraction and capitalization of surplus value in a universe that consists of a closed isolated capitalist economy. Our call for going beyond this universe while retaining Marx's discovery and looking at capitalism in its global setting still acknowledges the absolute necessity of keeping Marx's perspective of a "spontaneous system" intact. The case for socialism arises from this "spontaneity," for if capitalism were a malleable system (as the liberal tradition from Smith to Keynes believed), then there would be no need to overthrow it. Ours therefore is a call for a broader analysis that incorporates imperialism as an essential feature of the system, within Marx's perspective of a "spontaneous" system.

Marx himself, as we have suggested, had been moving in this direction. Indeed, if a distinction has to be drawn between an "early Marx" and a "late Marx," a more appropriate way of doing so would be between the Marx who looked at capitalism as a closed self-contained system and a Marx who saw it as the center of an imperial system, an idea that has been carried forward by other Marxists but not to the desired extent.

### The Case for Socialism

The case for socialism has until now been entirely in terms of liberating mankind from the "spontaneous" system that capitalism is, which is not only exploitative but also antagonistic in a deeply ontological manner, in the sense that even when, for instance, a rise in wages does not reduce profits, capital is still opposed to it. Any improvement in the conditions of the workers, even if it does not come at the expense of profits, poses a threat to the system by making the workers more resilient and powerful. And this ontological antagonism is not due to any malice; it is inherent in the system itself, which the capitalists, themselves an alienated entity within the system, are coerced into accepting.

But if primitive accumulation at the expense of the petty producers is a phenomenon that characterizes the system throughout its existence, and is also an immanent tendency within it, then this provides an important marker to socialism differentiating it from capitalism, namely that the journey toward it is one where petty producers are defended, protected, and promoted instead of being destroyed. To be sure, socialism is not a system marked with substantial petty production, but petty producers have to voluntarily come together to move toward more collective forms of property along this journey to socialism . Socialism rejects primitive accumulation, while capitalism's immanent tendency is to inflict it. Thus the journey toward socialism is undertaken by workers in alliance with petty producers facing primitive accumulation under capitalism, in particular by a worker-peasant alliance under the leadership of the workers whose distinguishing characteristic is that they, having no property of their own, can move directly to collective ownership of property.

The idea of a worker-peasant alliance was put forward by Lenin in his *Two Tactics of Social Democracy*, in which he argued that in countries coming late to capitalism (like Russia at that time), the bourgeoisie, haunted by the fear that an attack on feudal property could rebound into an attack on bourgeois property, makes common cause with the feudal lords and thereby thwarts the democratic aspirations of the peasantry.[6] These aspirations can be fulfilled only by the proletariat, which alone can break up feudal property and distribute land among the landless peasantry.

The case for a worker-peasant alliance, however, arises not just because of the bourgeoisie's compromise with landlordism. It also arises because of the process of primitive accumulation of capital from which the peasantry must be rescued. The bourgeoisie's culpability lies not just in its alliance with the landlord elements, but in the fact that the leading echelons of it directly squeeze the peasantry through primitive accumulation of capital, which becomes clear only when we see primitive accumulation not as being confined to the prehistory of capitalism but as being associated with capitalism throughout its life. And this requires looking at the capitalist system in its global setting, not in its closed isolation.

The case for socialism in countries where a substantial sector of petty production exists is that *the only way this vast mass of people, including the laborers engaged in this sector (for even peasant agriculture uses laborers), can be saved from destitution is by following a socialist trajectory.* Such a trajectory overcomes the spontaneity of capitalism; it negates all its immanent tendencies and its animosity toward state activism for introducing land-augmentation measures. Socialism thereby overcomes the problem of increasing supply price through land augmentation, while capitalism, by contrast, overcomes it by increasing absolute poverty through the imposition of an income deflation.

There has been a tendency within the Marxist tradition to underestimate the revolutionary potential of the peasantry. Most often this has taken the form of restricting the allies of the working class primarily to the small peasants, semi-proletariat, and the agricultural laborers, while excluding or being skeptical of any positive role of the middle and rich peasants in the revolutionary process, which has thereby circumscribed and enfeebled the revolutionary challenge. Whatever merit there may have been in this tendency, the era of neoliberal capitalism, which unleashes primitive accumulation upon large segments of the peasantry, robs it of this merit. It opens the possibility of forming a broad worker-peasant alliance that can take a major step toward transcending capitalism.

As to who can be counted as a peasant rather than a rural capitalist or proto-capitalist it is a question that has to be answered from the perspective of forming this alliance. Those who may be engaged in agriculture but whose major source of income comes from non-agricultural activities, because of which they do not feel the impact of the primitive accumulation of capital that is squeezing the agricultural producers, will not be a part of this alliance and will not qualify as peasants in any meaningful sense. On the other hand, those who are engaged primarily in agriculture and bear the brunt of the primitive accumulation of capital will be a part of this alliance. The term "peasants" should be reserved for them.

To be sure, even when worker-peasant alliances have been formed and have led to successful revolutions, maintaining these alliances during the journey toward socialism has proved to be an exceedingly difficult task, which has contributed greatly to the collapse or derailment of several of these revolutions. But here again the objective difficulties, which are undeniable, have been compounded by erroneous theory.

A well-known proposition is that commodity production gives rise to differentiation among the producers, which throws up a class of capitalists or proto-capitalists from the ranks of petty commodity producers. Taken together with a definition of commodity production as any production for the market, this proposition has led to the revolutionary movement being haunted by fears of capitalist restoration from the ranks of peasants and petty producers. To prevent such restoration, extremist policies have been used against sections of the peasantry that have so weakened the revolutionary movement that the possibility of capitalist restoration ironically has been greatly strengthened.

What is wrong with this extremist position is that *any production for the market does not constitute commodity production.* Petty producers in the form of sweet-sellers, eatery-owners, grocers, vegetable sellers, and inn-keepers have been operating in India for millennia and transacting through cash in the market, but this did not produce capitalism or proto-capitalism in medieval let alone ancient India. The commodity production that does produce differentiation and a tendency toward the creation of capitalists on the one side and a semi-proletariat on the other from the ranks of petty producers is a particular type of market participation, one where the product for the seller is pure exchange value and not a use-value, where it represents to the seller only a certain sum of money. For this there has to be an impersonality to the act of exchange that is typically associated not with local exchanges but with long-distance trade.[7]

It follows, therefore, that if the historical possibility of transcending capitalism that exists today, especially in view of the impasse of capitalism and the worldwide push toward fascism that it is generating, has to be realized, then the tendency of skepticism toward a broad worker-peasant alliance that is so prevalent within the Marxist tradition has to be overcome.

# CHAPTER 21

# The Road Ahead

We have argued that the hegemony of international finance capital has to be overcome if the current conjuncture is to be transcended. Doing so within the framework of capitalism is clearly not possible. Hence, the process of overcoming this hegemony will have to be part of a process of transcending capitalism itself. Different countries will have to follow their own paths for doing so. In what follows, we focus attention only on the case of a third world country like India. Our remarks, however, have general relevance.

## The Need for De-Linking

One way of overcoming the hegemony of international finance capital, the ideal way in fact, would be if a world state came into being, based on the support of the world's workers and peasants, which then confronted international finance capital to introduce measures for reviving the world economy and ensuring a basic minimum of living standard for all the world's people. This would mean that instead of a withdrawal from the current globalization for escaping domination by global finance, this globalization itself is carried to a higher level, even while the domination by finance is transcended.

But this is clearly out of the question at present. There is no internationally coordinated struggle of the working class, let alone of the peasantry;

so the question of a world struggle against the hegemony of global finance is not on the agenda at present, and waiting for such a struggle to develop would be like waiting for Godot in Samuel Beckett's play. Struggles, whether of workers or of peasants, are largely organized within particular countries, and because of such struggles, what is feasible, and has happened repeatedly of late, is the coming into power in particular countries of progressive governments committed to taking their countries out of the impasse that capitalism has currently engulfed them in.

Such a government, if it is to remain loyal to the interests of the working people on whose support it came to power, has to put restrictions sooner or later upon the free flow of finance out of the country. No matter what this government's suppositions, this would be a necessity, for any agenda for bringing about an improvement in the conditions of working people would arouse opposition from global finance. And even if the eyes of global finance happen to be closed toward such efforts, financing such an agenda, which would require an increase either in the fiscal deficit or in taxes upon the rich, would open these eyes, giving rise to an exodus of finance and offering the government a stark choice between two alternatives: either roll back such efforts and thereby boost the confidence of investors in the economy or put controls on capital outflows. If the government wishes to remain true to the promise to its class base then it will have to choose the second option.

This, itself, will mean a degree of de-linking from the current globalization. But matters would not end there. Even if capital flight is prevented through capital controls, meeting the current account deficit, which several third world countries including India habitually have, will be difficult if capital inflows dry up because of such controls. It would become necessary then to have some import controls as well. These would become all the more necessary if sanctions are imposed by advanced countries owing to the imposition of capital controls, which make the balance of payments even more precarious. For all these reasons there will be a dynamic movement of modification of the neoliberal regime that is currently in force in that country, involving de-linking from the process of globalization and putting in place trade and capital controls.

A new regime would necessarily have to rely on the domestic market for its economic growth. And though the initiative for stimulating the domestic market will have to be taken by the government, the manner of doing that must be through government expenditure that brings about land-augmentation and an increase in agricultural output through it, so that inflation is controlled without any recourse to income deflation of the working people.

This would not mean a return to the old dirigisme, which had avoided undertaking any radical land redistribution and had sought to develop agriculture along capitalist lines, though the capitalism it sought to develop was to come from within this sector itself rather than through the intervention of multinational agribusiness or the domestic big bourgeoisie. It is this development of capitalism in the countryside that widened economic inequalities there, keeping the mass of the people in a state of continued deprivation and leading to an atrophy of the domestic market. What a strategy for transcending neoliberal capitalism must do instead is to undertake land redistribution and develop agriculture along cooperative or collective lines through the voluntary consent of the peasants. (Extreme land concentration is inimical to the development of genuine cooperatives; the need for land redistribution is fundamental for this reason, too.)

The development of agriculture on the basis of voluntary collectives would not only effect land augmentation to a much greater extent than the dirigiste regime had done, it would also enlarge incomes in the countryside, and in a more egalitarian manner than earlier, and thereby expand the home market. Because the goods demanded would be employment-intensive, this alternative strategy will also entail using up labor reserves rather than adding to them.

But the increased supply of such goods for which demand would have increased due to the expansion of the home market would also have to come from a reenergized state sector, apart from petty producers, small capitalists, and various collective and cooperative units. This is because the imposition of trade and capital controls and of heavier taxation of the rich would lead most likely to an "investment strike" by big capital. In other words, even if we do not start with an emphasis on the public sector, we are bound to accord this emphasis to it sooner or later because of the logic of the situation.

An additional point is that the essence of a path of democratic transition is not just that working people become better off, but that their being better off should not be a matter of largesse by the government. It should rather be a matter of their rights. Hence, while the trajectory of development will have to be along the lines suggested above, this trajectory must be shrouded in the institution of economic rights. The regime that transcends the neoliberal development strategy must introduce a set of universal, justiciable economic rights on a par with the political rights typically enshrined in a democratic constitution. A minimal set of five such rights, namely the right to employment (or of wage payment if the state fails to provide employment); the right to food at affordable prices; the right to free, quality, public healthcare; the right to free, quality public education up to at least the university level; and the right to old-age pension and disability assistance of an adequate magnitude can be immediately implemented. And for this no more than an additional 10 percent or so of GDP will be required. Ironically, it has never been attempted before. Indeed, it is a telling comment upon the growth effected by the neoliberal trajectory that, despite its supposedly high rate, it has not met these basic requirements in countries like India. On the contrary, it has actually been accompanied by an absolute decline in per capita total absorption of food grains, that is, of direct and indirect absorption taken together, the latter through processed foods and animal products into which food grains enter as feed grains.[1]

The kind of development trajectory we have outlined appears at first sight to have little to do with socialism. But if socialism is seen as the ultimate destination of a trajectory of development, then its pursuit must be characterized by the measures we have just discussed. But even the pursuit of such a trajectory will face serious obstacles. Let us discuss some of these.

### Obstacles to an Alternative Trajectory

The most obvious obstacle, as one would expect, is the direct political intervention by the metropolitan countries, and in particular the leading one, the United States. This was the case vis-à-vis the postwar dirigiste regimes in the third world that sought to control their own resources and their destinies by de-linking from metropolitan hegemony. And this remains the case even today, except that the need for intervention has gone down greatly, at least in the non-oil-rich third world, because of the "spontaneous" obstacle to de-linking that arises in any country that is caught in the grip of a neoliberal regime. But if spontaneity fails, then the C.I.A. steps in.

This spontaneous obstacle is our second point. In any country that has a neoliberal regime and is open to the vortex of global financial flows, even before the political formation backing such an alternative regime has come to power, the very prospect of its doing so would start a capital flight. And the opponents of that formation would raise the question: If the country is already facing financial difficulties before the votaries of change have come to power, what a disaster it would face if these votaries did come to power. At this point the pro-change political formation would have to assure financiers and capitalists that it would not harm them an iota; it would be forced to backtrack from its vision. And in case it does not back off, many in the electorate will be persuaded by the prospects of disaster in the event of its coming to power and therefore vote against it, preventing it from coming to power.

Coming to power is itself fraught with difficulties. And if a pro-change formation does come to power despite these, then financial outflows will become a torrent, causing a financial crisis that would bring it much unpopularity and encourage the pro-capitalist formations, with the backing, needless to say, of the United States, to plan coups against it, including parliamentary coups of the sort that we have witnessed in Latin America.

These transitional difficulties arising from capital flight, which a country is bound to face in attempting an alternative development strategy, constitute the most powerful force keeping third world countries in thralldom to neoliberalism. It is their overwhelming deterring effect that makes any 1950s- and 1960s-style armed imperialist intervention for thwarting dirigisme unnecessary.

Countries once caught in the grip of neoliberalism simply find it exceedingly difficult to escape that grip. And their state of helplessness, of being trapped, is then held up by the spokespersons of neoliberalism as vindicating the desirability of the neoliberal economic arrangement, that there is no alternative (TINA), and that there is a consensus among all political formations in favor of neoliberalism. What is held up as "consensus" is, in reality, the helplessness that most political formations know they would experience when they try to escape from the clutches of a neoliberal regime.

There are, of course, certain exceptional circumstances when the international context is propitious for such an escape. A primary commodity price boom is one of them. The turn to the left in Latin America was made possible because of such a boom. The rise in oil prices was a factor that facilitated the leftist projects in Venezuela, Bolivia, and Ecuador, by making their problems of transition easier to handle. By the same token, the collapse of the primary commodities boom, and the collapse in oil prices in particular, has had the opposite effect, enmeshing the Latin American economies that had made a turn to the left in serious difficulties, for no fault of the left, resulting in setbacks.

To be sure, one can criticize these progressive regimes that, while pursuing laudable redistributive measures to ensure that working people benefited from the commodity price boom, they did not take steps toward a structural transformation of their economies. This would have better prepared them to face the consequences of the end of the primary commodity boom; but the point is that the collapse has hurt them and made the transition to an alternative regime that much more difficult.

The left has to prepare the people of the third world better, to take them into confidence that a price has to be paid in the period of transition for their emancipation, instead of promising the moon to them as bourgeois formations habitually do.

But in addition to these problems of transition, there is also an obstacle to the pursuit of an alternative path that arises from a certain ideological ambiguity within the left to the phenomenon of contemporary globalization. Let us examine this.

### The Concept of Nationalism

An important manifestation of ideological ambiguity is the opposition within the ranks of the left to any alternative strategy to neoliberalism that involves de-linking from the current globalization. De-linking, it is argued, would involve a revival of nationalism, which is reactionary and unacceptable to the left, whose essence lies in being internationalist. The implicit presumption here is that while the domination of current globalization by international finance capital is objectionable, there is nonetheless something positive about it, since it transcends nationalism.

The problem with this position is that it sees nationalism as one homogeneous category that is unambiguously reprehensible. It misses the distinction between nationalism that was invoked for the imperialist project in Europe, prompting Rudolf Hilferding (writing, on the eve of the First World War) to argue that the ideology of finance capital was a glorification of the "national idea," and the nationalism that was invoked by the anti-imperialist struggle in the colonies and semi-colonies. It misses, in short, the distinction between the nationalism of a Hitler and the nationalism of a Ho Chi Minh or a Gandhi, implicitly holding both to be reprehensible. This is a basic mistake.[2]

Not only were the two nationalisms fundamentally different in their objectives, but they differed in their nature as well. The nationalism that came into vogue in Europe in the aftermath of the Treaties of Westphalia, which also saw the beginning of the imperial project with Cromwell's conquest of Ireland, was not inclusive: it always located an "enemy within," the Catholics in Northern Europe, the Protestants in Southern Europe, and the Jews everywhere. It also perceived the nation as "standing above the people": the nation was not to serve the people, rather the people had to make sacrifices for the nation.

By contrast, the concept of nationalism that underlay the anti-imperialist struggle over much of the third world was inclusive: it *had to be inclusive* in order to mobilize an entire people against the might of imperialism. It did not entertain imperial ambitions; on the contrary, it had to have fraternal links with anti-imperialist struggles elsewhere, and therefore could not have ambitions of dominating them. Usually it developed a kind of "freedom charter" (such as the Karachi Congress Resolution in India in 1931), which defined how the new nation would serve the people's interest, instead of demanding that the people become subservient and only make sacrifices for a metaphysical entity called the "nation." In every single respect, then, anti-imperialist nationalism in the third world differed from the post-Westphalian nationalism of Europe, which was so blatantly reactivated at a later date by finance capital for its own ends, in a world of inter-imperialist rivalry.

To be sure, within the third world countries themselves the nationalism of the anti-imperialist struggle had to contend with a European-style exclusionary, anti-minority, and aggrandizing nationalism. This nationalism was not anti-imperialist but was directed against a religious, ethnic, or linguistic minority at home, and was *usually encouraged by imperialism to counter anti-imperialist nationalism.* The Hindutva nationalism in India, whose votaries were conspicuous by their absence from the anti-colonial struggle, is an obvious example. The struggle between these two nationalisms, an anti-imperialist and an exclusionary nationalism within most countries of the third world, still continues; and in the current era of globalization, the aggrandizing and anti-minority nationalism has gained the upper hand precisely because anti-imperialism has been rendered temporarily helpless by the hegemony of international finance capital.

The revival of the concept of nationalism that underlay the anti-imperialist struggle and that is *not* reactionary as is alleged, on the basis of a new agenda that transcends neoliberaism, is essential for reenergizing an inclusive concept of the nation. For this, the welfare of the people must be its main preoccupation, thereby halting the process of disintegration that afflicts much of the third world. To debunk it as "reactionary" is a gross error, particularly because the only force capable of carrying forward such a new agenda in today's world is the left, and its political leadership should prevent the development of this "nationalism" in a direction that is anti-internationalist.

The left can play this role of reviving an inclusive nationalism around an agenda that can constitute a new freedom charter, and make this nationalism a bridge to internationalism, as the Bandung spirit in an earlier period had attempted, only if it overcomes its ambiguity toward globalization by distinguishing between the different concepts of nationalism. Nationalism in the European context may carry unsavory connotations, but this is not universally true.

### The Pitfalls of Productionism

A second reason for the ambiguity toward globalization among sections of the left, especially within the third world, is the view that it has brought about a massive development of productive forces over much of the third world, measured in terms of the growth rate of the Gross Domestic Product, and is still capable of doing so. Since a mode of production according to Marxist understanding, it is argued, becomes historically obsolete and ripe for transcendence only when it becomes a fetter on the development of the productive forces, the view that globalization, and hence by implication capitalism itself, has become historically ripe for transcendence, is erroneous.

This view is often expressed alternatively, in mundane parlance, as follows: when globalization has brought enormously high growth rates, indeed unprecedented growth rates, to at least some countries of the South, for the people in such countries to demand de-linking from globalization would be nothing short of folly. It would be like chopping off the branch on which one is comfortably ensconced. And people in other countries of the South should await higher growth from globalization rather than de-link from it.

The first problem with this argument is that the historical obsolescence of a mode of production has nothing to do with the growth rates of the Gross Domestic Product. Economic historians have pointed out that in the period before the First World War Russia was experiencing high growth rates, with its industrial output rising by 50 percent over a period of merely five years. As far as world capitalism was concerned, the Victorian and Edwardian booms had brought high growth rates. And yet Lenin had no compunctions about calling capitalism "moribund" and asking for its overthrow at its weakest link at the time, namely Russia.

The reason was that he saw the system in its monopoly phase as being punctuated by devastating wars as a consequence of inter-imperialist rivalry, where the workers of the belligerent countries were offered a stark choice: either to kill fellow workers across the trenches or to turn their guns against the system that forced them to do so.[3] Exactly the same choice was offered to the people recruited from the colonies to fight on behalf of their metropolitan "masters." Or, in Rosa Luxemburg's words, the system had come to a pass where the choice was between socialism and barbarism. The historical obsolescence of the system was established by these outstanding Marxist writers not in terms of GDP growth rates, but in terms of the fact that it had brought mankind to a state of barbarism, from which socialism alone could rescue it.

This distinction between a phase of capitalism when it is historically progressive and a phase when it is historically regressive and hence obsolete is not very apposite, especially when one looks at capitalism in its world setting. Capitalism has always developed the productive forces on the one side and created growing absolute poverty on the other. Its "progressive" and "regressive" roles have always gone together, and not sequentially in phases. The earlier accepted proposition that the distinction between the two phases corresponds to one between pre-monopoly or free-competition capitalism and monopoly capitalism, though it appeared compelling at the time it was put forward, that is, in the context of imperialist wars, would scarcely appear convincing today.

The distinction between the two phases, even if interpreted in terms of the growth of productive forces as measured by GDP growth rates, will not pass muster, since the so-called Golden Age of Capitalism occurred, after all, in a period that belongs to the monopoly phase. Even if the distinction between the two phases is interpreted in terms of capitalism's descent into barbarism in one phase compared to the other, no temporal division of its history is possible on these lines. Capitalism was always barbaric in the colonies in the pre-decolonization period. And it continues to be barbaric even today, despite the absence of formal colonies, because of its ruthless imposition of income deflation on the working people of the third world.

The overthrow of capitalism for achieving human freedom comes on the agenda when theory has unraveled the deadly logic of its working, when the need for its overthrow for achieving human freedom has become apparent. True, some periods are more propitious for this purpose than others, but that is quite different from postulating a binary between a progressive phase and a phase of historical obsolescence. Our argument has been that the current period is a propitious one for the socialist project, because not only is capitalism at an impasse from which it does not appear as yet to find a way out, but also because, caught in this impasse, it is conjuring up the forces of fascism everywhere. This fascism, while it will not replay the history of the 1930s and early 1940s, will be sinister nonetheless because it will have an abiding presence. What we shall witness, in other words, is not necessarily wars and death camps, but a more or less protracted period of fascification of society, from which socialism alone can rescue mankind.

We have called this idea of judging the potential of capitalism in terms of the rate at which the productive forces are developing "productionism." Left ambivalence toward globalization on the basis of a "productionist" argument is wrong in our view for two reasons. First, productionism itself is wrong, and the potential of capitalism cannot be judged on this basis. And second, the two-phase conceptualization of capitalism on the productionist criterion lacks any substance. Of course, such a two-phase conceptualization based on any other criterion also lacks any substance. But productionism is usually the criterion in terms of which this twofold conceptualization is done, and de-linking from globalization is opposed typically by invoking this criterion. If productionism is inapposite for judging the potential of capitalism, then it follows that the ambiguity with regard to globalization and the opposition to de-linking from it represents an erroneous trend within the left.

Unless the left overcomes this ambiguity toward contemporary globalization and mobilizes the working people around an agenda of transcending the neoliberal order by de-linking from it, and thereby commencing a journey toward socialism, mankind will be long mired in crisis and fascism.

# Notes

## 1 A MONEY-USING ECONOMY

1. While this is clear and obvious, the theoretical apparatus that Keynes had developed, around the concept of marginal efficiency of capital, to give expression to this, is logically flawed. The marginal efficiency schedule in competitive conditions would not slope downwards; the reason given by Keynes for it, namely that the cost of producing capital goods at the margin increases as investment increases, is invalid, because the marginal efficiency of capital being an *ex ante* concept, its sloping down for this reason can happen only under oligopsony. But while the Keynesian apparatus is wrong, this does not negate the proposition that greater liquidity preference must cause a fall in the production of investment goods even under competitive conditions.

2. Prabhat Patnaik, T*he Value of Money* (New York: Columbia University Press, 2009).

3. They are discussed in detail in ibid.

4. Nikolai Bukharin, *Imperialism and the Accumulation of Capital*, ed. Kenneth Tarbuck (London: Lane, 1971).

5. This distinction between accumulation and investment was drawn clearly in Paul Sweezy, *The Theory of Capitalist Development* (New York: Oxford University Press, 1942).

6. Karl Marx, *Theories of Surplus Value, Part II* (Moscow: Progress Publishers, 1968).

7. Roy Harrod, "An Essay on Dynamic Theory," *Economic Journal* 49, no. 193 (March 1939).

8. Michał Kalecki, "Observations on the Theory of Growth," *Economic Journal* 72, no. 285 (March 1962); Prabhat Patnaik, *Accumulation and Stability under Capitalism* (Oxford: Clarendon, 1997).

9.   R. M.Goodwin, "The Non-linear Accelerator and the Persistence of Business Cycles," *Econometrica*, Volume 19, No.1 (January 1951).

10.  This argument was first advanced by Joseph Steindl, *Maturity and Stagnation in American Capitalism* (New York: Monthly Review Press, 1979, originally published in 1952).

11.  It may be thought that though lowering the price to sell more may invite retaliation from rivals, firms may still do that if the overall demand for the good is price-elastic. But if the overall demand is price elastic then the original price itself would not have prevailed; it would have been lowered even in the absence of any innovation

12.  Michał Kalecki, "Observations on the Theory of Growth," *Economic Journal* 72, no. 285 (March 1962); Prabhat Patnaik, *Accumulation and Stability under Capitalism* (Oxford: Clarendon, 1997).

13.  W. Arthur Lewis, *Growth and Fluctuations 1870–1913* (London: Allen and Unwin, 1978).

14.  Since $Mv = pQ$, it follows that with v, the income velocity of circulation of money, constant, $\dot{p}/p$ must equal $\dot{M}/M - \dot{Q}/Q$. The growth rate $\dot{Q}/Q$ in turn can only equal the rate of growth of the labor force in "efficiency units," as full employment is always assumed to prevail. This growth rate is called the "natural rate of growth."

15.  Joan Robinson, *The Accumulation of Capital* (London: Macmillan, 1956).

16.  Michal Kalecki, *The Theory of Economic Dynamics* (London: Allen and Unwin, 1954)

17.  Ashok Mitra, *The Share of Wages in National Income* (Bloomington: Indiana University Press, 1954).

18.  Michał Kalecki, "Class Struggle and the Distribution of National Income," *Kyklos* 24, no. 1 (February1971), republished in *Selected Essays in the Dynamics of the Capitalist Economy 1933–1970* (Cambridge: Cambridge University Press, 1971).

## 2 MONEY IN SOME THEORETICAL TRADITIONS

1.   Frank Hahn, *Equilibrium and Macroeconomics* (Oxford: Clarendon, 1984).

2.   Robert W. Clower, "A Reconsideration of the Microfoundation of Monetary Theory," *Western Economic Journal* 6, no. 1 (1967).

3.   Clower's lead has been followed by others, notably Bryce Hool, "Liquidity, Speculation and the Demand for Money," *Journal of Economic Theory* 21, no. 1 (1979), in conceptualizing a transactions demand for money in a Walrasian world with an auctioneer.

4.   David Ricardo, *Works and Correspondence of David Ricardo*, vol. 1, ed. Piero Sraffa (Cambridge: Cambridge University Press, 1951); Maurice Dobb, *Theories of Value and Distribution since Adam Smith* (Cambridge:

Cambridge University Press, 1973). See also Marx, *Theories of Surplus Value*, Part I (Moscow: Progress Publishers, 1969).

5.    Adam Smith, *An Inquiry Into the Nature and Causes of the Wealth of Nations*, 2 Vols. (Indianapolis: Liberty Fund, 1981), 466.

6.    Dobb, *Theories of Value and Distribution since Adam Smith*.

7.    Ricardo, *Works and Correspondence of David Ricardo*, vol. 1.

8.    Joan Robinson, *Economic Heresies* (London: Palgrave Macmillan, 1972).

9.    Karl Marx, *A Contribution to the Critique of Political Economy* (London: Lawrence and Wishart, 1971).

10.   Joan Robinson, *The Accumulation of Capital* (London: Macmillan, 1956).

11.   John Maynard Keynes, *The General Theory of Employment, Interest and Money* (London: Macmillan, 1936).

## 3 THE MARXIAN SYSTEM AND MONEY

1.    The discussion that follows is based on Prabhat Patnaik, *The Value of Money* (New York: Columbia University Press, 2009).

2.    Michał Kalecki, *Theory of Economic Dynamics* (London: Allen and Unwin, 1954).

3.    Nicholas Kaldor, "Monetarism and U.K. Monetary Policy," *Cambridge Journal of Economics* 4, no. 4 (December 1980).

4.    Ashok Mitra, *The Share of Wages in National Income* (Bloomington: Indiana University Press, 1954) provided an argument for why money wage increase would lead to real wage increases even within a broadly Kaleckian framework without going into the question of the value of money.

5.    The contradiction between these two properties of a money-using economy and an isolated capitalist sector is discussed at greater length in Prabhat Patnaik, "'Capital' and the Labour Theory of Value," in *Reading 'Capital' Today*, Ingo Schmidt and Carlo Fanelli, eds. (London: Pluto 2017).

6.    For a discussion of tax-financed appropriation of surplus from India under colonial rule, see Utsa Patnaik, "Revisiting the 'Drain,' or Transfers from India to Britain in the Context of Global Diffusion of Capitalism," in *Agrarian and Other Histories*, Shubhra Chakrabarti and Utsa Patnaik, eds. (Delhi: Tulika, 2017), and our chapter 10 below.

7.    This, to recapitulate, means that starting from any initial situation that is not on the warranted growth path, which itself has a knife-edge property, the economy would tend to converge to a stationary state. This is a *property* of the system, so that any observed positive trend, through cycles, can only be explained by exogenous stimuli.

## 4 CAPITALISM AND ITS SETTING

1.    Josef Steindl, *Maturity and Stagnation in American Capitalism* (New York: Monthly Review Press, 1976, originally published in 1951).

2.   R. F. Harrod, "An Essay on Dynamic Theory," *Economic Journal* 49, no.193 (March 1939).

3.   This argument can be formally expressed as follows. Denoting the level of capacity utilization in period t by $u_t$ which is a pure number $(O_t/K_t\beta)$, with O and K denoting output and capital stock respectively and $\beta$ the technological output-capital ratio, the desired level of capacity utilization by $u^*$, and assuming that a ratio $\delta$ of capital stock "dies" every period, we can say

$$[I_{t+1} - \delta K_{t+1}] / K_{t+1} = [(I_t - \delta.K_t) / K_t]. [1+ b (u_t - u^*)] \ldots (i)$$

The output in any period is determined by the multiplier, that is:

$$O_t = I_t / s \ldots (ii)$$

where s is the (constant) savings ratio. Equations (i) and (ii) yield two possible steady-state solutions or uniform trends, which, expressing $(I-\delta K)/K$ as i, are given by: (a) i = 0; and (b) $i = u^* s\beta - \delta$. The first of these trends is a stable trend, while the second, analogous to Harrod's "warranted growth rate," is an unstable trend.

4.   This conclusion, which draws on Rosa Luxemburg's argument, was derived by Michal Kalecki, "Observations on the Theory of Growth," *Economic Journal* (March 1962), for a range of investment functions which take into account the sensitivity of investment to demand.

5.   Josef Steindl, *Maturity and Stagnation in American Capitalism.*

6.   W. Arthur Lewis, *Growth And Fluctuations 1870–1913* (London: George Allen and Unwin, 1978).

7.   P. A. Baran and P .M. Sweezy, *Monopoly Capital* (New York: Monthly Review Press, 1966).

8.   S. B. Saul, *Studies in British Overseas Trade 1870–1914* (Liverpool: Liverpool University Press, 1960).

9.   W. Arthur Lewis, *The Evolution of the International Economic Order* (Princeton: Princeton University Press, 1978).

10.  E. J. Hobsbawm, *Industry and Empire: From 1750 to the Present Day* (Harmondsworth: Penguin, 1972).

11.  Utsa Patnaik, "Revisiting the 'Drain,' or Transfers from India to Britain in the Context of Global Diffusion of Capitalism," in *Agrarian and Other Histories*, Shubhra Chakrabarti and Utsa Patnaik, eds. (Delhi: Tulika, 2017).

12.  This argument is set out in detail in Prabhat Patnaik, *Accumulation and Stability under Capitalism* (Oxford: Clarendon, 1997).

13.  Michal Kalecki, *Theory of Economic Dynamics* (London: Allen and Unwin, 1954); *Selected Essays on the Dynamics of the Capitalist Economy 1933–1971* (Cambridge: Cambridge University Press, 1971).

14.  Kalecki gives figures to show a constancy in the share of wages in national income in the United Kingdom between 1881–85 and 1924. For the United States, however, no comparable figures exist, though the share of wages in

344 NOTES TO PAGES 64–74

U.S. manufacturing declines between 1879 and 1937. This decline, however, would be moderated if we take labor incomes inclusive of salaries. Kalecki, *Selected Essays in the Dynamics of the Capitalist Economy,* pp. 66–77.

15. The model that follows is only for illustrative purposes, to show how the existence of price-takers makes multiple NAIRUs possible. The question of why the inflationary process through which the price-takers are squeezed does not threaten the value of money is not addressed here.

16. Raúl Prebisch, *The Economic Development of Latin America and Its Principal Problems* (New York: United Nations Economic Commission for Latin America, 1950); H. W. Singer, "The Distribution of Gains Between Investing and Borrowing Countries," *American Economic Review* 40, no. 2 (May 1950).

## 5 INCREASING SUPPLY PRICE AND IMPERIALISM

1. David Ricardo, *Principles of Political Economy and Taxation* (1817), in *Works and Correspondence of David Ricardo,* vol.1, Piero Sraffa, ed. (Cambridge: Cambridge University Press, 1951).

2. Karl Marx, *Theories of Surplus Value, Part II* (Moscow: Progress Publishers, 1968).

3. See Iqbal Husain, ed., *Karl Marx on India* (Delhi: Tulika Books, 2006).

4. A simple model derived from that in chapter 4 illustrates the point. Let the price in the capitalist (manufacturing) sector be $p$, raw material and labor coefficients per unit of its output $a$ and $l$, respectively (with raw material produced by peasant agriculture); let its money wage rate of manufacturing workers be such as to give, at the expected price, a desired real wage rate (we abstract for simplicity from any labor productivity increase), which is a function of the unemployment rate. Let $w_a$, and $l_a$ denote, respectively, the money return per unit of labor and the labor input per unit of product in the agricultural sector. The system can be set out as follows:

$$(ap_a + wl)\,(1+\pi) = p \ldots \text{(i)}$$
$$w = f(u)\,p^e \ldots \text{(ii)}$$
$$w_a\,l_a\,\alpha = p_a \ldots \text{(iii)}$$

where $\alpha$ denotes traders' markup, assumed to be constant, over the unit prime cost of the agricultural product.

$$w_a = w^* p(t-1) \ldots \text{(iv)}$$

$w^*$ being the real income (in terms of manufactured good) that peasants try to maintain at the previous period's price. The expected price of the manufactured good by the workers in the metropolis is given by the formula

$$p^e_t = p_{t-1} \cdot p_{t-1} / p_{t-2} \ldots \text{(v)}$$

which, as mentioned earlier, simply assumes adaptive expectations, namely an extrapolation of the previous period's inflation rate into the current period.

It is clear that for any given level of unemployment $u$ in the manufacturing sector, and given the set of input coefficients, there would be a steady rate of inflation in this universe, which would be equal for both the sectors. The reason for such a steady rate of inflation is that one group of the working population, namely the agriculturists, acts as "price-takers." At this steady rate of inflation, corresponding to a given $u$, there would be a particular level of the terms of trade between manufacturing and agriculture. But as $l_a$ increases because of "diminishing returns," the real income of the agriculturists goes down; this happens through the rate of steady inflation at the given rate of unemployment $u$ increasing, while the terms of trade remain unchanged. Now, if $l_a$ *keeps increasing*, then we have accelerating inflation even at the given unemployment rate.

5.  This argument was initially given in Utsa Patnaik and Prabhat Patnaik, *A Theory of Imperialism* (New York: Columbia University Press, 2016). The argument made by some critics against that book, namely that it ignored the rate of interest, is obviously beside the point. If money is assumed to earn nothing, then what is said above would hold. Even if money is assumed to earn an implicit rate of return, commodities can also be assumed to earn exactly the same implicit rate of return as they are freely convertible into money. And even if commodities are not assumed to earn such a return while money is, this only raises the threshold, in addition to carrying costs, above which the shift to commodities would occur. Our argument above, however, establishes that with accelerating inflation any such threshold would invariably be crossed, leading to a collapse in the value of money. This collapse therefore has nothing to do with the rate of interest.

6.  There have been several important works of late on the question of empire and imperialism, such as Michael Hardt and Antonio Negri, *Empire* (Cambridge, MA: Harvard University Press, 2000) and John Smith, *Imperialism in the Twenty-First Century* (New York: Monthly Review Press, 2016). The argument of the present book, however, is completely *sui generis* in the sense that it focuses on the *necessity* of imperialism (a point not covered in writings in the Leninist tradition) and hence asserts an element of continuity between colonial times and the present.

## 6 PERIODS IN CAPITALISM

1.  S. B. Saul, *Studies in British Overseas Trade 1870–1914* (Liverpool: Liverpool University Press, 1960).

2.  Joseph A. Schumpeter, *Business Cycles*, 2 vols. (New York: McGraw-Hill, 1939).

3.  Alvin Hansen, *Full Recovery or Stagnation?* (London: Norton, 1938).

4.  Paul A. Baran and Paul M. Sweezy, *Monopoly Capital* (New York: Monthly Review Press, 1966).

5.   Charles Kindleberger, *The World in Depression, 1929–1939* (Berkeley: University of California Press, 1973).

6.   Harry Magdoff, "Militarism and Imperialism," *Monthly Review* 21, no. 9 (February 1970).

7.   As Baran and Sweezy point out in *Monopoly Capital*, state expenditure in other, non-military, sectors is opposed by capitalists, *inter alia*, because it entails providing competition to the capitalists already engaged in those sectors.

8.   Prabhat Patnaik, "On the Economic Crisis of World Capitalism," in *Lenin and Imperialism*, Prabhat Patnaik, ed. (Delhi: Orient Longmans, 1986).

9.   "Has Capitalism Changed?" was, in fact, the title of an international symposium edited by Shigeto Tsuru (1961) and containing articles by several well-known authors apart from himself, such as John Kenneth Galbraith and Paul M. Sweezy, where the dominant view was that it had. Shigeto Tsuru, ed., *Has Capitalism Changed?* (Tokyo: Iwanami Shoten, 1961).

10.  Michał Kalecki, *Selected Essays on the Dynamics of the Capitalist Economy 1933–1971* (Cambridge: Cambridge University Press, 1971).

11.  Joseph A. Schumpeter, "John Maynard Keynes," in Joseph Schunpeter, *Ten Great Economists* (Chicago: University of Chicago Press, 1952).

12.  Nicholas Kaldor, "Inflation and Recession in the World Economy," *Economic Journal* 86, no. 344 (December 1976).

13.  John Spraos, "The Statistical Debate on the Net Barter Terms of Trade Between Primary Products and Manufactures," *Economic Journal* 90, no. 357 (March 1980).

14.  Kaldor, "Inflation and Recession in the World Economy."

15.  It may be thought that since the most prominent outbreak of inflation began with the wage explosion in 1968 (Kaldor, "Inflation and Recession in the World Economy"), the inability to impose income deflation on the periphery had little to do with inflation. But the wage explosion itself arose because inflation had already been eroding real wages for some time (see Patnaik, "On the Economic Crisis of World Capitalism").

16.  Prabhat Patnaik, "Neo-liberalism and Democracy," *Economic and Political Weekly* 49, no. 15 (April 2014).

17.  Joan Robinson, *Economic Philosophy* (London: Watts, 1962).

18.  John Maynard Keynes, "National Self-Sufficiency," *Yale Review* 22, no. 4 (June 1933).

19.  Paul Krugman, "Running Out of Planet to Exploit," *The New York Times*, April 21, 2008.

20.  The FAO figure for the average output for the triennium in each case is divided by the population for the mid-triennium year.

21.  We are grateful to Souvik Chakravarty for giving us this figure based on research for his doctoral dissertation.

22.   Joseph Stiglitz, "Inequality is Holding Back the Recovery," *New York Times,*
      January 13, 2013.

## 7 THE MYTH OF THE AGRICULTURAL REVOLUTION

1.    J. D. Chambers and G. E. Mingay, *The Agricultural Revolution 1750–1880*
      (London: Batsford, 1966).
2.    Ralph Davis, *The Industrial Revolution and British Overseas Trade*
      (Leicester: Leicester University Press, 1979), Table 31.
3.    R. D. Lee and Roger S. Schofield, "British Population in the Eighteenth
      Century," in *The Economic History of Britain Since 1770*, vol. 1, Roderick
      Floud and David MacCloskey, eds. (Cambridge: Cambridge University
      Press, 1981).
4.    Angus Maddison, *The World Economy* (Paris: OECD Development Centre
      Studies, 2006).
5.    Chambers and Mingay, *The Agricultural Revolution 1750–1880.*
6.    Mark Overton, "Re-establishing the English Agricultural Revolution,"
      *Agricultural History Review* 44, no. 1 (1996); M. E. Turner, J. V. Beckett,
      and B. Afton, *Farm Production in England 1700–1914* (Oxford: Oxford
      University Press, 2001), though Liam Brunt, "Estimating English Wheat
      Production in the Industrial Revolution," *University of Oxford Discussion
      Papers in Economic and Social History* no. 29 (June 1999), suggests a
      somewhat higher rise.
7.    W. A. Cole, "Factors in Demand 1700–80," in *The Economic History of
      Britain Since 1770*, vol. 1, ed. Floud and MacCloskey.
8.    Turner, Beckett and Afton, *Farm Production in England 1700–1914.*
9.    Overton, "Re-establishing the English Agricultural Revolution"; Mark
      Overton, *The Agricultural Revolution in England* (Cambridge: Cambridge
      University Press, 1996).
10.   Overton, "Re-establishing the English Agricultural Revolution." Emphasis
      added.
11.   See Robert C. Allen, "Agricultural Output and Productivity in Europe
      1300–1800," discussion paper no. 98, Department of Economics, University
      of British Columbia (1998), "Tracking the Agricultural Revolution in
      England," *Economic History Review* 52, no. 2 (May 1999); Gregory Clark,
      "The Agricultural Revolution and the Industrial Revolution: England
      1500–1912," unpublished paper (2002), http://econ.ucdavis.edu.
12.   Calculated from FAO data. See Food Balance Sheets/Supply Utilization
      Accounts (FBS/SUA); available at faostat3.fao.org/faostat.gateway/go/to/
      download/F/FO/E.
13.   1 quarter = 28 pounds, 1 bushel = 2 quarter of wheat (corn) = 56 pounds.
      The bushel is a volume measure and the weight of different crops per bushel
      will vary, and of wheat will vary depending on moisture content. On average,

one bushel (Imperial measure) of wheat with standard moisture content weighs 56 pounds, or 25.45 kg. The conversion from bushels to kilograms above has been made on this basis to allow comparison with present-day grain output and availability. Population for 1701, 1801 and so on is shown against output for 1700,1800 and so on.

14. E, L Jones, "Agriculture 1700–1780" in R. Floud and D.N. McCloskey, *The Economic History of Britain since 1700 Vol.1 1700 to 1860* (Cambridge: Cambridge University Press, 1981).

15. Annual series on Exports and Imports in B. R. Mitchell and Phyllis Deane, *Abstract of British Historical Statistics* (Cambridge: Cambridge University Press, 1962), up to 1820–29 in thousand quarters; five-year averages from E. J. Hobsbawm, *Industry and Empire: From 1750 to the Present Day* (Harmondsworth: Penguin, 1972), from 1820–29 to 1885–89. Units of 10,000 cwt were converted to units of thousand quarters and ten-year averages taken to splice the series with the first series; 1 quarter = 28 lb., 4 quarters = 1 cwt = 112 lb.

## 8 CAPITALISM AND COLONIALISM

1. See, for instance, R. E. Rowthorn and J. R. Wells, *De-industrialization and Foreign Trade* (Cambridge: Cambridge University Press, 1987).

2. E. J. Hobsbawm, *Inudustry and Empire: From 1750 to the Present Day* (Harmondsworth: Penguin, 1972).

3. Utsa Patnaik, "Capitalism and the Production of Poverty," T. G. Narayanan Memorial Lecture, *Social Scientist* (January–February 2012).

4. Amiya Kumar Bagchi, "Some International Foundations of Capitalist Growth and Underdevelopment," *Economic and Political Weekly* 7, nos. 31–33 (August 5, 1972).

5. For statistical evidence on such retrogression in the case of India, see Shireen Moosvi, *The Economy of the Mughal Empire c.1595: A Statistical Study* (Delhi: Oxford University Press, 2015), in which the author compares the per capita income of India at the end of the sixteenth century with that in 1910 to find that the latter was somewhat lower.

6. W. Arthur Lewis, *Growth and Fluctuations 1870–1913* (London: Allen and Unwin, 1978).

7. This argument is set out in greater detail in Utsa Patnaik and Prabhat Patnaik, *A Theory of Imperialism* (2016).

8. Bipan Chandra, "Reinterpretation of Nineteenth Century Indian Economic History," *Indian Economic and Social History Review* 5, no. 1 (March 1968).

9. Paul A. Baran, *The Political Economy of Growth* (New York: Monthly Review Press, 1957).

10. This proposition is argued in the case of Asia by Tapan Raychaudhuri,

"Historical Roots of Mass Poverty in South Asia," *Economic and Political Weekly* 20, no. 18 (May 4, 1985).

11. We shall come back to this particular argument of Baran in a later chapter.

12. Shireen Moosvi, *The Economy of Mughal India c.1595: A Statistical Study* (Delhi: Oxford University Press, 2015).

## 9 COLONIALISM BEFORE THE FIRST WORLD WAR

1. Dadabhai Naoroji, *Poverty and Un-British Rule in India,*(London: Swan Sonnenschwein & Co. 1901), reprinted by Publications Division, Government of India, 1969; Romesh Chunder Dutt, *Economic History of India Volume 1: Under Early British Rule 1757–1837* (London: Kegan Paul, 1903), and *Volume II: In the Victorian Age 1837–1900* (London: Kegan Paul, 1905), reprinted by Publications Division, Government of India, 1970. The literature discussing the drain, whether directly or tangentially, includes A. K. Bagchi, "Some International Foundations of Capitalist Growth and Underdevelopment," *Economic and Political Weekly* 7, nos. 31–33 (August 5, 1972), *The Presidency Banks and the Indian Economy, 1876–1914* (Delhi: Oxford University Press, 1989), and *Perilous Passage: Mankind and the Global Ascendancy of Capital* (Delhi: Oxford University Press, 2005); A. K. Banerjee, *India's Balance of Payments: Estimates of Current and Capital Accounts 1921–22 to 1938–39* (Bombay: Asia Publishing House 1963), and *Aspects of Indo-British Economic Relations* (Bombay: Oxford University Press, 1982); D. Banerjee, *Colonialism in Action* (Delhi: Orient Longman, 1999); S. Bhattacharya, *The Financial Foundations of the British Raj* (Delhi: Orient Longman, 1971, reprint 2005); K. N. Chaudhuri, "Foreign Trade and Balance of Payments 1757–1947" in D. Kumar, ed. (with the editorial assistance of Meghnad Desai), *The Cambridge Economic History of India, Volume II c.1757–c.1970* (Delhi: Orient Longman, in association with Cambridge University Press, 1984); B. N. Ganguli, *Dadabhai Naoroji and the Drain Theory* (New York: Asia Publishing House, 1965); S.Habib "Colonial Exploitation and Capital Formation in England in the Early Stages of the Industrial Revolution," *Proceedings of the Indian History Congress*, Aligarh (1975); J. M. Keynes, "Review of T. Morrison's *The Economic Transition in India*," *The Economic Journal*, Volume 22 (1911); Angus Maddison, *The World Economy* (Paris: OECD Development Centre Studies, 2006); T. Morison, *The Economic Transition in India* (London: Murray, 1911); A. Mukherjee "The Return of the Colonial in Indian Economic History: The Last Phase of Colonialism in India," *Social Scientist*, Volume 36, No. 3-4 (March-April 2008) and "Empire: How Colonialism Made Modern Britain," *Economic and Political Weekly*, Vol. XLV, No.50, December 11, 2010; Y. S. Pandit, *India's Balance of Indebtedness* (London: Allen and Unwin, 1937); Utsa Patnaik, "Tribute Transfer and the Balance of Payments" in *The Cambridge Economic History of India Volume II, Social*

*Scientist,* Vol. 12, No.12 (December 1984), and "The Free Lunch: Transfers from the Tropical Colonies and Their Role in Capital Formation in Britain during the Industrial Revolution," in K.S.Jomo, ed., *Globalization Under Hegemony: The Changing World Economy* (Delhi: Oxford University Press, 2006); Sunanda Sen, *Colonies and the Empire: India 1890–1914* (Delhi: Orient Longman1992).

2.    The exceptions include Paul A. Baran, *The Political Economy of Growth* (New York: Monthly Review Press, 1957); Maddison, *The World Economy*; H. Heller, *The Birth of Capitalism* (London: Pluto Press, 2011); and Branco Milanovic "Ethical Case and Economic Feasibility of Global Transfers" (2007), available at mpra.ub.uni-muenchen.de/2587/1/MPRA-paper-2587.pdf.

3.    See Folke Hilgerdt, "The Case for Multilateral Trade," *American Economic Review,* Vol. 33, No.1, Part 2 (March 1943), and S.B.Saul, *Studies in British Overseas Trade 1870–1914* (Liverpool: Liverpool University Press, 1960).

4.    Quoted by B.N.Ganguli, *Dadabhai Naoroji and the Drain Theory,* 9. (Emphases added.)

5.    Both Adam Smith and Karl Marx had stressed that the rent of land arose from the ownership of land in a few hands, which enabled the owner, who did not necessarily have to make any outlay in production at all, to extract surplus for its use from the actual producer. Ricardo, however, inverted this concept and labeled as rent surplus profit over and above average profit obtained in production. For Marx's critique of Ricardo's concept, see Karl Marx, *Theories of Surplus Value*, Part II (Moscow: Progress Publishers, 1968), and Utsa Patnaik "Introduction" to U. Patnaik, ed., *The Agrarian Question in Marx and His Successors* (Delhi: Leftword Books, 2007).

6.    Paul Mantoux, *The Industrial Revolution in the Eighteenth Century* [1928], translated by Marjorie Vernon (London: Methuen, 1970); R. C. Dutt *Economic History of India,* Vol. II (1905).

7.    D. Kumar, ed., *The Cambridge Economic History of India,* Vol. II.

8.    See E. J. Hobsbawm, *Industry and Empire: From 1750 to the Present Day* (Harmondsworth: Penguin, 1972); David Landes, *The Unbound Prometheus: Technological Change and Industrial Development in Western Europe from 1850 to the Present* (Cambridge: Cambridge University Press, 1969); P. Deane and W. A. Cole, *British Economic Growth 1688–1959: Trends and Structure* (Cambridge: Cambridge University Press,1969); and B. R. Tomlinson, *The New Cambridge Economic History of India: The Economy of Modern India 1860–1970* (Cambridge: Cambridge University Press, 1993).

9.    See Friedrich List, *The National System of Political Economy,* translated by G. A. Matile (Philadelphia: Lippincott & Co., 1856); R. C. Dutt, *The Economic History of India,* Vol. I (Delhi: South Asia Books, 1990); Mantoux, *The Industrial Revolution*; and Baran, *The Political Economy of Growth.*

10.   Mantoux, *The Industrial Revolution,* p. 256.

11. Ralph Davis, *The Industrial Revolution and British Overseas Trade* (Leicester: Leicester University Press, 1979); Utsa Patnaik, "India's Global Trade and Britain's International Dominance," in S. Sen and M. C. Marcuzzo, eds., *The Changing Face of Imperialism* (Delhi: Routledge, 2018).

12. Phyllis Deane, *The First Industrial Revolution* (Cambridge: Cambridge University Press, 1965).

13. Deane and Cole, *British Economic Growth*.

14. See Table B.2 in U. Patnaik, "New Estimates of Eighteenth Century British Trade and Their Relation to Transfers from Tropical Colonies," in K. N. Panikkar, T. J. Byres, and U. Patnaik, eds., *The Making of History: Essays Presented to Irfan Habib* (Delhi: Tulika Press, 2000).

15. Simon Kuznets, "Foreign Trade: Long-term Trends," *Economic Development and Cultural Change,* Vol. 15, No. 2, Part 2 (January1967).

16. Though he put "special trade" against the Deane and Cole figures, he did not explain what "special trade" meant.

17. U. Patnaik, "Misleading Trade Estimates in Historical and Economic Writings," in P. Patnaik, ed., *Excursus in History: Essays on Some Ideas of Irfan Habib* (Delhi: Tulika Books,2011).

18. E. Backhouse and J. O. P. Bland, *Annals and Memoirs of the Court of Peking* (Boston: Houghton Mifflin, 1914), 322–331.

19. Ricardo's theory serves a very useful *apologetic function* for advanced countries by obfuscating the reality of possible adverse welfare outcome for the less developed country obliged to trade for extra-economic reasons. I. Kravis, in his "Availability and Other Influences on the Commodities Composition of Trade," *Journal of Political Economy* Vol. LXIV (April 1956), had provided an alternative theory to comparative advantage, but he did not critique Ricardo's theory adequately.

20. Samuelson's "linear programming" interpretation of Ricardo, in which with free trade the vector of world output (namely for all the trading countries together) increases, is obviously not valid in a situation where (taking just two countries) one country cannot produce one good at all. If the production of this good in the other country is constrained by the non-augmentability of fully used-up land area, then the total "world" output of this good will remain unchanged after trade, while that of the other will *contract;* this was the case with colonial trade. Paul A. Samuelson, "A Modern Treatment of the Ricardian Economy: I. The Pricing of Goods and of Labor and Land Services," *The Quarterly Journal of Economics*, 73/1 (February 1959), 1–35. See U. Patnaik, "Ricardo's Fallacy," in K. S. Jomo, ed., *The Pioneers of Development Economics* (Delhi: Tulika Books, 2005) for a critique.

21. Estimated by U. Patnaik in "The Free Lunch," using data in B. R. Mitchell and Phyllis Deane, *Abstract of British Historical Statistics* (Cambridge: Cambridge University Press, 1962).

22. Maddison, *The World Economy*.

23. See Utsa Patnaik, "The Free Lunch."

24. Davis, *The Industrial Revolution and British Overseas Trade*, 1979.

25. Calculated from Davis, *The Industrial Revolution and British Overseas Trade*, Statistical Appendix. See Utsa Patnaik, "India's Global Trade and Britain's International Dominance," in Sunanda Sen and Maria Cristina Marcuzzo, eds., *The Changing Face of Imperialism* (Delhi: Routledge, 2018).

26. A. H. Imlah, *Economic Elements in the Pax Britannica: Studies in British Foreign Trade in the Nineteenth Century* (Cambridge: Harvard University Press, 1958).

27. See Utsa Patnaik, "The Free Lunch."

28. Imports are taken here at f.o.b. values, namely values at port of origin, thus attributing freight, insurance, and commission as incomes to Britain. This figure is therefore lower than that mentioned in an earlier estimate.

29. While our procedure for calculating the present value of the "drain" D for say a five-year period should ideally have been $D = [d_1(1+r)^{T-1}+d_2(1+r)^{T-2}+....d_5(1+r)^{T-5}]$, where T is the date to which the sum is being calculated, we use the shortcut of taking D as $[(d_1+d_2+...d_5)](1+r)^{T-3}$, since year 3 is the mid-point of the period.

30. Quoted in R. C. Dutt, *Economic History of India*, Vol.1, 285. At Martin's 12 percent interest rate, the drain from 1765 to 1836 alone, by 1947 would amount to £5200 trillion (compare with 1947 GDP of the UK of £10.5 billion).

31. Quoted in R. C. Dutt, *Economic History of India*, Vol.1, 285.

32. Up to 1874, the exchange rate was close to £ 1 = Rs.10, so the figures in the first column in Rs. crores give the value in £ million. For the second column £1= Rs.15 will give a rough idea of the sterling equivalent.

33. Irfan Habib, *Essays in Indian History* (Delhi: Tulika Books,1995).

34. Reverse Councils were bills payable in sterling against rupees tendered for imports in India, but other than two years after the First World War, since India always posted export surplus, the net flow was of Council Bills.

35. M. de Cecco, *The International Gold Standard: Money and Empire* (New York: St. Martin's Press, 1984).

36. S. Panandikar, *Some Economic Cosnequences of the War for India* (Bombay, 1921), 203.

37. A. I. Levkovsky, *Capitalism in India: Basic Trends in Its Development* (Delhi: People's Publishing House,1966), pp. 96–97, quoting S. Panandikar, *Some Economic Consequences of the War for India*.

38. Dutt, *Economic History of India* Vol.II, 154–155.

39. Some writers have ignored the specificity of the macroeconomics of a colonized economy subject to such a drain, and therefore they were misled

into applying standard reasoning to it. K. N. Chaudhury, "Foreign Trade and the Balance of Payments 1757-1947" in D. Kumar ed., *Cambridge Economic History of India*, for instance, says that India's export surplus should have given rise to foreign trade multiplier effects. In fact, however, since the export surplus was matched by a budgetary surplus (with the drain items being shown in both cases to balance the accounts), and the overwhelming bulk of the tax burden fell on the working people, especially the peasantry, whose savings propensity was negligible, the aggregate demand in the colony, even on Keynesian reasoning, would not increase with the size of the drain. In addition, since exports were of products that were grown on the limited tropical landmass, products whose particular output rather than the level of aggregate demand determined overall employment and output in the economy, the export surplus would have a deflationary effect. See P. Patnaik, "On the Macroeconomics of a Colonial Economy," in P. Patnaik, ed., *Excursus in History* (Delhi: Tulika Books, 2011) for a critique.

40.   Bhattacharya, *The Financial Foundations of the British Raj*.

## 10 FURTHER ON COLONIAL TRANSFERS

1.    John Kenneth Galbraith, *A View from the Stands: Of People, Politics, Military Power, and the Arts* (New York: Houghton Mifflin, 1986), 315-16.

2.    Quoted in A. Chandavarkar, *Keynes and India* (London: Palgrave Macmillan, 1989), p. 57.

3.    Note that the value of Council bills represented India's balance of commodity trade, comprising the (positive) balance of merchandise trade plus the (negative) balance of commodity gold. Financial gold flows belonged to the capital account.

4.    S.Bhattacharya, *The Financial Foundations of the British Raj*, 260-61, 303-20).

5.    Utsa Patnaik, "The Free Lunch," Appendix.

6.    From Pandit, *India's Balance of Indebtedness;* and, A. K. Banerjee, *India's Balance of Payments*.

7.    See Pandit, *India's Balance of Indebtedness,* and A. K. Banerjee, *India's Balance of Payments*.

8.    Folke Hilgerdt, "The Case for Multilateral Trade"; S. B. Saul, *Studies in British Overseas Trade 1870-1914*.

9.    S. B. Saul, *Studies in British Overseas Trade 1870-1914*.

10.   Saul, *Studies in British Overseas Trade 1870-1914*, 56.

11.   Saul, *Studies in British Overseas Trade 1870-1914*, 58, Table XX .

12.   Saul, *Studies in British Overseas Trade 1870-1914*, 62.

13.   The regulation with respect to Council Bills had to be modified to allow their issue to exceed actual annual expenditure by Britain, which could no

longer absorb such fast-rising sums under normal heads of current spending. Whether the absorption took the form of using India's gold earnings to add to Britain's reserves requires investigation.

14.     Saul, *Studies in British Overseas Trade 1870–1914*, 62.

15.     Saul, *Studies in British Overseas Trade 1870–1914*, 203.

16.     Hilgerdt, "The Case for Multilateral Trade."

17.     Saul, *Studies in British Overseas Trade 1870–1914*.

18.     Balances in millions of dollars, calculated from adjusted frontier (imports valued c.i.f., exports f.o.b.). Both import and export balances are shown; the smaller of the two figures in each square represents the export balance of the group from which the arrows emerge, and the larger figure the import balance of the group to which the arrows point. The difference between the amounts in question is due largely to the inclusion in imports of transport costs between the frontiers of the exporting and importing countries.

        The figure for the import balance of the "Regions of Recent Settlement in the Temperate Belts" from the United States should be 690 instead of 670 as indicated in the figure.

        The United Kingdom, the United States, and Germany are shown separately; the other countries were grouped in three categories: the Tropics (including Central Africa, the tropical agricultural and the mineral producing countries of Latin America, and tropical Asia), the "Regions of recent settlement in the temperate belts" (including the British dominions of South Africa, Canada, Oceania, and Argentina, Uruguay, and Paraguay), and "Europe" with the exception of the United Kingdom and Germany. See League of Nations (1942), table 20–23, table 44, and Annex III for details on the classification and country data.

19.     United Nations, *International Trade Statistics 1900–1960 on International Merchandise Trade Statistics*,1962; available at www./unsd/trade/imts/ Historical data 1900-1960:pdf.

20.     A. I. Levkovsky, *Capitalism in India: Basic Trends in its Development* (Delhi: Peoples Publishing House, 1972).

21.     Charles Kindleberger, *The World in Depression 1928–1938* (Harmondsworth: Pelican, 1987).

22.     S. G.Triantis, *Cyclical Changes in the Trade Balances of Countries Exporting Primary Products 1927–1933* (Toronto: University of Toronto Press, 1967).

23.     B. R.Mitchell and Phyllis Deane, *Abstract of British Historical Statistics*.

24.     S. Sivasubramonian, *The National Income of India*.

## 11 THE UNRAVELING OF THE COLONIAL ARRANGEMENT

1.      Nicholas Kaldor has a model of the world economy where the rate of growth of one part of the world, the so-called "manufacturing sector," is tethered

to the rate of growth of the other part, the so-called "primary producing sector." Nicholas Kaldor, "What Is Wrong with Economic Theory?" in Nicholas Kaldor, *Further Essays in Economic Theory* (Cambridge: Cambridge University Press, 1978).

2. Amiya Kumar Bagchi, *Private Investment in India 1900–1939* (Cambridge: Cambridge University Press, 1972).

3. W. J. Macpherson, "Investment in Indian Railways 1845–1875," *Economic History Review* 8, no. 2 (1955).

4. Paul A. Baran, *The Political Economy of Growth* (New York: Monthly Review Press, 1957).

5. There is an enormous literature on Britain's return to gold. D. E. Moggridge, *The Return to Gold, 1925* (Cambridge: Cambridge University Press, 1969), is a very useful reference.

6. The real wage argument can be set out as follows. The price-level p is given by
$$p = (ame + w.l)(1+\pi), \text{ or } 1 = (ame/p) + wl/p)\ (1+\pi)$$
where a is the physical amount of imported input per unit of output, m its dollar price and e the exchange rate (pound-sterlings per dollar); w is the money wage rate; l the labor coefficient and $\pi$ the markup margin. Suppose at the initial exchange rate, there is a balance of payments deficit for the United Kingdom, and that a reduction in p in terms of dollars by 5 percent, *in the absence of any retaliation,* will bring about payments equilibrium. With floating exchange rates, since sterling must depreciate, e/p must rise, for which, with given $\pi$, w/p must fall. With fixed exchange rate, the same would hold for any e greater than the initial rate, that is, at any parity with a lower value of sterling than the initial rate. But with fixed parity at an overvalued sterling, that is, with an e that is, say, 5 percent lower than the initial rate, p, if it is to fall in dollar terms by 5 percent, must be lowered by 10 percent in sterling terms. Since the first term (ame) would have gotten lowered by only 5 percent (owing to over-valuation), w must fall by more than 10 percent for this to happen, that is, w/p must fall. Real wages would thus have to fall no matter what policy was pursued. But even if they do, retaliation would negate the effects of the policy.

7. John Maynard Keynes, *The General Theory of Employment, Interest and Money* (London: Macmillan, 1936), 381–82.

8. Britain's situation in this respect was different from that of today's United States, which can oblige countries to hold dollars, because Britain, though the leading capitalist *economy* of that time, was not the *military* leader of the capitalist world. On the contrary, it was locked in intense inter-imperialist rivalry with other capitalist powers.

## 12 A PERSPECTIVE ON THE GREAT DEPRESSION

1. J. A. Schumpeter, *Business Cycles*, 2 vols. (New York: McGraw-Hill, 1939).

2.    See Paul A. Baran and Paul M. Sweezy, *Monopoly Capital* (New York: Monthly Review Press, 1966), in which they refer to this exchange.

3.    Oskar Lange, Review of *Business Cycles*, by J. A. Schumpeter, *Review of Economic Statistics* 23, no. 9 (1941).

4.    Michał Kalecki, *Selected Essays on the Dynamics of the Capitalist Economy 1933–1971* (Cambridge: Cambridge University Press, 1971).

5.    Charles Kindleberger, *The World in Depression, 1929–1939* (Berkeley: University of California Press, 1973).

6.    Kindleberger, pp. 289–91.

7.    Richard F. Kahn, "The Relation of Home Investment to Unemployment," *Economic Journal* 41, no. 162 (June 1931).

8.    Kalecki, "Political Aspects of Full Employment" (1943), in Michal Kalecki, *Selected Essays on the Dynamics of the Capitalist Economy 1933–1971*.

## 13 PUBLIC POLICY AND THE GREAT FAMINE
## IN BENGAL, 1943-44

1.    John Maynard Keynes, *A Treatise on Money* (1930), in *Collected Writings*, vol. 5, Elizabeth Johnson and Donald Moggridge, eds. (Cambridge: Cambridge University Press, 1979), and *How to Pay for the War* (New York: Harcourt, Brace,1940).

2.    John Maynard Keynes, *Indian Currency and Finance* (London: Macmillan, 1913).

3.    Keynes, *A Treatise on Money*, in *Collected Writings*, vol. 5, 152–53; emphasis added.

4.    Keynes, *A Treatise on Money*, in *Collected Writings*, vol. 5, 153.

5.    Keynes, *A Treatise on Money*, in *Collected Writings*, vol. 5, 153, 154.

6.    Keynes, *A Treatise on Money*, in *Collected Writings*, vol. 5, 155; emphasis added.

7.    Keynes, *A Treatise on Money*, in *Collected Writings*, vol. 5, 155; emphasis added.

8.    Keynes, *How to Pay for the War*.

9.    Quoted in Chnadavarkar, *Keynes and India*, 119.

10.   Up to 1941–42, Total Government Outlay is the sum of Expenditure plus the absolute value of Total deficit as indicated. From 1942–43, Total Govt. Outlay is found to exceed this sum slightly, as there was rupee borrowing by government not shown in the RBI's table. The rupee-sterling exchange rate was approximately Rs.13.6 = £ 1. In the *Cambridge Economic History of India*, vol. 2, ed. Dharma Kumar and Meghnad Desai (Cambridge: Cambridge University Press, 1984), some data were reproduced (943, Table 12.11) from the same Table 15 of the RBI *Report* for 1946–47, but the figures in cols. 1, 3, and 4 were excluded. No idea of the actual increase in central government revenues and expenditure, or of total outlays and total deficit, can be obtained from the *CEHI*.

11.  India's national income estimates from S. Sivasubramonian (2000), adjusted for British India coverage by the authors.

12.  Amartya Sen, *Poverty and Famines: An Essay on Entitlement and Deprivation* (Oxford: Clarendon, 1981), 56.

13.  Bhowani Sen, *Rural Bengal in Ruins (*Peoples Publishing House, 1945) quoted in Rajani Palme Dutt, *India Today* (Delhi: Peoples Publishing House, 1947), 263; *Report on Currency and Finance 1945–46* (Bombay: Reserve Bank of India, 1946); Sen, *Poverty and famines*, 54.

14.  P. S. Lokanathan, *India's Post-war Reconstruction and Its International Aspects* (Delhi: Indian Council of World Affairs,1946), 42.

15.  Sen, *Poverty and Famines*.

16.  P. C. Mahalanobis, R.K Mukherjee and A.Ghosh, *A Sample Survey of After-effects of the Bengal Famine of 1943* (Calcutta: Statistical Publishing Society, 1946).ˎ

17.  Sen, *Poverty and Famines*, 75.

18.  See Utsa Patnaik, "Food Availability and Famine: A Longer View," *Journal of Peasant Studies*, Vol.19, Issue 1 (1991), reprinted in Utsa Patnaik, *The Long Transition* (Delhi: Tulika Books, 1999); and Anand Chandavarkar, *Keynes and India: A Study in Economics and Biography* (Houndsmills: Macmillan, 1989).

19.  We thank Arundhati Chowdhury for making available the digitized RBI reports.

20.  S. Sivasubramonian, *The National Income of India in the Twentieth Century*.

21.  Utsa Patnaik, "Food Availability and Famine."

22.  George Blyn, *Agricultural Trends in India 1891–1947: Output, Availability and Productivity* (Philadelphia: University of Pennsylvania Press, 1966), Table 5.3, 102.

23.  Lokanathan, *India's Post-war Reconstruction*, p. 49.

24.  Robert Skidelsky, *John Maynard Keynes*, vol. 3, *Fighting for Freedom, 1937–1946* (Harmondsworth: Penguin, 2001), 84–88.

25.  See Table 5, 251, of Geoff Tily, "John Maynard Keynes and the Development of National Accounts in Britain, 1895 to 1941," *Review of Income and Wealth*, 55, 2 (June 2009), 331–59.

26.  For Indian national income, S. Sivasubramonian's estimates adjusted for British India by the present authors.

27.  Some of the data Hunter had compiled was reproduced in U. Patnaik, "Food Availability and Famine."

28.  Sen, *Poverty and Famines*.

29.  Madhusree Mukerjee, *Churchill's Secret War: The British Empire and the Ravaging of India During World War II* (New York: Basic Books, 2011).

30.  Skidelsky, *Fighting for Freedom, 1937–1946*, 413–14.

## 14 POSTWAR DIRIGISME AND ITS CONTRADICTIONS

1.  J.M.Keynes, "National Self-Sufficiency," *The Yale Review*, Vol. 22, No.4 (June 1933).

2.   Joan Robinson, *The Accumulation of Capital* (London: Macmillan, 1956).

3.   Arghiri Emmanuel, *Unequal Exchange: A Study of the Imperialism of Trade* (New York: Monthly Review Press, 1972); Samir Amin, *Accumulation on a World Scale* (New York: Monthly Review Press, 1974).

4.   V. I. Lenin, *Two Tactics of Social Democracy in the Democratic Revolution* (1905), in *Selected Works*, 3 vols. (Moscow: Progress Publishers, 1977).

5.   Michał Kalecki, "Intermediate Regimes," in Michal Kalecki, *Selected Essays on the Economic Growth of Socialist and Mixed Economies* (Cambridge: Cambridge University Press, 1972).

6.   Prabhat Patnaik and C. P. Chandrasekhar, "India: *Dirigisme*, Structural Adjustment, and the Radical Alternative," in *Globalization and Progressive Economic Policy*, Dean Baker, Gerald Epstein, and Robert Pollin, eds. (Cambridge: Cambridge University Press, 1998).

## 15 THE LONG POSTWAR BOOM

1.   Paul A. Baran and Paul M. Sweezy, *Monopoly Capital* (New York: Monthly Review Press, 1966).

2.   Michał Kalecki, "The Problem of Effective Demand with Rosa Luxemburg and Tugan-Baranovsky," in Michal Kalecki, *Selected Essays on the Dynamics of the Capitalist Economy 1933–1971* (Cambridge: Cambridge University Press, 1971).

3.   Baran and Sweezy, *Monopoly Capital*; Paul M. Sweezy, *The Theory of Capitalist Development* (New York: Oxford University Press, 1942); and Paul A. Baran, *The Political Economy of Growth* (New York: Monthly Review Press, 1957).

4.   Nicholas Kaldor, review of *The Political Economy of Growth* by Paul A. Baran, *American Economic Review* 48, no. 1 (March 1958).

5.   Andrew Glyn and Bob Sutcliffe, *British Capitalism, Workers and the Profit-Squeeze* (Harmondsworth: Penguin, 1972).

6.   H. A.Turner, Dudley Jackson, and Frank Wilkinson, *Do Trade Unions Cause Inflation?* (Cambridge: Cambridge University Press, 1972).

7.   Prabhat Patnaik, "On the Economic Crisis of World Capitalism," in *Lenin and Imperialism*, Prabhat Patnaik, ed. (Delhi: Orient Longmans, 1986).

8.   Josef Steindl, "On Maturity in Capitalist Economies," in *Problems of Economic Dynamics and Planning: Essays in Honour of Michał Kalecki*, Tadeusz Kowalik, ed. (Oxford: Pergamon, 1966).

9.   In general, if the following three inequalities hold: (a) $\Delta G/\Delta Y \geq G/Y$; (b) $\Delta W/\Delta Y \leq W/Y$; and (c) $\Delta T_w/\Delta W \geq T_w/W$, where G is government expenditure in the initial situation, Y output, W the pre-tax wage bill of productive workers and $T_w$ the taxes paid by productive workers, then, if any one of three holds as a strict inequality, the *ex post* share of surplus in output would have increased because of government intervention.

10.  R. E. Rowthorn, "Conflict, Inflation and Money," *Cambridge Journal of Economics* 1, no. 3 (September 1977).

11.  W. Arthur Lewis quoted in Nicholas Kaldor, "Inflation and Recession in the World Economy," *Economic Journal* 86, no. 344 (December 1976).

12.  The pricing formula for manufactured goods is

$$p = (p_a a + p w^*.l)(1+\pi)(1+t)$$

where $p_a$ is the price per unit of primary commodity, $a$ is the primary commodity input used per unit of manufactured good, $w^*$ the wage rate expressed in terms of the manufactured good, $l$ the labor coefficient per unit of manufactured good output, and $\pi$ and $t$ the profit and indirect tax markup respectively. The terms of trade would move against the primary commodity if the rise in profit-cum-indirect tax margin is not sufficiently offset by a decline in $w^*.l$ or a. The share of pre-tax wages in gross value added at market prices will also fall if the rise in profit-cum-indirect tax margin is not offset by a sufficient fall in $a/w^*.l$.

13.  To avoid any confusion, we should make it clear that by "land-augmenting" measures we mean all measures that raise the productivity per unit of physical area (and not "land augmentation" in the sense of driving away existing land owners and augmenting its availability for capitalist producers). We sharply distinguish, in other words, between "land augmentation" and "primitive accumulation of capital."

## 16 THE END OF POSTWAR DIRIGISME

1.  Nicholas Kaldor, "Inflation and Recession in the World Economy," *Economic Journal* 86, no. 344 (December 1976).

2.  Paul M. Sweezy and Harry Magdoff, "Keynesian Chickens Come Home to Roost," *Monthly Review* 25, no. 11 (April 1974); Hyman Minsky, *John Maynard Keynes* (London: Palgrave Macmillan, 1975); Irving Fisher, "The Debt-Deflation Theory of Great Depressions," *Econometrica* 1, no. 4 (1933).

3.  Paul Krugman, "Running Out of Planet to Exploit," *The New York Times*, April 21, 2008.

4.  We are grateful to Dr. Shouvik Chakraborty for making this figure available to us.

5.  Of course, imperialism has been fighting wars in the third world of late. Some may argue that these wars are different from interventions that used to occur earlier against third world governments attempting economic decolonization, trying to escape the economic regime politically imposed by imperialism. But the point is that the kind of economic regime that imperialism used to impose politically is now imposed more or less through neoliberalism, a phenomenon that represents a triumph of imperialism, not its negation, as is often suggested.

## 17 THE NEOLIBERAL REGIME

1. Rudolf Hilferding, *Das Finanzkapital* (Vienna: Wiener Volksbuchhandlung, 1910).

2. Ragnar Nurkse, "International Investment Today in the Light of Nineteenth-Century Experience," *Economic Journal* 64, no. 256 (December 1954).

3. Interestingly only 10 percent of British capital investment came to India throughout the colonial period even though India was its largest colony.

4. Paul A. Baran, *The Political Economy of Growth* (New York: Monthly Review Press, 1957); A. K. Bagchi, *The Political Economy of Underdevelopment* (Cambridge: Cambridge University Press, 1982).

5. Michał Kalecki, "Intermediate Regimes," in Michal Kalecki, *Selected Essays on the Economic Growth of Socialist and Mixed Economies* (Cambridge: Cambridge University Press, 1972).

6. Prabhat Patnaik, "The Economics of the New Phase of Imperialism," in Prabhat Patnaik, *Re-Envisioning Socialism* (Delhi: Tulika, 2011).

7. We are assuming here for simplicity that the natural rate of growth of the workforce is the same as the rate of population growth.

8. The reduction in per capita consumption of food grains owing to primitive accumulation of capital can be denoted by $c(x) - c(y)$ where $c(x)$ and $c(y)$ denote food consumption at incomes x and y. Let N be the number of persons affected by primitive accumulation. Then if $N\{c(x) - c(y)\}$, the total reduction in food demand exceeds some threshold level $S^*$, then land augmentation slackens, such that $g_f \le n$, that is, the rate of growth of food grain production becomes less than or equal to the rate of growth of population (workforce). Since N is large, this condition is satisfied, which means that the displaced peasants neither can be absorbed in the capitalist sector nor even get back to the income level x from y to which it has fallen.

9. When a peasant goes to an expensive private hospital while earlier he would have gone to a cheaper pubic one, and pays for the greater expense by consuming less food, some may conclude that he is better off, since he is going to a more expensive hospital. This, however, is misleading as he has no choice in the matter: the public hospital he went to earlier is now run down or wound up under the neoliberal dispensation. Since he is getting the same amount of healthcare as he did earlier and yet consuming less food, the basket of goods he consumes is vector-wise smaller; he is therefore poorer according to us.

10. In fact, one of the present authors has found an inverse relationship between export-orientation of agriculture and domestic food availability to be a *universal phenomenon*. See Utsa Patnaik, "Export-Oriented Agriculture and Food Security in Developing Countries and India," *Economic and Political Weekly*, Vol. 31, Issues 35–37, September 1996.

## 18 INEQUALITY AND *EX ANTE* OVERPRODUCTION

1.  W. Arthur Lewis, *The Evolution of the International Economic Order* (Princeton, NJ: Princeton University Press, 1978).

2.  A. K. Bagchi, *The Political Economy of Underdevelopment* (Cambridge: Cambridge University Press, 1982).

3.  For some evidence on movements in the share of wages in the United States and the United Kingdom from the late nineteenth century to the end of the 1930s, see Michal Kalecki, *The Theory of Economic Dynamics* (London: Allen and Unwin, 1954).

4.  Joseph Stiglitz's finding that a typical male worker's real income in the United States in 2011 was marginally lower than it had been in 1968 is highly significant in this context. See his article "Inequality Is Holding Back the Recovery" in the *New York Times*, January 13, 2013.

5.  Thomas Piketty, *Capital in the Twenty-First Century* (Cambridge, MA: Harvard University Press, 2013).

6.  Luigi L. Pasinetti, "Rate of Profit and Income Distribution in Relation to the Rate of Economic Growth," *Review of Economic Studies* 29, no. 4 (October 1962).

7.  A comprehensive critique of Piketty's theoretical argument is contained in Prabhat Patnaik, "Capitalism, Inequality and Globalization," *International Journal of Political Economy* 43, no. 3 (April 2015).

8.  Michał Kalecki, *Theory of Economic Dynamics* (London: Allen and Unwin, 1954); Paul A. Baran and Paul M. Sweezy, *Monopoly Capital* (New York: Monthly Review Press, 1966).

9.  W. Arthur Lewis, *Economic Survey 1919–1939* (Philadelphia: Blackiston, 1950); Prabhat Patnaik, Introduction to *Lenin and Imperialism* (Delhi: Orient Longmans, 1986).

## 19 CAPITALISM AT AN IMPASSE

1.  Charles P. Kindleberger, *The World in Depression, 1929–1939* (Berkeley: University of California Press, 1973).

2.  John Maynard Keynes, *The General Theory of Employment, Interest and Money* (London: Macmillan, 1936), 381.

3.  Palmiro Togliatti, *Lectures on Fascism* (New York: International Publishers, 1976).

4.  Rosa Luxemburg, *The Accumulation of Capital* (London: Routledge, 1963, originally published in 1913).

## 20 CAPITALISM IN HISTORY

1.  R. M. Goodwin, "A Growth Cycle," in *Socialism, Capitalism and Economic Growth: Essays Presented to Maurice Dobb*, C. H. Feinstein, ed. (Cambridge: Cambridge University Press, 1967).

2.   The argument that follows is based on Utsa Patnaik and Prabhat Patnaik, *A Theory of Imperialism* (New York: Columbia University Press, 2016) and Utsa Patnaik, "Capitalism and the Production of Poverty," T. G. Narayanan Memorial Lecture, *Social Scientist* (January–February 2012).

3.   Anwar Shaikh, *Capitalism: Competition, Conflict, Crises* (New York: Oxford University Press, 2016).

4.   Marx's articles on India have been brought together by Iqbal Husain in *Karl Marx on India* (Delhi: Tulika, 2006).

5.   Marx's exact words are quoted in *Marx-Engels Correspondence*, www.marxists.org.

6.   V. I. Lenin, *Two Tactics of Social Democracy in the Democratic Revolution* (1905), in *Selected Works*, 3 vols. (Moscow: Progress Publishers, 1977).

7.   This argument is developed at greater length in Prabhat Patnaik, "Defining the Concept of Commodity Production," in *Studies in Peoples' History* 2, no. 1 (May 2015).

## 21 THE ROAD AHEAD

1.   This is borne out at the global level by the decline in per capita cereal output figures mentioned earlier. Since a larger proportion of grain output has been diverted for biofuel production over the period covered, per capita cereal availability for consumption purposes must have declined even more rapidly. In India, per capita availability of cereals and pulses in no subsequent year has reached the level it had reached in 1991, when neoliberal reforms were introduced.

2.   Prabhat Patnaik, "Two Concepts of Nationalism," in *What the Nation Really Needs to Know*, Rohit Azad, Janaki Nair, Mohinder Singh, and Mallarika Sinha Roy, eds. (New Delhi: HarperCollins India, 2016).

3.   György Lukács, *Lenin: A Study in the Unity of His Thought* (London: New Left Books 1970 [1924]).

# Index

authoritarianism, 304–5

automobile, as epoch-making innovation, 19, 57

Bangladesh, market competition for, India as, 92

banks, during Golden Age of capitalism, 93

Baran, Paul, 126, 176

Bevan, Aneurin, 214

Bhattacharya, S., 155

booms: *see* economic booms

Brazil, as emerging country, 290

Bretton Woods system: collapse of, in postwar *dirigiste* regimes, 253–54; in *dirigiste* regimes, 224–26, 230–31; exchange rate depreciation and, 225; Golden Age of capitalism and, 92–93; Keynes and, 202; nominal exchange rate system and, 225–26; war financing and, 216

British colonialism, before First World War: drain of wealth as result of, 128–35; global exchange earnings, appropriation of, 138–44; import-substitutes, 135–36; production capacity asymmetry, 135–38

British Empire: *see* colonial economies; colonial markets; colonial period; colonialism; India

British sterling: *see* sterling

Bukharin, Nikolai, 16–17

business cycles: Juglar, 88, 186; Kitchin, 88, 186; Kondratieff, 88, 186

*Cambridge Economic History of India*, 134

Cambridge Quantity Equation, 20

canal colonies, of India, 175, 245

capacity utilization, 343n3; accumulation and, 17; exogenous stimuli and, 55–56

capital: finance, 95, 256–57; migration of, 271; primitive accumulation of, 315–16; social legitimacy of, 95; *see also* capital goods

*Capital (Das Kapital)* (Marx), 51, 323–24

capital exports: colonial transfers and, 159–62; in Great Britain, financing of, 87

capital goods: employment levels and, 13; income levels and, 13; metropolitan, 173–74; in money-using economies, 13; new, 13; old, 13; in oligopolistic conditions, 13; price levels of, 13; production rates of, 13

capital stock, exogenous stimuli and, 55–56

capitalism: alternative trajectories to, 332–34; during colonial period, 86–88; colonialism and, 51, 115–27; conceptual representation of, 11–12, 54; crisis periods, 98–99; development of, 69; diffusion of, 159–62, 251, 272; during *dirigiste* regime, restructuring of, 221–24; exogenous stimuli, 55–60; external market requirements in, 16; fascism and, rise of, 302–8; finance capital as highest level of, 301–2; globalization of, 300; globalization regimes and, 94–98; Golden Age of, 88–94; ideological justification for, 306; increasing supply price